THE DOUBLE-DARING
BOOK FOR GIRLS

The DOUBLE-DARING Book for Girls

Andrea J. Buchanan & Miriam Peskowitz

Illustrations by Alexis Seabrook

COLLINS

An Imprint of HarperCollins Publishers

The publisher and authors acknowledge the inspiration of
The Dangerous Book for Boys for the concept and design of this book
and are grateful to Conn and Hal Iggulden for their permission.

THE DOUBLE-DARING BOOK FOR GIRLS

HarperCollins books may be purchased for educational, business,
or sales promotional use. For information, please write:
Special Markets Department, HarperCollins Publishers,
10 East 53rd Street, New York, NY 10022.

FIRST EDITION

NOTE TO PARENTS: This book contains a number of activities that may be dangerous
if not done exactly as directed or that may be inappropriate for young children. All
of these activities should be carried out under adult supervision only. The authors
and publishers expressly disclaim liability for any injury or damages that result from
engaging in the activities contained in this book.

Illustrations by Alexis Seabrook

Designed by MADA Design Inc., and The Stonesong Press, LLC

Library of Congress Cataloging-in-Publication Data has been applied for.

ISBN: 978-0-06-174879-0

09   10   11   12   13 ❖/RRD   10   9   8   7   6   5   4   3   2   1

CONTENTS

Introduction

NOT OFTEN IN HISTORY have girls and women been encouraged to be daring. It's a remarkable word, daring: old-fashioned and forward-looking all at the same time. With all the rules we're given about what girls should and shouldn't do, a little daring can go a long way.

As we learned in the original *Daring Book for Girls*, daring comes in many flavors. It can mean seeking adventure and being bold when bold is called for. It can mean being confident and brave and saying yes to the good risks that life brings your way. It is true that some daring happens on a grand scale, such as rafting down a raging river, surfing monster waves, saving lives, or traveling on a worldwide expedition. But everyday daring, courage, and bravery are no less important, whether it's trying something new, sticking up for someone who is being teased, or taking a small chance that winds up making a big difference.

When we put together *The Double-Daring Book for Girls*, we discovered daring girls and women everywhere we looked. Cowgirls who dared to ride horses and rope cattle. Bicycle-riding women who traded their Victorian hoopskirts for bloomers at a time when women weren't allowed to wear pants. Women and girls who risked their lives escaping slavery on the Underground Railroad—and who then, daringly, helped others escape, too. Women who looked to the skies and discovered the secrets of the universe, and daring girls who became musicians and scientists and leaders when no one thought women should do these things.

In addition to inspiring stories like these, *The Double-Daring Book for Girls* is bursting with crafts and games, sports and knowledge, and facts about the world. In these pages, girls can discover everything from how to make an electric buzzer game to how to create lightning in your mouth; from car camping and star gazing to turning your backyard into a farm; from making your own piñata out of papier-mâché to creating your own fun at slumber parties. Daring girls can learn to run a magazine or paint a room, run off and join the circus, or put on a show. With chapters on scoubidou braiding, dream catchers, card games, and even a whole chapter of stuff to do when you're bored, no girl will ever be at a loss for things to do.

Daring is all around us. It is in girls who break barriers and girls who help out friends. It is in girls who scale mountains and girls who speak their minds. It is in girls who make things and girls who ask questions, girls who set their sights on adventure and girls who find adventure in their own backyards. Daring is about finding your journey and following your dreams—getting off the sidelines and getting in the game, whatever your game may be.

So fire up your inner daring, turn the page, and remember the daring girl credo: Enjoy yourself, learn new things, and lead an interesting life.

Go on—we double-dare you!

—Andrea J. Buchanan & Miriam Peskowitz

Stargazing

ON ANY GIVEN NIGHT, close to five thousand stars are visible. Of that number, perhaps half of them may be seen by the naked eye. If you live in a city or an area with lots of light at night, you may be able to see only two hundred or so at the most. Still, it is possible to observe the stars the way people have since the dawn of time.

All you really need to go stargazing is a pair of eyes, a curious mind, and a dark night. Beyond that, there are just a few other things that you can bring if you have them handy: a pair of binoculars; a star chart, which is a basic map of the stars; and a flashlight, to help you read a star chart in the dark. Covering the light with red plastic is a good way to minimize light-interference while still allowing you to read the chart.

The best place to look for stars is one that is high and far from city lights. A hill, a mountaintop, or even (with your parents' permission) your roof: the higher and closer to the wide-open dark sky, the better. To best see the stars, you will need to let your eyes get used to the dark. Spend about ten minutes in the dark letting your eyes adapt to the lack of light. Once you've done this, you'll be able to see the fainter stars much more easily. Then, look up: With or without your binoculars, you can scan the sky for stars.

The old nursery song "Twinkle, Twinkle, Little Star" describes stars as twinkling for a reason: They actually do twinkle. The scientific name for it is "stellar scintillation." Stars appear to be twinkling at us because we see them through the moving air of Earth's atmosphere, which bends their light and sends it in random directions. Planets, on the other hand, don't twinkle, as they are closer to us and their light has less air to move through.

As for locating the constellations and other stars, a star chart or map is very helpful. One of the best kinds of maps is a planisphere, a kind of portable, configurable star map that can be adjusted for any date and time (and bought at a bookstore). But any star chart, map, or book will do. On every star chart, you will find several things: dots representing the stars, a circle around the stars representing the horizon, and direction markings (north, south, east, and west). The bigger the dots on the map, the brighter the stars. Many of these dots are connected by lines, outlining the constellations and asterisms. The stars, constellations, and asterisms are also labeled with their descriptive or numerical names.

HOW TO READ A STAR CHART

Face south, look up, and hold the chart over your head so that the side marked *North* is toward your forehead and the side marked *South* is toward your chin. (Remember, if you're using a flashlight, make sure the light is red or covered with red plastic so that the brightness of the flashlight doesn't interfere with your ability to see the stars in the night sky.) Then, see if you can match the star shapes on your map to the star shapes in the sky above you. The star maps are obviously quite a bit smaller than the actual sky and stars, so the stars on the map will look more squished-together than they do in the sky. But they're up there—and then some. You may even see stars that aren't on your map at all.

Here are two star charts: one for the Northern Hemisphere and one for the Southern Hemisphere. (The sky looks different depending on where you are on Earth.)

Northern Hemisphire - North

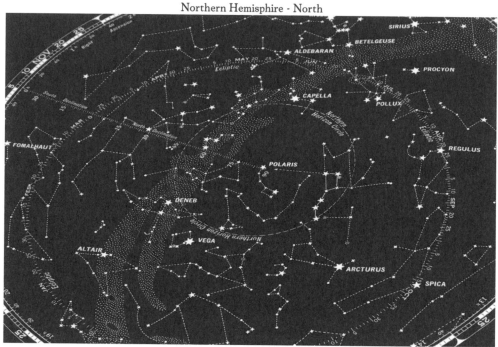

Northern Hemisphire - South

Southern Hemisphire - North

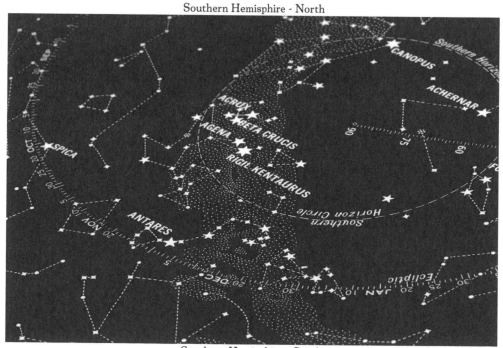

Southern Hemisphire - South

Constellations

THE WORD *CONSTELLATION* means "set with stars." Long ago, for reasons both practical and philosophical, people came up with the idea of identifying stars in groups or patterns to help them map out the terrain of the sky. Many of these star groups, or constellations, resembled dot-to-dot shapes of animals, objects, or people, and each one was given a name, usually from classical mythology. (Today, stars are named for their coordinates in space, as determined by the International Astronomical Union.) There are eighty-eight officially recognized constellations. Some of the star patterns we know best, such as the Big Dipper, are actually *asterisms*—groups of stars that, although they may create recognizable shapes and have descriptive names, are not officially constellations.

CONSTELLATIONS OF THE ZODIAC

The sun's orbit (its trajectory through space, as seen from Earth) follows a circular path, called an *ecliptic*, which is kind of like an imaginary belt across the sky. In addition to the sun, other heavenly bodies lie along that beltlike path: the moon, all of the other planets (except Mercury), and thirteen constellations. The constellations on this circular pathway are collectively known as the zodiac, which means "circle of little animals."

Before we discuss the thirteen constellations of the zodiac, a word about astronomy and astrology, if we may. Astronomy is not astrology, and the two should not be confused. Astronomy uses physics and math to observe, measure, and quantify the universe. Astrology attempts to find meaning—predictions of the future or explanations of the past—in the stars. Astronomy is based in science, while astrology is simply for fun.

Actually, astrology has been out of sync with what's actually in the sky for most of modern history. Some 2,300 years ago, the astrological signs were devised to coincide with the time that each constellation of the zodiac was prominent in the sky. But the charts and tables made by astrologists thousands of years ago have never been updated, and between now and then not only has the way we keep track of time with calendars been changed radically, but because of the way the Earth is tilted on its axis, we see the skies differently today from the way people did then. (And in 1930, when the International Astronomical Union officially set the boundaries of the zodiac constellations, they added a thirteenth constellation, Ophiuchus, which is not recognized by horoscope astrologers.) So the "signs of the zodiac" that we know from horoscopes in the daily newspaper have nothing to do with the current constellations of the zodiac and their locations during the course of the year.

Having said that, let's take a closer look at the thirteen constellations in the sun's ecliptic.

Pisces ("Two Fish") This constellation is named for the Greek legend of Venus and her son, Cupid, who, legend has it, escaped from the clutches of the wind monster Typhon by turning themselves into fish and swimming away, tied together by a rope so they wouldn't lose each other. The brightest star of this constellation, Alpha Piscium, is sometimes called "the knot," as it appears to tie the rope between the two fish on either side of it.

Pisces

Aries

Taurus

Gemini

Cancer

Aries ("The Ram") Aries is named for the winged ram in the story of the Golden Fleece. In the story, a flying ram is sent by the gods to carry a brother and sister far away from their jealous stepmother. The girl falls off along the way, but the boy makes it to the Black Sea, where he sacrifices the ram and gives its fleece to a dragon. Later, a man named Jason and his band of hero adventurers, the Argonauts, retrieve the golden fleece and return it to the children's father, the king of Thessaly.

Taurus ("The Bull") This constellation is one of the easiest constellations to spot. The bull figures in the Greek myth of Europa and the Bull. The god Zeus disguised himself as a white bull to woo the princess Europa, who saw the bull at the water's edge one day and hopped on its back. Once she was on it, the bull kidnapped her and took her to Crete.

Gemini ("The Twins") Gemini is named for the Greek heroes Castor and Pollux, who were members of Jason's team of Argonauts. The "twins" were actually half brothers. According to mythology, when Castor died, Pollux was despondent, so Zeus took pity on him and placed the brothers side by side in the heavens. The brightest stars in the Gemini constellation are named after them.

Cancer ("The Crab") This faint constellation between Gemini and Leo is named after the crab ("cancer" in Latin) sent to kill Hercules. In this Greek tale, Hercules fought the many-headed Hydra—no easy task, because each time he cut a head off the deadly water creature, two more grew back—as part of his twelve Labors. The goddess Hera rooted against Hercules and sent a crab to bite at his feet and distract him. Instead, Hercules crushed it with his foot. Grateful for the crab's efforts, Hera placed it in the heavens.

Leo ("The Lion") This constellation is named for yet another creature killed by Hercules, the lion. The lion, which lived in Nemea and devoured any person in his path, had a special hide that couldn't be pierced by iron, bronze, or stone. It took Hercules three months to defeat him. The brightest star in Leo is called Regulus (which means "little king").

Leo

Virgo ("The Maiden") Named for Astraea, who was known as the goddess of justice, Virgo is the second-largest constellation. Long ago, the constellation was visible around harvest time, so ancient names for her included Ishtar, Inanna, Isis, Athena, Ceres, Persephone, and Demeter—all goddesses connected with agriculture. In keeping with her harvest-time origins, Virgo is often depicted with a sheaf of wheat, marked in the constellation by its brightest star, named Spica. This is the only constellation representing a female.

Virgo

Libra ("The Scales") Long ago, Libra was part of the constellation Scorpius. It was called Chelae Scorpionis, Greek for "scorpion's claws," until around the first century BCE, when the Romans set it off as its own constellation. Unattached to Scorpius, the claws looked more like a set of scales. Libra's two brightest stars point to its early life as part of Scorpius. The first, Alpha Librae, is its second-brightest star, even though it's called "alpha," which usually means "first." This star is traditionally called Zubenelgenubi ("ZOO-ben-ell-jen-NEW-bee"), Arabic for "the southern claw." The second and brighter star, Beta Librae, is also known as Zubeneschamali ("ZOO-ben-ess-sha-MAY-lee"), meaning "the northern claw."

Libra

Scorpius ("The Scorpion") Scorpius is one of the oldest constellations, recognizable by its noticeable scorpion's tail. It's named for the legendary scorpion sent by Hera to kill Orion the hunter, who had boasted that he would kill all the animals on Earth. The scorpion stung Orion, killing him before he could make good on that promise, and the two were elevated to the heavens to continue their chase in the sky. Scorpius's brightest star, Antares, is located right at the heart of the Scorpion and appears red in color.

Scorpius

Ophiuchus

Sagittarius

Capricornus

Aquarius

Ophiuchus ("The Serpent Holder") This faint constellation represents Aesclepius, the Greek and Roman god of medicine and healing, usually depicted holding a wooden staff with a snake wrapped around it. The snake symbolizes renewal (due to the way it periodically sheds its skin), and Aesclepius's staff is used as a medical symbol to this day.

Sagittarius ("The Archer") This constellation depicts a centaur (a creature half man and half horse) named Chiron shooting an arrow. Chiron was Hercules's teacher. He was fatally injured when Hercules inadvertently shot him with a poison-tipped arrow. Sagittarius has two asterisms: to the east of Scorpius, a teapot, and just above that, a teaspoon.

Capricornus ("The Sea Goat") The faint constellation Capricornus was one of the earliest constellations identified in ancient times. Drawings of a goat-fish show up on Babylonian tablets from three thousand years ago. Babylonians also wrote about the water god Ea, known as "the antelope of the sea," whose symbols were a goat and a fish and who was often depicted as stepping out of the water wearing a cloak made to resemble a fish. Capricornus literally means "horned goat," and this constellation is also associated with Amalthea, a goat whose broken horn figured in many Greek and Roman legends and came to symbolize inexhaustible riches. (That origin lives on today in the word *cornucopia*, "the horn of plenty.")

Aquarius ("The Water Bearer") This constellation is another of the oldest constellations identified by the Babylonians, who saw it as an urn overflowing with water. To other cultures, it resembled other things, but the common thread throughout them all is the association with water. The Egyptians saw a resemblance to Hapi, god of the Nile. Another ancient symbol for Aquarius was of Ouranos (Uranus, the original sky god) pouring water from the heavens to Earth. Greek mythology also associated Aquarius with Ganymede, a young man who was taken to Olympus by Zeus to fetch wine for the gods. Appropriately enough, this constellation has an asterism of a water jar.

Notable Women I: Astronomers

WOMEN ASTRONOMERS IN ANTIQUITY

Enheduanna, who lived sometime around 2300 BCE, is the first female name in recorded history. The daughter of the Akkadian King Sargon, she was appointed High Priestess of the Moon Goddess, the pinnacle of astronomy at that time. She was also the first author to write in the first person, identifying herself in her writings. Her Sumerian hymns and other works were revered for hundreds of years after her death, leading some historians to call her "the Shakespeare of Sumerian literature." Her most famous quote: "What I have done here no one has done before."

Theano of Thurii was born in Greece in 547 BCE. She studied with, and later married, the mathematician Pythagoras. She was a mathematician, astronomer, and teacher of math, physics, and child psychology. One of her most important contributions was developing the principles of the Golden Mean. She was also known for her treatise "The Construction of the Universe," which made the case that the eight planets known at the time orbited around a "central fire" and that the distances between these planets and the central fire were in the same proportion as intervals of the musical scale.

One of the best-known early woman astronomers was **Hypatia of Alexandria,** a woman who lived in ancient Greece and was famous even in her own time as a mathematician, philosopher, inventor, and teacher. She wrote a book defining the astronomical knowledge of the times and also charted the heavens, mapping the planets and stars. Although she was revered as a scholar and recognized for her knowledge, she was also viewed with suspicion. She was killed in 450 CE by an angry mob that feared her erudition and knowledge had more to do with witchcraft than science.

GERMAN ASTRONOMERS

In the late 1600s, Germany emerged as a hospitable place for women interested in studying astronomy: At that time, one out of every seven astronomers in Germany was female. One of these was **Maria Cunitz,** a German astronomer who was homeschooled by her father in languages, classics, science, and the arts. She is most well known for her 1650 book, *Urania Propitia.* Published when she was just thirty, the book featured a set of astronomical tables and a more elegant solution to a question of physics known as "Kepler's Problem." Her book became so well known (and her achievement in writing it as a woman so astonishing) that her husband, who was also an astronomer, wrote a preface for later editions testifying that the book was indeed written entirely by his wife. And in keeping with the contemporary view on women's scientific abilities, she herself reassured her readers that her work was accurate, even though it was done by, as she put it, "a person of the female sex."

Another German astronomer, **Maria Margarethe Kirch,** was the first woman to discover a comet, "the comet of 1702." Sadly, she never got credit for this momentous event: When word was sent to the king that "Kirch" had discovered a comet, it was assumed that the discovery had been made by her husband, Gottfried Kirch—who did nothing to discourage that assumption. (He did finally admit the truth eight years later.) Maria continued her work, publishing astronomical findings under her own name in German scientific journals. In 1716 her son was named director of the Berlin Observatory of the Royal Academy of Sciences, and Maria and her daughters were appointed as his assistants. But members of the academy complained that she acted more as a director than an assistant, and eventually they forced her to retire, even though it meant her giving up her home, which happened to be on the observatory grounds. She continued her work privately until her death in 1720.

Caroline Herschel worked with her brother, the astronomer William Herschel, in the late 1700s. She not only helped discover the planet Uranus but also discovered nebulae and eight comets—no small feat, given the state of technology at the time. She became the first woman ever to receive a salary for her work in astronomy when King George III gave her a pension of fifty pounds a year. In 1798 she published her seminal "Catalogue of Stars," which indexed every star earlier cataloged by John Flamsteed, corrected errors in Flamsteed's list, and included more than 560 new stars that hadn't been recorded. In honor of her work, the Royal Astronomical Society presented her with their gold medal in 1828. (The next time a woman would receive this honor would be 1996, when it was awarded to astronomer Vera Rubin.)

AMERICAN ASTRONOMERS

Maria Mitchell was the first professional woman astronomer in the United States. One of nine children, she was introduced to astronomy by her father, a Quaker who believed in equal education for boys and girls, and who was also an astronomer in his own right. In 1847 she discovered a comet, becoming the first woman since Caroline Herschel to do so and winning a prize from King Frederick VI of Denmark, who had promised gold medals to anyone who discovered a comet with the aid of a telescope. She went on to become the first-ever professor of astronomy at Vassar College and was the first female member of both the American Academy of Arts and Sciences and the American Association for the Advancement of Science.

In 1881 Edward Pickering, the director of the Harvard College Observatory, became so impatient with a male lab assistant's work that he announced his maid could do a better job. Rather than be insulted by that jab, his twenty-four-year-old maid, **Williamina Fleming,** took him up on the offer. She ended up working at the observatory for the next thirty years, supervising the tedious work of cataloging more than 200,000 photographic plates, discovering 222 variable stars and 10 novae, developing a method of classifying 10,351 stars—and, perhaps even more important, hiring female "computers," many of whom went on to have distinguished scientific careers.

Annie Jump Cannon was hired to work at the Harvard Observatory as a human computer in 1897. She had a degree in physics from Wellesley (the women's college founded in 1870), but her first job with Edward Pickering was cataloging photographic plates (pictures) of the sky. Soon she developed a classification scheme based on stellar temperature that is still used today. Pickering even allowed her to sit in on his physics lectures, although women were officially barred from attending such events. By the time she was thirty-three, she had established her own physics lab and was a renowned star expert. Pickering acknowledged this by giving her (and the other women "computers") a salary of twenty-five cents an hour. She became the first recipient of an honorary doctorate from Oxford and was the first woman elected as an officer of the American Astronomical Society. She finally attained a Harvard appointment (as William C. Bond Astronomer) in 1938, just two years before her death.

Henrietta Leavitt also worked in Edward Pickering's lab. She began as a volunteer at age twenty-five in 1893. After five years, she was given a salary. Profoundly deaf, she battled illness while at the Harvard Observatory, but she made several important discoveries. Most notable was something called

"Cepheid variable star period-luminosity relation." Cepheid variables are stars with cycles of brightness and darkness. In 1904 Leavitt discovered that the length of the brightness cycle corresponded to the size of the star, which made it possible to measure distances between stars and the earth. By the time of her death in 1921 at age fifty-three, she had discovered 1,777 variable stars in the Magellanic Clouds. She has both an asteroid and a moon crater named in her honor.

Rock Towers

CAIRNS, OR ROCK TOWERS, come from the Irish and Gaelic word *càrn*, which means "any kind of natural rock pile or small hill." Some cairns are tall mounds. Some are shaped like pyramids rising from the ground. Some are built of a single tower of rock, and others are more free-form. In some parts of the world, piles of rock mark burial spots or memorials to the dead. Across the Canadian tundra, rock towers called *Inuksuk* are sometimes shaped like people. The word *Inuksuk* combines *inuk*, "man," and *suk*, "substitute," and they've been used for 4,000 years as guideposts through the wilderness.

On hiking trails, rock towers are commonly used to mark the trail and show which way to go, especially on rocky ledges where trail signs can't be marked on trees. Called *trail ducks*, they point the direction the path takes, and are a big help. These rock towers have long been interpreted as a sign of peacefulness and friendship. They let people know you've been at that spot and appreciated its beauty.

Rock towers stand without glue—always. That is their beauty. The stones are carefully stacked and balanced. To start, have many rocks around you to choose from, as well as a great deal of patience. It's easier if the stones are relatively flat. Balance works when you can find at least three points of contact between the rocks. In some towers, you can add stability by inserting smaller rocks in the gaps between the larger ones.

Balancing is done by feeling the connection between two stones in your fingers as you place one on top of the other, moving very slowly and carefully. Your intuition will tell you when it works—as will the sight of the top stone staying put.

Lacrosse

DON'T LET THE UNIFORM of skirts fool you—lacrosse is one tough sport. As with many sports, the object is to toss the ball into the goal while braving the other team's effort to prevent you from doing so. What makes lacrosse unique is the netted stick, and the finesse and skill it takes to use it.

Originally, lacrosse was an event held by native tribespeople in North America to train young warriors. More a spiritual journey than a simple game, it was played over vast acres of land by hundreds of players and lasted for days. The Cherokee called it "Little Brother of War." In Oneida mythology, it was a ritual to please the seven honored Grandfathers—or Thunders—who traveled across the sky and sent wind and rain to the earth.

In the 1700s, French settlers and missionaries to North America took to the game. They created new rules and time limits. Ten players were assigned to a team, and leagues were organized for European players. They renamed the game *lacrosse*, which referred to the stick (*la crosse*), and the name stuck when English speakers adopted the game.

Lacrosse for women and girls was jump-started by Constance Applebee. A British woman who had learned lacrosse and field hockey as a schoolgirl, Applebee moved to the United States to take a class at Harvard University in 1901 (women would not be admitted to Harvard until 1970, but they were permitted to take an occasional class, especially in the summertime). Looking around for a lacrosse game, she found that the sport had lost its popularity. Undaunted, and inspired by her love of the game, Applebee started a summer lacrosse camp for girls. In 1931 she established the U.S. Women's Lacrosse Association, which remained active for about fifty years.

Women's lacrosse differs from men's lacrosse in several ways. The net on the stick is shallower, which makes it harder to catch and hold the ball. Women's lacrosse is a noncontact sport, so players don't need helmets and layers of protective gear. Women's lacrosse also stays truer to the game's Native American origins. Until 2005, the field for women's lacrosse was played with soft boundaries, meaning the ball could be carried or passed anywhere so long as it wasn't dangerous and it didn't go beyond the umpire's sight. Today, the regulation field does have fixed measurements, but the area behind the goal remains open for play, a throwback to the earlier days.

PLAYERS

A lacrosse team has twelve positions.

	Position	Abbreviation	What She Does
Attackers	First Home	1H	Scores
	Second Home	2H	Scores, makes plays from everywhere
	Third Home	3H	Scores, moves the ball from defense to attack, passes to everyone
Midfielders	Attack Wing, Left and Right	AW	Moves up and down the field to get the ball to Attackers, speedy and filled with stamina
	Center	C	Takes control of the starting draw so her team gets the ball; runs a great deal, like all Midfielders. A position of attack and defense
	Defense Wing, Left and Right	DW	Marks the opponent team's Attack Wings, sends the ball back into the attack zone
Defenders	Third Man	3M	Marks the opponent team's Third Home; all defenders prevent shots on the goal at close range; they run fast, intercept passes, keep the ball away from their goal, and get it back to the Wings, who can get it to the Attackers
	Cover Point	CP	Marks Second Home
	Point	P	Marks First Home
	Goalkeeper	GK	Watches the ball like a hawk, field-coaches the Defenders, and keeps the ball out of the 6-by-6-foot goal she defends

THINGS TO KNOW ABOUT LACROSSE

BUTT END

The replaceable rubber cap at the bottom of the stick.

CATCH

As simple as it sounds: Catch the ball in the net at the end of the stick. Let your stick "give" a little bit, so it follows the trajectory of the ball. That makes the ball less likely to bounce out. Start cradling immediately to keep the ball in the net (see below for how to cradle).

CHECK

Women's lacrosse is officially a noncontact sport. Checking brings you just short of touching another player's body. To bodycheck, stay so close to a player on the opposing team that she is blocked from moving toward the goal or is intimidated into dropping or passing the ball, thus giving your team a chance to regain possession. Do all of this without ever touching her. To stick-check, "tap" your stick against your opponent's stick as many times as necessary to knock the ball from her net and gain control of it. No heads or bodies are involved. Naturally, you can't check another girl if she doesn't have the ball.

CLEAR

A ball caught by the goalkeeper and turned back into play.

CRADLE

Cradling is a lacrosse mystery, and it's a big part of what makes the sport look so graceful. The net on a women's lacrosse stick is shallow. To keep the ball in the webbing, or net, players rock the stick from side to side as they run, activating centripetal force to keep the ball inside the net. There are several ways to cradle, one in which you use your arm to move the stick across the front of your face, as if from ear to ear, and another in which your wrist does more of the work to turn the stick back and forth.

CREASE

The goal circle.

CROSSE

A fancy French word for the stick and the leather webbing, or net. The strings at the bottom of the net can be pulled to make the pocket tighter.

DRAW

To start the game, or restart play at the half or after a goal, two players stand in the center circle. Their sticks are at the ready, with the backs of the nets touching. The umpire puts the ball between their sticks. At the whistle, each player pulls her stick upward to gain control of the ball for her team.

8-METER ARC

The arc in front of the goal. A defender cannot stay in the 8-meter arc for more than three seconds unless she's within a stick's length of her opponent.

EYE MASK

Players are required to wear a wire mask, because the ball can travel as fast as 60 miles per hour.

FOULS

Minor fouls are called when a player does something dumb on the field, like rakes the ball or touches it with her body, or does an empty cross-check, which means checking someone's stick when the ball isn't anywhere nearby.

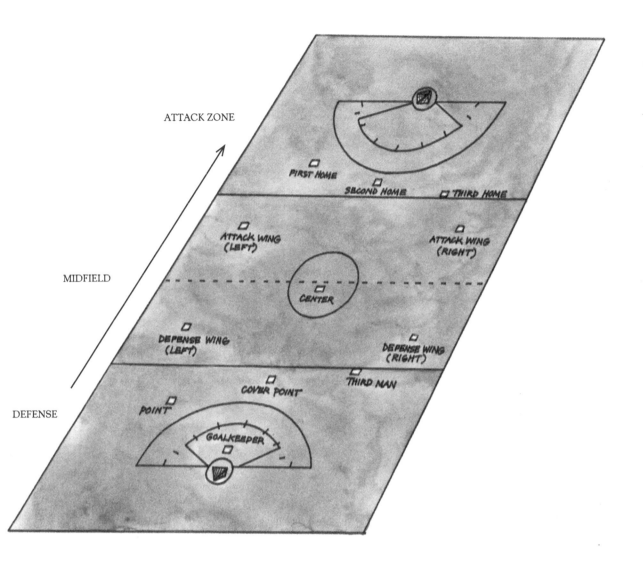

ATTACK ZONE

FIRST HOME

SECOND HOME   THIRD HOME

ATTACK WING (LEFT)   ATTACK WING (RIGHT)

MIDFIELD

CENTER

DEFENSE WING (LEFT)   DEFENSE WING (RIGHT)

THIRD MAN

COVER POINT

DEFENSE

POINT

GOALKEEPER

Major fouls are called when a player violates the spirit of the game and does something physically dangerous, like pushing or barging, or recklessly slashing a stick at another player.

Repeated fouls may persuade the referee to hand a yellow card to a player, who must leave the field for three minutes and is warned that what comes next is a game-suspending red card.

FAN
The 12-meter semicircle around the goal.

HEAD SPHERE
An imaginary 7-inch circle around each girl's head. No sticks should come inside this circle. The head sphere rule allows girls to play lacrosse without helmets, and keeps them out of the emergency room

MARK

To guard your opponent by staying less than a stick's length away from her.

MOUTH GUARD

In a crunch the mouth guard saves your teeth. Even more important, it prevents concussions. Wear at all times, unless you're just playing catch with a friend.

"NO HANDS"

The rule that only the goalkeeper can touch the ball with her hands.

PARENTS

Tell your parents not to yell directions at you while you're on the field and they're on the sidelines. Good coaches will enforce this rule. Also, be very nice to parents, because if you are an athlete, you will be asking them to drive you and your teammates to many a game and practice before you earn a license (not to mention a car) to drive yourself.

PASS

Get the ball to a teammate who can move it farther down the field and toward the goal. Pass when the time is right, and don't throw if no one on your side is ready to catch it. As long as you keep moving, even back and forth, and cradle the ball in your stick, your team has the ball and the other team can't score. Always stand ready for when a teammate passes to you.

POISE

Among with reminding players never to wear earrings and never to be tentative, one of our favorite coaches, Coach Cheryl, tells her girls to be poised on the field, which means knowing the wherewithal of the field and feeling your place on it. It's the first of the three Ps: poise, possess, pass.

THROW

Work the stick like a lever. Push the top of the stick forward while pulling the bottom of the stick back toward you. Follow through with your body weight. To throw farther, move your hands toward the bottom half of the stick. Find a tennis wall or a pitch back to practice on.

RAKE

When a player covers the ball on the ground with the net of her stick, protecting it from other players' reach while pulling it toward her on the ground. This may seem like a good idea, but, sadly, it is not allowed in games.

TOLI AND SHINNY

Toli is another Native American stick-and-ball game. It has fallen out of favor, but the Choctaw Nation organizes a national tournament each summer. Like early lacrosse, a single game of toli can include hundreds of players. It can last all day long on a field stretching several miles. Each player carries two sticks, called *kapucha*, which are made from a single piece of hickory, a strong wood that can be curved to hold the net. The ball, or *towa*, is a rock wrapped in cloth and leather strap. The goal is a single post that the ball must hit. Toli is a full-body-contact sport.

Traditionally, girls played shinny, a form of the sport with less body contact, also played on a boundless plain. The ball is hit and pushed along the ground with a plain or curved stick. Shinny is the ancestor of both golf and hockey and, today, can refer to any kind of informal or pick-up hockey game played in an open field or the street.

SCOOP

It's how you get the ball off the ground. Bend your knees and keep your body low, and scoop the ball up off the grass and into your net. Begin cradling immediately.

SHOOT

Get the ball past the goalkeeper to score. Be patient and wait for the right moment. Aim away from the goalie and toward the top corners of the net.

AND FINALLY, SKIRTS

If lacrosse players are so tough then why do they wear skirts? Called a kilt, the skirt is a holdover from the days when all female athletes wore skirts to play ball. Some lacrosse players like the skirt because it combines being feminine with being sporty. Some feel that it stays true to what Native Americans wore when they played the game and that it connects them to the tradition of women lacrosse players. Pull on a pair of bike shorts underneath and get ready to be fierce, fast, and agile.

Hula-Hoops

WHEN WE THINK OF HULA-HOOPS in America, the image that springs to mind is of the 1950s poodle-skirted teenagers who popularized the craze. But hooping has been around for thousands of years, whether as a way to exercise (in ancient Greece), as toys (Egyptians made hoops out of grape vines), or even as tools for target practice (Native Americans).

HOW TO HULA-HOOP

First, choose your hoop. Size is important: When you stand the Hula-Hoop up on its end, it should reach between your navel and chest.

Stand with legs shoulder-width apart and one foot slightly in front of the other. Hold your Hula-Hoop against your back, just above your waist. Give the hoop a push either left or right (whichever direction you prefer) with your hands, and then let go, keeping the hoop circling your waist by shifting your weight back and forth from one foot to the other.

Rather than make a circle with your hips, try to think of rocking back and forth. That keeps the hoop moving much more efficiently. Once you have the hang of hooping in one direction, try hooping in the other direction. And once you've mastered that, try these hula tricks.

HOOP TRICKS

THE KNEE KNOCKER
Start with your legs together and the Hula-Hoop at knee level. Give the hoop a push to start it circling around your knees. Move your knees to keep the hoop moving while holding both arms out at your sides.

UP AND DOWN
Begin in the normal hooping stance (legs shoulder-width apart, hoop around waist) and begin Hula-Hooping. Continue to keep the hoop circling as you ease the hoop down to your knees, and then bring the hoop back up again.

FOOTSIE
Spin the hoop around one ankle, and try to hop over the hoop with your other foot as the hoop spins around.

DECORATE YOUR HOOP
Customizing your hoop means decorating your Hula-Hoop to reflect your own personal style. You can tie ribbons around your hoop (using shiny ribbon every few inches can make for pretty hooping), wrap your hoop using colorful sticky tape (or use plain tape that you spice up with designs using permanent markers), or use glue to decoupage your hoop in decorative paper.

The Greek Alphabet

THE EARLIEST GREEK ALPHABET comes from a special time in history. Written languages did not yet exist, but around the globe, people were tentatively experimenting with letters, hoping to create a kind of communication that could last longer than the spoken word, and which might be a bit more specific than a drawing on a rock or the wall of a cave. What archaeologists call Minoan Linear B was one of these early attempts.

Minoan Linear B flourished on the island of Crete in the second millennium BCE. Sometime around 1200 BCE, the people who used it disappeared from history. Their language wasn't passed on, and no one in the modern world even knew it had existed. Then, in 1900, the British archaeologist Sir Arthur Evans discovered a stash of clay tablets during an excavation on Crete. The tablets were covered with a language he had never before seen. It took fifty years for scholars to crack the code of Minoan Linear B and to realize that it was an early form of Greek. Linear B has both syllables and logograms, which are symbols that refer to whole words.

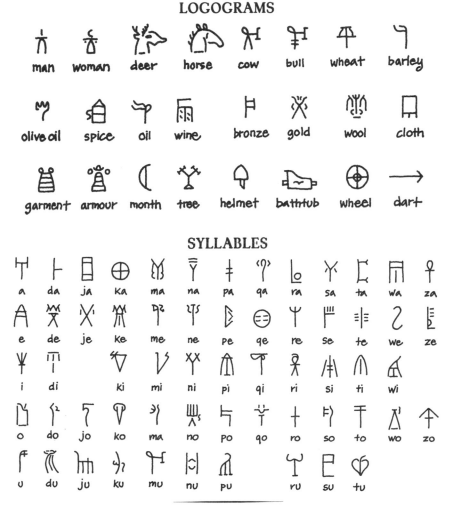

LOGOGRAMS

man   woman   deer   horse   cow   bull   wheat   barley

olive oil   spice   oil   wine   bronze   gold   wool   cloth

garment   armour   month   tree   helmet   bathtub   wheel   dart

SYLLABLES

a   da   ja   ka   ma   na   pa   qa   ra   sa   ta   wa   za

e   de   je   ke   me   ne   pe   qe   re   se   te   we   ze

i   di   ki   mi   ni   pi   qi   ri   si   ti   wi

o   do   jo   ko   ma   no   po   qo   ro   so   to   wo   zo

u   du   ju   ku   mu   nu   pu   ru   su   tu

A few centuries later, around 800 BCE, a second version of Greek developed. The new alphabet was based on letters from the Phoenician and Canaanite languages, which were used by people who lived in lands east of Greece. The new form, Attic Greek, became the language of the great philosophers Socrates, Plato, and Aristotle, and of all Athens during the Greek Golden Age.

Αα	Ββ	Γγ	Δδ	Εε	Ζζ	Ηη	Θθ
Alpha ("alpha")	Beta ("bay-ta")	Gamma ("gamma")	Delta ("delta")	Epsilon ("epsilon")	Zeta ("zeta")	Eta ("ay-tah")	Theta ("thay-ta")
a as in *father*	B	G	D	*e* as in *end*	Z	*ay* as in *hay*	Th
Ιι	Κκ	Λλ	Μμ	Νν	Ξξ	Οο	Ππ
Iota ("eye-o-tah")	Kappa ("kappa")	Lambda ("lamb-da")	Mu ("moo")	Nu ("new")	Xi ("k'sigh")	Omicron ("ohm-ee-cron")	Pi ("pie")
i as in *it*	K	L	M	N	*ks* or *x* as in *fox*	*o* as in *off*	P
Ρρ	Σσ	Ττ	Υυ	Φφ	Χχ	Ψψ	Ωω
Rho ("row")	Sigma ("sigma")	Tau ("tow" as in *tower*)	Upsilon ("up-si-lon")	Phi ("f-eye")	Chi ("k-eye")	Psi ("p'sigh")	Omega ("oh-may-ga")
R	S	T	*u* as in *put*	Ph/F	*ch* as in *Bach*	Ps	*o* as in *grow*

How to Conduct an Orchestra

AN ORCHESTRA CONDUCTOR IS A LITTLE BIT LIKE A TRAIN CONDUCTOR: Her job is to take people on a journey and make sure everyone gets there safe, sound, and at the same time. The conductor's ideas about the music, and her ability to indicate to the players what to do when, makes it possible for a group of sixty or so musicians to be on the same page in terms of how each piece of music is played.

THE BATON

The conductor's main accessory is recognizable to anyone who's been to a classical music concert or has watched Bugs Bunny on Saturday morning cartoons: a long, thin white stick, anywhere from just under one foot to two feet long, used by the conductor to mark time and give direction to the musicians. But the conducting baton wasn't actually standard until the 1830s. The first known instance of a baton being used to conduct music was in 1594, by a nun in San Vito Lo Capo who led her group of female musicians with a "wand." In the 1600s, the composer Jean-Baptiste Lully used a long stick, but instead of pointing with it, he thumped it on the ground to keep time and accidentally stabbed himself in the toe with it. He later died from the wound. After that, musicians rightly stayed away from batons, but in the early 1800s conductors such as Daniel Turk and Louis Spohr began to use batons in rehearsals, and Felix Mendelssohn, the famous pianist, composer, and conductor, made the baton legit for performance when he conducted the London Philharmonic with one in 1832. Since then, it has been the standard to use a baton when conducting.

Do you have to have a baton to conduct? Not necessarily: There are conductors today who do not use batons. But most conductors feel a baton helps make their movements more clear and visible to the orchestra. You can buy a baton at a music store, but for conducting around the house, a pencil, chopstick, or anything else long and thin will do just fine.

Do you need an orchestra to conduct? Most professional conductors would agree that an orchestra is necessary but not crucial. In fact, you can practice conducting to any music, whether it's played by live musicians or played over the loudspeaker at the grocery store.

CONDUCTING

Hold the baton in your right hand. With this hand you'll be indicating tempo (speed), dynamics (whether the music is loud or quiet), and articulation (whether notes are smooth or detached). You'll use your left hand to cue players (pointing with your index finger to prepare the player for an entrance) and indicate changes in volume (raising your left hand palm-up tells the orchestra to play louder; lowering your hand palm-down tells players to play quieter).

There are several basic conducting patterns: a two-beat pattern, a three-beat pattern, and a four-beat pattern. Whichever pattern you are conducting, begin by raising both arms in preparation, and emphasize the beat by bouncing your hand slightly when you get there. Otherwise it will look like you are simply flailing your arms rather than marking out a beat. Once you have the patterns down, you will be able to inject your own personal style. When the music gets louder, a conductor makes larger motions; when the music gets softer, she makes her motions smaller. When the notes are short and staccato, her movements become sharp and hard; when the notes are smoother and flowing, her movements become more fluid as well. These are the kinds of things you can experiment with once you know the basic conducting patterns.

THE FOUR-BEAT PATTERN

The four-beat pattern - 4/4

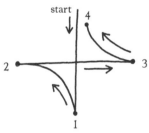

This is used for music that has four beats per measure. (When listening to it, you can count up to four before the rhythmic pulse of the music begins again. The song "Row, Row, Row Your Boat," for example, has a four-beat rhythm.) Begin with your right arm up, with your baton held just about at the level of your forehead. Bring it straight down to about chest level to mark the first beat. Then, bounce your hand over to the left, no farther than your left shoulder, to mark the second beat. Then, bring your hand across to the right (again, no farther than your right shoulder) to mark the third beat, and up again toward your starting position to mark the fourth beat. Practice this in slow motion, stopping sharply on each beat.

THE THREE-BEAT PATTERN

The three-beat pattern - 3/4

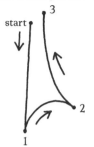

THE TWO-BEAT PATTERN

The two-beat pattern - 2/4 or 2/2

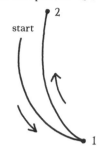

This is used for music that has three beats per measure (if you can't think of one, try humming "We Wish You a Merry Christmas"). Basically, you will be outlining a triangle with your baton. Begin with your right arm up, with your baton held at the level of your forehead. Bring it straight down to chest level to mark the first beat. Then, bounce it out to the right for the second beat. Then, swoop it back up to the starting point for the third beat. As with the four-beat pattern, make sure to practice by stopping sharply at each beat to make your pattern clear.

This is used for music with two beats per measure (think of the nursery rhyme "This Old Man," for example) and is a simple up-and-down movement. Begin with your baton held about as high as your forehead. Then, bring it down, but not straight down as in the other patterns. Instead, arc slightly to the right, as if you're drawing a crescent moon in front of you. Then, follow that same shape in reverse as you bring your hand back up to your starting point.

A Short History of the Bicycle

FROM THE DAY THE TRAINING WHEELS COME OFF until the day you get your driver's license, your fastest way of getting from here to there on your own is your bicycle. In 1896, the social reformer Susan B. Anthony said that bicycling gave girls everywhere "a feeling of freedom and self-reliance," and that it had "done more to emancipate women than anything else in the world." The bicycle is now quite taken for granted, but historically the bicycle was quite a revolution. It was the first vehicle to replace horses. And, when bicycles were invented in the nineteenth century, they became a way for girls and women to travel independently. Bicycles paved the way for women to wear pants—and to win the right to vote.

1817 The *dandy horse* is invented. It is a wooden walking machine with two wheels. People start to see the Dandy Horse on dirt roads, alongside wagons pulled by horses and oxen.

1844 The process for making rubber tires is invented by Charles Goodyear.

1860s The pedal and crank are developed.

1865 Steel technology advances. The *boneshaker bicycle* has wheels of steel that replace the earlier ones made of wood. The pedal is connected to the front wheel. The ride is uncomfortable, especially over cobblestones.

1870s The *high wheel bicycle* has a huge front wheel that is much, much larger than the tiny back wheel. The rider sits way up high. Also called the *ordinary*, this bicycle is made possible by the Industrial Age's production of ever stronger metals. The front wheel is so big because the larger the wheel, the farther a single push of the pedal will make the bicycle go. The pedal is still attached to the front wheel, because bicycle gears have not yet been invented. The high wheel bicycle is easily toppled and thus dangerous. It is

expensive, and its ridership is limited to the most affluent men (and to women and girls seeking scandal).

1870s The *high wheel tricycle* is suggested as an appropriate vehicle for women to use while wearing their Victorian-era, full-skirted, long dresses, and for dignified men seeking to avoid the ordinary's topple.

1880s So-called *safety bikes* are invented. This new bicycle has two wheels of equal size. For the first time ever, the pedals are attached to the back wheel, making good use of the newly invented bicycle chain. The metal in the frame is stronger. The safety bike's ride is bumpier than the high wheel, but more people live to have dinner that night.

1880s Wheeling becomes more popular. Bicycling clubs start to form. The clubs argue that cobblestone streets are far too bumpy. They lobby governments to pave the roads.

1888 A patent is filed for the first air-filled and inflatable pneumatic tire. The new tires make cycling much more comfortable.

1890s The bicycle craze is in full swing. In 1897 alone, more than two million bicycles are sold. Women in particular love bicycles, and bicycling becomes identified with the New Woman, who seeks more from life.

1890s   Women start to wear bloomers, blousy pants that tie at the ankle, covered by wide skirts that hit just below the knee. Bloomers had been popularized a few decades earlier by Amelia Jenks Bloomer, an American reformer. But with the bicycle, bloomers become a necessity. Women wear them instead of the old fashions of ungainly hoopskirts, bustles, petticoats, and whalebone corsets laced so tight it was almost impossible to breathe. Commonsense dressing becomes the new rage. Some people complain, fearing bloomers may usher in the end of the world.

1894   The social crisis provoked by women bicycling reaches a fever pitch. People worry that bicycling does grave damage to women's kidneys and livers, and that bicycles make women do bad things. In an 1894 editorial, the *Chicago Daily News* rises to the defense of female bicyclers, writing that "when a woman wants to learn anything or do anything useful or even have any fun, there is always someone to solemnly warn her that it is her duty to keep well. Meanwhile, in many states she can work in factories ten hours a day, she can stand behind counters in badly ventilated stores from 8 o'clock to 6, she can bend over the sewing machine for about 5 cents an hour and no one cares enough to protest. But when these same women, condemned to sedentary lives indoors, find a cheap and delightful way of getting the fresh air and exercise they need so sorely there is a great hue and cry about their physical welfare."

1894   Annie "Londonderry" Kopchovsky becomes the first woman to bicycle around the world. She pedals out of Boston in June 1894, and returns on September 12, 1895. She collects a $10,000 prize from a Boston man who bet his friend that she couldn't pull it off (and that he would give her the $10,000 if she could).

1895   At fifty-three, Frances Willard, founder of the Women's Christian Temperance Union and a suffragist, learns to ride a bicycle. In her 1895 book *A Wheel Within a Wheel: How I Learned to Ride the Bicycle*, she writes about the wider world she has entered and about her "natural love of adventure, a love long hampered and impeded."

1898   Coaster brakes are invented, making it easier to stop a bicycle on demand.

1900s   Hoping to shoo women off public streets and keep them indoors safe and sound, women-only indoor riding rinks are opened. They are outfitted with slalom courses, called "ten pin rides" because they are set up with bowling pins. Special cycling music is piped in. Riding sessions are followed by afternoon tea.

1920s   Children's bikes are first manufactured. These big bikes often weigh 60 or 65 pounds, but they are the right size for small legs.

1950s   Three-speed bikes are invented.

1970s   Leaner and lighter ten-speed bikes become popular.

1980s   Mountain bikes, with tougher, wider wheels and even more gears, take biking off-road and into the woods.

Picnic Games

CATCH THE BABY

A ball game for three or more people. Each player is given a number (1 through however many players there are). One player is "it," and she gets the ball; the other players form a circle around her. "It" throws the ball up in the air and calls out a number. The player whose number is called must catch the ball before it bounces. If she doesn't, she is now "it."

WATER BALLOON VOLLEYBALL

Just like regular volleyball, but with water balloons. And splashing.

THREE-LEGGED RACE

For any number of teams of two people. Each team prepares by having the two team members stand side by side, facing the same direction. The team member on the left-hand side ties her right ankle or knee to the left ankle or knee of the team member on the right-hand side using a bandanna or scarf. Then each team must race to the finish using their three legs.

TOE-AND-HEEL RACE

Players "run" by stepping so that the heel of the stepping foot touches the toes of the other foot.

POTATO SACK RACE

A game for any number of players, who must hop the course with their legs and feet inside a sack or pillowcase.

WHEELBARROW RACE

For any number of teams of two people. Each team must have one player who is the wheelbarrow and one player who pushes the wheelbarrow. The person who is the wheelbarrow places her hands on the ground; the person who pushes the wheelbarrow holds the wheelbarrow's feet. To race, the teams must walk to the finish line, with the wheelbarrow walking on her hands and the wheelbarrow pusher walking and holding up the legs. The team that crosses the finish line completely first wins.

WHAT TIME IS IT, MR. WOLF?

One person is the wolf. She stands with her back to the rest of the players, who are lined up at the opposite side of the field (or playing area). The group of players yells, "What time is it, Mr. Wolf?" The wolf calls out a time (for instance, "ten o'clock"), and the other players take one step forward for each hour (in this case, ten steps). Then the players ask again, "What time is it, Mr. Wolf?" The wolf can either continue to respond with more times, or she can call "Dinnertime!" At this point, the wolf turns around to chase the players, who must run back to the starting line without getting caught. Players who are caught become wolves, and the last nonwolf player left wins.

"MUSHROOM" PARACHUTE GAME

If you don't have a parachute, you can try this with a big picnic blanket or sheet. Lift it as high as possible, and then (still holding on to the fabric) run underneath the parachute and pull it behind as you sit down to create a kind of mushroom shape.

EGG RACE

This can be either an individual race or a relay race, and can be played several ways. Players can be required to: roll the egg down the course using only her nose; carry the egg on a spoon held in one hand; carry the egg on a spoon held by her teeth; or even all three in that order.

MESSY BALLOON RACE

This can be played with several teams and involves balloons filled with water or shaving cream. Each teammate gets a balloon and runs from a starting point to a predetermined ending point, and then sits on the balloon until it pops. Then she must run back to the start and have her next teammate do the same. The team that pops all their balloons first wins.

CRAB WALK SOCCER

This game is played like regular soccer (in which each team tries to score by kicking a ball into the opposing team's goal), except that all players must be in "crab" position (walking on their hands and feet with their heads and stomachs facing up).

MARBLE TOES

Use a rope to mark a circle on the ground, and then dump a bag of marbles within the circle. Four people at a time have one minute to pick up as many marbles as they can with their toes.

TUG-OF-WAR

Two teams face off against each other with a rope. Everyone holds on to the rope, and each team pulls backward to try to get the other team over the middle and onto the other team's side.

CATS IN THE CORNER

One player has a ball (such as a soccer ball), and the other players are "cats." The ball thrower stands in the center of a square play area, and the other players stand in the "safe zones" at each of the corners. The ball thrower calls out, "Cats in the corner!" and throws the ball as the cats run to a different corner of the play area. Any cat who is hit by the ball is out. The winner is the last cat standing.

OBSTACLE COURSE

Use materials you have on hand to create an obstacle course. This can involve anything from zigzagging between trees to crawling through cardboard boxes to stepping through a series of jump ropes or Hula-Hoops. Time each player as she runs the course. The fastest player wins.

RED ROVER

For two teams of any number of players. Each team forms a line and holds hands. One team begins by calling, "Red Rover, Red Rover, will [the name of a person on the other team] come over?" The person whose name is called runs over and tries to break through the line of the other team. If she succeeds, she gets to take someone from that team back with her to her home team; if she can't break through, she must stay with the opposite team. The other team has a turn to call "Red Rover." The game is over when all the players are on one team.

CARTWHEEL RACE

Race to see who can get to the finish line first by doing cartwheels.

KNOTS

Divide into any number of teams of six or more people. Each team stands in a circle with all players facing the center. Players then shake hands with the people directly across from them, and then grab left hands with a different person. The goal is then to untangle without letting go of anyone's hands.

FRISBEE

This can be as simple as tossing the Frisbee from friend to friend or dividing up into teams and playing a Frisbee version of football. In this kind of Frisbee, sometimes called Ultimate Frisbee, teams try to get the Frisbee into an end zone. Running with the Frisbee or tackling another player is not allowed. If a player drops the Frisbee or has her throw intercepted, the other team gets the turn. Another variation is Frisbee Golf, which involves throwing the Frisbee at a target or into a basket along a course.

OVER, UNDER, OVER, UNDER

A relay race whose goal is to pass a beanbag or ball down the line and be the first team to finish. The first person in line on each team passes the beanbag over her head to the person behind her. Then that person passes the beanbag under her legs to the next person. The next person passes over, the next person passes under, and so on. When the beanbag gets to the last person in line, that person runs to the front and the whole process begins again, until the person who first started the race is back at the head of the line.

Paper Cup Candles

THIS IS A CRAFT that can be made from materials that happen to be lying around the house. To make a paper cup candle, first gather materials related to the wax, the wick, and the mold.

The wax can be melted down from old candle stubs or from candles you've bought for cheap at a yard sale. Paraffin wax can be purchased at a craft store, along with candle wax dye.

The wick is made from twisted cotton. You can find special wick twine, but ordinary cotton string seems to work just fine. You may also recycle wicks by melting down old candles

The mold we use is a small paper cup (plastic is okay, if that's what you have). To make a taller or wider candle, cut a milk carton to the height you want, or use the tallest paper or plastic cup you can find. If candle making becomes a hobby, you can experiment with other kinds of candle molds.

You will also need an assortment of old pots, spoons, and tongs. Wax inevitably spills and sputters. Head to the nearest thrift store or yard sale or basement stash for old pots that can be devoted to candle making. In no event should you melt wax directly in your parents' good saucepan.

A FEW OTHER THINGS YOU'LL NEED:

- A double boiler, which is a set of two pots. The bottom pot holds an inch or so of boiling water. This provides an indirect heat to the top pot—which holds the wax. We prefer to use a metal can to hold the wax. Use a separate can for each color of wax. Pinch a spout in the can's rim so it's easier to pour.

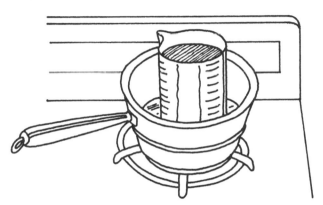

- Tongs and potholders

- A low tray or baking pan, to hold the molds

- Pencils, craft sticks, or plastic straws, needed to hold the wick straight while the wax hardens

- Masking tape, regular tape, or hot glue

MAKE THE CANDLE

To start, set out newspapers to protect the countertop and get the molds ready. Cut the wick so that it is a few inches longer than the cup or mold, and attach it to the bottom of the mold. There are a few ways to do this. We like wrapping the wick around a pencil or craft stick and resting it across the top of the cup so that the wick hangs straight down. Here's another method: Melt a few drops of hot glue at the bottom of the mold. Hold the wick in the glue it until it dries.

Fill the bottom of the double boiler with an inch or two of water. Put the wax in the can (or top pot), and put that in (or over) the bigger pot of water. Set both on the stove, and start boiling the wax. Hot wax can hurt, so ask for help if you are too young to use the stove alone.

The solid wax will turn to liquid. Pour it slowly into each mold. But save some wax, and don't fill the whole mold. Leave a little bit of the top of the mold empty, maybe an eighth of an inch. It's a good trick to know, and here's why.

In about twenty minutes, the wax will begin to set. That's when you'll heat the leftover wax. Pick up a stick and poke holes in the top of the candle all around the wick. (Do this carefully so that hot wax does not spurt up at you.) The candle will look messy, but do not despair. You are getting rid of air bubbles, so that your candle won't develop a deep spiraling crevice down the middle. Pour leftover wax over the mess. This tops off the candle. When it dries, the old and new wax will meld together nicely. The top will be smooth and flat.

In about four hours the candle will be ready. Unwrap the wick from the pencil, tear or cut the cup away, and cut the wick to size.

GLASS JAR CANDLES

Glass jars make good containers for candles. One thing to know: Once the wax melts in the double boiler, let it cool just a bit before pouring it into the glass so the glass won't break.

There's a trick for holding the wick down in a glass jar. When the wax is ready and melted, dip the wick in up to the height that the candle will be (in other words, leave lots of room for winding extra wick around a pencil, if you still need to do this). Set the waxy wick aside for a few minutes. The wax will harden, and this will help the wick stand up straight. In the meantime, pour the wax into the glass jar, and follow the same directions as for the paper cup candle. As the candle begins to set, put the wick in place.

HOW DOES A CANDLE WORK?

A burning candle is a circle of continuous reactions and more complicated than one would imagine.

❧ Paraffin wax comes from crude oil, and it's the fuel that keeps a candle flame burning.

❧ When the wick is lit, the heat from the flame melts the solid wax near it. This creates a pool of liquid wax. The wick absorbs and pumps the liquid wax up toward the heat of the flame. It does this by capillary action (which was described in the "Paper Flowers and Capillary Action" chapter in the original *Daring Book for Girls*).

❧ Liquid wax reaches the top of the wick, which also holds the flame. The hot flame turns the liquid wax into a vapor, which is a state between being a liquid or a gas.

❧ The vapor spreads out from the wick. It is this specific form of wax fuel that keeps the flame burning. The smoke that wafts upward after a flame is snuffed out is wax vapor that, in the absence of the flame's heat, condenses and becomes visible to the eye.

❧ The end of the wick burns and curls and comes to rest in the outer part of the flame. The light blue color at the flame's edge is hottest—1,670 on the Kelvin scale for measuring temperatures—and the flame cools toward the center, where it turns yellow, orange, and then red. Air pulls the hotter vapors up and out.

Why doesn't the whole candle burn? Because paraffin wax has a very high combustion point, so if it isn't near the wick, the wax won't burn up. The wick is relatively small, so only the wax closest to the flame melts.

Why doesn't the wick burn faster, since it's only cotton, which usually would burn to a crisp in a minute? Because the wax vapor cools the wick.

Why does the flame travel upward? Because it is lighter and less dense than air.

Tic-Tac-Toe Around the World

TIC-TAC-TOE HAS BEEN PLAYED worldwide for centuries. It has many alternative names in English: "tick-tat-toe" in Canada, "noughts and crosses" in Australia and South Africa, "Xie-Osies" in Northern Ireland, even "kisses and hugs" in some parts of the United States. Tic-Tac-Toe emerged from a category of ancient games called Three Men's Morris. (The word *morris* in the title comes from the Latin *merelius*, meaning "game piece." It's called "Three Men" because the simplest version is played with three game pieces.) These games have been played since the time of the Roman Empire in Europe and Confucius's day in Asia. Here are some other versions of Tic-Tac-Toe from around the world.

ACHI (GHANA)

In *Achi*, each player has four game pieces. They take turns placing these pieces on the board's nine intersections. Each player tries to get three pieces in a row. During this round, pieces cannot be moved, only "dropped" on the board. Say neither player can win this first round. One after the other, the players slide one of their game pieces along the board's lines into an empty spot on the board. They take turns until someone lands three pieces in a row and wins—and someone will always win. As with all Three Men's Morris games, taking the center has its advantages, especially when the pieces begin to slide.

YIH (CHINA)

The Chinese game of *Yih*, or *Luk Tsut K'ii*, is also a Three Men's Morris game. Its board is similar to the board in *Achi*, but with only three game pieces per player. In round one, both players lay down their three pieces. Then the sliding portion of the game begins. Players move a game piece to any open spot and use strategy to land all three in a row.

NINE MEN'S MORRIS

A related and more complex game is Nine Men's Morris. The board can be drawn on paper or cardboard (or even painted on a piece of wood, for a longer-lasting version). Each player has nine game pieces (and in a homemade version of the game, these may be two contrasting kinds of buttons or coins).

Like *Achi* and *Yih*, Nine Men's Morris has two stages. In the placement stage, each player puts her nine pieces on one of the twenty-four intersections on the board.

The goal of the game is to form three-piece rows. These are called mills, and you also need to block your opponent from forming mills. Once a player forms a mill, she gets to capture one of her opponent's pieces. This means she picks a piece and removes it from the board forever. The rule is, she has to choose a piece that is not a part of a mill (if no other pieces on the board can be removed, she can take a piece from a mill).

The movement stage begins when all game pieces are on the board. Players slide pieces to adjacent intersections. Each player makes mills, blocks mills, and outsmarts her opponent.

To win, reduce your opponent to fewer than three pieces. Or, push to the point where she has no more legal moves left. In other words, your opponent loses when she can no longer move any pieces, when she is blocked into a portion of the board, or when she has two pieces left and can no longer form a mill and capture your pieces.

Tips: Keep your pieces moving around the board. Don't get stuck in one sector. You might try to arrange your pieces with two nearby mill structures so that one piece can move back and forth. This will give you a mill—and a chance to remove one of your opponent's pieces—each turn.

WINNING AT TIC-TAC-TOE

1. Go first. This is the simplest way to win, because you will have five chances to play while your opponent has only four.

2. If you go first, grab the center. This is the clearest way toward tic-tac-toe victory there is. Alternately, take one of the four corners. **Never ever take an edge as your first move.** In your next moves, watch your opponent's moves, always block him or her from winning, and to the extent you can, continue to take corners.

3. If you go first and take a corner and the other player takes the center, your second move should be to take the corner diagonally across from your first move. This is counterintuitive. It works because it sets up two possible ways to win, because in your next move you will grab a corner that will give you two ways to win and your opponent only one way to block.

4. If you are the second player: If your opponent took a corner, you should take the center. If the center has been taken, grab a corner. In subsequent moves, block your opponent and take as many corners as you can. Take an edge only to nab your tic-tac-toe.

5. Always block a potential win (of course).

Don't show these strategies to anyone or else all tic-tac-toe games will end in a draw. When that starts to happen, try the French rules. They prohibit the first player from taking the center spot.

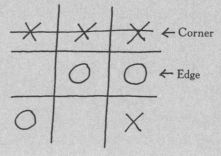

Collective Nouns About Animals

COLLECTIVE NOUNS ARE TERMS—usually colorful, descriptive words—to describe groups of animals, people, ideas, or things. Here are some of our favorites.

An aerie of eagles
An army of caterpillars
An array of hedgehogs
A band of coyotes
A bed of clams
A bevy of quail
A blessing of unicorns
A bloat of hippos
A brace of ducks
A brood of chickens
A business of ferrets
A cartload of chimpanzees
A cast of falcons
A charm of finches
A charm of hummingbirds
A clan of hyenas
A clash of bucks
A cloud of bats
A clowder of cats
A colony of ants
A company of moles
A congregation of birds
A congregation of crocodiles
A congress of baboons
A conspiracy of ravens
A convocation of eagles
A corps of giraffes
A coterie of prairie dogs
A covey of partridges
A crash of rhinos
A culture of bacteria
A dazzle of zebras
A deceit of lapwings
A doom of dragons
A dray of squirrels
A drove of cattle
A drove of donkeys
A drove of goats
A drumming of grouse
An exaltation of larks
A family of otter
A flange of baboons

A flight of cormorants
A float of crocodiles
A flock of camels
A flock of sheep
A gaggle of geese
A gang of elk
A gaze of raccoons
A glint of goldfish
A gulp of cormorants
A herd of antelope
A herd of boar
A herd of buffalo
A herd of deer
A horde of gerbils
A horde of mice
A host of sparrows
A hover of trout
A husk of hares
An intrusion of cockroaches
A kettle of hawks
A knot of toads
A labor of moles
A leap of leopards
A lodge of beavers
A lounge of lizards
A mob of emus
A murder of crows
A murmuration of starlings
A mustering of storks
A nest of hornets
A nest of vipers
A nuisance of cats
A nursery of raccoons
An ostentation of peacocks
A pack of dogs
A paddling of ducks
A parcel of penguins
A parliament of owls
A passel of hogs
A piteousness of doves
A pitying of turtledoves
A plague of locusts

A pod of dolphins
A prickle of hedgehogs
A pride of lions
A quiver of cobras
A rabble of butterflies
A rafter of turkeys
A rhumba of rattlesnakes
A richness of martens
A rookery of penguins
A rumpus of baboons
A school of fish
A scold of jays
A scurry of squirrels
A shiver of shark
A shoal of bass
A shrewness of apes
A siege of cranes
A skein of geese
A skulk of foxes
A sleuth of bears
A smack of jellyfish
A sneak of weasels
A spring of seals
A stable of horses
A string of ponies
A surfeit of skunks
A swarm of bees
A swarm of butterflies
A swarm of eels
A swarm of flies
A team of horses
A tiding of magpies
A troop of kangaroos
An unkindness of ravens
A wake of buzzards
A warren of hares
A watch of nightingales
A wedge of swans
A wing of plovers
A wisp of snipe
A yoke of oxen
A zeal of zebras

Card Games

CAMICIA ("SHIRT")

This Italian game for two players uses an Italian deck. If you don't have an Italian deck of cards handy, you can either swing by the local *tabaccheria* (tobacco shop) on your next trip to Italy and pick one up, or simply use your regular fifty-two-card deck with the 8, 9, 10, and joker cards removed.

In this game, there are two kinds of cards: *attack cards* and *normal cards*. The attack cards are aces, 2s, and 3s; the rest of the cards are normal. To play, deal the cards facedown to each player so that both have twenty cards each. Player 1 flips her top card over and places it faceup on the table in a middle pile between the players' card piles. If the card is normal, player 2 takes her turn. If the card is an attack card, player 2 must put a number of cards equal to the value of the attack card into the middle pile (one card for an ace, two cards for a 2, three cards for a 3). If the last card player 2 puts down in response to an attack is normal, then the attacking player (player 1) gets to take the whole pile and put those cards facedown at the bottom of her card pile and begin play again. But if the last card is an attack card, player 2 gets to keep her cards, and player 1 must put down the number of cards required by the attack card. The game continues until one of the players runs out of cards.

SPIT

This is a game for two players using a regular fifty-two-card deck. Deal the cards evenly, twenty-six cards to each player. To begin, each player sets up five piles of cards facedown directly in front of her, with one card in the first pile, two cards in the second, three cards in the third, four cards in the fourth, and five cards in the fifth. Turn over the top card in each of the five piles. The eleven cards left over for each player are their *spit cards*, which should be held by the players at all times. (If you're right-handed, hold the spit cards in your left hand; if you're left-handed, hold them in your right hand.)

When both players are done setting up their five piles, the game is started by saying, "One, two, three, *spit!*" Then both players must take the top card from their spit cards and place it down in the middle of the playing area, between the players' five-pile setups. These are now *spit piles*.

Using the cards facing up on their five-pile setup, players can play either spit pile by putting down a card either one rank higher or one rank lower than the card on the spit pile. (For instance, if a spit pile has a seven, a player can put down an eight or a six.) After taking a card from the five-pile setup, turn over the next card from that pile so that you have five cards facing up at one time. The goal is to play as fast as you can, to get rid of all the cards in your setup. If neither player can play a card on either spit pile, say, "One, two, three, spit!" and draw two new spit cards for the spit piles.

When a player has no cards left in her setup, pause the play and pick up the spit piles (the smaller pile goes to the player with no cards left; the bigger pile goes to the other player). Shuffle the cards and make another five-pile setup, as in the beginning of the game. Count, "One, two, three, *spit!*" and begin again.

Continue play until one player has too few cards to make a complete setup. When this happens, she should lay out as many of the five piles as possible and turn over the top card of each. Since she won't have any cards left over for a spit pile, there will only be one spit pile (the other player's) instead of two. Play on until one person wins by getting rid of all her cards.

SPOONS

For this game, which can be played with three or more players, you will need a standard deck of cards and (as you may guess from the name of the game) some spoons. How many spoons you need depends on how many players you have, as you'll need one less spoon than the total number of players (for instance, if you have four players, you'll need three spoons). Each player is dealt four cards, and the goal of the game is to have all four cards in your hand be the same rank (that is, *four of a kind*).

To play, put all the spoons in the center of the table and choose one player to be the dealer. The dealer gives each player four cards and places the rest of the cards in a *draw pile* next to her. The dealer is in charge of the draw pile, and the player to the left of the dealer is in charge of the *trash* (the cards that are unused after play).

The dealer begins the game by drawing a card from the draw pile. She can either pass it, facedown, to the player on her right; or she can swap it with a card from her hand, which must then be passed facedown to the player on her right. As that next player picks up the card (which she then must swap or pass to her right in the same manner), the dealer draws a new card from the draw pile to swap or pass. The play continues as each successive player picks up the card passed by the player next to her and either swaps or passes it along. (When the play reaches the trash player, she places the swapped or passed card in trash pile instead of passing it along to the dealer. If the dealer runs out of cards in the draw pile, the player in charge of the trash shuffles the trash pile and gives it to the dealer to use as the new draw pile.) Play continues until a player has four cards that are all the same rank, at which point she is allowed to take a spoon from the middle of the table.

Once one player has grabbed a spoon, the other players are allowed to grab spoons as well, often prompting a mad dash for the spoon pile. The player left without a spoon is out of the game. One spoon is then taken away from the spoon pile, and the game continues with one less player and one less spoon in each successive round until only one person is left.

(Another version, making for a much longer game: Once one player has a hand with four of a kind, she grabs a spoon. The other players are then allowed to grab a spoon, and the player who doesn't get one loses that round and earns the letter S (the first letter in *spoons*). Each time a player loses a round, she earns the next letter in the word. When a player has lost enough rounds to have collected all the letters in *spoons*, she is out of the game, and one spoon is taken away from the spoon pile. The game continues until only one person is left.

CARD GAMES

Scrabble Words

TWO-LETTER WORDS ARE THE SECRET ingredients to Scrabble success. Laying down a well-placed two-letter word can often net you more points than a straightforward five- or six-letter word. So knowing the list of which two-letter words are allowed in Scrabble can stand you in good stead the next time you're faced with a rack of Xs, Qs, and Zs. The following words are deemed acceptable for American tournament play by the National Scrabble Association.

AA rough and jagged basaltic lava
AB abdominal muscle (abbreviation)
AD advertisement (abbreviation)
AE one (from Scottish Middle English)
AG agriculture (abbreviation)
AH an interjection ("Ah!")
AI a three-toed sloth
AL an Indian mulberry tree
AM first-person singular form of the verb to be
AN indefinite article
AR a spelling of the letter r
AS a bronze coin; or the adverb meaning to the same degree
AT preposition meaning "in or near a particular location"
AW interjection ("Aw!")
AX another spelling of axe
AY yes (another spelling of aye)
BA in Egyptian mythology, a person's soul, repesented as a bird-headed figure
BE to exist
BI two
BO a martial arts stick
BY preposition meaning "near or next to"
DE of or from
DO to perform or execute, or the first tone of musical scale
ED education (abbreviation)
EF a spelling of the letter f
EH an interjection ("Eh?")
EL a spelling of the letter l

EM a spelling of the letter m; also, a unit of measurement in typesetting equal to the width of the lowercased letter m
EN a spelling of the letter n; also, a unit of measurement in typesetting equal to the width of the lowercased letter n
ER an interjection ("Um, er, well, . . .")
ES a spelling of the letter s
ET colloquial past-tense version of the verb eat
EX a spelling of the letter x
FA the fourth tone of the musical scale
FE Abbreviation for iron on the periodic table of elements
GO to leave
HA interjection ("Ha!")
HE referring to a male person
HI greeting or interjection
HM interjection ("Hmm . . .")
HO interjection ("Ho!")
ID one of the three components of the personality according to Freud
IN a preposition; an abbreviation for influence
IS third-person-singular form of the verb to be
IT an indefinite pronoun; or, in a game such as tag, the person who must tag other players
JO darling or sweetheart (from the Scottish jo, meaning "joy")
KA in Egyptian mythology, the spiritual soul that survives even after death

KI a plant native to Pacific Islands and China; also, an alternate spelling of *chi* or *qi*, the fundamental life force in Chinese philosophy

LA the sixth tone of the musical scale

LI a Chinese unit of distance

LO interjection ("Lo and behold!")

MA abbreviation of *mother*

ME myself

MI the third tone of the musical scale

MM interjection ("Mm!")

MO abbreviation of *moment*

MU a Greek letter; also, the Japanese word for "nothingness"

MY possessive pronoun

NA a variant of no

NE born with the name of

NO negative

NU a Greek letter; also, a Yiddish interjection ("It's good, nu?")

OD a hypothetical force or power

OE a small island

OF a preposition meaning belonging to, associated with, containing, coming from

OH an interjection ("Oh!")

OI interjection ("Oi!"); alternate spelling of *oy*

OM a sacred syllable used in prayer and meditation

ON a preposition

OP a style of abstract art (short for *optical*)

OR a conjunction; also, the gold on a coat of arms

OS a bone; an opening

OW interjection ("Ow!")

OX a bovine animal (a cow or bull)

OY interjection ("Oy!")

PA abbreviation of *papa*

PE a Hebrew letter

PI a Greek letter; also, the ratio of the circumference of a circle to its diameter (approximately 3.14159), usually written as π

QI the Chinese concept of fundamental life force energy

RE the second tone of the musical scale

SH interjection ("Sh!")

SI the seventh tone of the musical scale (also called *ti*)

SO the fifth tone of the musical scale

TA an exclamation, abbreviation of *thanks*

TI the seventh tone of the musical scale (also called *si*)

TO toward

UH interjection ("Uh . . .")

UM interjection ("I, um, don't know . . .")

UN one

UP to raise; risen

US first-person objective pronoun for *we*

UT another name for the first tone of the musical scale (commonly called *do*)

WE first-person plural pronoun

WO interjection ("Wo!"); alternate spelling of "Whoa!"

XI a Greek letter

XU a unit of currency in Vietnam

YA you

YE you ("Hear ye, hear ye")

YO interjection ("Yo!")

ZA abbreviation for *pizza*

Fun Things to Do with Paper

1. SPITBALLS

We shouldn't be telling you how to do this, but we can't resist. Wad up a piece of paper so it is smaller than the opening of the straw you're going to shoot it from. Put the paper in your mouth (that's the spit part), form it into a ball, and then push the spitty wad of paper into the end of the straw. Aim and shoot. As with the rest of life, practice makes perfect.

2. NEWSPAPER TREE

Newspaper trees go by lots of names. We've heard "fountain," "cornstalk," "log and torch," to name just a few. Whatever you call it, the first step in making it is to create one continuous roll, as if you had taped the sheets of newspaper together. Spread out a large sheet of newspaper, and start rolling it tight. When you are about six inches away from the end of the sheet, bring out the second piece of newspaper. Lay it over the end of the first piece. Start incorporating the new sheet of paper into the roll. Use a minimum of two to four sheets of newsprint, or many more if you would like.

When that's finished, wrap a piece of tape around the bottom and middle of the roll, or snap on a few rubber bands. This creates the "trunk" of the tree. Now it's time to make the fringes (or "branches") on top. With a pair of scissors, start cutting five to six slits, from the end of the roll to about a third of the way down the roll. When this is done, reach down through all the fringe into the center of the roll. Grab hold and start pulling the tree to life.

3. DOTS

This paper-and-pencil game is an easy way for two or more people to pass the time. Draw a 10-by-10 array of dots (although, really, your game board can be any size). Take turns connecting two adjacent dots with a line (no diagonals). As more and more lines fill the board, try to finish off a square—before someone else gets in your way. Even if another player has marked off two or three edges, if you finish a square, it's yours. Mark your first initial in the square and take a bonus turn. When the board is full, count the initialed squares. The person with the highest number wins.

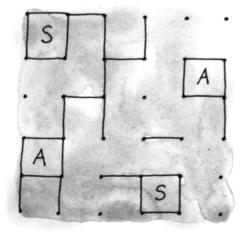

4. SECRET NOTES

Fold a top-secret communiqué into a tightly guarded square.

Step 1. These directions work best with an ordinary 8½-by-11-inch piece of paper. Start by holding the paper the long way, that is, with the longer edge on top (and the shorter edge to the side). Fold the page in half the long way. Then, fold the paper in half the long way again, to get the long strip of paper that can be folded into a secret note. The writing is hidden on the inside, and the paper has turned into a long rectangle (Figures 1a and 1b).

Step 2. Fold the bottom left corner up to meet the top edge. Fold the top right corner down to meet the bottom edge. The stars in the illustration are to get you ready for the next step, which can be tricky (Figure 2).

Step 3. In this step, the shape of the note changes to a kind of "S" shape. Fold the bottom left corner up to meet the top edge of the note. Doing so will form the left side of the center square. Follow the stars on the illustration: The lower corner folds up, and as you fold, the stars will match up (Figure 3).

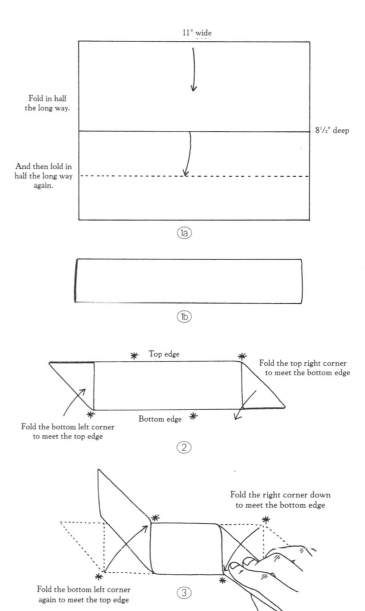

Do the same fold with the right side. Fold the top right corner down so it meets the bottom edge. The stars will match up. This fold will form the right side of the center square.

The "S" shape will emerge.

We've marked the top of the left triangle "A." We've marked the bottom of the right triangle "B."

These labels will come in handy for the next step.

Crease all the folds with your fingernail so they lay flat.

Depending on what size paper you started with, you may need to jiggle the folds in Steps 3 and 4 somewhat, keeping in mind that the important thing is to form the square in the center.

Step 4. Fold A back and toward the right. It will end up behind the center square. Fold B forward and toward the left. It will end up in front of the center square. The note should now look like a square with a triangle at the top (that's A) and a triangle at the bottom (that's B). There will also be a diagonal line across the center, from the folds (Figure 5a).

Step 5. To finish the secret note, fold the bottom triangle B up and behind the center square. Tuck it between the center square and the bottom part of A (you'll have to unfold A for a moment to do so). Next, fold the top triangle A down over the front of the center square. Tuck it inside the diagonal flap (Figures 5b and 6).

Voilá! Your secret note is ready to travel.

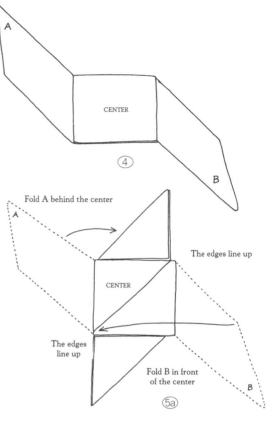

CENTER

④

Fold A behind the center

A

The edges line up

CENTER

The edges line up

Fold B in front of the center

B

⑤a

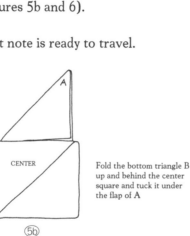

A

CENTER

Fold the bottom triangle B up and behind the center square and tuck it under the flap of A

⑤b

For the final step, fold the bottom triangle B up and behind the center square and tuck it in under the flap of A, and fold the top triangle A in front of center square and tuck it in. Voilà, your note is ready to travel.

⑥

5. MARBLED PAPER

Marbled paper is often used for bookmarks, wrapping paper, or the inside covers of books. To achieve that signature marbled look, ink or paint is floated on water in a shallow tray. Then paper is gently laid upon it, transforming the inky, marbled pattern to the paper.

When making marbled paper, the challenge is to get the ink to stick to the paper. One way professional crafters do this is by painting the paper with a mixture of alum and water. Alum is ordinarily used to crisp pickles and to help maraschino cherries keep their shape. It can be hard to use, though, and even harder to find at the local grocery store. We were admittedly skeptical when introduced to a surprising but reliable substitute: shaving cream. It's weird, but it works.

You'll need paint, paper, and a container. If you have marbling paints, that's great. But any type of paint will do: tempera, latex, acrylic, craft paint, watercolor, or any kind of ink, dye, or food coloring. The container you use should be slightly bigger than the paper. It can be a baking dish, a brownie pan, a watertight serving tray, or anything that's an inch or so deep.

Squirt an inch-deep layer of foamy shaving cream into the container. Use a plastic knife (or spoon or spatula or the flat edge of cardboard) to smooth the top surface of the shaving cream.

Sprinkle drops of paint over the smoothed shaving cream. The color will stay on top of the shaving cream, and the paper will rest on top of the shaving cream. With the tines or the side of a fork (or with a toothpick or stick or straw), make swirls and whorls in the paint and shaving cream. Hold the piece of paper in both hands, and place it gently down and onto the shaving cream, letting the center touch the shaving cream first. To prevent air bubbles, press your fingers gently from the center toward the edges once the paper is fully down.

When the paper seems to have picked up color (it will do so quite quickly), pull it away. Wipe away the excess shaving cream with the flat edge of a piece of cardboard. You can also rinse the paper under a water faucet—the color will stay. Lay the paper on a dish towel to dry, and get another paper to make the next batch, although you will need to start with a fresh layer of shaving cream every so often.

---

6. PAPER YOU CAN WALK THROUGH

Fold an 8½-by-11-inch page in half the short way. This means that you start with the long side on top and fold it as if you were folding the paper into a book.

Step 1. Start the first cut from the folded edge of the paper, about one half inch down from the top. Stop cutting about an inch shy of the unfolded edge of the page. The next cut starts from the unfolded edge of the paper. Start a half inch down from the first cut. As before, stop cutting about an inch away from the other edge.

Step 2. Continue making cuts in this back-and-forth way, from one side of the paper and then from the other, until you reach the bottom. Turn the paper, if that makes it easier to do the cutting. As you get close to the bottom of the paper, pay attention and watch out that the final cut gets started from the folded side of the paper.

Step 3. To finish, cut along the folded edge, but without cutting the very top or the very bottom (if you do slit any of these by mistake, just tape them together afterward).

Let the paper unravel, and you'll see how a single page can open wide enough for almost anyone to scoot through.

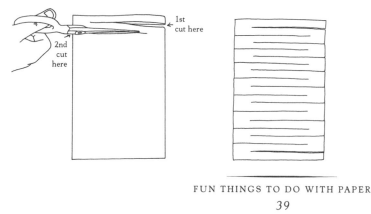

1st cut here

2nd cut here

Cut all folds except the very top and very bottom

7. PAPER BAG BOOK COVERS

You can make book covers in a jiffy with paper bags from the grocery store. To prepare, slit open a paper bag open along one of the creases and cut off the rectangular bottom. If there are no paper bags around, that's okay. You can cover a book with newspaper or wrapping paper or any paper you might have on hand.

Put the paper on a table or floor and place the book you want to cover on top. If there's more than a few inches of paper bag coming out the top or bottom, cut away the extra.

With the book open, mark the paper along the top and bottom so that it matches the height of the book. Push the book aside for a moment, and fold the paper along those two marks (Figure 1).

Put the book back on the paper. Mark the left edge and the right edge (Figure 2).

Take the book away. Fold along the marks on the left and right. You have just created a pocket on either side that the covers of the book will fit into. (Figure 3).

For the final step, tuck the front cover into the pocket created by the left-hand fold. Fiddle with the book's back cover until it too fits into the pocket on the right side (Figure 4).

Smooth everything out. Your book is now covered!

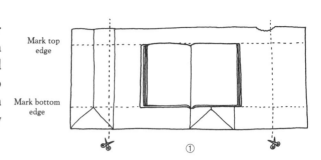

Mark top edge

Mark bottom edge

①

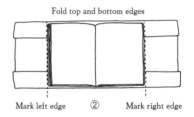

Fold top and bottom edges

Mark left edge   ②   Mark right edge

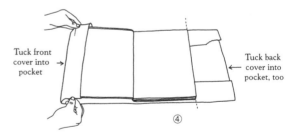

Fold here   Fold here

③

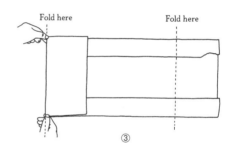

Tuck front cover into pocket →

← Tuck back cover into pocket, too

④

8. PAPER BEADS

To make paper beads, wrap strips and scraps of paper tightly around a straw or pencil. Glue down the edge, when it dries, cover the bead with varnish (like Mod Podge or watered-down white glue).

First method: Cut triangular pieces of paper. Put glue on the inside, place the larger end around a drinking straw, and wrap around it. Cut the straw to the same size as the bead, and go on to make the next bead.

Second method: Cut rectangular strips and use any kind of stick (or straw, nail, knitting needle, or pencil) as the center. Wrap any size rectangle paper around it. Put some glue on the last inch to hold the paper down. Slide the stick out. Apply the varnish.

When all is dry, thread the beads onto a string.

9. PAPER CHAINS

The classic paper chain is usually human figures or stars. Fold a long piece of paper into half, and in half again, and once more. On the front, draw the design. Start to cut, either through the whole batch at once or through half at a time, depending on how thick it is. Nearly any design will work, though. The only caveat is that the design must reach to both sides and be large enough to hold together when the paper strip is unfurled. Just think of the way that paper dolls seem to hold hands and you'll know what we mean.

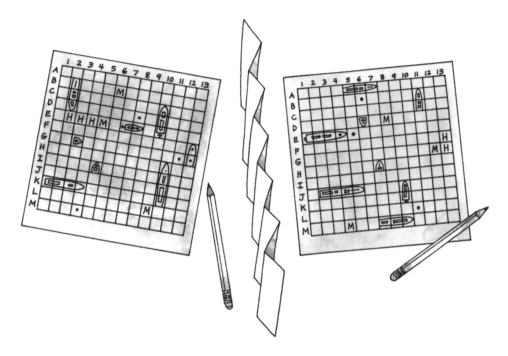

10. BATTLESHIP

Pull out a piece of grid paper, or draw your own grid on a plain piece of paper. Across the top, write the numbers 1 through 13. Along the side, write the letters *A* through *M*. This is your battleship game board and the sea on which your ships will sail. Each player colors in twenty squares on the board. These colored boxes are ships, and a ship can be from one to four adjacent squares long.

To play, take turns calling out points on the grid, like B-10, G-12, or L-9, and having the other player respond. So, player 1 might call out B-6. Player 2 would say, "Miss!" and mark a dot at B-6 on her board. Player 1 would mark an "M," for *miss*, on her board. Then player 2 takes her turn, and the play continues.

Each player keeps track of the spaces that her opponent calls by marking a small dot in each one. The boards get filled up during the game. Each player's game board begins to show her twenty ships, as well as a developing map of the other player's board.

If a player sinks a battleship, she gets an additional turn.

The first player to sink the other player's battleships wins the game. Not to mention, she is now in control of the high seas!

If the caller ...	The other player says ...	The caller ...
misses	"Miss!"	marks M
hits part of a ship	"Hit!"	marks H
hits the final part of a ship	"You sunk my battleship!"	blackens the boat's squares

Cowgirls

THE STEREOTYPE OF A cowgirl is that she's a cattle rustler and horse thief, like Belle Star, who rode with outlaws the likes of Jesse James. Or she's a gunslinging bank robber, like Etta Place, who ran with Butch Cassidy and the Sundance Kid before she mysteriously disappeared. More often than not, however, the original cowgirls of the 1800s were law-abiding women who mostly just broke some social conventions. Cowgirls liked cattle, loved horses, and enjoyed roaming free outside. They wanted an acreage of land to call their own and a herd to graze upon it. They prized their independence. To make that happen, cowgirls got creative.

Life on the prairie and the frontier was tough. Cowgirls worked hard, day and night. They could take crazy risks when they needed to, or just do a ranch's grunt work to learn the ropes and work their way up. Some cowgirls owned their own ranches. Others married and worked their ranch with a husband, taking charge when he was away, as cowboys often were. Some cowgirls disguised themselves as boys every so often so they could get hired as ranch hands or drive cattle on the Chisholm Trail. They would use a man's name to buy land in places where the law didn't yet allow women to own property. However they did it, these women, who were called "cowboy girls" for the longest time, liked making their own rules. Many had colorful life stories to tell.

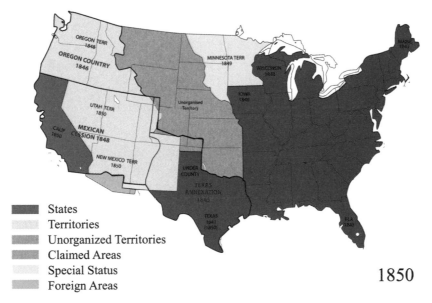

- States
- Territories
- Unorganized Territories
- Claimed Areas
- Special Status
- Foreign Areas

1850

LIZZIE JOHNSON, THE TEXAS CATTLE QUEEN

Lizzie Johnson was born in Missouri in 1840, but her family moved to Texas, where she grew up. Her dad was a teacher, and he founded the Johnson Institute. Lizzie studied there and then at the Chappell Hill Female College, and when she finished, she became a teacher. She settled into a two-story house and made the first floor rooms into a school. On the side, though, she did some bookkeeping for local cattle ranchers. She learned about ranching from them, and she published articles about cattle raising. Lizzie led a respectable life.

But what Lizzie really wanted was to be a cowgirl. She saved the money she earned as a teacher, accounts keeper, and writer, and she bought herself some land. She often had to use a man's name to buy and trade cows, as certain men wouldn't sell cows to a woman. In 1871 Lizzie Johnson became one of the first women in Texas to register a cattle brand in her own name. In those days in Texas, cattle ranchers shared an open range. Each spring the cows would be sent out to wander free on the range until fall. Then the roundup would begin. The cattle would be sorted according to which ranch's brand they carried. The cattle brand is how other legitimate ranchers knew whose cattle were whose. Having one allowed a rancher to use the range's open land for her cows.

It is also said about Lizzie Johnson that, honest ranching aside, she was an accomplished and notorious brush popper, a phrase which bears some explanation. Without a brand, cattle were considered by some cowboys and ranchers to be fair game. Brush poppers would routinely saddle up a horse, ride out to the range, and round up any unbranded cattle they came upon. A fire would be quickly started and stoked, the branding iron heated, and before anyone could see, those cows would be branded and claimed as one's own.

Lizzie Johnson was also probably the first woman to take her own cattle down the Chisholm Trail. The Chisholm Trail was the path through the vast open range of Texas. It led to the railroad depot in Abilene, Kansas. This was as close as the railroad came to the vast cattle ranges of Texas. (The railroad didn't reach Texas until 1887. By that time, overgrazed lands and some harsh winters had killed off many head of cattle and sent many ranchers bankrupt, but that's a different story.) To get their longhorn cattle to market, Texas ranchers moved them along the Chisholm Trail. The trail took a month or two, and it meant living outdoors with the cattle, driving them across rivers, down canyons, and up hills. It was considered men's work. By driving her own cattle on the trail, Lizzie was in charge of her cattle from start to finish: buying, raising, and selling them on her own. She was independent, and that's how she liked it.

FANNY SEABRIDE

As a young girl, Fanny Seabride looked out the windows of her home in Chicago and daydreamed about being a cowgirl. She just wasn't sure how to make it happen. One day she picked up the newspaper and studied the Classifieds section. One of the listings was a job as the governess for the children at the Horseshoe XX Ranch. It wasn't exactly what she wanted, but she circled it and bought a ticket for the next train to Texas.

At Horseshoe XX, Fanny was frustrated. The job kept her indoors with the children when she wanted to be out on the range. Soon enough, though, she had her big break. She was visiting a nearby ranch one day when a report came in that there was a hole in the ranch fence that needed mending before all the cows got out. The cowhands gathered round. All of them looked to the ground as if it were the most interesting artwork in the world, trying to avoid being picked for the job.

Fanny saw her chance. She grabbed a hatchet and saddled up before anyone could stop her, taking off for the far reaches of the ranch. She got the job done and in record time. This was how she became a cowhand, by starting at the bottom. She left her job as a governess and hired herself out as a fence mender. She also developed a sideline job as a sharp shooter and bounty hunter. While she was out on the range, she would shoot wildcats, coyotes, and wolves that threatened the cattle. Fanny earned a great deal of money doing this. Within a few years she was able to purchase her own ranch and one thousand head of cattle, making her dream come true.

JOHANNA JULY

Johanna July was a Black Seminole. This community was made up of black people who had escaped lives as plantation slaves in the Old South. They had run to freedom in Florida and, once there, lived with members of the Seminole tribe. In the early 1800s, the Seminoles were pushed out of Florida and relocated to a reservation in Oklahoma, then an Indian territory. The Black Seminoles went with them. Once in Oklahoma, Johanna July and her family left to start a free colony in Mexico. Like many Black Seminoles, they moved back and forth between Mexico and Texas. Her family learned great horse skills from the Mexican cowboys, and was often employed by the U.S. Army and its scouts.

As a girl, Johanna became an expert rider. She learned to ride bareback with only a simple rope looped around the horse's neck and nose. When her father died and her brother left home, it was up to Johanna to take care of her mother and her sisters. Johanna started working as a *domodora*, or horse tamer, for the U.S. troops stationed at Fort Duncan, Texas. Johanna was famous for her knowledge of horse folklore and all the ways to keep a horse healthy. She had unique ways of taming horses, like putting them into the Rio Grande until they were tired from swimming and begged to come out and behave.

Johanna had thick braids in her hair and wore bright dresses, gold earrings, and flashy beaded necklaces. She married, but she wasn't the best housewife. The beans always seemed to burn, and her sewing tended to unravel. When she'd lived with her mother and sisters, they had always kept house for her while she tamed horses. But her husband wasn't as forgiving. He became angry at Johanna's shortcomings in the kitchen, and he was a violent man. One afternoon Johanna decided she'd had enough. She slipped quietly away from her home. In a nearby field she picked a long stalk from a Spanish dagger plant, braided it into a bridle, and rode a pony straight out of town. She did marry two more times, but only to men who shared her passion for taming horses and mules, and that's how she lived her life. She preferred walking barefoot over wearing shoes and, on more than one occasion, caught the local train (which didn't stop in her small village) by standing in the tracks when she wanted to get on.

CATTLE KATE

Ellen Liddy Watson was called Ella by those who knew her well, and Cattle Kate by those who didn't. She was born in Ontario, Canada, and her family moved to Kansas in the 1860s. In 1862 the U.S. government passed the Homestead Act, which said that any citizen could claim 160 acres of government-surveyed land. If they built a house, planted crops, and stayed for five years, the land was theirs to keep. Ella's family became homesteaders. Aside from the move to Kansas, little is known about her early life, other than that her first marriage was when she was very young and ended in divorce. When the marriage was over, Ella headed to Nebraska, then Colorado, and then to Wyoming.

It was still rare for a woman to travel independently, even in the West. In Wyoming, Ella took on work as a seamstress, a cook, and a waitress. In 1886 when she was twenty-five, she met James Averell, a homesteader whose first wife and young child had died from fevers. Averell ran a road ranch, which was a combination roadside restaurant and general store. He was also the local postmaster. Ella wanted to work her own ranch, not just help run his. She went ahead and married James Averell, homesteaded the land next door to his, and set about building herself a herd of cattle.

Ella soon ran up hard against the big cattlemen of the Wyoming Stock Growers Association. The Association was trying to drive small cattle owners out of the trade so they could control it all. They denied her application for her own cattle brand. Cattle Kate ranched anyway. She was helped by her adopted son, Gene, and by some other men and boys she had hired.

Things went from tough to worse, however. The big ranchers accused Ella of stealing cattle, a charge she denied and no one could ever prove. In 1889 they had the local sheriff arrest her, and she and James Averell both were lynched in front of many witnesses. This was one of several killings that resulted in the Johnson County War of 1892. Small ranchers rebelled against the wealthy ranchers' associations. President Benjamin Harrison ordered in the U.S. Cavalry to stop the fighting, although the Cavalry ended up rescuing the powerful big ranchers of the Wyoming Stock Growers Association instead of coming in on the side of the smaller ranchers and homesteaders like Cattle Kate.

DALE EVANS

When the movies started there were many roles for actresses playing cowgirls, and Dale Evans was one of the best known. She had this to say about being a cowgirl:

I never intended to become a cowgirl. Sure, I grew up on a ranch, and I loved riding horses when I was a child. I knew my way around a milk cow all right, but never, ever did I dream cowgirl dreams. Cowgirl just wasn't a career option back then, at least not a very glamorous one. Movie star—that's what little girls of my generation longed to be.

Over the years I've discovered that there's more to being a cowgirl than punching cows, or winning rodeo trophies, or galloping off into a movie sunset with Roy. Cowgirl is an attitude, really. A pioneer spirit, a special American brand of courage. The cowgirl faces life head on, lives by her own lights, and makes no excuses. Cowgirls take stands. They speak up. They defend the things they hold dear. A cowgirl may be a rancher, or a barrel racer, or a bull rider, or an actress. But she's just as likely to be a checker at the local Winn Dixie, a full-time mother, a banker, an attorney, an astronaut.

Children of my generation longed to be movie stars. Today, even movie stars want to be cowgirls. I'm in my golden years, as they say, but I still sometimes find myself thinking about what I'd like to be when I grow up. It's sort of silly, I know, but—I think I'd like to be a cowgirl.

SHARLOT HALL

Sharlot Hall was born in Kansas in 1870, and she was a cowgirl from a very young age. Her father hunted buffalo on the plain. All the Hall kids learned to ride horses and keep watch over a herd. It was hard for the family to make a living, though. They moved from territory to territory, seeking out easier places to settle down.

When Sharlot was around eleven, her father took the family down the Santa Fe Trail to claim a homestead in Arizona. Around this time, Sharlot found some bad luck. She was thrown from a horse that she had been riding sidesaddle, as all girls and women were supposed to. Her spine was badly injured, and she spent a year in bed recovering.

A few years after that accident, Sharlot's father and brother both took ill. She was still in her mid-teens when she took over managing the family ranch. But once she was in charge, she decided that she would also homestead her own personal ranch nearby.

The thing about Sharlot is that she pursued many dreams. She was a cowgirl and a farmer who knew how to grow crops and keep the herd fed, watered, and healthy. She was also a writer, whose essays and poetry were published in a magazine called *Land of Sunshine*. She loved the outdoors, once writing to a friend that "just the sunshine on the sand is beautiful enough to keep one giving thanks for eyes to see with."

Sharlot served as the first official historian of the territory of Arizona (which didn't become a state until 1912). In her later years, she planned and opened a museum to preserve Arizona's history. The Sharlot Hall Museum in Prescott, Arizona, still exists. She was also active in politics. In 1925 she served as the elector from the state of Arizona. She traveled to Washington to deliver Arizona's three electoral votes for President Calvin Coolidge.

How to Dye Your Hair Using Kool-Aid

PEOPLE HAVE BEEN USING DYE to alter, decorate, and customize their hair for thousands of years. The first hair-coloring concoctions were made from minerals, insects, and plants. Like these early hair color techniques, Kool-Aid is only temporary, and it can only darken hair, not lighten it, so this will work better on hair that is lighter in color.

WHAT YOU NEED

- Two to four packets of your favorite Kool-Aid color (the longer and darker your hair, the more packets you'll need)
- Conditioner
- Vinegar
- Shower cap or plastic wrap
- Plastic gloves
- Mixing bowl
- Vaseline

BEWARE! This project is messy, and Kool-Aid will stain. Wear an old T-shirt to protect your clothes, and have a buddy help you.

In a medium-sized bowl, mix two to four packets of unsweetened Kool-Aid with several generous dollops of hair conditioner (about twice as much as you would normally use on your hair). Stir it until it forms a nice paste, with no lumps. If it's too thick, you can add a few drops of water; if it's too gritty, add more conditioner. For more vibrant color, and to help the dye stick, you can also add a teaspoon or two of vinegar.

Dampen your hair and then apply Vaseline along your hairline and on the tops of your ears. This will help prevent the Kool-Aid color from staining your skin. Put on plastic gloves, if you have them, and apply the Kool-Aid paste to your hair (*not* your scalp).

Once all the paste is on your hair, don a shower cap or use plastic wrap to cover your hair completely. On top of that, you can wrap an old towel around your head to keep your hair covered and to protect your clothes and furniture.

Leave the dye in for anywhere from a few hours to overnight. The longer you leave it in, the more colorful it will be. After you've left it in as long as you can stand it, rinse out the Kool-Aid mix with water, leaning over the sink or tub.

HIGHLIGHTS

Kool-Aid highlights are a great solution for darker hair, which doesn't absorb the Kool-Aid color as dramatically as lighter shades. For this, you'll be applying concentrated amounts of Kool-Aid color to dry strips of hair, rather than drenching your whole head in color. Use the same ingredients as above, but with just two packets of Kool-Aid. You'll also need tin foil and either a pipe cleaner, paintbrush, or new toothbrush for application.

Mix the Kool-Aid and conditioner as described above. Grab a small section of hair, and use the pipe cleaner, paintbrush, or toothbrush to apply the paste from the root to the tip. Once you have the paste spread on evenly and generously, wrap that section of hair in tin foil and go on to the next section. Once you've done that to all the sections you want to color, use a hair dryer (on low) on those foiled sections to bake in the color and dry the hair. Remove the foil when you're done.

REMOVING STAINS

Now that you've learned how to use a drink mix to dye your hair, would it surprise you to know that one of the best ways to remove color stains from your skin is with toothpaste? Just take a dab of regular toothpaste (no special kind needed), and gently rub it on the stained skin. Rinse it off and repeat until the stain is gone.

Make a Decoupage Bowl

DECOUPAGE (PRONOUNCED "DAY-COO-PAHZH") first began in Venice in the 1750s. People called it l'arte del povero, "the poor man's art," because it was a cheap imitation of the coveted lacquer furniture, bowls, and vases that were being imported from China and Japan at the time. To create these highly-prized items, artists would apply lacquer (a shiny coating or varnish) in upward of 150 layers, building a surface that was thick enough to carve.

Decoupage became popular among the leisure class in Victorian England. Queen Victoria herself loved the craft. In that era, women would often travel to one another's homes and visit for weeks on end. To pass the time they would work on crafts together, including elaborate decoupages. They used razor-sharp sewing scissors to finely cut out the paper images of landscape scenes, flowers, and birds. Then they laid these images on wood. Next, they covered the images with layer upon layer of varnish, each layer sanded before the next was added. This produced a smooth surface and a highly prized shine—and a treasured piece of artwork made among friends.

In France, Queen Marie Antoinette was an enthusiastic *decoupeur*. In fact, decoupage became associated with royalty and decadence. After the French Revolution of 1789, French culture was democratized, and decoupage understandably became less popular.

In the United States, decoupage experienced a renaissance in the 1960s, after an Atlanta woman named Jan Wetstone invented Mod Podge (the name comes from "modern decoupage"). Mod Podge glues, seals, and finishes just like varnish does, but it is easier to use. As a result, and for better or worse, many American homes in the 1960s and '70s became filled with decoupaged lampshades, dressers, wall art, and serving trays.

To decoupage like Queen Victoria and Jan Wetstone did, choose a paper image and a surface. Make sure the surface is clean, dry, and smooth. Use the sharpest scissor or craft knife you can find to cut the paper, then lightly glue the paper to the surface. Paint over it with varnish (or Mod Podge). When the varnish dries, rub the layer with industrial steel wool or sandpaper. (Industrial steel wool is purchased at the hardware store, and it doesn't have soap in it, like kitchen steel wool does.) Then apply the next layer of varnish, and continue until the project is done.

TISSUE PAPER BOWL

To make a decoupage bowl, here's what you need:

- A bowl. Any size will do, but try a small one first. This is just to be used as the mold.
- Plastic wrap or a plastic bag, to cover and protect the bowl
- Tape
- Nonstick cooking spray, cooking oil, or petroleum jelly, to dab on the bowl so the plastic slides off more easily
- Paintbrush

- Tissue paper that has been cut or torn into one-inch pieces, or pieces of other kinds of paper like newspaper and magazines
- Glue or varnish, such as Mod Podge, either matte or glossy; Matte Medium, which is made by the Liquitex company and found in art stores and used by painters to add texture to their paint; or a mix of 4 to 5 tablespoons of white glue and enough water so it becomes loose enough to be applied with a brush.

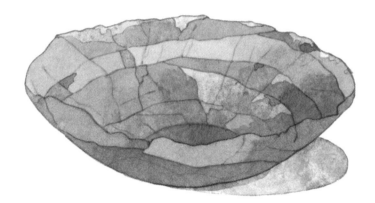

Step 1. Wrap the outside of the bowl in plastic. Tape the plastic on the inside to help keep it wrapped, if necessary. If you want, apply a bit of nonstick spray to the bowl before the plastic goes on, to make it easier to release the plastic at Step 4.

Step 2. Turn the bowl upside down. Place a piece of tissue paper wherever you want it on the bowl. Brush varnish over it. Continue doing this until the outside of the bowl is fully covered. This first layer is what you will see when you look inside the bowl. (Although even here, you can always add more layers to the inside once the bowl and plastic are removed.) Go outside and kick a soccer ball until this layer dries.

Step 3. When the first layer is dry, add a second layer. And a third and another, until you like what you have. The varnish will dry strong and hold the bowl's shape, so that even a single layer of tissue paper will make a bowl.

Step 4. When the layers are dry, untape the plastic. Remove the bowl from the decoupage. Any tears can be fixed with a dab of glue over a small piece of paper. Or, another layer can be added.

Dangerous Volcanoes

CHAITEN VOLCANO, SOUTHERN CHILE

The Chaiten volcano, one of some three hundred volcanoes in the Andean Arc region (which encompasses Chile, Peru, Ecuador, and Colombia), erupted in May 2008. The town of Chaiten, just six miles away from the volcano in the Gulf of Corcovado, was destroyed by ash and floods. Scientists believe the last eruption of the Chaiten volcano before this was sometime around 7420 BCE.

MOUNT VESUVIUS, ITALY

Located just east of Naples, this volcano famously destroyed the cities of Pompeii and Herculaneum in 79 CE. It has been dormant since 1944, but volcanologists believe it may be due for an eruption. There are two other volcanoes in Italy: Mount Etna, on the east coast of Sicily, and Stromboli, on one of the Aeolian islands off the north coast of Sicily.

POPOCATÉPETL, MEXICO

Nicknamed "Popo," this volcano is the second highest in North America, with an elevation of 17,802 feet. Popo has had more than twenty major eruptions since 1519, when Spanish explorers arrived and made note of volcanic activity. At just forty-two miles southeast of Mexico City, the city with the world's highest population, Popo is definitely one to watch. And you don't have to be a volcanologist to do so: The Mexican government has set up a "Popo-Cam" so people can view the volcano live on the Internet.

MERAPI, INDONESIA

This volcano's name means, appropriately, "Mountain of Fire." Lying on the border between Central Java and Yogyakarta, it is the most active volcano in Indonesia, emitting smoke an average three hundred days a year. It has erupted regularly since 1548, with small eruptions every two to three years and larger ones every ten to fifteen years. Some of the most notable eruptions took place in 1006, 1786, 1822, 1872, and 1930, with thousands of people killed each time. Dangerous eruptions took place more recently in 1994 and 2006, when the volcano erupted for several months; its most recent eruption was in January 2008.

NYIRAGONGO, AFRICA

Located in the Virunga Mountains of the Democratic Republic of Congo, this volcano and its nearby sibling, Nyamuragira, are responsible for nearly half of Africa's volcanic eruptions. Nyiragongo has erupted more than thirty-four times since the late 1800s, and features a churning lake of lava at its center. In 1977, this lava lake streamed out of the volcano at roughly 60 miles per hour, devastating everything in its path. In 2002, the volcano erupted again, sending lava gushing through the nearby town of Goma and swallowing the runway at Goma's international airport.

NAVADO DEL RUIZ, COLOMBIA

This is the northernmost volcano in Colombia, just eighty miles west of Bogota and right in the heart of the Pacific "Ring of Fire" (the area in the Pacific Ocean where some of the most active volcanoes in the world are located). The volcano last erupted on November 13, 1985, killing 23,000 people and wiping out the town of Armero with volcanic landslides (called *lahars*) of ash, mud, and volcanic rocks. This prompted Colombian officials to create an early warning system: Today, acoustic flow monitors placed inside the volcano can alert officials that instability is present, giving people time to evacuate the area before a full eruption occurs.

MOUNT FUJI, JAPAN

Japan has more than one hundred volcanoes, and there are many small eruptions each year. But Mount Fuji, the largest by far, hasn't erupted since 1707, when it spewed volcanic ash and cinders for more than a month, blanketing the towns around it for hundreds of miles. Today, Mount Fuji is a well-known symbol of Japan, and hikers can scale its 12,000-foot heights. But volcanologists are keeping tabs on it: Mount Fuji once went for four hundred years without an eruption; at three hundred years since its last big one, they worry another may be due.

MOUNT RAINIER, USA

This volcano in Washington state, just fifty-four miles southeast of Seattle, is 14,411 feet tall, the highest peak in the Cascade mountain range. The summit actually has two volcanic craters, each more than one thousand feet in diameter. Geothermal heat keeps the crater rims ice-free, but the mountain itself has twenty-six glaciers, more than any other place outside of Alaska. The volcano was active in the 1800s, with its last documented eruption in 1894. But with modern cities now built on top of the old mudflows from previous eruptions, scientists worry about the possibility of what a new eruption would mean today.

MOUNT ST. HELENS, USA

Another volcano in Washington state did erupt after a 120-year hiatus: Mount St. Helens, whose explosion on May 18, 1980, was equal to the force of 30,000 atomic bombs. The nine-hour-long eruption left a huge crater in its wake and caused a massive avalanche, diminishing the height of the volcano by more than one thousand feet. Ashes from the volcano were scattered as far away as New Mexico. Between 2004 and 2008, the volcano was in a state of continuous, low-level eruption, but as of July 2008, scientists determined that the period of activity had concluded.

KRAKATAU, INDONESIA

This volcanic island in the waters between Java and Sumatra in Indonesia erupted in 1883 with an explosion so loud, it was heard in places as far away as Australia and India. The ash expelled from the volcano blanketed the world so much that global temperatures plummeted: 1884 was called "the Year Without Summer" because of the layer of ash that prevented much of the sun's heat from reaching the ground. The ash and other volcanic matter in the atmosphere also turned sunsets red the world over. The event triggered tsunamis felt as far away as South Africa. The term *blue moon* came from Krakatau as well: The ash in the sky made the moon appear blue for two years after the eruption. Although the volcano hasn't had another big eruption, it is still active, having erupted in the fall of 2007, releasing lava, hot gases, and rocks, and again, more recently, in 2008.

Tennis

THE GAME OF TENNIS evolved from a handball game invented by bored monks in twelfth-century France. First it was played with bare hands and a ball (and was called *jeu de paumme*, "the game of the palm"); then with special gloves and a ball; and eventually with racquets and a ball. Once racquets were introduced, players began announcing their serves by shouting, "Tenez!"—basically, "Take heed!" or "Watch out!"—which is where our word tennis comes from.

The game steadily gained in popularity and moved out of the cloisters, until, by 1596, there were 250 tennis courts in Paris alone. In England, Henry VIII was a fan and avid player; in 1625 he had a court built at his Hampton Court Palace, which still stands today. The game thrived among seventeeth-century royalty in France, Spain, and Italy (in fact, it was called "royal tennis" or "real tennis"). But in England it began to die out in favor of other racquet sports such as squash—until the game was brought outside. Yes, tennis was played for most of its history indoors: Courts were narrow, enclosed rooms, with nets five feet high on the ends and three feet high in the middle, and points were scored by hitting the ball off the walls. Only in the nineteenth century did outdoor courts spring up in England, Australia, and America. After that, tennis became popular worldwide, and by the 1900s, it was a professional sport.

Here is a little bit about how to play the game, and the things you need to know before you take to the court.

TOOLS OF THE TRADE

The Racquet. Tennis racquets were originally made out of wood. In 1967 the first metal racquet was introduced, followed in the next decade by racquets made from aluminum. With each innovation in materials, the racquet became lighter and more powerful, and the racquet face and "sweet spot" increased in size. By the late 1980s, most racquets were made out of graphite, which was even lighter in weight, and today graphite and titanium racquets are the standard.

When choosing a racquet, look for one that's light and easy to hold. The grip, where you hold the racquet, is anywhere from 4 to $4^5/_8$ inches around. To see which size fits you best, grab the racquet: If you can touch your thumb to the top knuckle of your middle finger, it's the right size. As for length, the standard 27-inch size is perfect for beginners ages twelve and up. (Kids younger than twelve should use a racquet between 21 inches and 26 inches long. The younger you are, the smaller the racquet.)

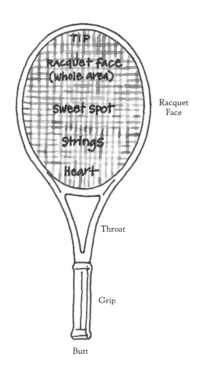

The Ball. You can find tennis balls at nearly any store for just a few dollars. Most tennis balls are made of rubber coated with felt and nylon, are 2 to 2⅝ inches in diameter, and are filled with pressurized air (you can buy pressureless balls, which don't depend on internal air pressure for bounciness, but they are a bit stiffer). If you have old tennis balls lying around, here's a simple way to check whether or not they're still good: Hold the ball at the height of your forehead, and then drop it. If it bounces up to about your belly button level, it's still good.

The Court. Tennis courts come in three basic kinds of surfaces: clay courts (commonly red or green and made of crushed stone or bricks mixed with rubber); grass courts (made with either synthetic grass carpets or very finely mown natural grass); and hard courts (made of asphalt or concrete). The courts are marked with widths for doubles games (36 feet wide) and singles games (27 feet wide).

STROKES

There are three main ways of hitting the ball: the forehand stroke, used when the ball is coming to the right side of a right-handed player or the left side of a left-handed player; the backhand stroke, used to hit balls on the left side of a right-handed player and the right side of a left-handed player; and the serve, which is the stroke that starts each point. Here's how to do them.

Forehand. Stand with your body turned sideways to the net (your free hand should be toward the net, and your racquet hand should be toward the baseline). Have your feet shoulder-width apart and knees bent slightly. Grip the racquet as though you are shaking hands with it—your fingers around the handle comfortably, not too tight and not too loose. Hold the racquet at about waist level, and be relaxed and ready.

When you're ready to hit the ball, bring the racquet back and down, then swing it forward and up, across your body, ending with the racquet pointing up above your head and over your other shoulder. The idea is to swing low to high, and to follow through with your swing even after the ball makes contact with your racquet.

Backhand. The backhand can be done with one hand or two hands. Two hands are easier to start with, and that's what we'll describe here. Stand sideways to the net with your knees slightly bent and your feet shoulder-width apart. This time, stand with the back of your racquet hand toward the net. Hold your racquet with both hands on the grip, your dominant hand holding the bottom and your other hand holding the grip just above your dominant hand. As with the forehand, stand relaxed and ready, with your eyes on the ball. To hit the ball, prepare by bringing the racquet back and down, and then swinging it forward and up, ending with the racquet up toward your shoulder. Like the forehand, swing from low to high and follow through.

The Serve. Players get two chances to hit a serve into the service box. The ball has to bounce in the service box diagonally across the court to be a "good" serve. Stand behind the baseline with your feet shoulder-width apart and your body turned sideways so that your free hand faces toward the net. Grab the racquet as though you are shaking hands with it, and hold a tennis ball with your non-racquet hand. Look at where you are aiming: the service box diagonal to you on the other side of the net. Lean back into your back leg as you prepare to serve.

Toss the ball straight up, but do not throw it: Instead, imagine simply lifting the ball and letting go, as though you are placing the ball on a high shelf. Swing your racquet back and bend your elbow to bring the racquet up behind you as though you are using it to scratch your back. From there, sharply bring the racquet up and forward over your head to hit the ball. Ideally, the backswing and the ball toss happen simultaneously. But you can work up to this by starting out first in the "back scratch" position and then tossing the ball up. Once you hit the ball, remember to follow through, just as in the other strokes. In this case, that means letting the racquet continue to move forward after you hit the ball, and finish in front of your body.

PLAYING THE GAME

If, unlike Henry VIII, you do not have your own private tennis court to play on, you may check your local recreation center, community park, or even a school or college for public courts. Otherwise, an impromptu game can be had in a backyard or a generous driveway; and for solo practicing, you can always hit tennis balls against a big wall, if there's one handy.

To begin a game of singles (two players competing against each other), first determine who will serve and who will receive—you can do this with a coin toss, if you like. Once it's determined who serves first, the players then stand on opposite sides of the court.

The server stands just behind her baseline, between the centerline and the sideline, and serves the ball so that it lands diagonally opposite in her opponent's service court. The server alternates sidelines for every point that is played. If the server steps on the baseline before she hits the ball, or if the serve does not land in the service box, it's called a fault. If the ball hits the net and still lands in the service box, it is a let (a do-over). The server has two chances at a serve; if she misses a second time, that is called a double fault, and she loses the point. The receiver can stand anywhere she likes, but the ball must bounce once in the service box before she hits it.

The receiver must hit the ball back over the net and have it land within the boundaries of the other side of the court. The ball can bounce once, but if it bounces twice before the receiver hits it, the point goes to the server. Once the ball is in play, it is okay to hit the ball before it bounces. The first player to win four points by a margin of two wins the game. Then the opponent gets to serve. The first player to win six games by a margin of two wins the set, and the first player to win two out of three sets wins the match.

SCORING

Originally, tennis scoring was based on the quarter numbers of a clock: 0, 15, 30, 45, and 60. It's been tweaked a bit since then, but the underlying idea is still there.

It takes four points to win a game, and the winner must win by at least two points. To win a set, a player must win six games, and must win by at least two games. If both players have six games, you either play until someone wins by two games, or play a tie-break game, in which the players take turns serving two points each. The winner of the tie-break game (and thus of the set) is the player who wins seven points, with at least two more points than her opponent.

There are special terms for the points won in a game. Zero points is called love. (It gets its name from the French l'oeuf, meaning "egg," which is what the number zero looks like.) The first point is called 15, the second point is called 30, and the third is 40. The server's points come first. So when you hear the score called as "15-love," that means the serving player has one point and the opposing player has zero; a score of 15-40 means the server has one point and the receiver has three. If the players are tied, the score is called all, as in 15 all or 30 all—except when the players are tied at 40, when it's called deuce. Deuce comes from the French word for "two," and when the players reach deuce, they must win the next two points in order to win the game. Whoever wins the point when the score is deuce has advantage, (for example, the score becomes "Advantage Rebecca"). If she wins the next point, she wins the game, but if the other player wins the point, the score goes back to deuce.

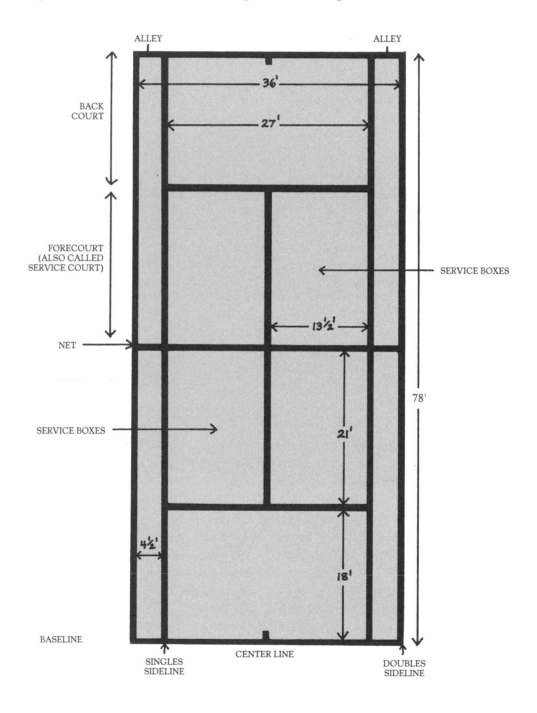

Make a Lava Lamp

THE LAVA LAMP has mesmerized people since it was first invented in 1964. Its signature look is due to the lava-like blobs of wax that rise and fall through an illuminated, water-like mix of chemicals. When heated by the lamp at the base, the wax blobs rise through the chemical mélange to the top, only to fall back down as they cool. It can be hypnotic and relaxing to watch, but it turns out that the chemicals in the official Lava Lamp are fairly poisonous. To make one of your own, we recommend this decidedly low-tech, but non-toxic, technique.

WHAT YOU NEED

- Baby oil
- Water
- Food coloring
- Foaming antacid tablets (sold under the brand name of Alka-Seltzer)
- Glass jar with a lid, a water or medium-size soda bottle with a cap, or any container that closes securely enough to shake.

Fill the jar two thirds of the way full with oil, and fill the rest with water.

Add a few drops of food coloring.

Break the foaming tablet into 6 to 8 pieces. Drop one or two pieces into the bottle, and watch the bubbles form and float to the top. When the lava bubbles die down, shake the jar (make sure the cover is on!). Then, add more pieces of the foaming tablet to keep the action going.

To light up the lava, use your trusty flashlight, desk lamp, or any other light source you find that can be beamed through the bottle from below or behind.

(Corn or canola or any of the usual kinds of oils found in a kitchen can be substituted for the baby oil, but the mixture will be yellowish instead of clear. Salt can be added to the oil as an alternative to the foaming tablets, in which case you keep adding salt to keep the bubbles bubbling. But in our experience, the salt doesn't work as well.)

This lava lamp works because oil and water don't mix (the word for things that don't mix is *immiscible*). Oil is lighter than water, and so it stays on top while the water sinks to the bottom. The food coloring attaches only to the water. The foaming tablets introduce carbon dioxide gas into the mixture, and that reaction makes the bubbles. When the gassy colored bubbles get to the top, they burst and sink to the bottom.

Labyrinths

YOU MIGHT THINK A LABYRINTH is the same as a maze, but its history and definition are quite unique. The original labyrinth comes from the island of Crete in Minoan times, about 3,500 years ago (1450 BCE). According to legend, it was created to house the fearsome Minotaur, a creature who was half man and half bull. The story goes that King Minos of Crete had won a war against King Aegeus of Athens and therefore made Aegeus pay him tribute once a year. The tribute took the form of seven girls and seven boys from Athens who were sent to Crete, where they would have to enter King Minos's labyrinth. At the center of the labyrinth lived the Minotaur (who was, in a terrible turn of events, the son of Minos's wife). Each year, the Minotaur would devour the young Athenians.

One year, when the time for tribute came, King Aegeus's own son Theseus stepped forward. He intended to go to Crete, enter the labyrinth, and kill the Minotaur. Just as Theseus arrived in Crete, he met Ariadne. She was the daughter of King Minos, and she fell in love with Theseus and vowed to help him. Before Theseus entered the labyrinth, Ariadne tied the end of a very long string to his hand. She held the other end at the entrance of the labyrinth. By following it, Theseus would be able to find his way out. Theseus got through the tricky maze, slayed the Minotaur, and, thanks to Ariadne's string, he also found his way home again.

Modern labyrinths don't have Minotaurs. And the ancient story may have gotten its terms confused. Mazes present intricate and unending choices about which direction to turn. They are about getting lost and using your wits to find your way out. Not so with a labyrinth, which has one path from start to finish, guaranteed. At the center, the path turns about-face to head out again. In a true labyrinth, no one gets lost.

Is any part of the story true? A Bronze Age coin from the ancient city of Knossos in Crete shows a square labyrinth—and the city's pride in the labyrinth. A tablet written in the pre-Greek language that scholars call Minoan Linear B was found in Crete (see the chapter on the Greek Alphabet): It describes a woman called the Mistress of the Labyrinth—and how it was a good idea to offer her a jar of honey!

Labyrinths have been found all over the world. In a villa in Portugal, a mosaic pavement made during the late Roman Empire had a square labyrinth—with a picture of the Minotaur at center. The French medieval cathedral of Chartres, which was the tallest and grandest church of its time, has an intricate fifteen-circuit labyrinth on the floor inside. Labyrinths are found in Native American cave drawings in northern Arizona in the United States. Fishermen in Sweden marked stone labyrinths in fields, seeking good luck and help in keeping mischievous trolls away.

CREATING YOUR OWN LABYRINTH

These illustrations show how to draw a classic seven-circuit labyrinth. The labyrinth starts with a seed pattern of horizontal and vertical lines that cross. In each of the four corners, add a right angle and a dot. Start at the top of the central line and draw a loop to the dot to the right. Continue to make eight loops, as shown in yellow and green below, and the labyrinth will emerge. This is a left-entry labyrinth, because you enter to the left of the central line and your first turn is to the left. To draw a right-entry labyrinth, draw the first loop to the left instead and continue from there.

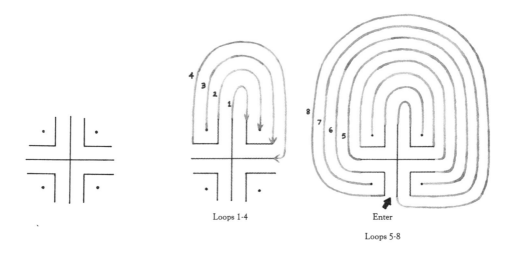

Loops 1-4

Enter

Loops 5-8

To make larger or smaller labyrinths, follow these other starting seeds:

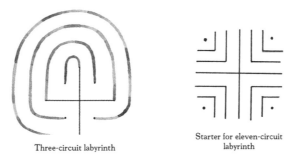

Three-circuit labyrinth

Starter for eleven-circuit labyrinth

If you want to make a human-sized labyrinth to walk through, chalk or paint these circuits on pavement. A seven-circuit labyrinth needs about twenty-five to thirty feet. Labyrinths can also be outlined in brick or stone, mown into tall grass, or cut into a late-season cornfield, if you happen to have one.

Turning Your Backyard into a Farm

TURNING YOUR BACKYARD INTO A FARM may seem far-fetched. During World War II, however, when the United States' food supply was tight, First Lady Eleanor Roosevelt asked everyone to plant Victory Gardens in their yards. Many answered her call. One growing season later, the nation harvested forty-four percent of its vegetables from home gardens. Even if you don't have a backyard, many plants can be grown in window boxes, in large pots, and even in self-watering containers on a terrace.

With some planning and stick-to-it-ness, you can create a working farm that grows all sorts of vegetables. It's widely believed that kids of a certain age don't like to eat vegetables. That shouldn't keep you from turning your backyard into a farm (and, in fact, we have witnessed actual children delighting in the taste and crunch of a fresh carrot or sugar snap pea). Plan crops with an eye toward producing what your family needs. You may also consider making a farm stand and selling your bounty of vegetables and flowers to neighbors and passersby.

PLANNING YOUR CROPS

Planning takes place before a spade is ever put to soil. Especially if you are thinking of making a farm stand, growing a little bit of everything is certainly a good plan. Here are some suggestions for specific farm stand–ready crops.

Lettuce is not a favorite of most kids, but adults seem to think it's rather special. In fact, the smaller and more weirdly named the lettuce, the more adults like it and the more they will pay you for it, especially if it is locally grown and organic (which it will be, because most kids don't add chemical fertilizers to their crops anyway). So consider growing different kinds of lettuce on your farm. The directions on the seed packets tell when to plant and what to expect. In early spring, sprinkle the seeds to the ground, cover with soil, and wait for the sprouts to peek out. Create a lasting crop by planting lettuce seeds every week until the weather gets too hot and the lettuce bolts and goes to seed. (You can even plant lettuce again in late summer, along with spinach, cabbage, and kale, and get a second harvest.)

Some people like broccoli and lima beans and radishes, but everybody loves flowers. Consider planting rows and rows of flowers. Zinnias, cosmos, sunflowers, sweet peas, and others grow from seeds that are planted directly in soil. Plus, the more you cut the blooms of these annual flowers, the more they grow. Zinnias are especially easy to grow from seed, and they come in many colors and varieties. Collect glass jars and vases from a local thrift store, where they will cost twenty-five cents, and use them as vases for the bouquets that you sell at your farm stand.

Fresh herbs are expensive in the grocery store, but you can grow them easily in your backyard. Popular herbs are basil, cilantro, chives, mint, oregano, parsley, dill, and tarragon. Many herbs can be kept in a glass jar with vinegar or oil, to give the vinegar and oil their flavor, and this is another item you can sell at your farm stand. Lavender is much loved, and its spikes are very fragrant, but it is a perennial plant that takes a few seasons to grow large. You should plant these perennials in a different place from the annual plot that, come fall, you will clean up and turn under to get it ready for next spring.

There are many additional possibilities, of course—watermelon, pumpkins, carrots, potatoes, tomatoes, squash, peppers, melons, and more. You can flip through seed catalogs for inspiration or talk to the folks at your local garden center to see what will grow best where you live, in the space you have. Whatever you decide to grow, the season before planting is a time to plan your crops. Draw a map of the rows and paths in your garden, and where each crop will grow. The rows can be long and narrow or short and wide. Your garden can be a circle with paths like spokes leading to the middle. Or it can be boxes, barrels, and tires lining your patio or porch. Life is long and has many planting seasons. There is no single right way to do this, and there are many seasons ahead in which to experiment.

PLANTING AND GROWING YOUR CROPS

1. Soil. Farming takes time, patience, and a good deal of trial-and-error learning, but the basic elements are soil, sun, and water. To get started, clear an area of grass and weeds. Grab a pitchfork, shovel, or hoe and break up the soil. Turn it over until the top 10 inches are loose and light. The soil will need to be improved and made more nutritious for the plants by adding mulch, manure, and exotic things like peat moss and special fish oils. Preparing the soil is hard work, but you'll appreciate it later on.

With your planting plan in mind, divide your plot into rows and paths. Put some weed protection down on the paths, which means laying down a thick layer of newspapers or some plastic. Let us tell you from experience that an hour spent doing this now will save you ten hours of bending over and weeding later in the summer.

Preparing soil for container gardening is clearly less labor intensive. Talk to experienced gardeners about getting the right composition of dirt for what you are growing, and get any tips on how densely to pack it.

2. Seeds and Seedlings. The directions on each packet of seeds, or that come with each seedling, will tell you how and when and where to plant. The seeds of some plants, such as carrots and peas and lettuce, are sown directly in the ground. Large seeds are often pushed into the ground, while small seeds may be sprinkled and then covered. Other plants, such as tomatoes, are better planted with seedlings. These are young plants that have been started indoors so they have a head start on the growing season.

A fun planting tip: Spread out a length of toilet paper (we're serious). Place the seeds in a line down the middle, however close or far apart you want them to be. Fold each side of the strip over the middle, lay it in the row, and cover it with soil. The paper keeps the seeds in place (and will biodegrade into the soil in about a week).

Some plants need special aids. Tomatoes need cages or stakes to keep them standing tall. Potatoes do especially well if you plant them inside a barrel or old tire and keep adding soil as they grow.

3. Harvest. All season long you'll be watering, weeding, weeding more, and waiting. One day, the first sweet pea pod will pop from the vine, the lettuce will sprout, and a few weeks later, three brilliantly red tomatoes will peek through the abundant green leaves, followed by tomatoes of yellow, orange, and purple hue. You realize the magic has happened. Bring along a basket and start your harvest.

4. Livestock. Farms aren't really complete without animals, so if you have a yard, consider a goat, pig, or some chickens. Of course, you will need to check the local zoning laws (not to mention ask your parents). Raising chickens isn't that hard—they tend to wander around your yard, laying eggs beneath the bushes where you can collect some each morning for breakfast. It's beyond what we can do here to explain how to raise chickens, but you can buy the eggs from a farm distributor, and to get started you will need a coop with a hatching box, a well-fenced yard that can protect the chickens from the local hawks and foxes, plus hay, food, water, and lots of sun. Oh, and agreeable neighbors.

Whatever you do, don't get a rooster.

5. Attitude. Never fear. Beginning farmers will undoubtedly make mistakes and accidentally kill their plants. But aside from set-up work, planting, and watering, nature does most of the work for you. Once you get started, you will figure many things out for yourself, and you will find good farmers and gardeners to learn from.

HOW TO SET UP A FARM STAND

To make a working farm, plan a farm stand where you can sell tomatoes, squash, lettuce, peas, and flowers to thankful neighbors and passersby. To get an idea of what to charge, check the prices at local grocery stores.

Your farm stand can open as soon as the harvest starts to come in. It can be as simple as a portable card table or a red wagon. Draw attention to your stand with a painted banner of fabric or paper. You can suspend the banner between two tall garden stakes. They push into the ground easily and have holes on top where you can connect the banner to the stake with pipe cleaners or string. Find some baskets or boxes for your vegetables, flowers, and bundles of herbs. Add other things to sell, if you like, such as crafts or baked goods, or put out some cups and a pitcher of iced tea or lemonade.

You can set your own hours and advertise that your stand is open every Friday afternoon (or whatever time you choose). You can try making it an on-your-honor farm stand, if your hometown is one in which you can do this sort of thing. You would set out the vegetables and flowers with the prices clearly marked, with a note that customers should leave the money in the cashbox. You can collect it when you return home from an afternoon at the pool.

Another plan is to work for hire. Some of your neighbors will appreciate fresh-from-the-garden vegetables if they don't have a garden of their own. Let them sign up for a weekly box of lettuce, tomatoes, flowers, and/or fresh herbs, or for a farmer's special, whereby you make up a box of whatever is ready to harvest that week. Larger farms do this through a system called community-supported agriculture, and you can do something similar at home.

Courage

COURAGE ISN'T ABOUT NOT FEELING FEAR. It's about feeling fear and doing the right thing anyway. Courage comes into play in all kinds of situations, big and small, from facing down a fast kick as the goalie of a soccer game, to being the first among your friends to try something new, to speaking your mind about something that matters. Many famous people have pondered the true meaning of courage. Here are some of their thoughts.

You gain strength, courage, and confidence by every experience in which you really stop to look fear in the face.

—Eleanor Roosevelt

Courage does not always roar. Sometimes it is the quiet voice at the end of the day saying, "I will try again tomorrow."

—Mary Anne Radmacher

Act boldly and unseen forces will come to your aid.

—Dorothea Brande

One isn't necessarily born with courage, but one is born with potential. Without courage, we cannot practice any other virtue with consistency.

—Maya Angelou

Only those who dare to fail greatly can ever achieve greatly.

—Robert F. Kennedy

Life is not easy for any of us. But what of that? We must have perseverance and above all confidence in ourselves. We must believe that we are gifted for something and that this thing must be attained.

—Marie Curie

Life is either a daring adventure or nothing.

—Helen Keller

He who is not courageous enough to take risks will accomplish nothing in life.

—Muhammad Ali

Patience and perseverance have a magical effect before which difficulties disappear and obstacles vanish.

—John Quincy Adams

I am not afraid of storms for I am learning how to sail my ship.

—Louisa May Alcott

There are three friends in life: courage, sense, and insight.

—Hausa proverb

All serious daring starts from within.

—Eudora Welty

If you hear a voice within you say "you cannot paint," then by all means paint, and that voice will be silenced.

—Vincent Van Gogh

A smooth sea never made a skilled mariner.

—English proverb

I learned that courage was not the absence of fear, but the triumph over it. The brave man is not he who does not feel afraid, but he who conquers that fear.

—Nelson Mandela

When you have confidence, you can have a lot of fun. And when you have fun, you can do amazing things.

—Joe Namath

Sundials

BEFORE MECHANICAL CLOCKS WERE INVENTED, people told time by gauging the position of the sun in the sky and watching the shadows. Ancient Egyptians used obelisks (four-sided monuments tapering to a point at the top), shadow clocks (movable devices with marks to track the progress of shadows throughout the day), and even water clocks (stone containers that allowed water to drip through a small hole at a constant rate) to track the passage of time. Greeks furthered the development and design of these early sundials using their knowledge of geometry, and the Roman playwright Plautus complained about how his days were hacked "so wretchedly into small portions" by sundials. Now our days are "hacked into bits" with watches, computers, and even cell phones. But sundials are still in use, even today.

The two basic parts of a sundial are the gnomon and the dial plate. The gnomon, the vertical part of the sundial, usually has a triangular, shark fin shape, although it can be as simple as a small straight rod and as fantastic as a giant staircase. The dial plate is the flat part of the sundial where the shadow falls. It is usually marked with notches or other notations to mark the daylight hours, although it can also contain other information (signs of the zodiac, compass points, the time of sunset and sunrise, and other such items sometimes referred to as *dial furniture*). Sundials work when the sun is out and the gnomon casts a shadow on the dial plate. Where exactly the shadow falls on the dial is dependent upon where the sun is in the sky. Because the sun follows a predictable daily path, the time of day can be told by where the shadow falls.

TO MAKE YOUR OWN SUNDIAL YOU WILL NEED

- Two pieces of thin but sturdy cardboard or card stock
- Pair of scissors
- Protractor
- Regular ruler
- Compass
- Marker or pen
- Tape

Make the dial plate: Measure and cut a length of cardboard 7½ inches tall by 8½ inches wide. Using your ruler, draw a straight line across the cardboard about a half inch from the bottom. Make a small mark on the middle of that line (4¼ inches from the edge), and then use your ruler to draw a straight line right up the middle from the bottom to the top of the cardboard. When you're done, it should look like an upside-down "T" (Figure 1).

Mark the hour lines: The placement of the hour lines on a sundial's dial plate depends on latitude (basically, how far away from the equator you are). The measurements below assume a latitude of 38°, which means this sundial will be more or less accurate in the continental United States, but not, for example, in South America or Australia.

Place the bull's-eye part of the protractor right in line with the intersection of your horizontal and vertical lines, and then make a small mark on the cardboard at each of the following degrees: 23°, 43°, 58°, 69°, and 80° (90° is already marked by your straight line up the middle); then 99°, 109°, 121°, 136°, and 156° (180° is marked by your straight line across the bottom). Then, use a ruler or straightedge to draw a straight line from the middle point on the bottom line to each of the marks you have made, out toward the edge of the cardboard. After you have drawn the lines, number them as follows, starting on the left-hand side: 6, 7, 8, 9, 10, 11, 12, 1, 2, 3, 4, 5, and 6 (Figure 2).

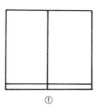

Make the gnomon: On the other piece of cardboard, draw a triangle 5½ inches tall and 4½ inches wide. A half inch below the bottom line, draw another horizontal line. This line should be slightly shorter than the one above it and centered beneath the line. Connect the bottom two lines by drawing diagonal lines on either end (Figure 3). Cut out this triangular shape, and fold along the line. For more stability, you can make a cut right in the middle of the part beneath the triangle, and then fold one side to the left and one to the right (Figure 4).

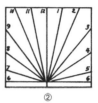

Put it together: On the middle, vertical line (the 12 line) of the dial plate, make a mark 4½ inches from the bottom of the cardboard, and use your scissors to cut along the line up to the 4½-inch point. Now take the gnomon (holding it by the straight up-and-down edge, with the sloping part going away from you), and slide it into the cut you made on the dial plate. Make sure it stands up exactly straight. When you've got it in position, use tape to secure it to the underside of the base (Figure 5).

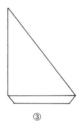

Final touches: You can decorate your sundial however you like—coloring it, putting stickers on it, painting it, or whatever else strikes your fancy. If you'd rather not mess with the sundial plate as you've already made it, you can dress it up by fixing your sundial to a larger piece of colorful cardboard or wood that you decorate separately.

Traditionally, sundials often have a motto. Sometimes these are about time; other times the mottoes are a way to express the personality of the dial maker. Here are some tried-and-true ones: "Let others tell of storms and showers; I mark only the sunny hours." *Tempus fugit* (Time flies). *Carpe diem* (Seize the day). *Amicis qualibet hora* (Any hour for my friends).

See it work: Grab your compass and sundial and go outside. Use your compass to find north, and then put the sundial down in a flat, sunny place with the 12 line pointing that way. Now you should be able to gauge the time by where the gnomon's shadow falls.

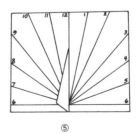

The Chinese New Year

THE CHINESE NEW YEAR FESTIVAL begins with the first new moon of the year—the Chinese year, that is. Legends tell of an ancient beast, *Nian*, that terrified a village. The villagers asked the great lion spirit to scare the beast away. The lion declined, as he was busy protecting the emperor's palace. And so the villagers conjured up the strongest dragon they could imagine. They made their dragon from long sheets of silk and held the dragon together with bamboo rods. Accompanied by the din of drums and shouts and firecrackers, the villagers and their bamboo-and-silk dragon frightened the beast away.

Now the New Year is celebrated with lion and dragon dances to the sounds of rhythmic drums and the sights of stilt walkers and colorful floats. Nearly one quarter of the world's people celebrate the Chinese New Year, whether they live in China or in the many places where Chinese people have emigrated, including American and Canadian cities and throughout Asia and Australia. The traditional Chinese calendar has relatively few festivals, which means that the New Year's festival takes pride of place. In Beijing and elsewhere, businesses shut down for those two weeks and even for a few days before and after. The snap of firecrackers is heard everywhere. The brilliant nighttime fireworks can, in some cities, last for days.

Homes are cleaned spotless and decorated with lanterns, blooms, and flowers. Bright citrus fruit such as oranges and tangerines are everywhere. Red ribbons are tied around plants. Tables are laden with food. People make New Year's visits to family and friends. Special red envelopes of gifts are exchanged.

At Chinese New Year, many homes sport the character "fu" on their front gates—upside down, making a pun. "Fu" means "good fortune" and "fu dao le" means "luck has arrived." "Dao" also means "to turn upside down." So, the character "fu" is playfully inverted, suggesting that luck has already arrived—been poured out—at that lucky household.

THE ANIMAL OF THE YEAR

Each new year is ushered in under the sign of one of the twelve animals of the Chinese zodiac. Each animal brings with it many legends. Whether a tiger, a dragon, or a sheep, the animal sign is seen as a way to predict the character, destiny, and fortune of that particular year, for everyone. The animal cycle repeats every twelve years.

COUNTING THE YEAR AND MONTHS: TRADITIONAL CHINESE STYLE

Since the Cultural Revolution of 1911, China has used the Western calendar for business, schools, and much of everyday life. Festivals, however, continue to be determined by the traditional Chinese calendar. For those used to the Western Gregorian calendar, the Chinese method of counting months and years may seem very complex, but here's a go at explaining it. In the Western system, although the word *month* comes from the word *moon*, the actual months never line up with the cycle of the moon. The Chinese calendar is lunisolar, which means that it follows the cycle of the moon, and every month is twenty-nine-and-a-half days long. Lunisolar systems need to be adjusted every so often, so that the months will always fall on the same seasons. To do this, the Chinese calendar adds leap months to keep the solar and lunar years matched up. Every nineteen-year cycle, seven months are added, similar to how the Western calendar adds a day to February every four years.

The Chinese calendar is counted from year one of the reign of the Yellow Emperor. That was 2698 BCE, which makes the Western year 2010 equivalent to the Chinese year 4708. Reckoning the start of calendar time since the Yellow Emperor has been in effect in China only since the Revolution of 1911. Before that, the Chinese calendar year was based on a sixty-year cycle of animals and elements.

WHEN IS THE CHINESE NEW YEAR?					
February 14, 2010	Year of the Tiger	4708	February 8, 2016	Year of the Monkey	4714
February 3, 2011	Year of the Rabbit	4709	January 28, 2017	Year of the Rooster	4715
January 23, 2012	Year of the Dragon	4710	February 16, 2018	Year of the Dog	4716
February 10, 2013	Year of the Snake	4711	February 5, 2019	Year of the Pig	4717
January 31, 2014	Year of the Horse	4712	January 25, 2020	Year of the Rat	4718
February 19, 2015	Year of the Sheep	4713	February 12, 2021	Year of the Ox	4719

THE LANTERN FESTIVAL

The Chinese New Year festival ends fifteen days after it starts. It is brought to a close with the appearance of the first full moon of the year and the Lantern Festival, called *Yuan Xiao Jie.* Lanterns represent the light of the full moon and everyone's hopes for good luck and joy in the year ahead. The lanterns also have riddles and puzzles on them, which everyone tries to solve.

MAKE A PAPER LANTERN

Red is the traditional color for a Chinese New Year lantern. To make one, you will need: paper, scissors, a stapler or tape, and string. Fold a piece of paper in half the long way (or book style). Starting at the folded edge, cut lines every inch or so, about two thirds of the way through. Unfold, and then roll the paper into a cylinder. Staple or tape the top and the bottom. Cut a smaller strip of paper, about a half inch wide and 6 to 8 inches long, and staple it to the top of the lantern. A piece of a different-colored paper can be rolled and taped into a tube and attached inside the lantern, too.

Hang the lantern with string, either by itself or with many other colorful lanterns. If you have the kind of string lights that stay cool and never burn, these can be attached to your lanterns, but be careful and ask an adult to double-check.

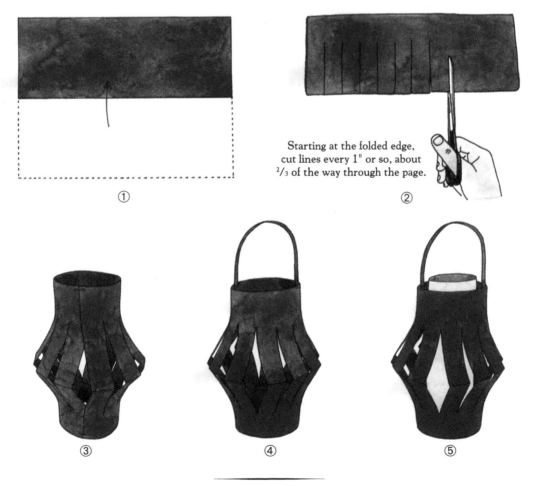

Starting at the folded edge, cut lines every 1" or so, about ²/₃ of the way through the page.

① ② ③ ④ ⑤

MAKE A RED ENVELOPE

Also traditional on the Chinese New Year are red envelopes, called *hong bao* in Mandarin Chinese and *lai see* in Cantonese. The envelope is filled with money or coins—but always in even numbers, for good luck. The money inside should never equal the number four, which is bad luck, but eight is a good amount, because the word for *eight* sounds the same as the word for *wealth*. Some envelopes are stuffed with chocolate coins. Whatever is inside, the red envelope is a symbol of good fortune both for the person who gives and for the person who receives. Some people put a dream list or wish list inside. Red envelopes are also given on birthdays and at weddings and other happy occasions.

To make an envelope, use the illustration to draw a template, which you can then cut out. Area 1 folds over area 2. Flaps A and B fold in and should be taped or stapled. Fill the envelope with something wonderful. Tuck flap C inside the envelope.

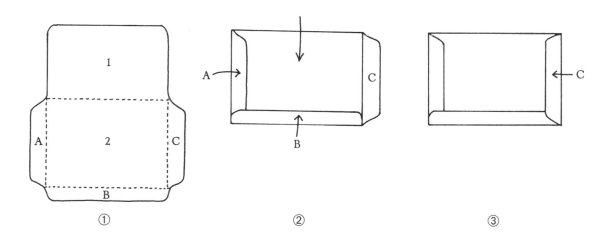

NEW YEAR'S GREETINGS

At Chinese New Year, in the Cantonese dialect of the south, "Gung Hei Fat Choi" is a wish for prosperity; and in Mandarin, the national dialect orginally native to the north, it's "Xin Nian Kuai Le," meaning simply "Happy New Year."

Notable Women II: Dancers

MARTHA GRAHAM was born in 1894. She did not start out as a dancer—in fact, she wouldn't begin her formal training in dance until she was twenty-two. But she would go on to become one of the pioneers of modern dance, an artistic innovator whose influence is still felt even today.

Martha was born in Pennsylvania and moved to Santa Barbara, California, with her family when she was in her teens. At sixteen, she saw her first dance performance, and she was so moved that she decided to devote her life to dancing. Her parents were not as enthusiastic, and so it wasn't until after she had graduated high school and attended college for three years that she was able to begin her studies. At the age of twenty-two, in 1916, she took her first class at the Denishawn Dance School, studying under the woman whose performance inspired her to dance at sixteen: Ruth St. Denis.

She was told she was too old, that her body was not the correct build, that it was too late for her to learn the proper technique. But Martha did not listen: She worked hard and she worked fast, and she came to have a reputation for detail and precision as well as perseverance. She toured with the Denishawn Company until she settled in New York in 1923. She dabbled in teaching on the dance faculty of the Eastman School of Music, but the academic life was not for her. Instead, she began choreographing and teaching at a classroom in the back of Carnegie Hall. The first performance of her new dance company premiered on April 18, 1926.

Graham's angular, raw movement stood in stark contrast to the refined and fluid technique of classical ballet. Shocking at first, and confusing for audiences, her choreography came to be embraced as distinctly American. It marked the beginning of an entirely new and modern viewpoint in dance.

She was the first dancer ever to perform at the White House; like Marian Anderson, she traveled abroad as a cultural ambassador and was awarded the Medal of Freedom, becoming the first dancer to receive such an honor. She was celebrated worldwide and given both the key to the city of Paris and Japan's Imperial Order of the Precious Crown. In 1951 she helped found the dance division of the world-famous Juilliard School. For a long while she resisted her dances being photographed or recorded, as she believed dance was a "live" creative event that should be experienced in the moment. Luckily for us, she relented, and some of her performances and choreography were preserved for posterity.

Her career spanned nearly seventy years and one hundred choreographed pieces, and she made her final performance at the age of seventy-six, dancing in a work called *Cortege of Eagles*. She died in 1991, at the age of ninety-six, but her famous dance company, the Martha Graham Dance Company, continues to perform around the world.

Maria Tallchief, born Elizabeth Marie Tall Chief on an Indian reservation in Oklahoma on January 24, 1925, was the first Native American prima ballerina.

Her father, who was of Osage descent, made sure his children had ballet and piano lessons from the time they were very young. Her mother, too, felt that artistic education was vital for her girls. Soon the family moved to California, so Maria and her sister, Marjorie, could study piano, as their mother hoped that one day they both might become famed concert pianists. But as much as Maria enjoyed her music lessons, she was more intrigued by dance. She studied with dance teachers like David Lichine and Bronislava Nijinska, the sister of the great dancer Vaslav Nijinsky. With Nijinska's encouragement, she pursued her dance training, which eventually took her to New York and the Ballets Russes de Monte Carlo.

Maria joined the Ballets Russes, where she quickly became a soloist and impressed audiences and critics alike with her performances. Particularly impressed with her was George Balanchine, who took over as the ballet master of the Ballets Russes in 1944. Maria quickly became his muse—inspiring many famous Balanchine ballets including *Symphonie Concertante, Orpheus, The Four Temperaments,* and *Scotch Symphony*—and, in 1946, his wife. They traveled the world together performing: In Paris she became the first American-born woman dancer to perform with the Paris Opera Ballet, both in Paris and on tour in Moscow. When they returned to the United States, Balanchine founded the New York City Ballet and made Maria its prima ballerina. This marked the first time any American had held the title of prima ballerina in any company, anywhere.

Maria enjoyed enormous popularity. She was particularly known for her performance in *The Firebird* and as the Sugar Plum Fairy in *The Nutcracker*, a role she originated in 1954. She was honored for her international achievements and for the visibility she gave to Native Americans by the state of Oklahoma, who in 1953 gave Tallchief the name *Wa-Xthe-Thomba:* "Woman of Two Worlds." That same year, President Dwight Eisenhower named her "Woman of the Year." After her marriage to Balanchine ended, she remarried in 1956 and became a mother soon after, taking the only leave of absence she ever permitted of herself during her career. Afterward, she returned briefly to Balanchine's New York City Ballet to work on his *Gounod*

Symphony, and then joined the rival American Ballet Theatre in 1960.

She continued to perform through the mid-1960s, debuting with Rudolf Nureyev on American television and touring America and the USSR with the American Ballet Theatre. She retired from dancing in 1966 and moved to Chicago, where she was artistic director of the Chicago Lyric Opera and later founded the Chicago City Ballet with her sister, Marjorie (who had also made a career of dancing). In 1996, she was honored at the Kennedy Center as one of America's most important artists. She lives in Chicago.

Raven Wilkinson was five years old when her mother took her to see her first ballet in 1941. The famed Ballets Russes de Monte Carlo was at New York's City Center Theater, performing the ballet *Coppelia*, about a doll that comes to life. This was the Ballets Russes of Balanchine and Maria Tallchief, and when the curtain fell after the final dancer took her last bow, Raven turned to her mother and told her she knew what she wanted to be when she grew up. Four years later, at age nine, she was able to take her first steps toward that goal: She began to study at the school run by the Ballets Russes.

A natural-born dancer, she was nurtured by her teacher Madam Maria Svoboda, and the director of the school, Sergei Denham, who both noted her refined, elegant form. In 1954 she was given a full contract and made a member of the Ballets Russes—the first African-American dancer to be a member of any major ballet company. She was quickly promoted to soloist, and she toured with the company for six years. Her time as a performer, however, was marred by prejudice and discrimination. Staying at a hotel with the company while on tour in Atlanta, Georgia, an elevator girl reported Raven to the management, and she was forced to leave: The hotel was "whites only." Her roommate on the tour protested, leaving with Raven as she was moved to a black hotel, but when they arrived, only Raven was allowed to stay: The hotel was "blacks only." Later, in Alabama, members of the Ku Klux Klan ransacked the Ballets Russes's bus, demanding to know where the African-American dancer was. Nobody would answer them, but afterward Raven would report a burning cross outside her hotel window. After that season, the company suggested to her that she might reconsider performing in the South in light of these kinds of threats. Raven, despondent after six years of touring under these tough conditions, took a break from dancing and joined a convent.

But her love for dance refused to go away. In 1967, after eight months of life as a Catholic nun, she left the order and returned to the stage. This time she went to Holland, where she was a soloist with the Dutch National Ballet.

Seven years later she returned to her hometown of New York, where she continued to dance on her own terms. Her most recent performance was in 2008, dancing in New York City Opera's production of *Madama Butterfly*.

Cricket

WHEN YOU TRAVEL AROUND THE GLOBE, it quickly becomes apparent that the world's most popular bat-and-ball game is not American baseball, or even softball. It turns out to be a long and seemingly eccentric game played with two runners, a half flat bat, three wooden sticks popping out of the ground, and fielder positions with names such as Silly Point, Gully, and Deep Square Leg. Yes, we're referring to cricket.

Cricket was once one of those games that men and boys played while their mothers and sisters watched from the sidelines. Not anymore. In the United Kingdom, Finland, Trinidad, and elsewhere, girls are playing cricket like never before.

Here are some things to know about cricket:

1. The field is a large ellipse, but there's no regulation shape or size.

2. In the middle of the field is a rectangle of grass that is carefully tended and mown short. This area is called the pitch. The pitch has two wickets, one at either side. Each wicket is made from wooden stumps that are set close enough to each other that the ball can't get through. The stumps are connected on top with a bail, which falls off when the stumps are hit.

3. A few feet in front of each wicket is a line on the ground. It's called the popping crease, which is where the batter stands to hit the ball. The batters must touch the popping crease with their bats to score a run. The pitcher (who in cricket is called a *bowler*) must never go past the popping crease when bowling the ball.

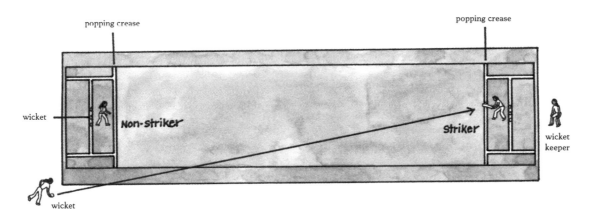

4. Newcomers to cricket may be surprised that a match lasts so long. Test matches are the highest level of professional games, and they last for five days. Each day, the game goes on for six hours until thankfully someone at last calls, "*Stumps*," and play ends. Even single-day cricket lasts longer than many other games. That's just the way it is.

5. Cricket matches are divided into innings. This word is always used in the plural, as in the sentence "That was a long innings." Each innings features ten batters and ends when all ten have gotten out. If the players are good, an innings can last a very long time indeed. In many cases, teams agree ahead of time on how many innings to play.

6. A cricket team has eleven players. When a team is in the field, nine players spread across the grass. One is the wicketkeeper. This is the only fielder who wears a glove or protective gear. Several players take turns bowling. There are no set positions. Fielders are constantly moved about as the captain changes strategy and chooses new tactics during the game.

7. When the bowler bowls the ball toward the striker, it is called a *delivery*. The ball is thrown a little lower than hip height. It will bounce somewhere along the pitch. This bounce makes the ball unpredictable and harder to hit. A bowler bowls six good deliveries. This set of six is called an *over*. After each over, the wicketkeeper moves to the opposite wicket. A new bowler comes to the pitch and bowls from this new direction. Bowlers can bowl many *overs* in a game, just not one right after the other. One thing, though, is that they must keep proper posture, avoiding a bent elbow and making sure the delivery arm is straight.

8. Batting and scoring runs works something like this: At all times there are two batters on the pitch. Each stands by a wicket. One is called the striker. The other is called the nonstriker. The bowler does a run-up from behind one of the wickets. Making sure not to step a toe over the popping crease, the bowler bowls the ball toward the striker. The striker tries to hit the ball so that she and the nonstriker can score runs. The striker also tries to protect the wicket from being hit by the ball.

That's the simple part of the explanation.

The ball is hit. Both batters run back and forth between the wickets. Each time they near a wicket they make sure to touch their bats across the popping crease before turning to head back from whence they came. Both batters keep running back and forth until the ball is *dead.* This means that the wicketkeeper caught the ball. Or a fielder caught the ball. Or the batters are in danger of being tagged out while away from their wicket, or for whatever reason they need to get back to their places so they can have a chance to strike again and score more runs.

Another difference from baseball: After scoring a bunch of runs, a striker bats again and again, scoring even more runs until finally making an out. Then the nonstriker takes the place as the next striker. The team's next batter walks onto the field to become the new nonstriker. And the innings continues.

9. Cricket scores often run into the hundreds, so don't be surprised. One point is scored each time a batter runs between the wickets when the ball is in play. Extra points are awarded, too. These are called, simply, *extras*. Hitting the ball to the boundary fence—that's four extras. Sailing the ball over the fence is six extras. A striker can also get an extra when the bowler oversteps the popping crease or bowls wide and too far away. Another term to know is the opposite of an extra: *short*. That's when a batter doesn't touch the crease with her bat, and so the run can't be counted.

10. These are a few of the ways a batter gets out (and the bowler gets to "take the wicket"):

- The ball is caught "on the full."
- The striker swings at the ball and misses, and the ball breaks the wicket. (If the striker swings and misses, but the wicket does not break, it is not an out!)
- The striker swings and misses and steps out of the popping crease, and the wicketkeeper gets the ball and breaks the wicket before the striker can get back behind the crease. This is called *stumped*.
- A fielder catches the ball, throws it to the pitch, and breaks the wicket while the batter is not safely in the popping crease. The nearest batter is called out.
- There's another situation called *Leg Before Wicket* (LBW). This is when the batter misses the ball but intercepts it with some part of her body (and, hence, the ball doesn't hit the wicket and cause an out). The team in the field believes that had the batter not gotten her body in the way of the ball, she would be out. They ask the umpire to decide.
- There are other ways to get out, but they are rare. The batter may unintentionally hit the wicket or touch the ball with a hand or get in the way of a fielder. Our favorite, though, is when a new batter times out by dillydallying and taking too long to get on the field.

11. There are two umpires. One stands by one wicket and watches the bowler. The other stands by the other wicket and watches the striker. In professional games there may be a third umpire who can check the video replay to see what happened. In cricket, everyone is supposed to be very polite to the umpire, asking "How's that?" in the rare event that a call is questioned. This rule is rarely followed.

Lightning

LIGHTNING, most simply, is electricity. We use electricity every day, from morning (when we hit the snooze button on the alarm clock) to night (when we turn on our reading lamps at bedtime) and nearly every moment in between. But if you've ever witnessed a flash of lightning forking through the sky on a stormy night, you know how powerful, and even frightening, electricity can seem when it isn't packed inside a battery or hidden behind a light switch. To understand how lightning works, first a quick review of clouds and a refresher on atomic particles. As you may remember from the original *Daring Book for Girls*, a cumulus cloud is a puffy, cotton-ball-type cloud whose name comes from the Latin word for "pile" or "heap." A nimbus cloud is a cloud that's full of rain. Combine these two types of clouds together and you have a cumulonimbus cloud—a giant, puffy, rain cloud, also called a thunder cloud.

You may also remember from the original *Daring* book our discussion of atoms and the small particles inside them, called protons and electrons. These are too small to be seen by the naked eye, but we know a few important things about them. Protons, which are found inside the center of the atom, are particles that have a positive charge. Electrons, which orbit around the atom's nucleus the way the planets orbit around the sun, are particles that have a negative charge. Protons and electrons are equal in strength, so if an atom has an equal amount of protons and electrons, it has no charge at all and is considered neutral. If it has more protons, that gives it a positive charge; if it has more electrons, it has a negative charge.

What does this have to do with lightning? It turns out that large cumulonimbus clouds are the perfect breeding grounds for lightning, because although they appear to be nothing more than dark and looming shapes in the sky, hidden within the clouds is a veritable electricity factory. Inside are air currents, paths of air moving up and down. Energy forms as the air currents inside the clouds move the water droplets and ice crystals that are also inside the clouds. The faster the air moves, the more the water and ice collide, breaking into pieces and releasing charged particles. The smaller particles, which are positively charged, float toward the top of the cloud, and the larger particles, which are negatively charged, sink toward the bottom.

We know something else about protons and electrons and the way positive and negative particles interact: *Opposites attract.* You can see this with magnets, the way like sides repel and opposite sides pull together. The same thing happens with charges. So when the buildup of energy in the cloud reaches its peak, and there is no more room inside the cloud for separation between the particles, the positive and negative charges rush toward each other, and the energy released as they make that leap is visible as lightning.

Sometimes this is contained within a cloud, and the flash of electricity moves from one part of the cloud to another part of the same cloud. Other times it sparks from one cloud to another nearby cloud. And, in its most recognizable form to us, it can zigzag through the sky between the cloud and the ground.

But this most characteristic version of lightning striking isn't exactly what it appears to be. We see lightning forking through the sky down toward the ground, but in reality, the lightning is actually traveling from the ground *up*. Remember how the negative particles accumulate in the lower part of the cloud? When there are enough negative particles there, some of them escape in channels of negatively charged air called *leaders*. Like the tentacles of an octopus searching for prey, those negative leaders are on the hunt for positive charges to grab onto. If the cloud is close enough to the ground, those leaders attract positive channels coming up from the ground, called *streamers*. When a leader and a streamer meet, the result is a brilliant flash of lightning that illuminates the forky downward path of the negative charges. We see only that downward path and not the upward path of the streamer, which is why it appears to us that the lightning is traveling down.

WHAT ABOUT THUNDER?

Thunder and lightning go hand in hand because thunder is the sound of lightning. Lightning is incredibly hot—hotter than the surface of the sun even—and as it singes through the air, the air around the lightning expands from the heat, and the cooler air on either side rushes in. This creates a sound wave that we hear as thunder. The only reason we don't hear thunder at the exact same time we see lightning is that light travels faster than sound: The light created by lightning reaches our eyes long before the sound created by lightning reaches our ears.

In a speed race, sound can't even compete. It travels at about 5 miles per second, while light travels at an incredible 186,282.397 miles per second. But the slower pace of sound can help you determine how far away a storm is and how quickly it is moving. Count the number of seconds between the moment you see the lightning and the moment you hear the thunder. Then, divide that number by 5. The result tells you how far away the storm is in miles.

LIGHTNING SAFETY

If the time between seeing lightning and hearing thunder is fewer than thirty seconds, immediately go indoors, even if it's not raining. Take shelter inside a house or, if you're away from home, in a car with the windows shut. The important thing is to be inside, as shelter can protect you from a lightning strike. Once inside, avoid using water or any electrical equipment, and stay away from windows. After the storm has passed, wait thirty minutes before going outside again.

If you cannot go indoors, try to be as safe as possible outdoors. Lightning strikes the tallest object it can find, so try to make yourself as small as possible. Get down on the ground, curling yourself into a ball with your hands over your ears and your head tucked in to your chest. If you are with other people, try to keep at least 15 feet between each person. Stay away from metal, water, and lone buildings or trees. If someone is struck by lightning, call 911.

LIGHTNING EXPERIMENTS

Benjamin Franklin conducted his famous lightning experiment with a kite and a key, but he was not the first to theorize about electricity. In fact, a few weeks before Franklin and his son went out on that stormy Philadelphia night in June 1752, a man named Thomas-François Dalibard performed the very same experiment in France. Both of these experiments sparked the imagination of other budding scientists, who were eager to see with their own eyes how lightning and static electricity worked. Here are some much safer experiments you can do yourself.

LIGHTNING IN YOUR MOUTH

For this you'll need some Wint-O-Green or Pep-O-Mint Life Savers (or other wintergreen-flavored or peppermint-flavored doughnut-shaped mints). Go into a dark room—a bathroom is ideal, because it has a mirror—and let your eyes adjust to the darkness. Then, put a mint in your mouth and crunch it using your teeth without closing your mouth. Look in the mirror while you chew and see if you can spot bluish sparks of light.

Sparks fly because as you use your teeth to break the candy, you're also breaking apart the sugars inside the candy. This releases tiny electrical charges, which attract the oppositely charged nitrogen in the air all around you. When those opposite charges meet in the middle, it creates a spark—just like lightning.

LIGHTNING IN YOUR HAND

Take a long flourescent lightbulb (not an incandescent bulb) and an inflated rubber balloon and go into a dark room. Rub the balloon on your hair for a few seconds and then hold the balloon next to the end of the fluorescent lightbulb. Be amazed as the bulb lights up.

This experiment works thanks to static electricity. Rubbing the balloon on your hair creates an electrical charge, but the charge has no place to go (hence, the term *static* electricity). When you bring the charged side of the balloon to the end of the fluorescent lightbulb, the electrical charge jumps from the balloon to the bulb, which causes the bulb to light up.

LIGHTNING FACTS

* Most lightning bolts are an inch wide or less and about a mile long.

* The longest recorded lightning bolt ever seen was 118 miles long, sighted near Dallas, Texas.

* The longest lightning bolt fossil ever unearthed was a 17-foot-long fulgurite found in 1997 in Gainesville, Florida. A *fulgurite* (from the Latin word for "thunderbolt") is a glassy tube formed by lightning underground as a lightning bolt hits the earth and tears through the soil.

* Somewhere, right now, someplace on Earth is being struck by lightning. Lightning strikes the earth about one hundred times each second. In the Democratic Republic of the Congo, near the small village of Kifuka, is the most lightning-struck place on Earth.

* In the United States, the area between Tampa and Orlando in Florida receives fifty lightning strikes per square mile each year, earning itself the nickname "Lightning Alley." In New York, the Empire State Building is struck by lightning about twenty-three times each year. During one storm, it was struck eight times in twenty-four minutes.

* The man holding the Guinness World Record for being the person most struck by lightning is Roy Sullivan, a forest ranger from Virginia, who survived seven lightning strikes before his death in 1983.

How to Waltz

I T MAY SEEM OLD-FASHIONED TODAY, but at the turn of the nineteenth century when the waltz came from Vienna to Britain and the United States, waltzing was considered scandalous. The dance allowed touching between the partners, but what was truly terrible, according to the aristocrats who complained about it, was that waltzing was easy to learn and didn't require the assistance of a dance master. Waltzing was a dance of the people.

The first waltzes were recorded in Germany in the 1750s, and the name comes from the German verb *walzen*, which means "to turn." Doing these turning dances to the music of Johann Strauss and other composers became a huge craze in Vienna, the city at the center of the Austro-Hungarian empire. While the waltz may no longer be considered a "craze" anywhere, it is still *the* classic partner dance, called "the queen of all dances." And one day, you never know when, you may be in a situation where partner dancing is required, and you will wish you'd spent ten minutes learning how to waltz before being dragged onto the dance floor.

STEPS AND BOXES

In a waltz, both partners move in a six-step forward-side-together, back-side-together pattern. They move and turn in a box shape, so it helps to imagine a square on the floor and then pretend to step on each corner. The dance has an up-and-down motion, too, which means that everyone's heels go down-up-up, down-up-up (but you might save this more advanced step for later).

Of the two partners, one leads and one follows, and their steps mirror each other. When one partner moves forward starting with the left foot, the other partner moves backward, starting with the right.

Two things to remember as you start: Always transfer your weight to the foot you step with, and don't under any circumstances ever look at your feet—that's a surefire way to a waltzing disaster.

POSITIONS

If you are the leader, place your right hand on the middle of your partner's back. Your left hand goes out to the side, elbow bent, ready to hold your partner's hand (you will hold hands at about your partner's eye level).

If you are the follower, your left hand will rest on the leader's right shoulder. Your left arm will rest on the leader's right arm. Your right hand holds your partner's extended left arm.

The two partners don't exactly face each other; the position is more of a "V," which is a good thing because it's just too easy to step on toes when you waltz. Your legs move between your partner's legs, rather than lining up with their toes.

Now that you are in position, the chart can help you take it from here. And once you have learned the count-to-six step, you can add the more advanced down-up-up motion; that's what the center row of the chart on the next page shows. Both partners go up on tiptoes for two counts, and then down on their heels for one count. Think of it in this way: At each opposite corner of an imaginary box you are dancing in, you will either be up or down.

	1	2	3	4	5	6
Leader	Left foot forward	Right foot to the right side	Left foot steps to meet the right	Right foot backward	Left foot to the left side	Right foot steps to meet the left
Both	Heels down	Up on toes	Up on toes	Heels down	Up on toes	Up on toes
Follower	Right foot backward	Left foot to the left side	Right foot steps to meet the left	Left foot forward	Right foot to the right side	Left foot steps to meet the right

TURNING

Once you get good at waltzing, you'll be ready to twirl across the dance floor with showy, fancy turns.

To do turns, the leader continues the forward-side-together step. The leader initiates the move. If you are the leader, let your shoulders lead with confidence. Pull your partner along with your right hand. Do a few regular waltz steps, move slightly, and then try a full quarter or half turn (Hint: Pivot and step wider on counts 2 and 5). The follower steps into a turn, and while we could try to describe here what happens next, rest assured that when you are dancing and decide to turn, you will know exactly what to do, and more.

Above all, the goal of waltzing is to be able to talk and laugh while you dance. Good luck!

THE "FAKING IT" WALTZ

If the special waltzing moment arrives and you haven't mastered the true waltz steps, never fear. Forget the sophisticated box step. Skim these directions and dance this basic folk waltz with aplomb.

	1	2	3	4	5	6
Leader	Right foot steps right	Left foot steps to meet the right	Shift weight to right foot	Return! Left foot steps left	Right foot steps to meet the left	Shift weight to the left foot
Both	Heels down	Up on toes	Up on toes	Heels down	Up on toes	Up on toes
Follower	Left foot steps left	Right foot steps to meet the left	Shift weight to left foot	Return! Right foot steps right	Left foot steps to meet the right	Shift weight to the right foot

Furoshiki

SOMETIME IN THE EIGHTH CENTURY, people in Japan began using sturdy square cloths to carry their clothes and serve as bath mats when visiting steam baths. By the seventeenth century, these bathing cloths, called furoshiki (from the words *furo*, meaning "bath," and *shiki*, meaning "to spread out"), were used by nearly everyone, from merchants to aristocrats, as a means to transport and carry anything. (The Japanese expression, "To spread a big furoshiki," means to brag that you can handle more than you really can.)

Furoshiki were so popular at one time that every Japanese home had several on hand. In the twentieth century, furoshiki began to be used less and less, reserved more for wrapping gifts to acknowledge formal occasions such as weddings and funerals. But today furoshiki are once again becoming popular as a reusable, environmentally sound alternative to plastic shopping bags.

Furoshiki come in many sizes, from as small as a handkerchief to as large as a bedsheet. The most common sizes today are small (18 inches) and medium (28 to 30 inches). Furoshiki can be made from any material, from cotton to synthetic fibers to silk, and the designs can range from the simple to the ornate, depending on the occasion and the season (for example, prints with cherry blossoms are often used in the spring).

WRAPPING WITH FUROSHIKI

The three basic ways of wrapping are hirazutsumi ("just wrapping"), hitotsumusubi ("with one knot"), and futatsumusubi ("with two knots"). All other methods are simply variations on these techniques. To encourage people to use furoshiki in the place of plastic shopping bags or gift wrap, Japan's Ministry of the Environment recently created a folding guide featuring fourteen different ways to use furoshiki.

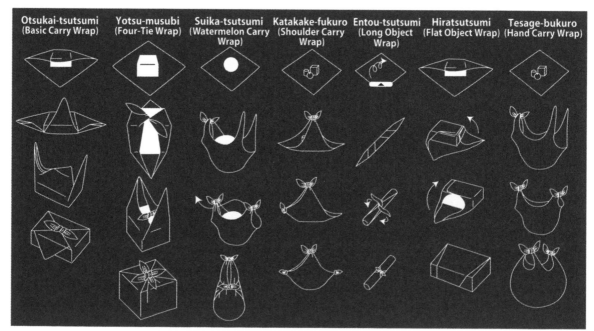

Otsukai-tsutumi (basic carry wrap)

Place the item in the center of the furoshiki, and tuck the top corner underneath it. Bring the bottom corner up and over the box. Then, take the two other corners, and tie them in a square knot across the top.

Yotsu-musubi (four-tie wrap)

Place a square item in the center of the furoshiki. Take the left and right corners, and tie them in a knot on top of the item. Then, take the other two corners (top and bottom), and tie those in a knot on top of the first knot.

Suika-tsutsumi (watermelon carry wrap)

Place a ball-shaped item in the center of a medium-sized (28-inch) furoshiki. Tie the top left and bottom left corners together, creating a loop. Then, tie the top right and bottom right corners together, creating a loop on that side. Then, take the knot on the right-hand side, and pull it through the loop on the left side to create a handle for carrying.

Katakake-fukuro (shoulder carry wrap)

Place several small items in the center of the furoshiki. Tie the top and bottom corners together. On the left side, twist the fabric to gather it and tie it in a knot. On the right side, twist and gather the fabric to tie a knot. With either side knotted, you can sling it over your shoulder and the items won't fall out.

Entou-tsusumi (long object wrap)

Place the object at the bottom corner of the furoshiki. Roll it all the way to the opposite corner. Lift the two ends, and bring them toward each other. Twist them around each other once, and then turn the object over and tie in a knot on the other side.

Hirazutsumi (flat object wrap)

This method uses only folding, no knotting or tying. Place item in the center of the furoshiki. Take the top corner, fold it over, and tuck it underneath the item. Fold the left corner over. Fold the right corner over. Bring the bottom corner up and over the item, tucking it underneath.

Tesage-bukuro (hand carry wrap)

Place items in the center of a medium to large (28- to 36-inch) furoshiki. As in the watermelon wrap, tie the left-side corners together, and then the right-side corners together.

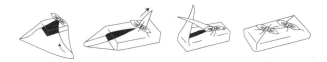

Kousa-tsusumi (slender object carry wrap)

Place item in the center of a medium-sized (28-inch) furoshiki. Tie the top corner and the right corner in a knot. Take the bottom corner, pull it through the knot, and tie that to the remaining corner.

Hon-tsusumi (two books carry wrap)

This works best with a larger (42-inch) furoshiki. Spread the furoshiki, and place one book on the left corner and one on the right. Fold the left and right edges over the books and then flip the books over until their edges meet in the center.

Lift the top and bottom corners and cross them in the middle. Then, flip the two books again so that they fold up together with the crossed fabric inbetween them. Stand them up on end so that the crossed fabric is on top. Then, twist the fabric and tie the ends in a knot to create a carrying handle.

Futatsu-tsusumi (two knots carry wrap)

This will work with a medium (28-inch) furoshiki. Place the item in the center of the furoshiki. Take the top and bottom corners, and cross them in the center so that one points left and one points right. Tie the left-side corners in a knot, and then tie the right-side corners in a knot.

Kakushi-tsusumi (hidden knot wrap)

Place the item in the center of the furoshiki. Tuck the top corner underneath, and fold the bottom corner over. Tie the left and right corners in a knot on top. Then, pull the fabric out from underneath the knot, and place it over the knot to hide it.

Bin-tsutsumi (bottle carry wrap)

Place a bottle in the center of a medium-sized (28-inch) furoshiki. Take the left and right

corners, tie a knot on top of the bottle, and then twist the ends of that tie and to make another knot, leaving a loop in between the two. Take the other two corners, cross them around the bottle, and then tie on the opposite side.

Bin-tsutsumi 2 (two-bottle carry wrap)

Stand two bottles side by side in the center of a large (36-inch) furoshiki. Then, holding them by the neck, gently lay them down, the right-side bottle pointing to the right corner and the left-side bottle pointing to the left corner. Making sure to keep the same distance between them, roll the bottles down toward the bottom, and then fold the bottom corner over them, and roll them in the fabric all the way up to the top. Grab the bottles by the neck and stand them up. Tie the ends of the fabric on top.

Sao-tsutsumi (padding carry wrap)

Place the item at the bottom corner of the furoshiki with the very edge of the corner folded on top. Roll the item all the way to the top corner. Pull the left and right corners up, twist them across the object, and turn it over. Then, tie the corners together on the other side.

The Double-Daring Girl's Guide to Getting Out of Trouble

IN A LIFE OF DARING AND ADVENTURE, you may need to wiggle out of a tight spot. Here are some solutions for when you find yourself in one. Start embellishing your tale of heroism now. Whatever happens, later on it will make for a darn good story.

1. Lost in the Woods. Dusk is falling and you find yourself alone in the woods. Before panic sets in, take a moment to STOP—that is, Stop, Think, Observe, and Plan. Then, put the trusty whistle that's been hanging around your neck to good use. The universal code for "I'm lost and in trouble" is three short blasts. Repeat it every five minutes until you are found. When you hear someone else's whistle, respond immediately with a whistle blast of your own.

2. Dog Ate Your Homework. Whether you've lost your homework or simply haven't done it, honesty is the best policy, although it's not always the easiest. What you need to know is that teachers don't like surprises. Approach the teacher before class. Don't make excuses. Don't whine. Do not under any circumstances tell a dramatic sob story. Just stick to a straightforward explanation, and try to look responsible. Suggest a plan for making good, as in, "May I hand in the essay tomorrow?"

3. Capsized Boat. Remain calm (and be glad you were wearing your life vest). Stay with your boat (unless you're just a few yards from shore, in which case you're not really in trouble, you're just wet). Gather any gear that floats by. Right the boat if you can. Flag down the nearest motorboat to tow you to shore. And if you happen to have a working cell phone packed away in a watertight plastic bag, use it to call the coast guard, and your mom.

4. Makeup Mess. It happens to the best of us, but it's easy to fix. Clean a mascara mess with olive oil or baby oil. Wipe off excess lipstick with a tissue and either try again or opt for the natural look. On your next attempt, remember that less is more.

5. Clothing Emergency. Your pants rip. Food spills on your shirt. Your coat gets a big muddy puddle splash. Here's where grace under pressure comes in. Keep your chin up. Pretend it's not there. Or mention it casually before someone else does, and continue on your way. Soon what everyone notices is not what's wrong with your outfit, but your cool, unflappable style.

6. Jellyfish Stings. Rub the area with sand or rinse with seawater to get rid of the lingering residue from the jellyfish's tentacles. (Don't use tap water or ice, which make the matter worse.) Soak a bandana in vinegar and hold it on the sting for 20 minutes. For a tried-and-true method, sprinkle on a layer of meat tenderizer.

7. Caught on Thin Ice. You're ice skating on a pond, when suddenly you see a slow crack forming in the ice. Get down on your hands and knees. This distributes your weight more equally and puts less pressure on the ice. Crawl carefully and slowly to the nearest shore.

8. Quicksand. In horror movies, one bad step and you are sucked forever into a milky morass. The good news is that most quicksand pits don't look anything like the movies, nor are they as deadly. Your body is less dense than quicksand, which means that you can float. Use slow, small motions to get on your back. Once you're floating, move yourself slowly to the edge of the pit and carefully hoist yourself onto firmer ground.

Japanese Tea Ceremony

THE FIRST RECORD OF TEA DRINKING in Japan dates from 729, when the Emperor Shomu invited one hundred Buddhist monks for tea at the Imperial Palace. But it wasn't until the late 1100s that "The Way of Tea" became established, when the Buddhist monk Eisai went to China to study with Zen monks and returned in 1191 with tea seeds and plants—and the ritual of drinking tea for health and clarity.

"The Way of Tea" was perfected by Sen no Rikyu in the sixteenth century, when he organized the tea ceremony around four basic principles that are considered to be the spirit of the tea ceremony even today: *wa* (harmony), *kei* (respect), *sei* (purity), and *jaku* (tranquility). These concepts are evidenced in every aspect of the ceremony, from the simple placement of flowers in a vase, to a host's creation of a comfortable, pleasant, clutter-free, and harmonious setting for her guests.

The study of the tea ceremony is a lifelong quest. Tea practitioners strive to become expert in not only tea, but also the arts of calligraphy, kimono, flower arranging, ceramics, and incense; even guests are expected to know the etiquette of taking tea. Here is a little bit about how to host your own Japanese tea ceremony.

HOSTING YOUR TEA CEREMONY

A tea ceremony is a relatively formal affair. Even the more casual ceremony is expected to last an hour; the fancier events can last as long as four. Given this, invitations are often sent a week in advance. Keep the guest list small: part of the beauty of the ceremony is its intimacy.

As a host, you are responsible for creating a pleasant atmosphere for your guests, which means making sure that the place where you'll be having your tea ceremony is clean and uncluttered, and that you are prepared ahead of time. Remember, nothing has to be fancy: The tea ceremony, for all its intricacy, is meant to be relaxing and simple.

The equipment used in the tea ceremony is called *chadōgu* ("tea tools"). The more formal the ceremony, the more *chadōgu* you will need. If you are planning a simple ceremony at home, you can use tea bags and regular cups or mugs. But here are a few of the more traditional tea tools:

- Tea whisk (*chasen*), for mixing powdered tea with hot water. These special whisks, carved from a single piece of bamboo, are about 5 inches long and 1 inch thick at the base.

Tea Whisk
(chasen)

- Tea bowls (*chawan*) and a simple rectangular white linen cloth (*chakin*) for cleaning the bowls. Small bowls are used to drink tea, rather than cups, and they come in a range of styles. In general, thin, shallow bowls are used during the summer, and deep, thicker bowls are used in winter.

- Tea scoop (*chashaku*). These long-handled spoons, used for scooping loose or powdered tea, are usually made of bamboo. It is considered impolite to touch the scooping part with your hand.

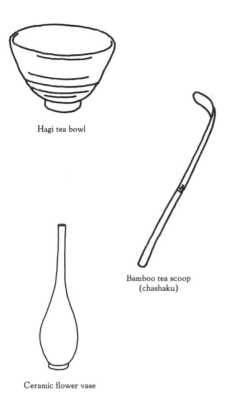

Hagi tea bowl

Bamboo tea scoop
(chashaku)

Ceramic flower vase

- Teapot (*kama*). This can be a regular teakettle. In a traditional Japanese tearoom, *kama* are heated over a hearth sunken into the floor.

- Green tea or black tea.

- Tray for small sweet treats.

- Vase with a simple arrangement of seasonal flowers. Nature is an important part of the tea ceremony.

- Artwork, such as a favorite painting.

- Calligraphy, usually written on a hanging scroll and showcasing a quote, saying, or message in keeping with the season or the occasion for the ceremony.

Things to Know: The Five Spaces

There are five different areas through which guests pass in a traditional tea ceremony. They are: the receiving room (*Yoritsuki*), the passageway (*Roji*), the space for symbolic cleansing (*Tskukubai*), the waiting area (*Machiai*), and the tearoom (*Chashitsu*). In traditional ceremonies, these spaces are both outdoors and indoors, embracing nature as part of the way of tea. These days, not many people have gardens with special tearooms in their backyards, but the five spaces aren't so different from the way you may welcome guests into your house any day. When you have a friend over for dinner, you most likely greet her at the door, bring her down the hall and into your home, perhaps point out where the restroom is in case she needs to wash up, take her to the living room to wait until dinner, and then into the kitchen or dining room to eat. The five spaces of the tea ceremony are very similar.

The room you use as your tearoom (*Chashitsu*) should be a special place, free of clutter. It should have a table that is clear of everything except your tea equipment, and an area for displaying flowers and perhaps a calligraphy scroll. Ring a bell to call your guests into the room. Once everyone is settled, enter the room and welcome your guests with a bow. Your guests will bow in return. Then you may say a few remarks, especially if this ceremony is celebrating a special occasion.

Starting the Ceremony

The traditional ceremony has many subtle rules about how to present the tea tools, brew the tea, and serve it to guests. For our purposes here, we will describe how to embrace the spirit of the ceremony without performing all of the rituals, which take even experienced tea practitioners years to learn.

Begin by bringing in a tray of sweets for guests to eat before drinking the unsweetened tea. Most guests who have attended tea ceremonies know to bring a small paper napkin with them to use as both a napkin and a plate for the sweet treats. As a thoughtful hostess, however, have some extra napkins on hand just in case.

Once your guests are done eating, remove the tray and any trash. Then, return with a tray holding your tea supplies. This may be simply the teabowls or cups for your guests, if you are brewing tea in tea bags; or, if you are using powdered tea, it may be one teabowl, a scoop, a whisk, and a tea caddy containing tea. Either way, the tray will also hold a *chakin* (a linen napkin). If you have a *fukusa* (a larger, fancier cloth), use it to cover the tray, and then lift it off to reveal the supplies to your guests. Fold it nicely, and use it to symbolically clean the tea scoop. Use the *chakin* to wipe the teabowls or teacups before you serve your guests.

If you are using tea bags, boil water in a teakettle and brew the tea. Rather than bring the hot teakettle to the table, pour the tea into a decorative ceramic teapot and bring that to the table. Pour tea into individual cups for your guests, just a small amount at a time. Pay attention to whether or not your guests need more, and pour as needed.

If you are using powdered tea, hold the scoop in your right hand and scoop one scoop of green tea for each person into a large teabowl. Pour hot water into the bowl, and then use the whisk to mix the tea. Whisk twenty-five to thirty times until there is a nice green froth on the top. The teabowl will be passed from guest to guest as they share the tea.

Ending the Ceremony

The closing of the tea ceremony should be as graceful as its start. When all the guests are done, bow and say to them, "I will finish." The guests will then return the cups, bowls, and utensils used in the tea ceremony to you. Place them on the tray in the orderly way they were placed at the start. Put the tray back in the kitchen, and return to the tearoom. Bow to your guests. Then, enjoy a few moments of conversation before thanking them and saying good-bye. Lead them to the door and watch them as they leave to be sure everyone is fine.

INSTRUCTIONS FOR GUESTS WHO ARE SHARING A BOWL OF TEA

- When you receive the cup of tea, bow to the person who gave it to you.

- Take the cup of tea with your right hand, and place it in the palm of your left hand.

- Turn the cup clockwise three times before you take a drink.

- It is considered polite to make a slurping sound when you are done, to let the host know you enjoyed the tea.

- Wipe the cup with your right hand.

- Turn the cup counterclockwise and pass it to the next guest, if you are sharing the tea. Otherwise, return it to the host.

WORDS ABOUT THE TEA CEREMONY

Cha no yu
Japanese tea ceremony

Chaji
Tea function; a more formal ceremony that can last as long as four hours and includes *kaiseki* (a full-course meal), sweets, *koicha* (thick tea), and *usucha* (thin tea)

Chakai
Tea meeting; a short and relatively informal tea ceremony that includes *usucha* (thin tea) and *tenshin* (a light snack)

Hiroma
Large room, about 15 square feet, used for formal tea ceremonies

Ichi za konryu
The unity created by a group of people coming together, as in a tea ceremony

Kokoro ire
Putting your heart into something, the spirit behind every action in the ceremony

Tokonoma
Alcove for displaying calligraphy scrolls

Friendship

FRIENDSHIP IS AN AMAZING part of girlhood. Friends are treasures, and true friends stick together through thick and thin. In good times, a friend makes life even more fun. In bad times, a friend can offer a hand up for a high five and help make things better.

But sometimes friendship can be tricky. When good friendships go bad and no one steps in to help, girls sometimes see friends gossip, talk behind people's backs, and tease. Some girls worry that the only way to be part of these friendships, and the only way to be popular, is to tease and manipulate other girls themselves.

When friendships are going well and girls are busy with friends, grown-ups often advise girls to be independent and think for themselves ("If Lori jumped off a bridge, would you do it, too?"). When girls are independent but shy, grown-ups prod them to find friends ("Why are you always by yourself? Why don't you make friends with David, or with Eileen?"). Add to this the shifting sands of ever-changing friend landscapes and friendship can be perplexing indeed. What to do when the close friend who used to play tetherball and sit next to you on the bus now snubs you? When the friend who once liked to joke around and kick soccer balls now talks nonstop about boys and who likes whom? When the boy who was once a buddy no longer wants to talk to girls, any girls, ever? Friends are supposed to be loyal, but sometimes friendship can be fickle.

It seems like there are three things to know about friendship: how to meet someone new and turn them into a friend, how to be kind to a friend, and how to keep a friend.

Meeting a friend tends to be easy when you are young. School is filled with girls and boys your age. Clubs and teams gather people together who have similar interests. Old-fashioned entreaties to friendship such as "Would you like to come to my house and play?" or "Can I join your four-square game?" are tried-and-true ways to make new friends. If you are shy or find it hard to speak up, meeting friends may take an extra effort. If this is the case, take a deep breath, find your courage, and give it a try. It will be worth it. When you are older, the words may change to "Would you like to meet for coffee, or for lunch, or for a walk?" Otherwise, the process remains the same. A friendship often begins with a simple question.

Sometimes two people meet and immediately feel like they've found a soul mate or a long-lost twin. Other friendships grow more slowly. You get to know each other over many weeks or months and realize one day, happily, that you can count on each other as friends. Both are equally good ways to start a treasured friendship. Sometimes a friend's interests change. You play tennis, and she takes up lacrosse. You both did environment club, and now she tries out for the school play and makes other friends. Your classes change, or she leaves for a new school. You learn that it's okay not to have everything in common and that a friendship can grow and change.

Kindness is something we tend to know when we see it, and feel when we don't. Some girls experience the less-than-pleasant twists and turns of friends in cliques. Some girls emerge from girlhood scarred from bad friendship behavior and are afraid to trust other girls as a result. But just as friendship can begin with a simple question, it can be helped along with simple kindness. If a friendship becomes mean, try to stay above the fray. That means not letting yourself become caught up in messy drama. Even when drama seems unavoidable, you always have the option of opting out, staying true to yourself, and keeping grounded in what's right and wrong. Above all, let kindness rule the day.

Being kind does not mean being a doormat. Being kind means extending generosity of spirit to other people—but also to yourself. It means not being cruel to others and not letting others be cruel to you, either. Saying "I'm sorry" to soothe hurt feelings is kindness in action—and so is saying "I'm sorry, too," and "That's okay, I forgive you."

Keeping a friend can take some attention. Occasionally, frustrations arise that can best be sorted out with words. Most of the time, though, friendship is easy, and it's nurtured with the simple act of spending time together. What you do is up to you. You could go fishing. You could make crafts or play a sport. You could organize a yard sale to raise money for your school or for people who are going hungry. You could put on a play or even just goof off at a sleepover. The point is having fun and doing things together—all of which makes your friendship stronger.

One last thing to keep in mind about friendship: It gets even better when you share it. Introduce your friends to each other, so that the circle of friendship can expand. Here, simple phrases like "Hilary, do you know Meredith?" make easy work of that.

Football

FOOTBALL HAS BEEN AN AMERICAN TRADITION ever since it started as an outgrowth of rugby in the late 1800s. By 1895, it was a professional sport, and by 1920, it had an official governing body. Historically, football has been a tackle sport played professionally by men, but that has been changing. In 2000, the Independent Women's Football League was established; today, it has more than three thousand players for eighty teams in sixty-seven cities. School-age girls have made headway in football as well: In 2003, eleven-year-old Jasmine Plummer famously became the first girl ever to play in the Pop Warner kids' football league (and the first-ever girl quarterback). And of course, anyone, boy or girl, can play a modified version of the game with friends: You don't need uniforms or referees, just a field, a ball, and friends who know how to play. Here are the rules of the game.

OVERVIEW

Professional football is played on a 53-yard-wide and 100-yard-long field, sometimes called "the gridiron," because of the gridlike lines marking each yard and every group of 10 yards. At each end of the field are *end zones*; behind each end zone are two 10-foot-high goalposts. The point of the game is for one team to get the ball from the middle of the field into the opposing team's end zone by carrying it, kicking it, or passing it. Each game has four 15-minute quarters of play, with a halftime break in the middle. The clock is stopped for fouls, when a player goes out-of-bounds, and for time-outs (which can be called up to three times by each team for each half of the game). If the score is tied at the end of four quarters, one last fifteen-minute quarter is played. This is called *sudden-death overtime*, because the first team to score during those fifteen minutes of play is the winner, and the game abruptly ends even if the quarter is not fully played out. (Note that the rules for college football overtime are slightly different.)

WHO'S ON THE TEAM

Each football team is allowed to have only eleven players on the field at a time. But most teams have more than that on their *roster* (or the list of total players belonging to a team)—they usually have forty-five players, although the number can be as high as fifty-three. Each team is divided into three groups: the offense (the part of the team, including the quarterback, that has the ball at the beginning of a play); the defense (the part of the team whose job it is to prevent the opponent from scoring); and the special team (team members who specialize in kicking the ball for kickoffs, free kicks, punts, and field goals).

PLAYING THE GAME

A coin is tossed to determine which team starts the game; the team that wins the toss can choose to either kick off or receive. The receiving team has to catch the kickoff and try to move the ball as far as possible in the direction of the kicking team before being tackled, an event which ends this first play. The spot where the play ended becomes what's called the *line of scrimmage*—basically, an imaginary line across the field where the teams face off against each other.

The teams now line up on either side of the line of scrimmage, and the team with the ball (the offense) has four chances to get the ball 10 yards closer to the opposing team's end zone (the defense). Each of these four chances is called a *down* (i.e., *first down, second down*, etc.). If the team succeeds at getting the 10 yards needed within four downs, the team then gets another four chances to move the ball another 10 yards. If the team gets the ball into the other team's end zone, that is called a touchdown. If the team runs out of downs (i.e., by not gaining the needed 10 yards), the other team gets the ball.

The teams move the ball by using *plays*, which, essentially, are strategies for moving all eleven players on the field in the most optimal way to score a touchdown, decided by the coach or quarterback. The offensive team has thirty seconds to start a play. Usually, this involves the center snapping the ball to the quarterback, who can either run the ball, hand it off to a running back, or throw it to a receiver. The ball must be caught by the receiver or else the play is considered "incomplete," and the down is lost.

SCORING
Teams score through touchdowns, conversions, field goals, and safeties.

Touchdown (TD; 6 points): Running with the ball into (or catching the ball within) the other team's end zone

Conversion (also called *extra points*; 1 or 2 points): After a touchdown, the scoring team can either kick the ball through the goalposts for one point or advance it into the end zone for two points.

Field goal (FG; 3 points): Kicking the ball through the goalposts. Field goals are often attempted on fourth downs, when the ball is close to the goal line or time is running out.

Safety (2 points): A defensive team can score two points by tackling a member of the offensive team who has the ball in her own end zone.

FOULS

When a foul occurs, the referee throws a yellow flag on the ground and blows a whistle. The penalty for fouls ranges from 4- to 15-yard losses. Some of the most common fouls are holding (holding onto or pulling a player other than the runner), grabbing another player's face mask, and being offside (on the wrong side of the ball when the snap happens).

FOOTBALL GAMES YOU CAN PLAY WITH FRIENDS

TOUCH FOOTBALL AND
FLAG FOOTBALL

Touch football and flag football are the noncontact versions of football, meaning that there is no tackling allowed. In touch football, players touch the player with the ball to end the play. This version is most commonly seen at picnics, on the afternoon of Thanksgiving, and at school recess. In flag football, offensive players wear flags (usually colored strips of cloth attached to a belt) and defensive players grab or otherwise remove the flag to stop play. Otherwise, the basic rules of the game are the same.

DUCK HUNT

To play, you will need six footballs and twenty-five short cones. There are seven players: two quarterbacks, two receivers, and three defenders. The goal is for the receivers to catch three balls as quickly as possible without getting caught by defenders.

Mark out a playing area about 15 to 20 yards long and 15 yards wide, and place five cones in a line across the field every 5 yards to create four grids. The two quarterbacks should be at the start of the first 5-yard grid, the two receivers and two defenders in the second 5-yard grid, and a third defender in the third 5-yard grid.

Give each quarterback three footballs. The quarterbacks throw the first balls to the two receivers in the second 5-yard grid. If a receiver successfully eludes the defenders and catches a ball from either quarterback, she can advance to the third 5-yard grid, where the third defender awaits. Her defenders can follow to the next grid as well, but only after both receivers have caught their balls. Once a receiver has moved to the next grid, the quarterback throws another ball. If the receiver catches the second ball in that third 5-yard grid, she moves on to the final grid; again, defenders can follow only once both receivers have caught the third-grid balls. The game is over when a receiver becomes the first to catch the third and final ball in the last grid. (Note: Players should toss all balls back to the quarterbacks after each play.)

ULTIMATE FOOTBALL

To play, you will need one football, cones to mark the playing area, and (if possible) different-colored shirts or vests for each team. With six players, the playing area should be 30 yards by 15 yards. With ten players, it should be 50 yards by 25 yards. Play is continuous (meaning everybody plays at once), and the goal is to score by getting the ball in the end zone. Divide the players into offense and defense. Other than that, there are no designated positions. Players are allowed to take two steps after getting the ball and can give the ball to another player only by throwing it. If the offensive team drops the ball, throws it out of bounds, or scores, the other team gets the ball; offense switches to defense, and play begins at the spot where the ball was dropped, thrown, or scored.

GOING DEEP

To play, you'll need one football and ten cones or yard markers. Put one cone 10 yards downfield, the next cone at 15 yards, the next at 20, and continue every 5 yards until you hit 50 yards or run out of room.

This game is for any number of players playing in groups of three (one quarterback, one receiver, and one defensive back) at a time. The quarterback starts at the beginning of the field, and the receiver stands some distance away; the defender must be at least 3 yards away from the receiver. The goal is to throw a pass as far as possible without the ball being dropped or intercepted. Each group of three gets five attempts. Add up the distances of each pass for a final score. The winning quarterback and receiver is the team with the highest score; the winning defender is the team with the lowest score.

How to Throw—and Catch—a Football

THROWING A FOOTBALL is easy once you break it down to its four basic components: Grip, stance, release, and follow-through.

How you grip the ball helps determine the amount of control you have over your throw. Hand size does factor into this, as bigger hands have an easier time spanning the ball, so try to find a football that's sized right for you. Put the football in your throwing hand with the lace side of the ball facing your fingers. Move your hand so that your pinkie finger is closer to the throwing

end of the ball (the point facing away from you), rather than in the middle. Spread out your fingers along the laces and seams. Your thumb goes along toward the bottom of the ball, and your index finger should be pointing straight up (think of making a "U" shape with your thumb and index finger).

The correct stance begins with your feet shoulder-width apart. Bring the ball to your chest, just under your chin, as you take a step back in preparation for your throw. (If you're throwing with your right arm, step back with your right foot; if you're throwing with your left, step back with your left foot). Keeping the elbow bent, raise your throwing arm to bring the football back and close to the side of your head. Extend your other arm in front of you for balance, and use your index finger to point in the direction you're going to throw.

To release the ball, shift your weight from your back leg to your front as you quickly extend your throwing arm in a forward motion. Let go of the ball when your arm is still slightly above your head. Flicking your wrist (rotating it slightly) as you release the ball will add speed and help the ball spiral through the air.

Follow through by keeping your arm extended even once the ball has left your hand, pointing toward the target with your index finger with your palm facing the ground.

Catching a football basically comes down to one simple rule that holds true for any kind of ball game: Keep your eyes on the ball. Here are a few other tips for being on the receiving end of a football pass.

When catching a throw that is chest-level or higher, form a triangle with your hands by holding them palms out with thumbs and index fingers touching. The open triangle space between your hands is where the tip of the ball should land. When making a low catch, hold your hands with palms facing out and pinkies touching.

Extend your arms toward the ball as it approaches you. The goal is to catch it with your hands, not your body.

Car Camping

SOMEWHERE BETWEEN A SLEEPOUT in your backyard and a two-month-long backwoods hike on the Pacific Coast Trail comes car camping. When going car camping, you pack the family tent, sleeping bags, and everything else into the car and drive right up to your campsite. Once you convince your parents to take you (it may not be hard—many parents love to be outdoors), here's what you—and they—will need to know, borrow, and bring.

MAKE RESERVATIONS

The first step is to decide where you're going and make reservations. At a few state parks you can just drive up and get a site. Most are very busy, and you may need to call as much as a year ahead of time to reserve a site. To do this, go online and check the home page for the state park you want to camp at. The site will show you a map of the campsites at that park. Here's where you will pick up the telephone and dial the ranger. You need a little inside information. Ask which sites the ranger recommends (and which to avoid). You'll want a site with flat ground and a great view, something near the bathrooms, but not too near. While on the phone, ask the ranger some other questions, too, like how remote the campground is, how far it is to the nearest store for supplies (like such as ice, milk, and midnight snacks), and whether they sell firewood onsite. You may learn that the state park has little cabins to rent, complete with the modern luxuries of refrigerators and bunk beds and maybe even some electricity (and you can bet that your parents will be interested in options like that). There are also private campgrounds, as well as large national parks.

Car camping is a relative luxury compared to the backwoods variation where you may be dehydrating your own food for weeks in advance and tracking down iodine tablets to purify your drinking water. Still, it takes some planning. Campsites usually come with a picnic table, a fire circle, and a water spigot. You'll have to bring everything else, and here's a list of the basics.

SHELTER AND SLEEPING GEAR

- Tent. When in doubt, bring the bigger tent. "Sleeps four" usually means four small people without a lot of stuff. If it's a tent that's new to you, set it up at home once, so you know it works and you know that all the stakes and poles are there. It's never fun to struggle with a tent when dusk is falling and it's starting to rain and your family's been in the car all day. When you get to the campsite, raise the tent on the flattest ground you can find, and keep it at least ten feet from the nearest firepit.
- Ground cloth or a tarp, for beneath the tent.
- Sleeping bags for everyone.
- Sleeping pads for everyone. Air-inflated mats, foam, a cot, or the cushions from the chaise lounge out back are all good, as are inflatable mattresses, although they have a reputation for leaking air when you least expect. You'll especially want something comfortable for your parents so they won't be grumpy in the morning and wish they hadn't agreed to go camping.
- Pillows, if you want, and if there's room in the car.
- A big lantern for the tent. (It's optional, but very nice.)
- A canopy tent, or a tarp to string between trees to cover your picnic table and cooking area and protect them from rain.
- Other things you may want to pack: camping broom and dustpan, a doormat for the tent, a sit-upon. Shock cord (the elastic that goes in tent poles) is good for a camping clothesline.

PERSONAL GEAR

- Clothing: shorts and jeans, underwear, several shirts, jacket and sweatshirt (since nighttime can be cooler than you expect), swimsuit, pajamas, a hat, many pairs of socks, and an extra pair of shoes should the first pair become drenched after playing in the creek.
- Everyone needs a flashlight, whether for exploring or simply getting to the bathroom in the middle of the night. Make sure to put in new batteries, and even bring along some extras for back-up. You may even want to pack the batteries in backward so the flashlight doesn't accidentally turn on during travel and run the batteries down.
- Toothbrush and other toiletries, such as soap, a hairbrush and hair bands, shampoo, etc.
- Toilet paper. Campsite bathrooms should have some, but you just never know.
- Any medicines you take.
- Water bottle.
- Rainwear, if rain is in the offing.
- Bandana, to protect your hair from ticks.
- Things to do and play with, like a deck of cards, a good book, a whistle.
- Plastic bag for dirty clothes.
- Fishing rods, if you like, or some fishing line and a hook wrapped around cardboard, for making your own rod once you get there.

- Binoculars, if there's a pair around.
- Bug spray.
- Sunscreen.
- Quarters, because some campsites charge to use the hot showers.

COOKING GEAR

- First and foremost, a cooking stove and some extra fuel. If it's your first time camping, see if you can borrow a camping stove from a neighbor. Set the stove on one end of the picnic table so no one has to stoop down to cook.
- A frying pan and a saucepan big enough to boil water and make spaghetti, or as many pots and pans as you want, without going overboard.
- Cooking utensils, such as spatulas and stirring spoons, a kitchen knife and cutting board, serving spoons and tongs, scissors, a can opener, and a bottle opener.
- A coffeepot for your parents, and their requisite coffee and tea. Toss in some hot cocoa.
- Gallon jugs to hold water (a few weeks ahead of time, start saving plastic milk jugs). You'll need water on hand to put out the fire, and at some campsites you may have to lug water from the main area to your site.
- Plates, forks, knives, and spoons, drinking cups and mugs, or a mess kit, if you have one.
- Heavy-duty aluminum foil, good for many things.
- Paper towels, dish towels, pot holders, and dishwashing liquid; a plastic basin or bin for doing the dishes, and a sponge or scrubby; a bag for trash and a supply of resealable plastic bags.
- Plastic tablecloth for the picnic table.
- First-aid kit.
- Towels, large and small.
- Twine or string, and duct tape.
- Matches or a lighter.
- Chairs, for relaxing.

FOOD

- A large cooler and either some heavy-duty long-lasting ice packs or a source of new ice cubes each day you've set up camp.
- Condiments such as ketchup, mustard, mayonnaise, salt and pepper, spices and seasonings, cooking oil and/or spray, salsa, maple syrup, and butter. Some families pack these and bagged lunches for the day of travel, and that's all. They buy the rest when they arrive at a store near the campsite, which they've checked out ahead of time. Other families bring everything from home, packing milk, yogurt, cheese, eggs, a sack of soup cans, boxes of macaroni and cheese, bread and sandwich makings, and whatever else they need, along with enough snacks to last the duration.
- Some easy camping favorites are, in no particular order, spaghetti and sauce, pancakes and French toast, hot dogs, grilled cheese, macaroni and cheese, cans of soup, cheese and bean quesadillas, cereal and granola, along with the usual helpings of fruits and vegetables (some very organized people cut the vegetables in advance and even remember to bring salad dressing). Almost everyone remembers the marshmallows, chocolate bars, and graham crackers for s'mores.
- Your favorite drinks. Check ahead to be sure that the campground water is safe to drink, and if it isn't, bring in your own water. Don't forget to ask your parents what drinks they want, too.

FUN FOOD TO MAKE

Hot dog on a stick

Use a strong-enough stick that you found nearby. Whittle away the bark and make a point at the end, then spear the hot dog and roast it over an open flame.

Trail mix

Also known as *gorp* (and called *scroggin* in New Zealand and Australia). Some combination of raisins, peanuts, M&Ms, chocolate chips, dried fruit, pretzels, cereal, sunflower seeds, and coconut, all tossed into a bag.

Frito chili

Slit open the front of a bag of corn chips, and then cut across the top and bottom so the whole front can be opened up into a makeshift bowl. Heat up some chili, and pour over the opened bag of chips.

Eggs in a bag

Mix eggs with a splash of milk or water and some salt and pepper. Pour into a resealable plastic bag, the stronger kind meant for the freezer. Add any mix-ins, like cheese, vegetables, or meat. Gently drop the bag into a pot of boiling water. You'll see when it's done, and lift it out with tongs.

Hobo packs

The basic recipe is some combination of meat, chicken, or fish, with veggies and chunks of potato or cheese (optional), and salt and pepper or other seasonings. Divide into individual portions. Wrap each in heavy-duty aluminum foil, closing the sides tightly to make a pack. Cook in the fire for 30 to 45 minutes.

HOW TO DO THE DISHES WHEN YOU'RE CAMPING

First off, try to get out of doing the dishes. If you can't, heat water on the stove until it is hot but not boiling. Pour it into a plastic basin or large bowl. The thing to know is that the water in the basin needs to stay clean, which means that all the cleaning and rinsing is down off to the side. With that in mind, scrape the plates over a trash bag or bin. Wash with a soapy sponge—but not over the basin. Rinse with clean water from the basin, letting the water run off to the ground. Lay the dishes on a towel to dry, or put them in a drop bag and hang from a clothesline or tree.

CAMPING OUT

It can be hectic, with all that planning and packing and following the map to get there. But soon enough you're at your new home in the woods. The tent is up. The sleeping bags are laid out. At night you can see the stars. You wake up to morning birds. By day, you explore, hike, play Frisbee and cards, go fishing, whittle, and swim if there's a lake. In the evening you sit around the campfire, read mystery stories aloud, talk, sing, play harmonica and guitar, and bring life back to its low-tech basics.

THE CAMPFIRE

The campfire is essential. Most campsites sell logs for fires, or can tell you where to get them. In the nearby woods you can scavenge for tinder (which is thinner than a pencil) and kindling (which is the size of a grown-up's thumb), both of which will get the fire started.

While it seems romantic to cook over the open fire, it can take a very long time. Try it, but know that when hunger is at hand, practicality should reign and you should use the camping stove. Use the campfire for special things like roasting marshmallows and hot dogs on a stick or using a forked branch to toast a piece of bread.

When you're done cooking and eating, put all the food away. If the bears don't get it, the ants, raccoons, and chipmunks will. Enterprising and experienced campers will attach a rope to the bags of food and hanging them from a tree.

GOING TO THE BATHROOM IN THE WOODS

It may happen while you are camping or hiking that you need to do something outside that, more often than not, you do inside and behind closed doors. The first thing to do is see if there are restrooms nearby. If you are far from a bathroom, the next step is to clarify your preferred level of privacy. Walk away from camp as much as you need to feel comfortable. Back up against a large rock or tree for even more privacy.

When you find the right place, glance down at your feet. Either your toes or your heels should face downhill, so that gravity can help what happens next trail away from you. Next, squat way, way down, as close to the ground as possible, keeping your knees as wide as possible. As you do this, pull down your shorts or pants, and scrunch them into the crevice behind your knees. If it helps, hold on to a rock or tree for balance.

If you have brought along something to help you clean up afterward, make sure you have a plastic bag, too, to dispose of it so the raccoons don't get it. If you didn't bring anything to wipe with, never fear. Intrepid hikers of the backwoods have learned to bounce up and down while squatting, which usually solves the problem. (You can also resort to the age-old trick of "air-drying.") If there is something on the ground—how may we be discreet here—that needs extra attention, dig a small hole, and use a rock or stick or leaves to tuck everything away.

Tying a Sarong

ORIGINALLY THE WORD *SARONG*, which means "sheath" in the Malay language, referred specifically to the skirtlike garment worn by the men and women of Malay. Sarongs are members of the same clothing family as togas, chitons, and kimonos—lengths of fabric draped and twisted around the body. Sarongs are usually made from brightly colored silk or cotton and tend to feature intricate patterns. Often, they are dyed using a technique called *batik dyeing*, whereby wax is applied in patterns on the cloth before the fabric is dipped into colorful dye. These days, a sarong can be worn by anyone, and the word in general refers to a length of cloth that can be tied or fastened into clothing. A sarong can be wrapped around the waist to make a skirt or tied across the chest to create a dress, hung on the walls as art, draped across the shoulders as a shawl, or fastened around the body as a sling for carrying a baby. In the United States, they are often worn as cover-ups over swimsuits.

WEARING YOUR SARONG

You can buy a premade sarong, or you can make one yourself. All you need is lightweight fabric. A sarong is 4 to 5 yards long and 1 to 2 yards wide, depending on how tall you are. Here are a few different ways to wrap it.

Around-the-neck dress

Hold the sarong out lengthwise against your back, just below your armpits, so that you are in the center of the fabric. Bring each side across your chest, crossing each other. Twist the ends of the fabric, and tie the twisted ends behind your neck.

Shoulder knot

Start with the sarong held lengthwise along your back. Move the fabric so that you have about one arm's length on the left side and all the rest on the right. Take the left side, and bring it across your chest and on top of or over your shoulder. Then, take the right side, wrap it across your chest (over the fabric) and behind your back, all the way across until it meets up with the left-side edge on your shoulder. Tie the two ends at a knot.

Front knot

Begin with the sarong held lengthwise along your back. Bring your arms forward to pull the fabric taut on your back. Then, instead of grabbing the ends of the sarong and twisting to tie, gather the fabric at a point about halfway between your armpits and the ends on either side, twist, and tie them together in a double knot in the center of your chest.

Batik

BATIK (PRONOUNCED "BAH-TEEK") is a way of dyeing cloth using melted wax to create patterns. The art originated perhaps one thousand years ago in Java, Indonesia, and continues to be practiced by craftspeople throughout Indonesia, West Africa, Malaysia, the Philippines, and Thailand. Batik, along with tie-dyeing, became popular in the United States during the 1960s and '70s. Contemporary batik dyeing often differs a bit from the traditional process—modern batik makers embrace synthetic fabrics and even use materials other than wax to create the intricate patterns characteristic of batik—but the basic methods of making batik cloth are still the same.

Traditionally, batik was made by women, who painted wax on fabric by hand. Sometime in the seventeenth century, the canting was invented. This bamboo-handled, penlike instrument has a nozzle at one end; melted wax is poured into a groove along the pen and released bit by bit from the nozzle. Using a canting, women painted fabric with intricate wax designs, some so complicated they could take six months to complete. As foreign interest in batik production increased, other methods of applying the wax were invented to hurry the design process along. The *cap*, a kind of stamp made of thin metal bands attached to a handle, was one such invention. The stamps, which started being used by batik makers in about 1845, could be dipped in wax and applied to fabric at a much quicker pace than canting. Rather than producing one batik every six months, batik makers could make several a day. Men, who had traditionally never had the patience for canting, eagerly took to using the cap process, which essentially meant taking over the majority of batik production from the women who had always done it. Today, batik textiles made using canting are highly valued, as each one, with the imperfections and irregularities that come with handmade crafting, is a unique work of art.

MAKE YOUR OWN BATIK

You can make batik without using canting or a cap, but you will need the following supplies:

- Length of plain cotton fabric
- Cold-water dye
- 1 beeswax candle
- 1 paraffin candle
- Metal soup can and a pot of water
- Paintbrush
- Pencil
- Bucket or large bowl for dyeing the cloth
- Some old newspaper
- Iron

A Note about the Supplies

For the fabric, an old white cotton bedsheet is ideal. If you use new fabric, you will need to boil it to remove the chemical finishes on it that would otherwise prevent the dye from taking. For the wax, it's best to use a mixture of 30% beeswax and 70% paraffin wax. Paraffin by itself is very brittle, and beeswax is sticky; mixing the two together helps the wax stick to the fabric and prevent the wax designs from breaking or cracking. If you don't have candles, you can buy sheets of wax at a craft store.

Make Your Design

Use a pencil to sketch out a design on your cloth. It doesn't have to be fancy. Many batiks feature repeating geometrical designs, which can easily be made using a ruler or by tracing the outlines of household objects such as cups or books. Once you've sketched out your design, lay the cloth taut on a durable flat surface (such as a countertop or a table in your backyard) with some old newspaper underneath the cloth to protect the surface.

Melt the Wax

For this part you will need a grown-up's help. Take a metal soup can (make sure it is free of soup, the lid, and the outer label), place the wax inside it (two parts paraffin and one part beeswax), and place the soup can in a pot of water on the stove. Turn the heat on. As the water boils, it will melt the wax inside the can.

Hot wax is very hot indeed, so be very careful. When the wax begins to bubble, turn the heat down to low so that the wax does not smoke. Test the wax to see if it's done by dipping your paintbrush in the wax and applying it to a scrap of test cloth: if the wax appears shiny and see-through, it's done. If it's white-ish and you can't see through it, it needs a little more time to melt.

Paint with Wax

Hot wax is hot, but it cools down fast. Try not to let it get completely dry on your paintbrush. Dip your paintbrush in the wax and then use it to paint wax on the design you outlined. If your design extends beyond the part of the cloth on your frame, move the cloth over, pull it taut, and paint the next part of the design. Keep going until you have traced your whole design.

Dye It

Prepare a cold-water dye bath according to the instructions on the dye—at its most basic, this amounts to filling a large bucket with cold water and stirring in the dye mix. Then add the cloth. Stir gently with a wooden spoon to move the cloth around and make it saturated. Then let it sit for a while. The longer you let it sit, the stronger and deeper the color will be. When it's time to take the cloth out of the dye bath, do not rinse it, wring it out, or put it in the dryer. Instead, let it drip-dry outside (or in an indoor place where you can hang it up and let it drip onto an old towel).

Remove the Wax

When the fabric is dry, iron the cloth between sheets of newspaper. This will heat up the wax and make it stick to the newspaper instead of the cloth. There may still be a bit of wax residue on the cloth. If it bothers you, you can scrape it off, being careful not to tear or cut the fabric. If that doesn't work, you can soak the cloth in strong laundry detergent, though this may wash out some of the dye.

Sand Castles

THE TRUE TREASURE OF ANY BEACH, water aside, is sand. Sometimes it's rough and rocky, and other times gorgeously silky and smooth. Sand comes in all shades of black, gray, pink, and white. Sand is the medium for building towers, cities, and villages; for making extensive channels and water works; and for castles surrounded by a moat. It's the surface for etching large pictures or labyrinths, or writing messages for low-flying airplanes.

If you didn't grow up at the beach, you may not know some of these basic tricks to the refined art of sand sculpting. So grab a shovel and a bucket and find your spot—hopefully not when high tide's coming in and splashing against your progress.

1. Water Supply. That's what the bucket is for. Sure, you can use it as a mold for castle turrets, but its biggest use is to hold water, which is crucial to sand sculpting. Fill the bucket with water, add sand, and keep filling with more water and more sand as needed. You can also create a water supply by digging a channel to water's edge and letting the tide bring you water, or by digging a hole in the sand deep enough to reach the water table. (If you are planning to build a moat, make it deep, and let the moat double as a water source.)

2. Sand Blocks. Fill a bucket with water and add sand. Stick your hands in and lift up a palmful of silty sand. Shake your hands a bit and let most of the water drain back to the bucket. Mold the sand in your hand into a rectangular brick, or a circle, and lay it into place on your castle, road, bridge, or tower. Repeat until done.

There is science behind sand blocks. Water creates bonds between the grains of sand. Molecules of water are held together by the physical force called surface tension, which is why when you slightly overfill a glass, instead of spilling, the water holds together over the rim. Of course, if you add too much

SOME MORE SAND CASTLE TIPS

☆ The best sand is not the very dry sand on the majority of the beach, nor the very wet sand right at water's edge, but the narrow strip of damp sand between them.

☆ To make the base, pack in sand and flatten the top. Build on top of that.

☆ Plastic buckets make natural molds. Pack in sand, add water as you go, fill to the brim, and turn over quickly.

☆ Don't forget to dig tunnels and construct bridges.

☆ To make a staircase, first make a ramp. Make horizontal and vertical cuts with the tip of the shovel to form the stairs.

☆ Carve intricate windows and doors on castles and details on animals or other shapes with ceramic tools and other small carving tools. Plastic straws are good for blowing extra sand away from detail spots.

water to the sand, everything collapses, just as the water in the glass will eventually spill over if you add more.

3. Sand Drips. This can help create a Gothic look for your castle and its turrets. Reach in the bucket and hold a batch of watery sand in your hand. Holding it above where you want to build, let the sand drip and fall from your closed fist.

SAND GARDEN

A sand garden is one way to create miniature sand castles and sand towns at home, all year long. This is what you need to make one:

- A box made of wood, cardboard, or plastic. The sides should be about 2 to 3 inches high, and each side should be around 12 inches long, but really, any size box can turn into something interesting. If the seams or corners of your box are at all leaky, seal them with Mod Podge or some other kind of sealer (white glue will do in a pinch) and let dry.

- Sand, to fill the box. This can be play sand (the kind that fills sandboxes) or beach sand. If you use rocky beach sand, you may want to shake it through a sieve to remove the larger pieces.

- Vegetable, canola, or baby oil

- Spoon, for stirring

- Things to make mini sand castles and designs: small stones, feathers, bottle caps, and cups, as well as sticks for tracing and drawing

Fill the box with sand. Start with a teaspoon of oil, mix, and add small amounts more while mixing the sand. You'll want to add enough so that the sand will stick together for shaping, as it does on the beach after you add some water. Don't add so much that it becomes a big mess. The sand is ready when it begins to hold shape on its own and can be molded with small cups and spoons.

Months and Days

WHERE DO THE NAMES OF THE MONTHS COME FROM?

The calendar we use today is called the Gregorian calendar, after Pope Gregory XIII, who came up with a calendar system in 1582. Before that, the calendar most widely used was the Julian calendar, after Julius Caesar, who formulated his own system in 45 BCE. But even before either of those calendars, there was the Roman calendar, devised by the Roman king Romulus, which had only ten months: Martius, Aprilis, Maius, Iunius, Quintilis, Sextilis, September, October, November, and December.

The Roman year began in March (Martius) with the spring equinox, when the sun passes over the earth's equator (this happens twice each year: once in the spring around March 20, and once in the fall around September 22). The last five months are named for their order of appearance: Quintilis is the fifth month, as *quint* means "five"; Sextilis's root is *sext*, which means "six"; September's root is *sept*, which means "seven"; and so on. These ten months spanned 304 days, with 61 "extra" winter days not included on the calendar. (The span between December and March was most likely not tracked on a calendar because it was a time when no harvesting could be done anyway.)

Around 713 BCE, the Roman king Numa Pompilius added the months January (Ianuarius) and February (Februarius) to the end of the calendar, bumping the calendar up to twelve months and making it 355 days long. That's still short of our 365-day year, but it synced up nicely with the actual lunar year (which was measured by the twelve cycles of the moon). Pompilius also took into consideration the Roman superstition about lucky and unlucky numbers—to the Romans, odd numbers were lucky and even numbers were not—and made each month twenty-nine or thirty-one days long. The sole exception was February, the last month to be added, which ended up with an unlucky twenty-eight days. To get around that "unlucky" even number, he split February into two parts, one that was twenty-three days long and the other five days long. And, because 355 calendar days still didn't match up to the actual seasonal year, every few years he threw in an extra month, Mercedonius, after the first part of February. The extra twenty-seven days helped average out the difference, but it was hard to implement because some people just plain forgot about it.

When Julius Caesar came to power, around 45 BCE, he did his own fiddling with the calendar, moving it from the lunar-based cycle Pompilius favored to one more aligned with the solar year. He made the calendar year begin with January instead of March (September, October, November, and December retained their original names even though they became the ninth, tenth, eleventh, and twelfth months of the calendar year); he introduced the concept of the leap year, adding an extra day to February every four years; he abolished the February split and the random

Thirty Days Hath September

Many schoolchildren learned the following nursery rhyme to help them remember how many days were in each month:

Thirty days hath September,
April, June, and November;
All the rest have thirty-one,
Excepting February alone,
And it has twenty-eight days time,
But in leap years, February has
twenty-nine.

extra inter-February month; and he assigned those extra ten calendarless days to existing months. He added two extra days each to Ianuarius, Sextilis, and December, bringing them up to thirty-one days each; and he added one extra day each to Aprilis, Iunius, September, and November, making each of those months thirty days long. February, at twenty-eight days, still remained the shortest month, probably by virtue of its being added last. These are the lengths of the months as we know them today. In about 8 BCE, Quintilis and Sextilis were renamed in honor of the emperors Julius Caesar and Augustus, becoming the months we know now as July and August.

The Julian calendar was widely adopted and used for centuries, but it was the Gregorian calendar that became the standard in most countries. It didn't happen overnight, however: Pope Gregory made his calendar mandatory for everyone to follow in 1582, but Britain and its American colonies didn't begin using it until almost two hundred years later, in September 1752; Russia used the Julian calendar until 1917; and Greece didn't make the switch until 1923.

WHY ARE THERE SEVEN DAYS IN A WEEK?

It was the Babylonians who more than three thousand years ago came up with the idea of a week being equal to seven days. They had already figured out the length of a month through observing the moon and noting that it took the moon twenty-nine and a half days to go from a new moon to a full moon and back again. But they felt it would be useful to have another unit of time somewhere between one day and a whole month.

Looking to the moon again, they saw that the moon's cycle could be broken down into four basic parts—new moon, first quarter, full moon, last quarter—each of which took about seven days or so to complete. Thus, it made sense to divide the month into these smaller parts, *weeks*, each of which was seven days long. Obviously, this idea stuck, but the Babylonians weren't the only culture to come up with the idea of dividing months into weeks.

The most practical idea about weeks came from cultures that had "market days," days when people gathered to buy and sell produce and other goods. The number of days in a week depended on how often the community came together to the market: In some West African tribes, that was every four days; in Egypt, it was ten days. The Roman week was called the *nundinae* (ninth day), as there were nine days between each market day. The ancient Mayans had a complicated calendar that used two different-length weeks: a thirteen-day week, for which the days were simply numbered, and a twenty-day week, for which each day had a name.

Much later in history, in France, the Revolutionary Calendar was introduced, with a ten-day week. This concept (which was used from October 24, 1793, until it was abolished on January 1, 1806) was developed by a team of mathematicians, astronomers, artists, poets, and even a gardener, all under the direction of a politician named Charles-Gilbert Romme. The mathematicians came up with the idea of equal month division (twelve months of thirty days, with five or six days left over), the ten-day week (of which the last day, the tenth, was the *weekend* and the only day off work), and a way of measuring time using units of ten (right down to the notion that there should be exactly 100,000 seconds per day). The poets and artists (and the gardener) were tasked with naming the days and months. The project lasted almost thirteen years before people became fed up with 100-minute hours and nine-day workweeks. Napoleon Bonaparte abolished the calendar, and France reverted to the seven-day week in 1806. (The

Revolutionary Calendar threatened to take hold again in May 1871, but luckily, never stuck.)

The Babylonian idea of the seven-day week prevailed simply because very powerful cultures enforced it. The Romans made it part of the calendar throughout their empire. The Christian church continued to further the notion. And the British Empire spread the seven-day week worldwide. Now the seven-day week is a global given, as our businesses, schools, and workplaces all function on the idea of seven-day groups: five days on and two days off.

HOW DID THE DAYS OF THE WEEK GET THEIR NAMES?

In Babylonian times, just as now, seven was considered a lucky number. It was a pleasing coincidence, then, that the seven days in a week corresponded nicely with another group of seven things: the seven planets in the sky (including the sun and the moon) that the Babylonians could see with the naked eye. And so it shouldn't surprise us to learn that the days were originally named for the seven planets.

The Greeks and Romans continued this tradition, naming the days after their names for the planets, which also happened to be named for the characters in Greek and Roman mythology. We can still see traces of this in the names we use today. But these ancient Greek and Roman names were revised by the Anglo-Saxons, who invaded Britain hundreds of years ago and replaced those names with the names of characters from their own mythology about the planets. So our current English names for the days of the week reflect a mix of the two traditions. (Other cultures named the days in the most practical way, by using numbers.)

NAMES OF THE DAYS OF THE WEEK

	MONDAY	TUESDAY	WEDNESDAY	THURSDAY	FRIDAY	SATURDAY	SUNDAY
Planet	Moon	Mars	Mercury	Jupiter	Venus	Saturn	Sun
Babylonian	*Sin*	*Nergal*	*Nabû*	*Marduk*	*Ishtar*	*Ninurta*	*Shamash*
Greek	*Hemera Selenes* ("Selene's Day," after the moon goddess)	*Hemera Areos* ("Ares's Day," after the god of war)	*Hemera Hermu* ("Hermes's Day," after the messenger god)	*Hemera Dios* ("Zeus's Day," after the highest of the Greek gods)	*Hemera Aphrodite* ("Aphrodite's Day," after the goddess of love and beauty)	*Hemera Chronos* ("Chronos's Day," named for the god of time, who was the father of Zeus)	*Hemera Heliou* ("Helios's Day," named for the god of the sun)
Roman	*Dies Lunis* ("Luna's Day," after the moon goddess)	*Dies Martis* ("Mars's Day," after the god of war)	*Dies Mercurii* ("Mercury's Day," after the messenger god)	*Dies Jovis* ("Jupiter's Day," after the god who, like the Greek Zeus, was king of the gods and the skies)	*Dies Veneris* ("Venus's Day," after the goddess of love and beauty)	*Dies Saturni* ("Saturn's Day," after the god of agriculture, who was the father of Jupiter)	*Dies Solis* ("Sun's Day," named for the god of the sun)

	MONDAY	TUESDAY	WEDNESDAY	THURSDAY	FRIDAY	SATURDAY	SUNDAY
Planet	Moon	Mars	Mercury	Jupiter	Venus	Saturn	Sun
French	*Lundi* ("Moon Day")	*Mardi* ("Mars's Day")	*Mercredi* ("Mercury's Day")	*Jeudi* ("Jupiter's Day")	*Vendredi* ("Venus's Day")	*Samedi* ("Sabbath Day")	*Dimanche* ("Day of God")
Norse mythology	*Mano* (*Mandag,* "Mano's Day," after the moon god)	*Tyr* or *Tiw* (*Tyrsdag,* "Tyr's day," after the god of war; *Tyr* is sometimes spelled *Tiw,* resulting in *Tiwsdag,* "Tiw's Day.")	*Woden* or *Odin* (*Wodnesdag,* "Wodan's Day"; also spelled as "Odin's day"; Odin and Mercury are both associated with poetic and musical inspiration.)	*Thor* (*Torsdag,* "Thor's Day," named after the god of thunder; Thor and Jupiter were both gods who wielded thunderbolts.)	*Freya* or *Frigga* (*Fredag,* "Freya's Day," named after Odin's wife and, like Venus, the goddess of beauty.)	*Sataere* (*Saterdag,* named, like Saturn, after the god of agriculture; today in Norwegian this day is called *Lørdag,* "Washing Day")	*Sol* (*Søndag,* "Sol's Day," named after the sun goddess)
German	*Montag* ("Moon Day")	*Dienstag* ("Assembly Day"; originally *Ziostag,* "Zio's Day," *Zio* being the German form of *Tyr*)	*Mittwoch* ("Midweek")	*Donnerstag* ("Donner's Day," or "thunder day," after the Germanic god of thunder)	*Frietag* ("Freya's Day")	*Samstag* ("Sabbath Day")	*Sonntag* ("Sunna's Day," after the sun goddess)
Old English	*Monandæg* ("Moon's Day")	*Tiwesdæg* ("Tiws's Day")	*Wodneesdæg* ("Wodin's Day")	*Thresdæg* ("Thor's Day")	*Frigedæg* ("Frigga's Day")	*Sæturnesdæg* ("Saturn's Day")	*Sunnandæg* ("Sun's Day")
Japanese	*Getsu Yo Bi* ("Moon Day")	*Ka-Yo Bi* ("Fire Day")	*Sui Yo Bi* ("Water Day")	*Moku Yo Bi* ("Wood Day")	*Kin Yo Bi* ("Gold-Day")	*Do-youbi* ("Earth-Day")	*Nichi Yo Bi* ("Sun Day")
Russian	*Ponedelnik* (After "do nothing")	*Vtornik* ("Second")	*Sreda* ("Middle")	*Chetverg* ("Fourth")	*Pyatnitsa* ("Fifth")	*Subbota* ("Sabbath")	*Voskresenye* ("Ressurection")

How to Catch Fish

WHEN YOU'RE ON THE TRAIL and hungry, you can find your own dinner in a nearby creek with a little luck, some patience, and of course your fishing gear. Here's how to haul fish for supper.

FIRST, KNOW YOUR GEAR

Rod: This long pole is the center of all things fishing. A modern one holds a fishing line that threads through a reel.

Reel: This keeps the line wrapped up and untangled, and holds the tension in your line. It spools out the line when you're casting and, in general, is essential for anything more than "drop it in the water off the end of the dock" fishing.

Line and Leader: The fancy name for line is *nylon monofilament.* The line starts at the reel, threads through some guides, and ends in a metal leader. The leader holds the hook, a lure, some weights, or whatever rig you need.

Tackle Box: This holds all the things that attach to the end of your line, collectively called *tackle* or *rig.* It includes special compartments for all your hooks, bobbers, sinker weights, feathery lures, and plastic fishlike jigs (which have a hook hidden inside), and for all sorts of swivels and spinners that twirl in the water and, hopefully, attract fish. Toss in a nail clipper for trimming the line.

Bait: We're talking worms, ants, crickets, or minnows. What you use depends on what you're trying to catch. Bait can be found at the nearest marine store or roadside bait shack, or even in your own backyard. Catch unsuspecting minnows with a seine or fish net. In a pinch, ask the first person you see with a rod and some fish on her line what she's using and where she got it. The bait should be the size of the hook. While you're gathering bait, grab a bucket, some cold water to drink (summer fishing gets hot), and an old towel, which you'll appreciate after you catch your first fish.

THEN, GET FISHING

1. **Choose a Rod.** Find one that's comfortable for you, and figure out how the reel works, as there are several different kinds. In general, for smaller fish, use a smaller rod. Bigger fish call for a bigger rod.

2. **String the Line.** Thread the line through your rod. Snap on a bobber, which will float on the water and keep the rig up until a fish grabs your bait, at which point it will bob up and down to let you know you've made a catch. Lower down, pinch on a sinker weight or two. This helps get the hook down to where the fish are.

3. **Find the Fish.** You've untangled your line, fixed up a rig, and got yourself some bait. Now

The cinch knot keeps everything attached, line to reel, leader to line, hook to line, and, thus, is worth knowing.

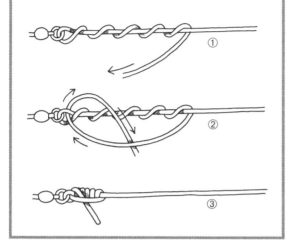

5. Reel in Your Fish. When the floater bobs under, there may be a fish at the end of the line. Let the fish pull the line for a moment; this sets the hook. Start to reel in, slowing down every so often to play the fish by reeling slow, then pulling sharp. You'll get the feel of it. Once you pull it out of the water, get the fish over the bridge, onto the boat, or onto dry land as soon as you can, and *then* finish reeling in, because it's no fun watching your fish wriggle free and swim away right at the end.

6. What Now? First things first: the hook must be removed. Grab the fish below the gills and jaw to calm it, and wiggle the hook out of the fish's mouth. If the hook doesn't come out easily, cut the line near the hook and toss the fish, hook and all, back in the water. It's not ideal, but it's much better than torturing the fish.

At this point you've either become addicted to fishing or have vowed to become a vegetarian. You need to decide whether to toss the fish back in the water or take it home for dinner. Some fish are protected, so know the local laws, and measure, because fish under a certain length have to be tossed back, no matter how hungry you are. Also, make sure that the waters aren't polluted and that fish from it are okay to eat. If you're tossing back, do it soon; the fish will appreciate it. If you're going to eat it, leave the fish in the bucket of water.

7. Prepare Your Supper. Someone once said that fishing is boring until you catch one, and then it's merely disgusting. Between now and your dinner plate looms cutting off the fish's head and cleaning out the guts. It's not for the squeamish, but fishing means learning to touch things that formerly seemed icky, like earthworms, bait, and live fish.

Here's how it's done. First, make sure the fish is dead. Then, wash the fish in tap water.

it's time to track down the fish. Easier said than done? Seek out the local lore about where fish are running, where and when high tide's coming in, whether or not the water is clean, and whether or not you need a government-issued license to fish. Head to a pier or riverbank or a low bridge over running water. Jump into a small boat and paddle to deeper waters, trolling your line adrift behind the boat. For more adventure, hitch a ride on a large boat, and head oceanward to cavort with the big fish.

4. Cast Your Line. Sometimes you simply drop the line in and see what happens. Sometimes you are more active, which means you'll cast to where you think the fish are, and let the line move with the current. If no fish bite, reel back in and cast again. Cast and reel until the magic happens and a fish bites.

Tip: Lots of rods end up in the water. Always hold the line with your thumb until right before you cast. And always hold onto your rod when you cast.

Remove the scales with the dull side of a knife or a special fish scaler. Now for the gross part. With a single slit below the gills, cut off the fish's head. The fish's organs will come out with the head. Push the knife into the fish's belly, and cut along the bottom to the vent hole near the tail. Rinse again, and scrape out anything left inside. The fish should look clean. You're almost done. Cut off the tail. With a knife or with scissors, cut off the top and bottom fins. Rinse again. Stoke the fire. You're ready to flour up the fish and toss in the frying pan, if you still want to.

The Snapper Are Running and Your Rod Is at Home: What Do You Do?

You can make a rod for yourself (or for your little sister) that's strong enough for snapper and other small fish. Bamboo makes for a nice pole because it is so flexible, but any decently strong branch or dowel will do. At the end of the stick, tie on the fishing line so it's long enough to reach the water. Tie the hook to the end of the line. If you have a tackle box nearby, snap on a bobber 2 feet from the end of the line, and pinch a weight on near the hook.

If you have some elastic and some duct tape, you can add some "give" to the rod that will come in handy when you have to pull in a fish. Find a small piece of elastic; 8 inches will do. Tie the elastic to the stick. Tie the fishing line to the elastic. Cover both knots with a few layers of duct tape to keep the connections tight and strong.

Notable Women III: Math and Science

Maria Gaetana Agnesi (pronounced "Anyesi") was an Italian mathematician who was the first person to write a textbook on differential and integral calculus. Such was her renown and her importance to the world of math that in her own time she was pronounced the most important woman mathematician since ancient Greece's Hypatia.

Born on May 16, 1718, to a wealthy family in Milan, Italy, Maria was the oldest of twenty-one children. Her father was a math professor, and the attitude in Renaissance Italy toward the schooling of women at the time was favorable, so Maria was able to receive an impressive education. By the time she was nine, she had mastered French, Latin, Greek, Hebrew, and several other languages, and by the time she was a teenager, she was considered a prodigy in mathematics. She was passionate about her studies, but she was equally interested in becoming a nun. Her father would have none of it.

She followed her father's wishes and continued her education in mathematics, studying with a monk named Ramiro Rampinelli. It was Rampinelli who introduced her to calculus and, impressed by her grasp of the subject, encouraged her to write her own book on it. She began her work on the book at age twenty, writing in Italian rather than Latin (which was the preferred "scientific" language for publication) and framing the book as a kind of textbook for her younger brothers. When *Instituzioni analitiche* (Analytic Institutions) was published in 1748, it was an academic sensation. The two-volume treatise had taken her ten years to write, and the book made higher math accessible to the learned (but nonexpert) reader. For a person to write a serious book on math without formal, university-based education was impressive; for a woman to write it—well, that was nearly impossible. And yet Maria had done it. For her contribution to the field, she was elected to the faculty of the Bologna Academy of Sciences as the chair of mathematics and natural philosophy. She was only the second woman ever to be appointed a university professor.

After her father's death in 1752, when she was just thirty-four, she finally turned to the subject that had long held her interest: theology. She became the head of the Hospice Trivulzio for Blue Nuns at Milan, where she spent her time ministering to the homeless, the poor, and the sick. Eventually, she joined the order, becoming a nun. She died on January 9, 1799. She has an asteroid and a crater on Venus named in her honor.

Maria's name lives on today in what was actually a mistake. She is best known for her work on an equation first investigated by noted mathematicians Pierre Fermat and Luigi Guido Grandi concerning something called a versed sine curve. In her text, she referred to the equation as *a versiera*, which means "to turn." But when her text was translated into English, the translator, John Colson, misread the word as *avversiera*, which means "witch." And thus, her most famous lingering contribution to mathematics is an equation known to students as "the Witch of Agnesi."

Augusta Ada Byron King, countess of Lovelace, was born Augusta Ada Byron in London on December 10, 1815. Her father was the famed poet Lord Byron, a writer who was regarded as one of the greatest European poets in his own time and is still revered today. (He was also famous for capturing the heart of many a woman, earning him the reputation of someone who was, as the novelist Lady Caroline Lamb put it, "mad, bad, and dangerous to know.") When Augusta Ada Byron was twenty, she married William King and gained the title countess of Lovelace; today, she is known as simply Ada Lovelace.

Ada's mother, Anne Isabelle Milbanke, was not as enamored with Lord Byron as his legions of female fans were. She left him a month after Ada was born, and Ada never knew her father outside of his published works. It was her mother's wish that Ada not be poetic and dramatic like her father, and so Ada was encouraged to study mathematics and music, disciplines her mother hoped would counter any poetic tendencies. Ada excelled in her rigorous studies, under the stern direction of her mother and the best tutors money could buy, but her logical mind had its own undeniable flights of fancies: In 1828, she used her knowledge of math to design a flying machine.

Ada and her mother were part of upper-crust London society, where noblemen spent their time studying astronomy, botany, or other scientific pursuits at their leisure. Noblewomen, of course, were not encouraged to be intellectual, but nonetheless Ada was a part of this casual scholarly environment. One of the gentleman scientists she met was Charles Babbage, who was known as the inventor of something called the *difference engine*, a complex mechanical calculator. He was a professor of mathematics at Cambridge, and when he met Ada, he was in the process of devising another invention, an elaborate mechanical calculator that could, in his words, not only foresee, but act on that foresight. It was all the more intriguing to Ada because of the simple fact that it hadn't yet been built. Her imagination was captured by the sheer possibility of such a machine. Although she was just seventeen when she met him, she and Babbage began a lively correspondence about the machine, logic, mathematics, and other subjects.

Ada married in 1835 and had three children with William King. In 1841, Ada began another course of intense mathematical study with noted mathematician Augustus De Morgan. Meanwhile, Babbage was trying to secure funding support for the further development of his difference engine and his second machine, the analytical engine. His partners in England were reluctant to put more money into the project, especially as the first machine wasn't fully finished, but he found support from mathematicians in Italy and France. When a lengthy article about his machine was published in French, he asked Ada to translate it. She spent much of 1842 to 1843 working on the project. But she took it just a step farther: She not only effectively described the way this early mechanical and general-purpose computer might work, but also put forth some theories about the things such a machine might be capable of beyond mere number crunching—ideas Babbage himself had not considered. In her notes, which turned out to be three times as long as the original article, she suggested a plan for calculating complex Bernoulli numbers (thereby creating the first computer program) and predicted that one day the machine might be used to generate music, create graphics, and even assist people in practical, not just scientific, activities. Today, these are in fact some of the many things computers do.

Ada died of cancer in 1852, at the age of thirty-seven, and was buried alongside the poet father she never knew in life. At the time of her death, Charles Babbage had still not constructed the machine she so eloquently described. In fact, he would die in 1871 without having built it. It wouldn't be until just before World War II that a professor at Harvard would draw on his knowledge of the analytical engine to create what came to be called the Harvard Mark I electromechanical computer. The inventor, Howard Aiken, would be assisted in his development of the computer by another woman following in Ada's footsteps: Grace Hopper. In 1979 the U.S. Department of Defense invented a computer software language and named it "Ada" in honor of Ada Lovelace, the first computer programmer.

Grace Murray Hopper was one of the very first computer scientists. Her accomplishments in both programming and the military (she was a rear admiral in the U.S. Navy) earned her the nickname "Amazing Grace."

Grace was born in New York City in 1906, the oldest of three children. A curious child, she entertained herself at age seven by taking apart her alarm clock—and then all of the alarm clocks in the house. Grace's parents encouraged her to explore her natural inclination for tinkering and also made sure that she and her sister had the same kind of education as their son. Still, Grace's high school years were spent at private schools whose aim was to turn out genteel young ladies (although she did manage to play basketball, water polo, and field hockey).

She graduated from Vassar College in 1928 with a degree in mathematics and physics. After graduating, she taught at Vassar while studying at Yale, where she was one of only four women in the doctoral program. She married in 1930 and earned her PhD in 1934. Nearly ten years later, she followed in the military tradition of her family and joined the U.S. Navy WAVES (Women Accepted for Volunteer Emergency Service). She was assigned to the Bureau of Ordnance Computation Project at Harvard University. She was the third person to join the research team headed by Professor Howard Aiken, who reportedly welcomed her with the words, "Here, compute the coefficients of the arc tangent series by next Thursday."

Her job was to work on the first electro-mechanical computing machine, called the Mark I. This early computer wasn't the slick screen, keyboard, and mouse we know today; rather, it was as big as a room, 55 feet long and 8 feet high, with nearly 760,000 separate pieces. It could carry out addition, subtraction, multiplication, and division, and it could perform logarithms and trigonometric functions, all stored and tabulated mechanically using 3,000 decimal storage wheels, 1,400 rotary dial switches, and 500 miles of wire. With all this power, it took the Mark I five seconds to perform a simple multiplication problem.

She took one look at the Mark I (perhaps remembering all those clocks she dismantled in her youth) and jumped right in, learning to program it and in the end creating a five-hundred-page manual of operations, in which she outlined and described the basic operating principles of computers. By the end of World War II, she had helped to develop the second version of the machine and was appointed to the Harvard faculty as a research fellow. In 1949, she joined

the Eckert-Mauchly Computer Corporation as a senior mathematician and remained there, even as the company changed names through the years, until she retired in 1971.

Throughout her life, she was known for not only her scientific mind but also her keen wit. As a creative and daring innovator, she was famous for saying, "It's easier to ask forgiveness than it is to get permission." Toward the end of her life, when asked if she had an open mind, she responded, "I believe in having an open mind, but not so open that your brains fall out."

Her best known contribution to the field was her invention of the compiler—a program that translates English instructions into computer language. She also developed the first commercial high-level language (a way of instructing computers to do certain tasks), which eventually evolved into COBOL (COmmon Business Oriented Language), a programming language for performing simple computations on large amounts of data. In this, she was the first software engineer, and her work has been described as the building blocks of modern computing.

In 1969, she was honored with the Man of the Year award from the Data Processing Management Association, and in 1991, she received the National Medal of Technology. When she died on January 1, 1992, Admiral Grace Hopper was buried with full naval honors at Arlington National Cemetery.

THE WOMEN COMPUTERS OF ENIAC

ENIAC, short for Electronic Numerical Integrator and Computer, launched the world into the computing age, but none of the fanfare centered on the people who actually helped it come into being: The six women who programmed it.

In 1945 the U.S. Army put out a call for "computers" for a top-secret job at the University of Pennsylvania. Eighty women math majors were hired to calculate ballistics trajectories by hand, but six women were selected for the highly classified, top-secret project: Jean Jennings Bartik, Frances "Betty" Snyder Holberton, Kathleen McNulty Mauchly Antonelli, Marlyn Wescoff Meltzer, Ruth Lichterman Teitelbaum, and Frances Bilas Spence.

The secret project was ENIAC, the first all-electronic computer, which was made up of some 18,000 vacuum tubes and forty 8-foot black panels. Because it was secret, the women weren't given access to it until they had received security clearance; and because they were the first programmers, they had no instruction manuals to explain the machine to them. They worked six days a week, looking at diagrams, creating their own flow charts, and physically programming the machine by hand, maneuvering cables, wires, and thousands of switches to route the data.

Their program worked: What had previously taken hours, weeks, and even years to calculate, ENIAC could do in seconds. In February 1946, the army unveiled ENIAC to the public, celebrating its inventors, Dr. John Mauchly and J. Presper Eckert. But there was no mention of the skilled mathematicians who had invented the field of computer programming from the ground up. The six women were included in the press pictures, but their pioneering work was left out of the story.

ENIAC is still on display at the University of Pennsylvania. The amount of information contained in the room-sized ENIAC in the 1940s can now fit onto a silicon chip just a fraction of a square inch in size. Women—and men—no longer walk along the physical hallways of an actual computer program. But thanks to these six women, who went on to teach other future computer engineers early programming techniques, females have an important place in both the history and the future of computer programming. And in 1997 they finally got their recognition: All six were inducted into the Women in Technology International Hall of Fame.

Make a Piñata from Papier Mâché

ALTHOUGH WE THINK OF PIÑATAS AS MEXICAN, they come from China, where they brought color to New Years celebrations. The explorer Marco Polo brought them back to Italy in the 1300s. There, piñatas became part of the spring Lent ritual; the first Sunday of Lent was commonly called "Piñata Sunday." These piñatas were not papier mâché, and they weren't stuffed with goodies, as they are today. They were clay jars or figurines that were smashed as part of the celebration; the Italian word *pignatta* means "a fragile bowl or vase."

Piñatas were brought to the Americas by Spanish missionaries and explorers. They may have been surprised to find that the Aztecs and the Mayans already had their own jar-smashing rituals. The Aztecs covered a clay vessel with colorful feathers and filled it with treasures for Huitzilopochtli, their god of war. The Mayans had a game in which the eyes of the clay smasher were covered with a blindfold, which is how our piñata games today are often played.

Piñatas are now made of cardboard or—preferably, since cardboard is hard to break open—from papier mâché. Papier mâché is the ultimate this-and-that craft. At every stage it's a trial-and-error process, with lots of room for vision and change. It can be started on the spur of a moment, and the ingredients are simple: newspaper, water, and flour, the latter of which can always be borrowed from a neighbor if the pantry at your house is bare. Papier mâché will make a mess, but that's okay. Life is messy, and this mess, luckily, can be easily cleaned up.

WHAT YOU NEED

To make a papier mâché piñata you'll need some combination of:

- Balloons
- Bucket or large mixing bowl
- Bowl to hold the balloon
- Spatula or large spoon for mixing
- Flour
- Salt
- Water
- White glue
- Masking tape
- Brushes
- String
- Newspaper or plastic sheets to protect working surfaces
- All kinds of household paper supplies such as crepe paper and construction paper to add features and decorations to the outside
- Paper cups, wads of crumpled paper, paper towel tubes, paper taped into a cone shape, empty food containers, or anything else you find around the house
- And not to be forgotten: candy, toys, and other treasures to put inside!

Step 1. The base for a piñata is a balloon, which you blow up and tie, and then tape the knot down (masking tape will do, as will a gluey strip of paper when it's ready).

Step 2. Time to shred the newspaper, lots of it. Don't use scissors, just tear, because the torn fibers make the papier mâché stronger. The strips should be about 1 inch wide and perhaps 6 inches long (longer or shorter, depending on your project). Newspaper is used for nearly all the layers, although strips of white paper or construction paper can be especially nice for the final layer.

Step 3. Make the glue. The quick-and-easy method for making glue mixes 1 cup of flour and 2 cups water in a bowl. When the mixture is right, it will be somewhere between soupy and thick, and will moisten the newspaper without destroying it. Add more water or flour as needed, and add ¼ cup of salt at the end. It acts as a preservative, which you'll appreciate about a month from now.

For a creamier and stronger glue, boil 5 cups of water then add 1 cup of flour. Stir until the lumps are gone. Once the flame is off, the glue will cool quickly.

These classic flour-and-water glues work because, in chemistry terms, the starch in flour is a long molecule that can wrap itself around other objects and in this way become "sticky." Water helps the starch in flour become sticky, and heat releases the starch even more, which is why some people prefer the stovetop method.

Step 4. The balloon is ready, the paper is in shreds, and the glue is mixed, so you're ready to bring your piñata to life. If you don't like the total mess that papier mâché can entail, place dry paper pieces where you want them, and apply the gluey mixture with a paintbrush. Put a bowl

beneath the balloon to hold it in place while you work. Dip the newspaper into the glue mixture. Wipe off the excess (or let it drip off), and start covering the form with the strips. Keep applying strips until the balloon is covered. Smooth the strips. Add layers to get the thickness you want.

Add features as you go, such as ears or a nose or legs. Tape on cups and paper tubes and crumbled paper to create shapes and dimension, and papier mâché over them, knowing that pretty much anything can be made to work. Brown paper lunch bags filled with crumpled newspaper are good for heads. Newspaper logs (several sheets of newspapers, rolled tightly together, and taped) are good for adding arms and legs.

Cover the balloon with two to four layers, which will make it strong, but not so strong that it becomes difficult to break. When done, set aside to dry, which may take a day or two.

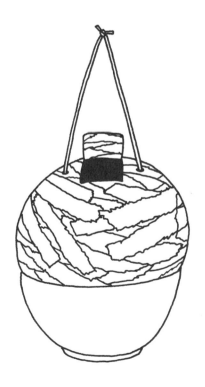

Step 5. When the glue is dry, cut a 2-inch hole at the top for putting in treasures. (This is a good time to pop the balloon, too.) Cut two smaller holes nearby, and tie on about a foot and a half of string, for hanging the piñata later. Decorate the outside of the piñata with paint; with glued-on rectangles of colorful paper, fringed over each other; or by wrapping crepe paper around the piñata in overlapping layers. Fill the piñata with candy and treats (a word to the wise: make sure that the inside is absolutely dry). Tape the cutout piece back into place.

Step 6. Play! Hang your piñata outdoors from a tree branch with line, pulley style. If indoors, make sure the space is truly large enough, and screw a 1-inch eyebolt into the ceiling for the line. Some people let the piñata hang steady in one place. Others play with someone controlling with the cord and pulling the piñata up and down, making the game harder. Hit with a fallen tree limb, a broomstick, or a plastic bat—and make sure everyone is out of the batter's way, especially if she is blindfolded and turned around several times to up the ante.

MAKE A PAPIER MÂCHÉ STATUE WITH CHICKEN WIRE

Once you know the directions for papier mâché, the sky is the limit when it comes to building statues, carnival floats, or anything. Chances are, if you can visualize it, you can make a rough model with some chicken wire and masking tape, and bring it to life. Big projects use tons of newspaper, so start stockpiling now. You'll look around and see that the world is filled with things that double as elements of papier mâché statues: plastic soda bottles, stacks of cereal boxes (to make a tall tree), paper bowls, paper towel tubes, cardboard boxes, wire hangers, and so on.

The trick to large statues (and carnival floats) is making an armature of chicken wire. This wire is sold in hardware stores, usually at a reasonable cost. Use a large piece for the body. You can start by making a cylinder and then cutting smaller pieces to attach for arms and legs. For some large statues you may try using a long piece of wood as a central "spine" and stapling the chicken wire to that. (To attach, twist together the pointy ends of the wire, or be creative; whatever works, works.) Shape the wire foundation into an animal, person, or imaginary creature. As with the piñata, gluey newspaper strips are laid over this foundation. If the first layer is challenging, put strips of masking tape over the chicken wire so the gluey newspaper has something easier to stick to.

When done, let dry fully. This can take a few days. White primer can be used for the first coat of paint. Continue with any kind of paint, from poster paints to latex wall paint, markers, or anything with color. Some people use white paper or colored paper for the last layer, to start the decorating early.

If you think your statue will be displayed outdoors, use water-resistant Portland cement as your glue. If you do use the usual flour-and-water glue and still want protection from rain, snow, sleet, and hail, after the chicken-wire statue has dried and been decorated, brush on a final layer of polyurethane varnish. Perhaps it's overkill, but if you want the statue to live outdoors absolutely forever, try marine spar varnish, which is used on seagoing vessels and is available at a boating store or marina.

Slumber Party Games

WHETHER YOU CALL IT A SLEEPOVER, pajama party, snoozer, or crash, a slumber party is the perfect setting for silly, fun, and sometimes challenging games with friends. Here are five of our favorites.

HA HA HA

As you may guess from its title, this game is all about contagious laughter. To play, everyone lies on the floor with each person's head resting on another person's belly. All it takes is for one person to start laughing, and pretty soon everyone else will be laughing, too. Another variation is to have one person to begin the laughter by shouting, "Ha!" Then the next person must say, "Ha ha!" The next person must say, "Ha ha ha!" and so on. It's impossible to get too far without everyone laughing.

TRUST FALL

Stand in a close circle, shoulder to shoulder and arms outstretched, palms out, with one girl in the center of the circle. The girl in the middle stands with her feet together, folds her arms against her chest, closes her eyes, and says, "I am ready to fall." The other girls answer, "We are ready to catch you." Then the girl in the center falls backward or forward toward the girls forming the circle. These girls should catch or stop the fall, gently pushing the falling girl back into an upright position.

ABC SENTENCE GAME

The goal of this game is to have a conversation in which each sentence begins with words using successive letters of the alphabet. Sit in a circle, and have someone choose a letter of the alphabet to start with. The person who goes first says a sentence that starts with a word using the letter that was chosen. (For instance, if the starting letter was "A," the person could say, "A nice day we're having, isn't it?") The next person has to

respond with a sentence beginning with the next letter of the alphabet. (For example, "But it was supposed to rain.") Then the next person does the same ("Can't you just enjoy it?"), and so on, until the starting letter is reached again.

VIKING

This game works best with six or more people. To begin, choose one person who will start out as the Viking. Then, have everyone sit in a circle, legs crossed, and clap their hands on their thighs, creating a constant beat. The Viking starts the game by pointing her index fingers up alongside her head (mimicking horns on a Viking hat). The players on either side of her must paddle (mime a paddling movement) to the right or to the left, depending on which side the player is on (the player on the right paddles right, the player on the left paddles left). The Viking chooses the next Viking by pointing her horns at another player. Then that player must make the Viking hat with her fingers and the players on either side of her must paddle. If a player forgets to make the Viking horns or paddle motions, or if she paddles the wrong way, she is out. The game continues until there are only two people left.

"THIS IS A WHAT?"

A game for five or more players. For this game you'll need an object for each player—and for everyone's sanity, each object should be one syllable (pen, book, clip, etc.). At first the game sounds deceptively easy: Players sit in a circle and pass each object to the person on their left. But tricky rules make this much harder to do.

There is a basic script that must be followed in order for an object to be passed to the next person. One player is a giver, and the other is a receiver.

> **Player 1** (Giver): "This is a pen
> [or other object]."
> **Player 2** (Receiver): "A what?"
> **Player 1** (Giver): "A pen."
> **Player 2** (Receiver): "A what?"
> **Player 1** (Giver): "A pen."
> **Player 2** (Receiver): "Oh! A pen!"

The object can be handed to the second player only when she acknowledges the object ("Oh! A pen!") after asking twice what it is. Then she must pass it along to the person next to her, following the same script.

The trick is that while the second player is passing along that pen (or other object) to the third player, the first player is now passing something else to the second player, making her both a giver *and* a receiver. So the second player must turn her head to respond to the first player ("A what?" "A what?" "Oh! A book!") as well as turn her head back to talk to the third player ("This is a pen"; "A pen"; "A pen"). More objects are added until all objects are in play and each player is participating in the script.

Tip: The first player is in charge of all the objects. Practice first with one object, going all the way around the circle, and then two objects; then, work up to putting all the objects into play.

The Nobel Prize

WHILE HE WAS ALIVE, the Swedish businessman Alfred Nobel was best known as the inventor of dynamite. When he died in 1896, he willed that his great fortune be used to create an international prize to honor "those who, during the preceding year, shall have conferred the greatest benefit to mankind." The first Nobel Prize was awarded in 1901 in each of five areas: physics, chemistry, physiology or medicine, literature, and peace.

Nobel Prize winners receive global attention for their causes or books or research—and a cash prize of Swedish *kronors*, equal to about $1.5 million. Except for the years during World War I and World War II, prizes have been announced each fall. In 1969 a sixth prize was added, in the field of economics. The Nobel Prize is often awarded to groups of scientists who work together.

Among the nearly 791 Nobel Laureates (and some twenty organizations) are thirty-five women (one of whom, Marie Curie, won the prize twice). It has not often been easy to be a woman scientist, doctor, or writer. Many of the Laureates pursued their passions for years and years, with little public support, before receiving the Nobel Prize. These Laureates were especially daring in their willingness to search for new scientific answers, to write great literature, or to put their very lives at risk to call attention to injustice and war.

YEAR	WINNER	COUNTRY	FIELD
1903	Marie Curie	France	Physics
1905	Bertha von Suttner	Austria-Hungary	Peace
1909	Selma Lagerlöf	Sweden	Literature
1911	Marie Curie	France	Chemistry
1926	Grazia Deledda	Italy	Literature
1928	Sigrid Undset	Norway	Literature
1931	Jane Addams	United States	Peace
1935	Irène Joliot-Curie	France	Chemistry
1938	Pearl Buck	United States	Literature
1945	Gabriela Mistral	Chile	Literature
1946	Emily Green Balch	United States	Peace
1947	Gerty Cori	United States	Physiology or Medicine
1963	Maria Goeppert-Mayer	United States	Physics
1964	Dorothy Crowfoot Hodgkin	United Kingdom	Chemistry
1966	Nelly Sachs	Sweden	Literature
1976	Mairead Corrigan	Northern Ireland	Peace
1976	Betty Williams	Northern Ireland	Peace
1977	Rosalyn Yalow	United States	Physiology or Medicine
1979	Mother Teresa	India	Peace
1982	Alva Myrdal	Sweden	Peace
1983	Barbara McClintock	United States	Physiology or Medicine
1986	Rita Levi-Montalcini	Italy	Physiology or Medicine
1988	Gertrude B. Elion	United States	Physiology or Medicine
1991	Aung San Suu Kyi	Myanmar	Peace
1991	Nadine Gordimer	South Africa	Literature
1992	Rigoberta Menchú Tum	Guatemala	Peace
1993	Toni Morrison	United States	Literature
1995	Christiane Nüsslein-Volhard	Germany	Physiology or Medicine
1996	Wislawa Szymborska	Poland	Literature
1997	Jody Williams	United States	Peace
2003	Shirin Ebadi	Iran	Peace
2004	Elfriede Jelinek	Austria	Literature
2004	Wangari Maathai	Kenya	Peace
2004	Linda B. Buck	United States	Physiology or Medicine
2007	Doris Lessing	United Kingdom	Literature
2008	Françoise Barré-Sinoussi	France	Physiology or Medicine

Pogo Sticks

AN OLD STORY HAS IT that a man traveled to Burma (which is now called Myanmar), where he met a farmer's daughter named Pogo. Pogo's family was poor, and she had no shoes. She liked to visit the local Buddhist temple each day, but the road was muddy. So her father built her a bouncing stick, and called it a "Pogo" after his shoeless daughter. Considering the fact that pogo sticks work terribly on mud and much better on hard asphalt and concrete, the story seems unlikely. What is true is that, in 1919, George Hansburg patented the pogo stick in the United States. In the 1920s, pogo sticks became a huge craze, with chorus-line girls in New York performing pogo stick shows on stage.

Pogo sticks are all about finding your balance and your center of gravity. Stake out a patch of concrete or asphalt or other very hard surface. Prepare for several hundred attempts and possibly a few days to get it right.

The easiest way to start: Hold the handlebars and keep the stick straight up. Put the foot of your non-dominant leg, whether left or right, on the foot bar. Very, very quickly get the other foot up and immediately start to jump. When you bounce, pull the pogo stick up with you.

There is a slightly harder way to start, but it's good to know. Place both hands on the handlebars. Jump up and land both feet on the foot bars at the same time. This gets you started with a good jump, but it can take some time to master.

To move ahead, push your body slightly forward. You'll see that the pogo stick will follow. What's important, though, is always to land with the stick straight. Don't push it away or lean sideways.

When pogo-ing starts to work, the stick will feel like it's part of your body. Still, pogo-ing can be harder than it looks. It can take a while, and many false starts, to feel balanced. Pogo-ing is definitely a time to remember that most things are doable if you stick with it and try two hundred times. Take small jumps at first, and start counting!

Tip: To keep your pogo stick working well, every so often put a few drops of motor oil or grease on the center shaft, bracket, and springs, and clean the rubber tip with soap and water.

How to Run Away and Join the Circus

THERE'S A RECURRING SCENE from an old-fashioned sort of book in which an unhappy child leaves home under the dark of night to become a lion tamer at the circus. It's not widely done anymore. Circuses now abide by child labor laws, and many are giving up their lions and tigers and bears. Still, were you to run off to join the acrobats and trapeze artists, jugglers and clowns, here are some skills you may want to know.

HOW TO JUGGLE

Like most circus skills, juggling looks so easy when someone else does it. The first thing to know is that the balls don't go in a circle. You don't shuffle the balls to a single hand that throws them while the other hand catches. Instead, the balls cross paths, and knowing this goes a long way in understanding how juggling is done. One other thing to watch out for: Everyone's tendency is to toss the balls too far ahead and, thus, to move forward as they juggle. Try to throw the balls straight up. It helps if you practice with your back against a wall.

Start learning to juggle by throwing with one ball. Toss the ball from one hand to another, in an arc. The ball should crest at the same height each time you throw it. You want to be able to rely on throwing the ball the same way and to the same height from both hands. Catch with the other hand—but make sure not to raise your hand to catch the ball; let the ball come to your hand. Then, toss the ball from hand two back to hand one, reaching the same height. As this becomes easier, find a rhythm by counting out loud: *Throw, catch, throw, catch* or *One, catch, one, catch.*

When you're confident with the throw and can do it almost with your eyes closed, add a second ball. You'll expand the rhythm, so that you will throw ball one, and when it reaches the highest point of the crest, you will throw ball two (from the other hand, of course), which will be inside the curve of the first ball. Try saying,

Throw, throw, catch, catch or *One, two, catch, catch.* Keep practicing.

At long last, pull out a third ball. Put two balls in one hand and the third ball in the other hand. Throw first from the hand with two balls. As with two-ball juggling, throw the next ball when the one before it crests. Relax, throw steady, and focus. Practice counting *One, two, catch, three, catch, catch,* and stop after one round. Each ball should end up in the opposite hand. After some celebrating, continue on until you're able to juggle three balls without stopping.

THE HIGH WIRE

Walking the high wire is called *funambulism*—from the Latin words *funis*, meaning "rope," and *ambulare*, meaning "walk." The wire is generally a half inch wide, and the safety wires are called the mechanics. The trick to the high wire is to get your center of gravity directly over that half inch as you walk, unicycle, juggle, or joust your way through a sword fight.

The balancing pole is key. It can be as long as 39 feet, with weights at each end. The balancing pole droops at both ends. This means that the walker's center of gravity is lowered below the wire, which makes it similar to balancing on ordinary land. Well, not exactly. The soft-soled suede shoes you wear will help your feet grip to the wire. It takes quite a few years to master working the wire—with lots of mechanics and safety wires until you can style effortlessly for the audience, which in the circus means to pose and take your bows.

PLATE SPINNING

To spin a plate, you'll need one with a ridged circle underneath. You'll also need a stick with a point at the end—a ski pole makes a good stick, or you can whittle a point at the end of a stick or dowel. Put the stick on the inside of the circular ridge. Hold the plate steady—and horizontal—in one hand. With the other hand, hold the stick very firmly and begin to move it in circles. If it works, you'll be twirling the stick so that the bottom stays put and only the top moves in a circle. Let go of the plate, and as it goes faster, the stick will move to the center of the plate. Eventually you'll be able to throw and catch.

It's probably a good idea to practice on plastic plates first.

STILTS

If you run away to become a stilt walker, the circus will no doubt issue you a pair of professional-quality stilts. In the meantime, so you can work up your stilting skills before you arrive at the big top, here's how to make a pair of practice stilts at home.

MATERIALS AND TOOLS

- For the two poles: Two 6-foot-long pieces of 1-by-3 pine, for the poles
- For the two platforms: Four 8-inch-long pieces of 2-by-3 pine. (The four pieces can be cut from a 4-foot-long piece of 2-by-3. Sometimes the hardware store will do this for you, which makes putting the stilts together a breeze.)
- Sandpaper (stapled or nailed to a block of wood)
- Four carriage bolts, $5/16$-by-5 inches
- Four $5/16$-inch washers
- Four $5/16$-inch wing nuts
- A drill with a $3/8$-inch bit, a saw, a pencil, a ruler, and duct tape

Each foot platform will be made from two 8-inch-long blocks of wood. You will drill two holes through each block, put them together, drill two holes through the pole, and then attach everything with the carriage bolts, wing nuts, and washers. Here are the step-by-step directions.

- On each of the two poles, mark a line 12 inches up from the bottom. Set the poles aside for the time being.
- Use a pencil to mark the top front side of each of the four 8-inch-long pieces of wood. On two of them, measure the centerline. Along that line, measure 1½ inches from both top and bottom. Use a ⅜-inch bit to drill the holes. These two will be the front block of each pair.
- Once that is done, put each of these drilled blocks on top of a second block. Put the drill bit into each already drilled hole, and drill through the second block. This helps ensure that all the holes line up exactly where they need to be. When you're done, all four blocks should have two holes each. Keep the pairs together, but set one pair aside.
- Take one of the pairs of blocks and one of the poles. Match a block (it shouldn't matter which one) up to the 12-inch mark you made on the pole. Set both on a place where you can drill without destroying anything, and go ahead and put the drill into the top hole of the block and drill a hole through the pole.
- Now put both blocks on the pole, with the one you just drilled on top. Put a carriage bolt through the top hole. It will go through the two blocks and the pole, and it will keep everything in place while you drill the second hole. Put the drill into the bottom hole of the blocks and drill through the pole. When the holes are clear, put a carriage bolt through the bottom hole. Tighten both the top and bottom bolts with a washer and a wing nut.
- Take up the other pair of blocks, and repeat these steps to make the second stilt.

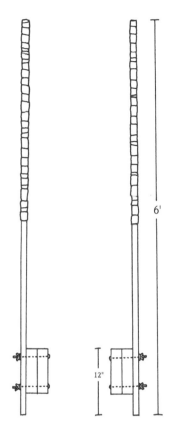

To finish, sand all the surfaces. You may decide to wrap the upper part of the pole with duct tape or duct tape over foam or some similar kind of covering, to create a more comfortable grip for your hands.

Finally, to walk on stilts: Wrap your hands around the poles, and use your arms to lift the stilt as you walk. Start against the wall where you can hold on as you take small steps. Ask someone tall to hold the stilts in front of you as you take your first steps and get the hang of it. All we can say, hopefully without sounding like a broken record, is that it takes lots of practice.

When you're ready to be higher up on your stilts, pull out the drill, repeat the steps above, and make a new set of holes where you want them.

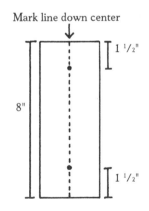

FIRE EATING

We admit, we're stymied by fire eating. We aren't sure why anyone would want to do it, and although we could find out, we have chosen not to know how it's done. Some things in life must remain a mystery.

How to Make a Rope Ladder

IN THE BOOK *The Penderwicks: A Summer Tale of Two Sisters, Two Rabbits, and a Very Interesting Boy*, the four Penderwick sisters—Jane, Rosalind, Batty, and Skye—hang a rope ladder from the stately tree outside their friend Jeffrey's window. With it, he can escape from the second floor of Arundel mansion when his mother isn't looking, and the sisters can climb up to visit him when he's grounded.

Ladders of all sorts come in handy, and with strong wood and secure knots, they are fairly simple to build. Here's a quick guide to making a ladder that best matches the Penderwicks' escape route. It is made of rope and, like theirs, can be stashed in the branches when not in use. It's based on an old design called a bathing knot, from ladders used to pull oneself out of the water onto a boat or dock, or up a lake's steep bank.

You may want to practice this knot first on thinner twine and then go for the real thing. When you're ready, get a very long length of rope, probably five or six times the height that you want it to be in the end. Cut the rope in half, and leave enough at the top so you can tie it to a tree branch when you're done.

Step 1. Working with the left-hand rope, arrange two long loops, as the bottom of the illustration shows.

Step 2. Push the right-hand rope into the loop that is marked A.

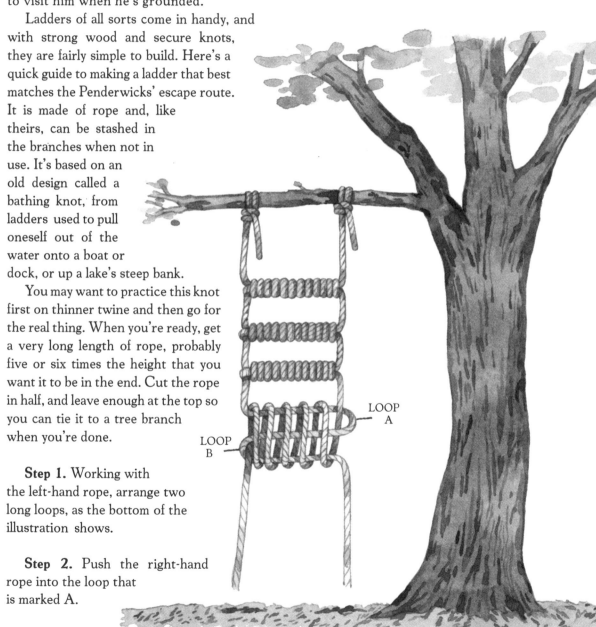

LOOP A

LOOP B

Step 3. Wrap this rope around the long loops. Do this a minimum of four times. If you want the steps to be wider, make even more wrapping turns. It can be a little tough, but hold the long loops in place while you are wrapping the other side of the rope around them.

Step 4. As you get to the other side, pull the rope to the front through the loop marked B. Pull it tight and, as you do, make sure the loops and the wrapping stay even.

Make as many planks as you want, always starting the long loops from the rope on the left side and starting the wrapping from the right.

When you're done, hang the ladder on a tree with this incredibly reliable knot: Round Turn and Two Half Hitches.

ROUND TURN AND TWO HALF HITCHES

Wrap the rope end around the tree branch once (from back to front). Once the rope is up and over, wrap it around the branch a second time. (If you want to be extra sure that it will hold, add another wrap here, which officially turns the knot into Two Round Turns and Two Half Hitches.) Pass the working end of the rope over and in front of the standing rope. Pull it around to make a half hitch (which is the ordinary knot that everyone knows). Pull tight, make a second half hitch, and pull tight again in the same direction. In short, two wraps around the branch, and two half hitches, and you have a knot that will hold your ladder up.

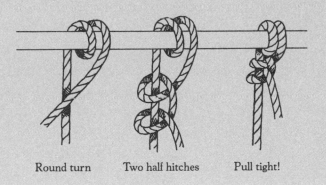

Round turn   Two half hitches   Pull tight!

Scoubidou

IT'S PRONOUNCED JUST LIKE the cartoon character Scooby Doo, but it's actually a string craft beloved by anyone who's logged time in summer camp. Scoubidou is the European version of the braiding and knotting craft that in the United States is known as gimp, boondoggle, or lanyard.

You can buy the flexible, colorful scoubi string in any craft store. Knotting and tying the stretchy, elastic plastic strings transforms them into anything from bracelets and necklaces to key chains, friendship rings, decorative shapes, and even animals. Here are a few stitches to get you started.

CHINESE STAIRCASE STITCH

Starting out. This stitch uses four strings: three different-colored strings that are all the same length and one clear string that is twice as long as the others. Gather the four strings, and tie them together in a regular knot at the top, leaving about an inch or two of string.

Tying the knot. Take the clear string and bring it across the front of the other three strings, leaving a bit of a loop near the place where all the strings meet. Wrap it around the other three strings, and bring the end of the clear string through the loop. Pull tight to make a knot. Repeat this several times (make a loop, wrap around, pull through), and you'll be able to see a spiraling staircase of knots developing.

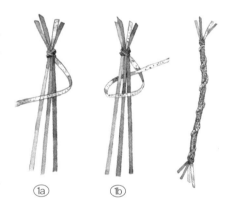

SQUARE STITCH

Starting out. Starting a stitch can be a little tricky, so we recommend beginning a square knot by tying two strands of scoubidou together. Find the centers of two different-colored scoubi strings that are the same length, and tie one string around the center of the other. Orient the strings so that the string you used to make the knot is pointing up and down, and the string you tied the other string around is pointing left and right. Now imagine the four strings as the points of a compass: The top string is North, the bottom string is South, the right string is East, and the left string is West.

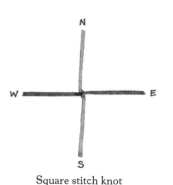

Square stitch knot

Tying the knot. To make a square stitch, bring the North string over and toward you, so that it hangs down over the South side, just to the right of the South string. Then, bring the South side up and away from you so that it hangs over the North side. (The ends of both North and South strings should now be directly below the knot you made at the beginning. If you use one hand to hold both the string ends at this point, you will see that you have made two loops: the North string loop on the right and the South string loop on the left.) Then, take the East string and thread it over the first loop next to it (North) and all the way through the second loop (South). Then, take the West string and thread it over the first loop next to it (South) and all the way through the second (North). Gently pull all the strings to tighten. You've now made your first square stitch, which looks like a little checkerboard pattern. Now turn the stitch over to the other side (which does not look like a checkerboard—it has a string going across the middle diagonally), and repeat the steps (flip North string South, flip South string North, weave East over and under, weave West over and under) to make another stitch. After the second stitch, just keep going (no need to turn the strings over), and repeat the stitch as many times as you like.

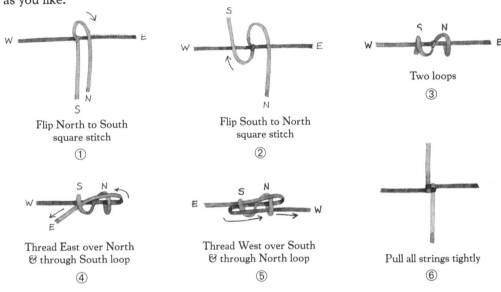

Flip North to South
square stitch
①

Flip South to North
square stitch
②

Two loops
③

Thread East over North
& through South loop
④

Thread West over South
& through North loop
⑤

Pull all strings tightly
⑥

TRIANGLE STITCH

Starting out. The triangle stitch uses three strands of scoubi string. Gather three different-colored strings together, and tie all three in a regular knot, leaving about an inch or two of string at the end. Then, grab that knotted short end and flip it over so that the long strings lay out on your hand. Orient the strings so that there is clearly one string pointing straight up, one pointing to the left, and one pointing to the right. Using our compass points as a guide, this would be a North string, a West string, and an East string.

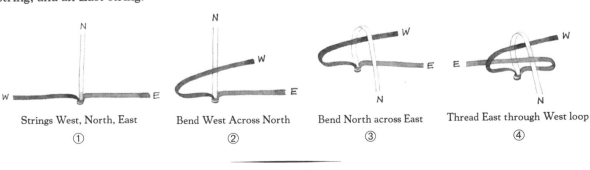

Strings West, North, East
①

Bend West Across North
②

Bend North across East
③

Thread East through West loop
④

Tying the knot. Take the West string and bend it across the North string, making a small loop between the two strings. (Note that West should be on top of North, laying across it, not underneath.) Then, take the North string, and similarly, bend it across the East string. (So West lies across North, and North lays across East.) Now take the East string and thread the end of it through that first loop you made between the West and North strings. Pull all three strings tight. Repeat those steps (West across North, North across East, East through West) to create another stitch. Keep going until you run out of string!

COBRA STITCH

Starting out. This stitch uses four strands of scoubi string. Begin by gathering all four strings and tying a knot an inch or two from the ends. Hold the strings by the short end, and let the four long ends dangle. The two middle strings will stay hanging down throughout the stitch, and the strings on the right and left are the working string. We'll call them right and left.

Tying the knot. Part one: Take the right strand and bring it behind the middle strands, leaving a small loop on the right side as in the Chinese Staircase stitch. Bring right in front of left strand. Bring the end of left strand up and over the front of the middle strands and through the loop made by right. Pull strings to tighten. This is the first half of the stitch.

Part two: Take the strand on the right, and bring it across in front of the middle strands, leaving a small loop on the right side. Bring right underneath/behind the left strand. Bring the end of the left strand back and behind the middle strands and up through the loop made by the right strand. Pull strings to tighten. To continue the stitch, repeat parts one and two.

Ending your stitch. When you're nearing the end of your scoubi string and want to tie off the stitch, for the last two stitches simply pull the scoubi strands tighter than normal to secure it and then trim the ends with scissors. For extra added security, you can always use a dab of glue to fasten the strands in place.

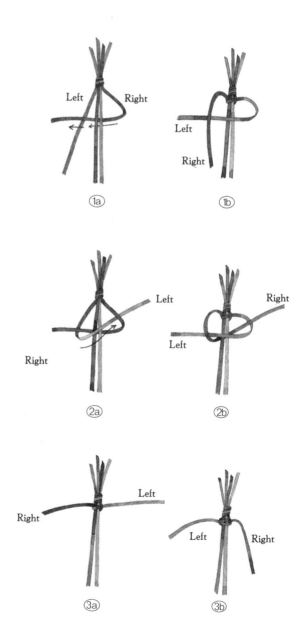

FOUR QUICK SCOUBIDOU PROJECTS

BRACELET

What you need: 2 different-colored scoubi strings, 3 feet long each

Type of stitch: square

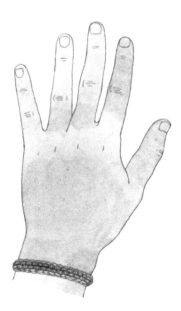

Follow the instructions for square stitching as noted above, and continue creating stitches until your square-stitched scoubidou is long enough to loosely circle your wrist. Bend the strings end and the stitch end of the bracelet together to make a circle and thread the strings on the string end through the stitches on the stitch end. (If those stitches are tight, use a blunt craft needle or a push pin to loosen the stitches enough to slip the strings through.) Pull the strings to tighten, and add a dab of glue to secure. Then, pull the strings even tighter and set the bracelet aside overnight (or at least eight hours). When dry, trim the ends off the strings.

KEYCHAIN

What you need: 1 keyring and two 3-foot-long strands of scoubi strings in contrasting color

Type of stitch: square

Tie one scoubi string in a knot around the key ring (make sure the knot is in the center of the string, so the amount of string on either side of the knot is equal in length). Slip the other scoubi string just underneath the knot, and pull through until you get to the center of that string. Start a square stitch: Use the knotted string as your North and South and the string you threaded through as your East and West, and follow the instructions above. Then, just repeat and repeat and repeat, until your keychain is as long as you like. To end, make a double knot with each string and trim the ends.

HAIR BAND

What you need: 1 hair band (cloth-covered, not rubber) and 1 strand of scoubi string (The length of string depends on the size of the hair band, but a 3-foot length should suffice.)

Type of stitch: Chinese staircase or cobra

Tie the end of the scoubi string around the hair band. Then, begin a Chinese staircase stitch: Make a loop on the right side of the band, wrap the string around to the left (through the middle of the hair band), and thread the end through the loop. Pull to tighten. Repeat until you reach the place where you started. Tie the ends together with a very tight double knot and trim.

PENCIL WRAP

What you need: 1 pencil, 1 strand of scoubi string, four pony beads (basic plastic craft beads)

Type of stitch: none, just wrapping

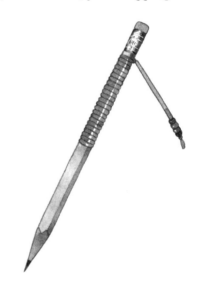

Tie the end of the scoubi string at about the midpoint of the pencil. Make it a tight knot. Then, wrap the string around the pencil, working your way up until you get to the top near the eraser. Then, tie another tight knot (you can also slip the end of the string around the last wrap to make a knot), thread the beads on the end of the string, tie a knot to make a stopper for the beads, and then trim the end.

The Underground Railroad

BETWEEN 1810 AND 1850 OR SO, anywhere from 25,000 to 100,000 people escaped slavery in the United States on the Underground Railroad. The Underground Railroad was not an actual railroad but a trail of of secret attics and straw beds in barns, and of safe houses and midnight horse-and-buggy rides to the next station. The railroad was underground in the sense of being a resistance to the status quo. The steam railroad was emerging during these years, and its image turned the word *railroad* into a powerful metaphor.

People escaped from slave conditions in the southern states to find relative freedom in the North. They were helped by abolitionists, a group made up of people who had already escaped from slavery, black people who were born free and were never slaves, and white people who detested slavery. People broke the law to help slaves travel from the South to find safety in the northern states and Canada. No one controlled the network. Most of the people involved in the railroad knew only a few

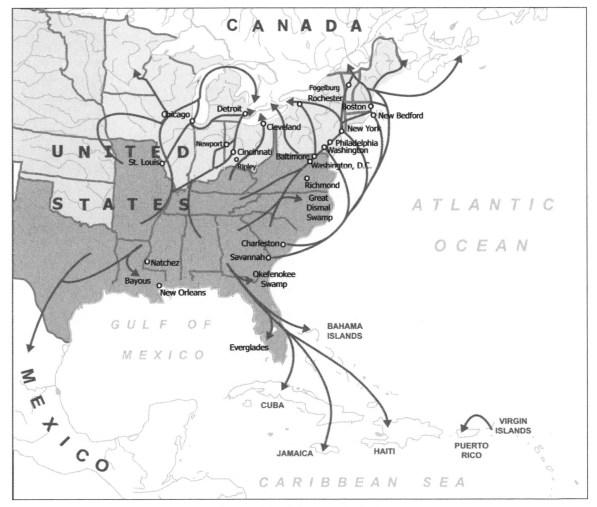

Routes of the Underground Railroad

trusted individuals. They knew a nearby farmer who could be called upon to saddle up some horses at midnight, or a schoolteacher who could guide a runaway slave through a few miles of swamps or backwoods paths to the next station.

The Underground Railroad became an even more dangerous venture after 1850. Prior to this, many northern states did not cooperate with slave catchers. But the U.S. Congress wanted the southern states to agree to let California enter the United States as a free state. In return for the support of the southern states, Congress passed the Fugitive Slave Act and the Compromise of 1850. This made it the responsibility of all states to catch and return runaway slaves. Anyone who resisted faced fines, prison time, and the potential loss of their homes.

This law slowed down the railroad and caused general mayhem. Freeborn blacks in the North were now routinely captured and sent South to be slaves. People no longer trusted that the northern states were safe enough. The traveled even farther north and crossed the Great Lakes into Canada. In 1860, the northern Union and the southern Confederacy went to war. Life for people in slavery wouldn't be safe until the end of the Civil War and the adoption of the Thirteenth Amendment to the U.S. Constitution in 1865, which finally abolished slavery.

STORIES FROM THE UNDERGROUND RAILROAD

ANNA MARIA WEEMS

Anna Maria Weems lived in Maryland. Her town, Rockville, was twenty miles from Washington, D.C., and about 45 miles south of the Mason-Dixon line that separated the slave-owning states from the northern states. She was born in 1840 and was owned by Charles Price. Abolitionists had already purchased the freedom of her mother and a sister. Her three brothers had been sold to slave owners in states farther South, but the Price family refused to sell fifteen-year-old Anna Maria. Fearing she would try to escape, her owners made her sleep on the floor of their bedroom to keep watch over her at night. Anna Maria escaped anyway. She was taken in by the Bigelow family of Washington, D.C. The Price family sent slave catchers to look for her. Anna Maria hid inside the Bigelow house for six weeks, afraid to step outside and be caught.

During those six weeks, William Still, a black abolitionist who was the chairman of a vigilance committee in Philadelphia, hatched a plan to free Anna Maria. Still persuaded his doctor to drive his horse-drawn carriage to Washington. He instructed the Bigelow family to find a carriage driver's uniform. The plan was to ask Anna Maria to cut her hair short and disguise herself as a boy named Joe Wright, a carriage driver and coachman, and pretend that she worked for the doctor.

Although risky, the disguise worked. A day after leaving Washington, D.C., the doctor and Anna Maria had crossed the Mason-Dixon line. When they reached Philadelphia, Anna Maria was introduced to the Still family and their four children. She lived with them for several weeks. The next station was New York, home of the affluent merchant Lewis Tappan, who was at the time seventy years old. Once again, Anna Maria buttoned up her driver's outfit, masquerading as a boy to outsmart any slave catchers.

Mr. Tappan convinced a minister friend of his to take Anna Maria on the last leg of her underground journey: the train ride to Canada. The railroad was a scary prospect. Its cars were always staked out by slave catchers and their spies. Both Anna Maria and the minister worried that they wouldn't make it. From the window they saw the narrow suspension bridge over Niagara Falls. Even as the train sped into the freedom of Canada, they feared they would be caught at the very last moment.

But nothing of the sort happened. Just two months after Anna Maria's escape from Maryland, Anna Maria and the minister passed gratefully into Canada. They hired a wagon driver to take them along muddy, slippery roads. They headed to Dresden, a town where Anna Maria's aunt and uncle had settled after escaping slavery several years before.

We know nothing about the rest of Anna Maria's life. Her story was recorded by William Still, who lost track of her once she was settled in Canada.

HARRIET JACOBS

In her memoir, Harriet Jacobs described her early life as relatively happy, even though she grew up as a slave in North Carolina, the daughter and granddaughter of slaves. She was taught to read and write, which was unusual (both for girls generally and for slave girls especially), and to sew. Her sense of well-being was shattered, though, when the woman who owned her died. Harriet had hoped that the woman's last will and testament would set her free. Instead, the will placed Harriet in the home of a man named Dr. James Norcom, who treated her with increasing violence.

In her late teens, Harriet sought protection from Dr. Norcom by becoming friendly with a white attorney who lived in a nearby town. His name was Samuel Tredwell Sawyer, and he would later become a congressman from North Carolina. Together, Samuel and Harriet had two children, a son named Jacob and a daughter named Louisa. But Samuel's protection was not enough.

POSITIONS ON THE UNDERGROUND RAILROAD

Conductors
People who guided runaways from one safe house, or station, to the next.

Passengers
People who escaped from slave owners and were heading either to the northern states or to Canada.

Stations
Safe houses, with hidden attics, secret rooms and closets, root cellars, water cisterns, haylofts, and barns with fake floors. Fugitives could sleep for a night or two, eat a warm meal, and move to the next station as soon as the coast was clear. Also called *depots*.

Stationmasters
People who housed the runaways in their homes, farms, Quaker meetinghouses, and churches, or who found outdoor hiding places for them.

Stockholders
Affluent Americans who gave a great deal of money to the efforts of the Underground Railroad.

Vigilance Committees
Groups of abolitionists who raised money for food and lodging of people escaping slavery. They provided money for train fares and boat trips, helped people settle into new communities in the North and in Canada, and sometimes raised money to purchase their freedom legally.

Dr. Norcom decided to take Harriet and Samuel's children to be his slaves and to make them work on his plantation. That was too much for Harriet, and she got up the courage to run away from him. Samuel built a secret room for Harriet in the tiny crawlspace over her grandmother's house. Samuel then purchased the freedom of his two children from Dr. Norcom; such was the craziness of slaveholding times that children of a slave were considered slaves, even if their father was free or white. Harriet lived in the tiny attic, although it was barely large enough to hold her. She watched her children grow up through a peephole in the floor and came out only in the thick of night.

After seven years of living like this, Harriet decided the time had come to move her family north. With the help of the Underground Railroad, she escaped from North Carolina on a ship leaving the harbor. The boat took her to Philadelphia, and then she went by carriage to New York City. Samuel sent their daughter Louisa there, and eventually she and Harriet were reunited. The two of them went even farther north, to Rochester, New York. Harriet's brother had settled in Rochester when he had escaped slavery a few years before. Samuel sent their son, Jacob, to Rochester, too.

Rochester was filled with antislavery activity. Harriet soon joined ranks with abolitionists there such as Frederick Douglass, who published the antislavery newspaper *The North Star*. A former slave himself, Douglass had just written one of the first true-to-life accounts of slavery, and his book became an international bestseller. This encouraged Harriet to write the story of her years in slavery, her years in hiding, and her daring escape, and she published her book *Incidents in the Life of a Slave Girl* in the 1850s.

HARRIET TUBMAN

Harriet Tubman was born Araminta Ross around 1820. She was a slave to the Brodas family of Dorchester County, on Maryland's eastern shore. When she was six, she was hired out to work as a house slave and a nursemaid. Later, she would work the fields. In her twenties she met and married John Tubman, who was a free black man. She took his last name and took her mother's name, Harriet, and that's how she became Harriet Tubman.

In 1849, Harriet started hearing rumors that she and other slaves on the Brodas plantation were to be sold. Fearing her life would turn worse than it was, she decided to run away. She was helped by a friend, a white woman who guided Harriet to the Quakers in neighboring Caroline County, and that's where her journey on the Underground Railroad began. It would take Harriet many stations and many nights spent walking to reach freedom.

To move north, Harriet used the knowledge that enslaved people passed to one another about how to follow Polaris, the North Star. Polaris is always in the north, and in the Northern Hemisphere, the Big Dipper is always in the sky. The two stars on the pouring edge of the Big Dipper point straight ahead to the North Star.

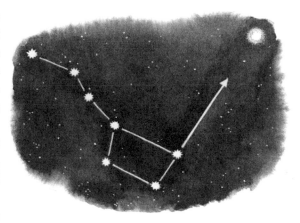

Night after night, Harriet followed the North Star through Delaware and into Pennsylvania. She made it to Philadelphia in seven weeks, and the Quakers there helped her to find work.

The next year, Harriet would return on the sly to Maryland. She ferried her children and her sister out of slavery. Her husband, John, was already a free man, and he decided to stay (he would later remarry). Harriet continued to return. She rescued her brothers and their friends, her niece, and many others. Before long, slave owners were offering a $40,000 reward for Harriet's capture. That didn't stop her. It just made her smarter and more wary and clever. All told, Harriet made nineteen trips and conducted more than three hundred people along the Underground Railroad. Some people called her Moses, after the biblical figure who led the Israelite slaves to freedom. Other people called her "the General."

Dreams and Their Meanings

WHY DO WE DREAM? It's a question that people have been asking since people have existed. An ancient Egyptian manuscript dating back to 2000 BCE, known as *The Book of Dreams*, discusses good and bad dreams and their significance. In ancient Greece, sick people would go to "dreaming hospitals," where they would spend the night and find solace and healing in dreams. In the third century, a man named Artemidorus wrote a book called *Oneirocritica* (The Interpretation of Dreams), explaining dreams as inspired by the daily life of the dreamer and varying from person to person.

Scientists today believe that dreaming happens while we sleep because of neurons firing in the brain. These firing neurons send bursts of electrical signals to the cortex, where higher thought and vision originate. The cortex tries to make sense of the signals by rearranging them, along with real memories, into a story. In the 1950s, scientists discovered that dreaming happens during a stage of sleep called REM, standing for rapid eye movement. During REM sleep, which occurs every ninety to one hundred minutes, three to four times a night, the brain is very active, and this is when we have our most vivid dreams. During an eight-hour night of sleep, fully two hours of that is spent dreaming.

Everyone dreams, even if they don't remember dreaming. Babies spend most of their time asleep dreaming. Even animals dream. So clearly, although we still don't understand exactly why dreaming happens, dreaming is an important part of being asleep—and being alive.

COMMON DREAMS

Artemidorus was generally accurate with his dream theory from thousands of years ago: The meaning of dreams ultimately depends on who's doing the dreaming. You and your friend may both have a dream about playing with a cat, but what that particular dream means to each of you will be different, because you are different people, with different circumstances. You may have a cat as a pet, which may make your cat dream a happy one. But your friend may be deathly afraid of cats, which may make her cat dream a nightmare. Figuring out what a dream means involves thinking about your own thoughts and feelings and about what is going on in your life during waking hours. It's like following clues to understand a mystery or reading a book to figure out a story.

But although dreams are personal, there are some common themes that nearly everyone has dreamed about at one time or another. Here are the most popular common dreams.

Falling	Dreams of falling usually indicate feelings of being overwhelmed by some situation in your waking life.
Being chased	A reaction to anxiety and pressure. If you are running away in your dreams, you may be wishing to avoid something in waking life.
Taking a test or exam	These dreams may arise from a fear of being unprepared or being "put to the test" in your waking life.
Flying	These dreams can literally be about perspective: You have risen above everything and see it from a higher place. How you feel in flying dreams can indicate how you feel about your own personal sense of power and control.
Being Naked	Dreams of showing up to school naked are, like "test dreams," about being vulnerable and unprepared. However, if you're not embarrassed in the dream, it may be a symbol of your confidence and openness.
Teeth	Dreams about teeth falling out are often interpreted as a metaphor for anxiety and powerlessness—although some cultures believe that dreaming about losing your teeth means that you have been gossiping in real life.

TYPES OF DREAMS

In addition to common themes that many people experience in dreams, there are also several types or categories of dreams that people have.

Daydreams	These are dreams that happen when you're not quite asleep and not quite awake. They can take place during waking hours when we let our minds wander and our imaginations carry us away.
Lucid dreams	*Lucid* means "clear," and in these dreams, the dreamer realizes that she is dreaming. Many people have moments of lucidity in dreams where they can change the course of the dream story and continue dreaming. But often the moment of realization that what is happening is a dream is exactly when a dreamer wakes up.
Nightmares	Nightmares have nothing to do with horses: The *mare* in *nightmare* comes from an Old English word meaning "goblin," which is a scary little creature—which is why we know nightmares as scary dreams.
Recurring dreams	These are dreams that repeat themselves with little variation. Some dreams recur once or twice, but there are people who report having recurring dreams throughout their entire lives.
Prophetic dreams	Prophetic dreams supposedly tell the future. These kinds of dreams are usually the stuff of stories—meaning they don't really occur in real life. It is true, though, that dreams have inspired artists, inventors, and other creative people who have the ability to take something they dreamed about and make it real.
Epic dreams	These are extremely vivid dreams that feel incredibly real to the dreamer.

READING A DREAM

Dreams are basically a story that your brain is telling you. And what those stories mean, if anything at all, depends on how you read them.

When trying to make sense of a dream, think of it the way you would a story. The best stories don't just provide a plot, or a series of events that happen over the course of the story. They use symbolism, metaphor, and other imagery to communicate the essence of the story being told. Dreams come from the most creative part of your brain, and it makes sense to read them with the same kind of creative eye you use when you read books.

To do this, write your dream down, in as much detail as you remember, as soon as you wake up. After that, see if you can pick out the main theme of the dream. If it was a movie, what title would you give it? Would it be a comedy, a romance, or a scary movie? What would you write on the movie poster to describe it in just a few words? Asking yourself those questions can help you figure out the big picture of your dream.

Then think about the details, the small things that stick out in your mind when you remember the dream. Some of these things may not make any sense, or their meanings may not be clear to you, if they even have any. You can figure out what those small details may mean through association (thinking about what something has in common with other things) and amplification (thinking about something's larger meaning). For instance, say you remember holding a candle in your dream. First, think about association: Ask yourself, what the first thing is that you think of when you think about a candle? (You may say "fire" or "light" or "seeing in the dark.") For amplification: Ask yourself, what does a candle mean to you when you think of it? You may say warmth, or happiness, or whatever springs to mind. Thinking about a small detail creatively helps you move from the particulars about a thing to what its bigger meaning may be.

Pull back to the big picture again and see if you can match up anything from the dream, either its details or associations or theme, with something going on in your regular life. Did anything happen the day before that was remotely similar to what happened in your dream? Connect the dots, if you can. Sometimes the scary dream of running away from a terrifying monster doesn't seem quite as frightening when you connect it to the day before, when you forgot to do your homework and felt nervous in class.

Dream Journal

THIS JOURNAL IS PERFECT for recording any kind of dream. The journal's binding is a rubber band threaded through two holes in the cover, and then looped around a twig. It has another nifty feature: The cover doesn't just fold in half. Two folds are made equidistant from the center. This creates a spine, so that the pages can lay flat when you write, like in an actual book in which the paper inside lays flat.

You may use any kind of paper (perhaps some heavier paper for the cover), and you will also need a pencil, scissors, ruler, rubber band, and a twig. To make holes, use a hole puncher or a paper awl, or even a pointy ballpoint pen or one end of a pair of scissors.

To make the journal, first cut the cover and the pages to size. Your journal can be as large as you like. The general rule is that the cover should be twice the length of the pages—plus an inch more, to make room for the binding.

The illustration shows how to put the book together. On the inside of the cover, measure where the two folds will be. Mark these lightly, and fold them a few times to make a right-hand side crease. Lay the pages on the right-hand side, and fold the top cover over the pages so the spine forms.

With everything lined up against the spine, make two holes through the cover and the pages. Pull a rubber band through the holes, and then push the twig through the loops of the rubber band that peek up through the journal. If there's no rubber band around, just use string, and tie it in the back.

Fold Here   Fold Here

Cover   Pages

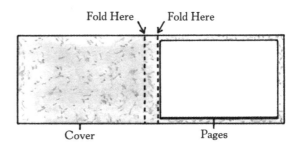

Pull rubber band through
the two holes

Make two holes
through pages &
cover

Push branch through rubber band loops

Dream Catchers

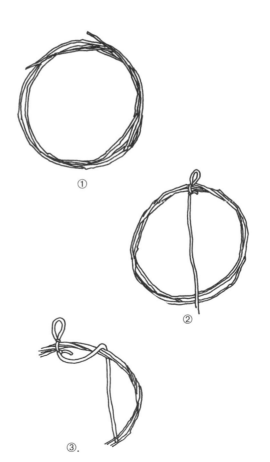

DREAM CATCHERS COME TO US from the Chippewa culture. These handmade objects have a long tradition, but they became popular in the 1960s and '70s, when they spread to other Native American nations and into popular culture.

The Chippewa words for *dream catcher* are *asabikeshiinh* ("spider") and *bawaajige nagwaagan* ("dream snare"), and these words conjure up an accurate image of what the dream catcher looks like: A woven web that catches and holds bad dreams just as a spider web catches and holds anything it comes in contact with. This web, however, allows good dreams to pass through.

To make your own dream catcher, you will need:

- 2 to 4 feet of grapevine (or any kind of flexible tree branch) that has been soaked in water until soft
- 4 to 16 feet of yarn (Twine will also work, but yarn is best.)
- 1 or 2 beads
- 2 to 4 feathers

Take the grapevine, which should be bendy after soaking, and gently curve it to form a circle. Traditionally, dream catchers are no wider than a grown-up's hand, so keep that in mind as you craft the size of your circle. Once you've made your circle, continue to wind the rest of the vine around it, going under and over. This both makes it sturdy and keeps the circle from uncircling back into a straight line (Figure 1).

Now for the string. The amount you need depends on how large your circle is: The larger the circle, the longer the string. Take the 4 to 16 feet of string and tie a loop on one end. This loop will be used to hang the dream catcher once you're done. Tie that end around the top of your circle so that the loop part sticks out. Then, use the long part of the string to start weaving the dream catcher's web (Figure 2).

Take the string and loosely drape it over the top of the circle about 2 inches from where it's

①

②

③.

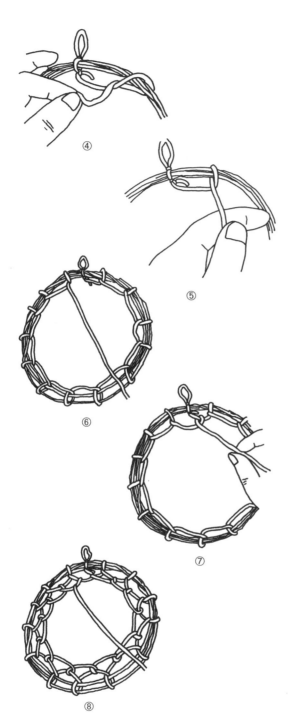

④

⑤

⑥

⑦

⑧

tied and let end of the string hang down on the back (Figure 3). Then, thread the end of the string through the loop you just made, pulling it through to the front again gently (Figures 4 and 5). Repeat this stitch, draping the string over and around the back just two inches from where it's attached, and pulling the end through the loop to the front again. Keep repeating the stitch around the circle until you are within a half inch or so from the hanging loop you tied on first (Figure 6).

Now you'll begin to make another circular layer of web using the same kind of stitch. But instead of stitching around the circle, you are stitching around the string from the previous round of stitching. So, to start the next round from the end of the first, loosely thread the string over the string from the very first stitch, and then pull it through the loop you just made (Figure 7). Repeat until you have stitched all the way around the circle again (Figure 8). Continue stitching another round. After the third or fourth go-round, thread a bead or two onto your string (creating a "spider" for the web), and continue stitching around and around until there is no more room to stitch. Leave a hole in the very center of the dream catcher for the "good dreams" to slip through, and end the stitching by tying a knot.

Do not trim the excess string: This is what you will use to tie the decorative feathers. Use as many feathers as you like—two or three will do it, but you can always use more if you have enough string. Tie a knot around the end of the feathers to attach them. Then, hang up your dream catcher over your bed. Sweet dreams!

Commonly Confused Words

AFFECT AND EFFECT

An *affect* is a feeling or emotion. As a verb, it means to act on, influence, or change something. An *effect* is the result of something. As a verb, it means to make something happen.

*Listening to the speech **affected** her profoundly.*

*The speech had a profound **effect**.*

*Her **affected** accent did not have the desired **effect** on her audience.*

IMPLY AND INFER

To *imply* means to indicate or suggest something indirectly. To *infer* means to make a guess about what that something may be.

*Her happy greeting **implied** she was glad to see me.*

*I **inferred** from her smile she was happy I was there.*

LAY AND LIE

To *lay* means to place or put something somewhere. *Lie* means to recline. (These two are especially tricky, but a good rule of thumb when you're not sure which to use is to try substituting *lay/lie* with a form of the verb "to place." If using *place* instead of *lay/lie* still makes the sentence work, then using the word *lay* is the right way to go.)

*She **lays** the book on her nightstand every night before she goes to sleep.*

*She **lies** down on the bed and shuts off the lights.*

PEAK AND PIQUE

A *peak* is the top of something. The word *pique* means to interest, excite, or rile up, or, as a noun, the state of being riled up.

*She had reached the **peak** of her career.*

*The story she heard the other day **piqued** her interest in backpacking.*

DISINTERESTED AND UNINTERESTED

To be *disinterested* means to be impartial, unbiased, and neutral. To be *uninterested* means to be, well, not interested in something.

*Let the **disinterested** judges decide the winner of our debate.*

*Our debate must be spirited; otherwise, the audience will become **uninterested**.*

NAUSEOUS AND NAUSEATED

Something *nauseous* makes people feel sick to their stomachs. Feeling *nauseated* is feeling sick to your stomach. So it is incorrect to say, "I feel nauseous"—unless you are trying to tell people that you feel like you're making everyone sick!

*The **nauseous** smell drove everyone out of the room.*

*The smell made her **nauseated**.*

FEWER AND LESS

The word *fewer* is about a number that can be counted: Use *fewer* to describe *how many* of something. The word *less* is about amount: Use *less* to describe *how much* of something.

*Our fourth-grade teacher assigns us **fewer** papers to write than our third-grade teacher.*

*Our fourth-grade teacher gives us **less** homework.*

FARTHER AND FURTHER

Farther is used to refer to distance, as it means "at a greater distance or more advanced point." *Further* is about time and degree and means a continuation, extension, or something additional.

*She walked until she could go no **farther**.*

*Her friends urged her to give the idea **further** consideration.*

How to Make a Scarecrow

AS LONG AS THERE HAVE BEEN FARMS, there have been birds delighted to find food—and farmers trying their best to keep those birds away. In ancient Egypt, scarecrows protected wheat crops along the Nile River from hungry flocks of quail. Japanese farmers hung cloth from bamboo stalks to keep birds away from their rice fields. (Medieval Japanese mythology tells of a scarecrow named Keubiko who stands outdoors all day and knows everything there is to know about the world.) In the early Americas, native peoples used human bird-scarers, scarecrows, and yucca lines. These yucca lines were cords that were stretched from pole to pole over the fields and tied with rags and bones that would click-clack in the breeze to frighten the birds.

The British scarecrow was born of the Great Plague of 1665. British farmers had often asked real girls and boys to run around the fields and frighten the birds. When the bubonic plague spread from village to village, many people died, and children became scarce. Farmers began to make scarecrows that looked like bird-scaring children, complete with faces, clothing, and shoes.

In the 1800s, immigrants from Central Europe brought to farms across the United States the now-common scarecrows: the man wearing overalls, a long-sleeved shirt, and a wide-brimmed straw hat, and the woman with her traditional Pennsylvania-Dutch long dress and sunbonnet. The two scarecrows would hold court at opposite ends of the cornfield in the never-ending task of keeping the crows at bay.

DIRECTIONS

A simple, straight-armed, T-cross scarecrow requires a long board or pole for the upright spine and a second board for the horizontal arms. These two pieces of wood can be attached with nails, or lashed together with twine. The simple scarecrow works best if your scarecrow wears a dress or skirt. If you have your scarecrow wearing pants, pull one of the pants legs onto the pole, and let the other leg hang free. The following directions show how to make a fully clothed scarecrow with movable arms and two legs.

MATERIALS AND TOOLS

⚙ **Wood.** Try to round up scrap wood, perhaps from a neighbor whose house is being renovated and has just laid a large pile of wood scrap on the curb. For a relatively permanent scarecrow, use pine boards. The exact measurements are not ultimately important—it's only a scarecrow, after all—but if you can, get 12 feet of 1-by-4 or a similar cut of wood and cut it into seven pieces:

- One 6-foot board for the main post or spine. If you are using different kinds of wood, this should be the strongest one, and of course, you can add footage to make your scarecrow even taller.
- Three 1½-foot boards for the bendable shoulders and arms

- One 1½-foot board for the hips
- Two 3-foot boards for the legs

✪ Hammer

✪ Nails that are long and strong enough to hold your wood. You'll need around twenty of them (but only three or four for the simple scarecrow). Here's how to prevent the wood from splitting when you bang in the nails. Turn each nail upside down. Rest it against the wood. Tap lightly with the hammer to flatten the point just a bit. Turn the nail right side up and hammer the wood pieces together.

✪ Clothing, the fun part: shirts, skirts, pants, shoes, and hat, in whatever style you desire. If you really want to keep the birds away, add pieces of mirror, light catchers, sparkly metal, or crystals for the eyes or elsewhere on the body.

✪ For the head: pillowcase or plastic bag; leaves or hay; twine; thick string or yarn; permanent markers.

1. Attach the Boards

The diagram illustrates how to set up the boards. Lay them out on the ground to see how they connect. Leave room at the top of the spine so the head can be attached. Start by nailing the shoulders and the hips and the legs. Before attaching, put the shirt or dress on the shoulders. Push up the sleeves and then attach the arms to the shoulders. Pull the sleeves down over the boards.

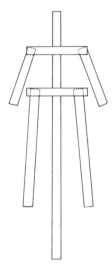

2. Dress the Scarecrow

The shirt is already on. Now you can pull the rest of the clothing on. Some scarecrows have stuffed clothing. If you go this route, use leaves, light twigs, or hay. Tie off the end of the sleeve or pants leg with some twine.

3. Make the Head

There are lots of options. The simplest is to stuff a pillowcase with a plastic bag full of leaves, branches, leaves, or hay, and attach it to the body with twine. (Leave the bottom of the pillowcase free so you have lots of room to tie it to the scarecrow.) Make

hair from string, and use permanent markers to draw the face. With a mask, hat, or bandanna, the scarecrow is ready to go.

A more complicated and time-consuming option is to make a papier mâché head. Follow the directions in the "Make a Piñata from Papier Mâché" chapter, using a round balloon as the base for your scarecrow's head. When you're done, use a special varnish to make the scarecrow's head waterproof.

4. Stand the Scarecrow

Your scarecrow can lean against a tree or be tied to a fence. But traditionally, scarecrows stand in the middle of a field, planted firmly in a hole in the ground. Here's how to dig a good hole.

Get a shovel from the garden shed and start digging. A special tool called a posthole digger makes easier work of this (it looks like a huge pair of scissors with scoops at the ends). Whatever tool you choose, dig really deep, because the scarecrow will need a 12-to-18-inch hole to keep it standing. Once you're done digging, place the scarecrow in the hole and repack the dirt very tightly. Stomp it down with the shovel and with your feet. Knowing how to dig a good hole comes in handy whether you're standing a scarecrow or burying a treasure. (It's also good for setting up campfire pits and booby traps—covered with lots of branches, of course!)

The Moon and Moon Lore

THE MOON, one of Earth's oldest companions, is the subject of many ancient stories. Depending on which myth you hear, it is made of cheese; there is a man in it (or a woman, or a rabbit, or a frog); it can make people go crazy; it can even be blue. The mystery and power of the moon lives on today in words like *moonshine* (foolish talk, or alcohol made by moonlight), *honeymoon* (the custom of drinking mead—a beverage made from honey and herbs—for a month following a wedding), and, yes, *lunatic* (a person made insane by the moon). Here are some facts and stories about the moon.

MOON FACTS

⇨ The moon is the second-brightest object in our sky (the sun, of course, is the brightest).

⇨ The moon is egg-shaped. It looks round to us because the large end points in our direction.

⇨ The moon's gravitational pull affects the oceans here on Earth. It is the reason that we have two low tides and two high tides each day.

⇨ Despite the gravitational forces between the earth and the moon, the moon moves away from the earth at a rate of 1.5 inches a year.

⇨ The moon is about 238,900 miles away from the earth. By space shuttle, it takes about three days to get there.

⇨ The moon is both very hot and very cold. For two weeks at a time, one side is baked in the sun, becoming as hot as 243° F. Then for two weeks, that side faces the cold darkness of space and is chilled to about -272° F.

⇨ The Sea of Tranquility on the moon is not actually a sea, but one of the dark areas of the moon (called the *maria*) that from far away looks like an ocean. There is no water on the moon.

⇨ The oldest map of the moon was discovered in a prehistoric cave in Knowth, County Meath, Ireland. It's estimated this lunar map is nearly five thousand years old.

⇨ The moon is the only extraterrestrial object to have been visited by humans. American astronauts Neil Armstrong and Buzz Aldrin were the first. They landed on the moon on July 20, 1969.

⇨ There are twenty-eight craters on the moon named after women scientists, all of whom made significant contributions to science and astronomy.

PHASES OF THE MOON

Because the moon is revolving around the earth, it doesn't always look the same to us. Half of the moon is always illuminated by the sun, but it's not always the portion that we can see. So, to us, the moon appears to grow from a sliver to a full moon and back again as the sun's light moves across it during the course of the month, even though the moon itself stays a constant size. We call the changes in the moon's appearance the phases of the moon. There are eight phases, and it takes the moon about 29.5 days to cycle through them.

1. New Moon
This is the start of the lunar cycle. At this point in the cycle, the moon is between the earth and the sun, and so to us it appears as though the moon is not there.

2. Waxing Crescent
A sliver of the moon's right side is illuminated by the sun. This crescent moon is halfway between a new moon and a half moon (or first quarter moon).

3. First Quarter
The moon and the earth are side by side in their orbits, and the moon appears to us as being half full. Because of this, it's sometimes called a half moon. But the name *first quarter* is apt because at this point in the lunar cycle, the moon has completed a quarter of its orbit around earth, and because even though it looks like a half moon to us, what we're seeing is actually just a quarter of the moon's surface.

4. Waxing Gibbous
The moon appears to be bulging, as more than one half of the right side is illuminated by the sun. This waxing gibbous moon is between a first quarter moon (half moon) and a full moon.

5. Full Moon
The moon is positioned behind earth and the sun, and we are able to see the entire half of the moon surface lit up. (To us, of course, it looks like the whole moon is lit up; but the other side of the moon that we can't see is totally in the dark.)

6. Waning Gibbous
Another bulging moon, no longer fully illuminated. In this phase, we can see almost the entire left side. This waning gibbous moon is between a full moon and a last quarter moon.

7. Last Quarter
The moon and sun are side by side in their orbits, and we can see the left half of the moon illuminated. The moon in this position has made three quarters of its orbit and has one quarter left to go before the new moon.

8. Waning Crescent
The moon appears as a small crescent, illuminated by the sun on the left side. This crescent moon is between a half moon (or last quarter moon) and a new moon. After this phase, the cycle begins again with the new moon.

BLUE MOONS AND OTHER MOONS

Native Americans gave each full moon of the year its own name as a way to track the seasons. These names, usually descriptively associated with the weather or farming, were used by tribes in the northern and eastern United States and by farmers from colonial times to the present. Here are the traditional full-moon names according to *The Old Farmer's Almanac*.

January: Wolf Moon
This moon gets its name from its appearance during a time of year when wolves were said to howl in hunger outside the villages. Also called the "Old Moon."

February: Snow Moon
So called because of the heavy snows that traditionally occur in February. Also called the "Hunger Moon," because of the heavy snows that made it difficult to hunt for food.

March: Worm Moon
So called because in early spring the ground softens enough for earthworms to emerge. Also called the "Sap Moon," because maple sap starts to flow around this time.

April: Pink Moon
The Pink Moon gets its name from pink wild ground phlox that grows in April. It is also called the "Sprouting Grass Moon," the "Egg Moon," and the "Fish Moon."

May: Flower Moon
This moon gets its name from the many flowers that blossom during the month of May. Also called the "Corn Planting Moon" and the "Milk Moon."

June: Strawberry Moon
So called because of the fact that strawberries are ripe for harvesting during this month. Also called the "Rose Moon" and the "Hot Moon."

July: Buck Moon
So called because this month is when bucks (male deer) start to grow new antlers. Also known as the "Thunder Moon" because of the frequency of thunderstorms in this month.

August: Sturgeon Moon
This moon's name grew from the availability of sturgeon in the Great Lakes and Lake Champlain during this time of year. It is also called the "Green Corn Moon" and the "Grain Moon."

September: Harvest Moon
So called because of its brightness and proximity to the autumnal equinox. The moon is so bright, people can work late into the evening to finish all the harvesting chores.

October: Hunter's Moon
This moon, also called the "Travel Moon" and the "Dying Grass Moon," gets its name from the hunting that took place in preparation for the long winter.

November: Beaver Moon
So called because this month was possibly the last month to set beaver traps (to catch beavers and make winter furs) before the waters froze. Also called the "Frost Moon."

December: Cold Moon
Also called the "Long Nights Moon," this moon is named for the long, cold nights of winter.

BLUE MOONS

There is such a thing as a blue moon, but it doesn't actually appear blue in the sky. Because the moon's phases take 29.5 days to complete, the cycle doesn't line up exactly with each calendar month. This means that every few years (about 2.7 years on average), two full moons will appear in one month. When this happens, the second moon has come to be called a *blue moon*. Originally, though, a blue moon described the third full moon in a season that had four full moons. (Seasons usually have three full moons, so *blue moon* meant, essentially, an extra moon.) Now, however, the first definition is more common, and we use the phrase *once in a blue moon* for something that happens rarely. This usage of the term became popular after the famous eruption of the Krakatau volcano in 1883: The volcanic ash that blanketed the sky worldwide caused the moon to appear to be blue for two years.

TIMELINE: REAL WOMEN ON THE MOON?

Twelve men have walked on the moon, but so far no women have been there. Perhaps some daring girl will be the first! Here are some women who have come close.

1959 Geraldine (Jerrie) Cobb passes all the preliminary physical and psychological tests for the Mercury astronaut training program, but NASA refuses to admit the aspiring female astronaut entry to the final round because it is men only.

1963 Valentina Tereshkova, a Soviet astronaut, spends three days in space, orbiting Earth forty-eight times. She is the first woman ever in space.

1978 NASA finally allows women to complete the astronaut training program. Six women are chosen as candidates: Rhea Seddon, Kathryn Sullivan, Judith Resnik, Sally Ride, Anna Fisher, and Shannon Lucid.

1983 Sally Ride serves as a specialist on a six-day space flight, making U.S. history as the first American woman in space.

1984 Soviet astronaut Svetlana Savitskaya and American astronaut Kathryn Sullivan become the first women to walk in space.

1986 Schoolteacher Christa MacAuliffe and astronaut Judith Resnik perish in a space shuttle crash. The *Challenger* exploded just 73 seconds after liftoff because of the failure of an O-ring seal on its right solid-rocket booster.

1992 Mae Jemison, physician and astronaut, becomes the first African-American woman in space.

1993 Ellen Ochoa, scientist and astronaut, becomes the first Latina-American woman in space.

1994 Chiaki Mukai becomes the first Japanese woman in space.

1995 Eileen Collins becomes the first woman to pilot a space shuttle.

1996 American Shannon Lucid becomes the first woman to receive the Congressional Space Medal of Honor. She had spent six months on the Russian space station *Mir*, a record stay in space for women and for American astronauts.

1998 The space shuttle *Discovery* launches in May with a flight control team composed almost entirely of women.

1999 Eileen Collins becomes the first female commander of a U.S. space shuttle when she commands the ninety-fifth launch of the space shuttle *Columbia*.

2003 Kalpana Chawla, the first Indian-born woman in space, is killed in the space shuttle *Columbia* disaster along with seven other crewmembers.

2006 Anousheh Ansari, an Iranian American, becomes the first female "space tourist" (a civilian who pays a fee to fly aboard on a space mission), flying to the International Space Station and back.

2007 Sunita Williams becomes the record holder for the longest spaceflight by a female traveler (195 days) and number of spacewalks by a female (four).

2008 Thirty-year-old Yi So-yeon becomes the first South Korean in space.

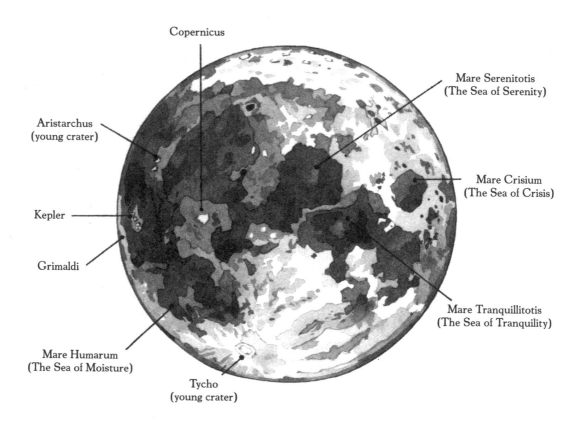

Copernicus

Mare Serenitotis
(The Sea of Serenity)

Aristarchus
(young crater)

Mare Crisium
(The Sea of Crisis)

Kepler

Grimaldi

Mare Tranquillitotis
(The Sea of Tranquility)

Mare Humarum
(The Sea of Moisture)

Tycho
(young crater)

Moon Craters

Make a Snow Globe

SNOW GLOBES BECAME POPULAR in the nineteenth century, and the most ornate of them showed intricate landscapes. Since then, they've been paperweights, collector's items, and, above all, fun things to have on your shelf and give as a present. It turns out they're very easy to make at home. You will need:

❄ A glass jar with a lid that screws tight. A small baby food jar does the job, as will a larger bottle with a secure lid. (Remove any sticky labels of the jar with vinegar and steel wool or a scrubby sponge. If the sticky stuff remains, fill the jar with water to weight it down, and leave it to soak overnight in a larger bowl filled with a water-and-vinegar mixture in it—filling the jar with water holds it down in the mixture. You can also try soaking the jar and label overnight with vegetable oil or peanut butter.)

❄ Fun doodads that will fit in the jar and can be glued to the inside of the lid, like plastic dolls, game pieces, or Lego accessories. Try just about anything that can be glued, won't come apart in water, and that's not too big to get into the jar.

❄ Glue or clay that's strong enough to keep the doodad connected to the lid. Try glue from a hot-glue gun, superglue, modeling clay, or florist clay, which you can purchase at craft stores.

❄ Glitter

❄ Water

First, glue the doodad to the lid of the jar with the strong glue of your choice. You can also use a large enough piece of modeling clay to fit the lid and to hold the doodad. Set it aside to dry fully. Make sure the doodad is really sticking.

Then, when the glue is dry, fill the jar most of the way to the top with cold water, leaving some room for air. Add a few teaspoons of glitter. You can also add a little bit of something called glycerin to the water. It's available at drugstores, and it thickens the water so the glitter will fall more slowly.

Finally, close the lid tight, and shake. Once you're sure you have the right amount of water and glitter, take the lid off and dry it well. Put some glue on the inside edge of the lid, and glue it tight to the jar. You can hold it tight with clay, too. Allow the whole thing to dry before shaking.

Phrases and Idioms and Their Origins

YOU'D HAVE TO BE COOL AS A CUCUMBER not to notice how often we rely on phrases and idioms (figures of speech), even when their meaning escapes us. So batten down the hatches and get ready to learn about some of our hands-down favorites. We're pulling out all the stops as we let the cat out of the bag about some of the common phrases we use every day without really knowing where they came from.

Bee in your bonnet

To have a *bee in your bonnet* means "to be preoccupied or obsessed with an idea." A bonnet is a hat that ties under the chin and usually has no brim and a poufy top. If you can imagine what it may be like to have a bee trapped inside your hat, you can see what a good description that is for an idea you just can't stop thinking about. (An earlier version of the phrase was a *bee in your head*, which sounds even less comfortable.) The phrase first appeared in a poem in 1648.

Beyond the pale

This refers to anything outside the limits of acceptable behavior. *Pale* (from the Latin *palus*, meaning "pole" or "stake") is an old word for a pointed stake or a fence made from these stakes. Long ago, some towns and cities were fenced off or walled off by a pale, enclosing the community within a physical boundary. To go *beyond the pale* meant going outside of the community, into a territory where the inhabitants would quite likely not share the same customs or values.

Busy as a bee

This phrase has come to indicate a person who is industrious or very busy. The association of hard work with the lightness and quickness of a bumblebee flitting about on a sunny day is a pleasing one. But the phrase actually originated in an attempt to describe how hard women supposedly worked at making men's lives difficult! It appears in a collection of stories called *The Canterbury Tales*, written by Geoffrey Chaucer sometime between 1386 and 1400. A section called "The Merchant's Tale" concludes with women being described as being "busy as bees" in their attempts to trick, deceive, and lie to men: "Lo, suche sleightes and subtilitees / In wommen be; for ay as busy as bees / Be thay us seely men for to desceyve, / And from a soth ever a lie thay weyve."

Cool as a cucumber

This describes a person who is calm, composed, and unflappable. The expression started in the eighteenth century, apparently derived from the fact that cucumbers are cool to the touch.

Dog days of summer

This phrase, referring to the hot days of July and August, has an ancient history. The brightest star in the constellation Canis Major (which means "big dog" in English) is Sirius, also called the "Dog Star." Ancient Greeks and Romans noticed that Sirius was most visible during the hottest days of the year, from mid-July to mid-August, and believed that the Dog Star's appearance might have had something to do with how hot it

was. So that time of year became known as *dog days*, or *canicular days*. (First noted in English in John de Trevisa's work *Bartholomeus de proprietatibus rerum* in 1398: "In the mydle of the monthe Iulius the Canicular dayes begyn.")

Get down to brass tacks

This means to focus on the most basic things. The phrase came into use in the United States sometime in the 1800s. Although many have tried to "get down to brass tacks" on the exact origin of it, there are a few likely explanations. One is that the expression comes from shopkeepers, who switched from measuring fabric by holding it against the shopkeeper's arm to measuring cloth exactly between brass tacks nailed into the counter. *Getting down to brass tacks* in that sense meant getting an exact measurement, no matter which shop you went to. Another explanation has to do with shoes: Soldiers' boots in the 1800s had leather soles secured to bottom of the boot by brass tacks. When the leather wore down, the tacks would poke through to the soldiers' feet. *Getting down to brass tacks* in that sense meant getting to the absolute (and uncomfortable) bottom of things.

Hands down

This expression is often used as part of the phrase *to win hands down* and originally comes from the sport of horse racing. Jockeys hold their horses' reins tight as they race; if the reins are held loosely, with hands down at their sides instead of up higher, the horses slow down. So winning *hands down* means winning easily indeed—a racer would have to be pretty far ahead to drop hands, slow down, and still win the race. *Hands down* was used in horse racing in the mid-1800s, and by the turn of the century, it had become well enough known that even nonracing people understood it to mean something along the lines of "having no trouble at all."

Let the cat out of the bag

This means "to reveal a secret" (or, in the words of another idiom, to "spill the beans"). This phrase came from a scam dating all the way back to the sixteenth century in which a pig bought at market would be replaced by a cat (cats being less costly for the pig sellers). The idea was that the customer wouldn't open the bag and discover he'd been sold a cat instead of a pig until he was far from the marketplace. (The expression *buying a pig in a poke* is also related to this: *Poke* meant "bag," and *buying a pig in a poke* meant buying something without checking first to make sure you're getting what you were promised. Evidently, the substitution of cats for pigs was so common that even the French have a similar expression, *acheter chat en poche* ("to buy a cat in a bag").

Mad as a hatter

This expression usually refers to a person who is crazy. You may think the phrase comes from antics of the Mad Hatter in Lewis Carroll's *Alice in Wonderland*, but in fact it's the other way around. In the 1800s, mercury was used as part of the process for making hats. What people didn't know then was that mercury was poisonous. Many hatters (people who made hats) became very sick from being exposed to the toxic fumes, developing shakes, tremors, mood swings, and other neurological problems. The name medical doctors gave to this disease, "Mad Hatter Syndrome," is still used to describe mercury poisoning.

Happy as a clam

Describing someone as being *happy as a clam* means that a person is happy and content. But how do we know that clams are happy? We don't, really, but looking at the early (and longer) version of the phrase gives us a clue. The original expression, which turned up in America in the early 1800s, is *happy as a clam at high water*. Being that high tide is when clams are usually free from predators—including humans, who catch clams at low tide—a clam at high water would be a happy clam indeed.

Put your nose to the grindstone

This expression, which means "to do hard work," is an old expression that dates back to the sixteenth century. It comes from the way knife grinders sharpened their blades: To hold the blades against the grindstone, they often bent very close to the stone, to the point that it looked like they had their noses right up against it.

In the limelight

This has come to mean "to be the center of attention," but it originally meant, quite literally, that a person was in the limelight. In the early 1800s, before the days of electricity, Victorian theaters used gaslight to light up the stage. An enterprising lighting director discovered that putting limestone in the gas flame made the light appear bright, which gave the actors a healthy glow. Not every gaslight on the stage could be equipped with limestone, so usually only the solo performers stood in front of those lights—which is why a person who is the center of attention is said to be *in the limelight*.

Pleased as punch

When someone is pleased as punch, it means she is inordinately pleased with herself. But what is so pleasing about punch? It turns out the punch in question is not a drink, but the name of the main character in a famous puppet show: Punch and Judy. The Punch and Judy puppet show is a British pastime that has been performed for the past four hundred years. It started as a version of a medieval Italian show starring a puppet named Polichinello. Although his name was changed when the show moved to Britain, the plot has stayed the same since the 1600s: Punch hits his wife (Judy), kills people, and outwits everyone who tries to catch him. Every time he does an evil deed, he calls out with glee, "That's the way to do it!" Being *pleased as punch*, then, means being very, very pleased—perhaps inappropriately so.

Pull the wool over your eyes

To pull the wool over someone's eyes means to trick him. This expression was first recorded in 1839 in the United States, and most likely refers to the wool wigs worn by men at that time. A wig slipping down over a person's eyes meant that he wasn't able to see because of the wool blocking his line of sight. Even though wool wigs are no longer worn today, the expression lives on.

Pull out all the stops

This means to make every possible effort. It comes from the world of music, specifically pipe organs. Pipe organs have a long pipe for each note of the keyboard, and each pipe has what's called a *stop*, something that can admit or block the flow of air to each pipe. Blocking the flow makes the volume quieter; removing the stop to let the air flow makes the volume louder. Stops are controlled by the organist, so playing while *pulling out all the stops* means playing at the fullest possible volume.

Get off scot free

Getting off scot free has absolutely nothing whatsoever to do with Scottish people. The word *scot* is actually a Scandinavian word meaning "tax or payment," and *scot free* simply means "not paying taxes." The expression has evolved from its early use as far back as the 1400s into what it means today: getting away with something or doing something without penalty.

How to Become President of the United States of America

THE PRESIDENT OF THE UNITED STATES enforces the nation's laws; commands the army, navy, air force, and marines; and makes treaties with foreign nations. The president establishes our national ideals, protects the United States' reputation abroad, nominates justices to the Supreme Court, and keeps watch over the federal government's three million employees.

The rules for becoming president were established in the U.S. Constitution. We elect our president every four years. When a presidential candidate wins the election in each state, he or she wins that state's electoral votes. The candidate with the greatest number of electoral votes then becomes president. A candidate for president must be a natural-born citizen, must have lived in the

United States for fourteen years, and must be older than thirty-five. (There's no upper age limit, though—Ronald Reagan was our oldest president when he left office at seventy-seven.)

The Federal Election Commission (FEC), created in 1975, provides additional rules for presidential campaigns. The FEC oversees the funding of presidential campaigns and keeps the campaigns as fiscally honest as possible throughout the eighteen months of a political campaign. The longest portion of the campaign is devoted to becoming the presidential nominee of one's chosen political party. This occurs through state elections or caucuses called primaries and then through national nominating conventions for each party. The general election comes after the primaries and lasts two months.

Who runs for president? Most people who want to be president have already served as elected officials. Many have been U.S. senators from or governors of their home states. Candidates can also have experience in the law, in community work, in business, or in other fields.

GETTING STARTED

About a year and a half before the election, a candidate launches a presidential exploratory committee to consider the prospects of raising sufficient money for the campaign and winning the election. The candidate either chooses a political party or decides to run as an independent. The formal campaign begins with a public announcement of the candidate's intention to run for president. Then she must file the Statement of Candidacy form with the FEC and turn her attention to staffing. Every candidate needs the help of a campaign manager, fund-raisers, pollsters, a press secretary and speechwriters, not to mention chairpersons for each state, seasoned advisers, and excited volunteers. As the campaign progresses, more forms are filed with the FEC, such as the Statement of Organization form, and forms that tally campaign contributions and donations each month.

Along with promoting a message and a vision and setting up campaign headquarters, a candidate needs to make sure her name gets on the primary ballot in each state. Each state has unique laws about how to do this. Some states require as many as 50,000 signatures from supporters in the state. Other states ask for a simpler petition or a single form.

PRIMARY SEASON

Public presidential primaries didn't always exist. In fact, the U.S. Constitution says nothing about primaries: In the first American elections, the president was the candidate who got the most votes, and the vice president was the candidate with the second-most number of votes. For most of American history, presidential candidates were picked by political party bosses in proverbial smoke-filled back rooms. In the early twentieth century, primaries were created to change that. They were invented in order to give the American people a greater role in choosing their political parties' presidential nominees. In the 1950s, the growing popularity of television and the national exposure it offered convinced more states to hold full primaries. By the early 1970s, primaries became the norm in all fifty states. Today, most states hold a primary election. Some states, such as Iowa, Alaska, and Nebraska, organize caucus votes, whereby delegates are assigned through conversation and a show of hands. Some states, such as Texas, do both.

The primary season starts in January of the election year, and it awards delegates to each candidate. (The delegates are individuals who will represent the state at the party's nominating convention.) Why delegates? Because when it comes to electing presidents, the United States does not use direct voting, as it does for nearly all other elected offices. Instead, we elect and empower delegates. Some states assign the delegates to each candidate based on the proportion of the actual vote each received. Other primaries are winner-takes-all.

The goal is to win more delegates than the other candidates in your political party, especially in big states such as New York and California, and to reach your party's qualifying number of delegates. To do this, a candidate will visit each state many times, produce television and radio ads, meet with the press, and shake the hands of many citizens.

It gets even more complex. Some delegates are *pledged* delegates. They have to vote for the candidate who won the votes in their state. Other delegates are *unpledged*. These are the so-called *superdelegates*, a position created in the 1980s. Superdelegates are party insiders and elected officials, and in the United States, the Democratic Party relies on them more heavily than does the Republican Party. No matter whom the voters in their states chose, these unpledged delegates can make their own decisions about which candidate to support at the national nomination convention.

As the primary season wears on, usually from January to June of the election year, many candidates will receive fewer votes and delegates than they had hoped. As they see their chances of winning the nomination dim, they drop out of the primary race. The first candidate to collect the qualifying number of delegates becomes that party's presumptive candidate for president, although it's up to the actual nominating convention to make it official.

THE CONVENTION

In August or September of the election year, each party holds a presidential nominating convention. The delegates and superdelegates meet for several days of inspiring speeches and politicking. Many times the party's candidate has been obvious for several months. Every so often, though, the delegates and superdelegates may become locked in pitched battle at the convention, as the final count to pick the presidential nominee goes down to the wire. Whatever the case, the delegates must formally nominate candidates at the convention. The convention ends in the official announcement of the party's candidate for president. In the final moments, massive amounts of colorful balloons and ticker tape are dropped from the ceiling.

THE GENERAL ELECTION

Election Day is the first Tuesday after the first Monday in November. As with the primaries, the vote is indirect. This means that a candidate must win more votes than her opponent in each state, so as to win each state's winner-takes-all electoral vote. A candidate needs 270 votes from the Electoral College to become president of the United States.

What is the Electoral College? The framers of the Constitution feared the popular vote and put a system in place in which, originally, the elected representatives and senators formed the Electoral College (in this case, *college* means an organization, not a school). We elect our presidents state by state. This means that whichever candidate gets the most votes in each state wins all the electoral votes from that state. Even if the winner wins by only two or three votes, he or she gets all the electors; only two states, Maine and Nebraska, divide the electors proportionally. Thus, it's not the number of actual votes that matters, but winning just enough in each state—and winning big states with lots of electoral votes.

Three American presidents lost the popular vote (the actual number of votes cast by citizens), but won more electoral votes and, thus, were inaugurated as president: Rutherford B. Hayes in 1876, Benjamin Harrison in 1888, and George W. Bush in 2000.

The system may seem bulky and indirect, but it's from Article 2, Section 1 of our Constitution, with some help from the Twelfth Amendment of 1804. Each state's number of electors equals the sum of its congressional representatives plus the two senators. Larger states have more electors than small states. Washington, D.C., gets three electors, even though it doesn't have any representatives in the U.S. Congress.

During the general election, the nominees crisscross the country on bus, train, and plane. They visit each state, some many times over. Town meetings and rallies are held. Speeches are given. Hands are shaken. Presidential debates are prepared for, and advertising spots are crafted for radio and television. The candidates look everywhere for new and creative ways to get their message to the voters. They make sure citizens are registered to vote. They keep their staff motivated and their volunteers enthusiastic. At every turn, they stay on their toes and seek a winning strategy to get voters to the polls to vote for them on Election Day.

WINNING

On the evening of Election Day the popular votes from each state are counted, the electoral votes are counted, and the winner is declared. According to the Constitution, the race isn't officially over until the 538 votes of the Electoral College are fully and officially counted on the first Monday after the second Wednesday in December. In addition, any voting irregularities or problems with the ballots or voting machines need to be sorted out so the winner can be declared.

The winner is called the president-elect until the inauguration, which takes place at noon on January 20. The president-elect will stand in front of the U.S. Capitol and be sworn into office by the Chief Justice of the United States with these words, straight from the Constitution:

"I do solemnly swear (or affirm) that I will faithfully execute the office of president of the United States, and will, to the best of my ability, preserve, protect, and defend the Constitution of the United States."

WOMEN WHO HAVE RUN FOR PRESIDENT OF THE UNITED STATES

1872, 1892 Victoria Woodhull is the first woman to run for president of the United States. She runs twice on behalf of the Equal Rights Party. She runs for president years before women even have the right to vote in U.S. elections.

1964 Margaret Chase Smith, a Republican senator from Maine, runs against Barry Goldwater, Nelson Rockefeller, Richard Nixon, and a host of others for the Republican nomination.

1972 Two women seek the Democratic nomination for president: Patsy Takamoto Mink, a Democratic congresswoman from Hawaii, and Shirley Chisholm, a Democratic congresswoman from New York (the first African-American woman to be elected to the U.S. Congress). A third woman, Bella Abzug, also a Democratic congresswoman from New York, announces her intentions to run, but drops out before the primaries. (Abzug had coined the saying, "This woman's place is in the House—the House of Representatives," during her run for Congress in 1970. She was also quoted as saying, "Women have been trained to speak softly and carry a lipstick. Those days are over.")

1976 Ellen McCormack ran as a Democrat in 1976, and as a third-party candidate in 1980.

1988 Patricia Scott Schroeder, a Democratic congresswoman from Colorado, runs competitively in early primaries but withdraws for lack of funds.

1990s Several Republican women run for their party's nomination, but none wins much voter support.

2000 Republican Elizabeth Dole organizes the first truly viable run by a woman for a major party nomination, although her campaign falters midway through the primaries. She is later elected to the U.S. Senate to represent her home state of North Carolina, where she served for eight years.

2004 Carol Moseley Braun, a Democratic senator from Illinois, runs in the primaries.

2008 Hillary Rodham Clinton, a Democratic senator from New York, becomes the first woman of either major party to finish the full run of state primaries with significant voter support.

In addition to women seeking the nomination of the two major parties, more than twenty-five women have run for president under the banner of smaller political parties.

Quilling

QUILLING IS A PAPER CRAFT that has been popular for hundreds of years with everyone from seventeenth-century monks to Colonial American girls to twenty-first-century scrapbookers. It involves rolling and coiling narrow strips of paper to create three-dimensional designs. Quilling gets its name from the tool that was first used to roll and shape the paper: an actual quill. Basically, to quill all you need to do is curl the very edge of a paper strip around your toothpick or other quilling tool, and then continue to wind the paper around and around until it is all rolled up. That's it! After that, it's all about creating shapes and designs out of the paper you've rolled.

WHAT YOU NEED

- A quilling tool. (There are quilling needles you can buy, but you can also just use a toothpick.)
- Paper strips (You can buy these, or you can cut your own from lightweight construction paper. They should be $1/8$ inch wide and 12 inches long.)
- Craft glue

BASIC SHAPES

Once you've rolled up the narrow paper strip, use any of these shapes to make a three-dimensional design of your imagination. You can quill paper into these shapes and leave it at that, or you can make these shapes as part of a larger design.

Tight circle

Coil the paper strip very tightly, and glue the end down before removing the paper from the toothpick or quilling tool.

Eye

Make a loose circle and then pinch both sides. This can also be made into a leaf, by bending the pointed sides slightly.

Loose circle

Coil the paper strip, and take it off the quilling tool. Let it loosen and then glue the end to make it a closed circle.

"V" shape (antennas)

Fold the paper strip into a "V" shape, and then use the quilling tool to roll just the ends on either side, rolling away from the "V" point.

Teardrop

Make a loose circle and then pinch one side.

Tendrils

Make a "V" shape with the paper strip, and roll each end of it in the same direction.

Spiral

Instead of rolling the paper on top of itself to make a coil, roll the paper around the toothpick or quilling tool in a spiral shape. When you pull the paper off, it should look like a twisting rope.

Heart

Make a "V" shape with the paper strip, and roll each end toward the center.

Peg/contoured peg

A peg is basically a small tight circle that can be used underneath another shape to give it a three-dimensional appearance. A contoured peg is made from a tight circle as well: After rolling a tight circle, gluing the end down, and taking it off the quilling tool, push the middle of the circle up from underneath. It should look like a small volcano.

"S" shape

Roll one end of the paper strip in one direction until you reach the middle of the strip; then, roll the other end in the opposite direction.

Square/rectangle

Make a loose circle and then pinch both sides to make an eye. Then, pinch the other two sides to make a square. To make a rectangle, make a loose circle and shape it into an oval before pinching the corners.

Triangle

Make a loose circle and then pinch it on one side, then the other, and then on top.

TIPS

• Be prepared: Have extra paper strips on hand in case something doesn't turn out the way you wanted. You can always redo it.

• When gluing the end of a paper strip, you can use a toothpick or narrow piece of scrap paper to dip in glue and apply to the end of the strip.

• Quill a batch of strips into coils, and after you have a bunch, get to work on shaping them and creating a design. This tends to go faster than coiling one strip of paper at a time.

• To glue your design onto background paper, take a piece of scrap paper and spread a thin layer of glue. Then, gently place your design on top of the glue to coat the bottom of it, and use tweezers (or very careful fingers) to pick up the design. Place it on the background paper and press down to fix it in place.

• To shorten a paper strip, tear it using your fingers rather than cutting it with scissors: A torn end is a softer end, which blends in better when you glue it. To make a longer strip, glue the ends of two strips together.

• Don't worry about being perfect! Like so many handmade artistic things, the small imperfections that may crop up in the quilling process make the final version that much more individual and special.

START QUILLING

Quilling can be used to make any kind of design. Here is what you need to make a simple butterfly:

- • Quilling strips:
  two 1-foot-long strips for the top wings
  two 8- or 9-inch strips for the bottom wings
  one 1-foot-long strip for the body
  one 6-inch strip for the antennae
- • Quilling needle or other tool to roll the strips
- • Craft glue
- • Toothpicks (for applying the glue)

Quill all of the strips into loose coils, except for the strip you are using for the antenna. Put a dab of glue on the ends to make each one a closed circle and to prevent the coils from unspooling. Take the strip you are using for the body and squish it down to create an oblong shape. For each of the wings, pinch one side to create a teardrop shape. Take the strip you are using for the antennae, fold it in the middle to mark the center of the strip, and then quill into a "V" shape. Then, glue the parts together to make your butterfly.

Playing the Harmonica

WHAT BETTER INSTRUMENT TO ACCOMPANY SONGS ON THE PRAIRIE, a campfire, or your next sleepout? Called the harp by those who love it, the harmonica is easy to toss in a pocket and, with some simple tips, you can play along while people sing, and then add in a repertoire of train sounds, field hollers, and howls.

What gives the harmonica its unique sound is that blowing out through a hole produces one pitch, while inhaling through that same hole produces another. Also, the harmonica doesn't just produce single notes, but whole chords. That makes it kind of like holding a full band or orchestra in your hand.

HOW TO HOLD THE HARMONICA

Stretch your left-hand thumb and fingers straight out like alligator jaws, and hold the harp in the space between them. The harp has the numbers one through ten on it. When the harp is in position, the numbers will be on top and on the side closest to your mouth. The low numbers—which correspond to the lower pitches—are on the left. If your harmonica doesn't have numbers, don't worry: Just test it out and hold the end with the lower notes to the left.

Your right hand will reach around to just about cover the back of the harmonica. You'll be sealing the back of the harmonica, and using your right hand and fingers to control the air coming in.

The harmonica actually rests inside your lower lip and close to your teeth—that's right, it really goes into your mouth, which is something that not everyone realizes. Your upper lip will come half way over the top of the harp, or even more. Your tongue will often rest on the bottom of your mouth, except when you're using it to make a special sound. And one more thing, the harp doesn't stay horizontal—tilt it up, to about a 30° angle.

TO PLAY

To breathe in through the harmonica is to *draw*, and it is the "ah" sound. To breathe out is to *blow*, and it is the "ooh" sound. As you draw and blow through the harp, think about adding consonants to the "ah" and "ooh" sounds, like such as *ha* and *hoo*, *ta* and *too*, *la* and *loo*, or *ma* and *moo*. This is one way to create different sounds.

In first position, your mouth is at the middle of the harp (around numbers 4, 5, and 6), and you blow or breathe out. To play in second position, hold the harp so your mouth is down by the lower numbers and lower pitches, and use the draw (breathing in).

Those are the basics, and now it's time to play. Try two counts of "ha" sounds and two counts of "hoo" sounds. To make a train sound: breathe out three times, and draw in once. Shake the harmonica as you play to see what happens. As you play, keep breathing in and out, and your hands and mouth will start making the sound happen.

Horses

THERE ARE HUNDREDS of different kinds of horses. Here are a few breeds you may recognize.

AMERICAN QUARTER HORSE

This breed of horses, developed in colonial America, is known for its speed and agility. It got its name because it could outrun any other horse in a quarter-mile race. The quarter horse turned out to be excellent for not only racing, but also ranching, which was crucial for Western explorers who needed horses to help them do everything from traveling great distances to roping cattle. Today, quarter horses are the most popular breed of horses, used not only for recreational riding but also on the racetrack, at rodeos, on ranches, and at horse shows.

ARABIAN

One of the oldest breeds in the world, these horses originated in the Middle East thousands of years ago. (They even appear in rock paintings in the Arabian Peninsula from as far back as 2500 BCE.) Arabians are famous for their intelligence, stamina, and speed, and are recognizable by their distinctive heads and high tails. Nearly every modern riding horse today has Arabian bloodlines.

CLYDESDALE

The Clydesdale is a kind of draft horse, a horse bred for difficult tasks such as ploughing, doing farmwork, or carrying heavy loads. Clydesdales originally came from Scotland about three hundred years ago and are notable for their formidable height and weight (they can be as much as 6 feet high and weigh nearly 2,000 pounds!), as well as for their large hooves and the white feathery hairs falling from knee to hoof like bell-bottomed pants. As recently as the 1960s, these horses were common sights in towns, where they pulled carts for vendors selling milk and vegetables. Nowadays, they are rarer (although they have starred in several television commercials): They have an estimated worldwide population of just five thousand.

LIPIZZAN

Lipizzan horses, also called Lipizzaners (pronounced "LIP-it-sahn" or "LIP-it-sahn-er"), are named for the Austrian town Lippiza, where the breed was first developed in the sixteenth century. Lipizzaners are sturdy horses. They are born dark brown or black in color, but by the time they are about ten years old, their coat is completely white. They are precise movers and are often trained to do dance steps. If you've ever seen "dancing horses" in a parade, they were probably Lipizzaners. These horses had a brush with danger during World War II, but the United States intervened under General George Patton and 250 Lipizzans were saved. Today, there are around three thousand of these horses worldwide.

SHETLAND PONY

Shetland ponies originated in the Scottish Shetland Isles, where they were used to plough farmland and pull carts in coal mines. They are strong, intelligent, and very small: Even the tallest Shetland pony is only about 42 inches high (just about the size of your average second- or third-grader). Shetlands are possibly the strongest of all horse breeds, as they can pull fully twice their own weight and can live as long as thirty years. Today, the ponies no longer have to work in the mines. They are mostly used as children's riding ponies and are seen at carnivals, fairs, and petting zoos. Some of the smaller Shetlands, called Miniature Shetlands, have also been trained as "guide horses," which, like guide dogs, help guide people who are blind.

THOROUGHBRED

Thoroughbreds are best known as racing horses. They were first developed in seventeenth- and eighteenth-century England and bred for their speed and hot-tempered spirit. Thoroughbreds are the fastest horses, able to run as much as 40 miles per hour. They are also able to race at a very young age: You can ride a Thoroughbred when she's just one year old. They are also excellent jumpers and are often used in traditional games of polo (where players ride horses and swing at balls with a mallet). There are millions of Thoroughbreds around the world, and nearly 120,000 Thoroughbred babies (called *foals*) born each year.

MUSTANG

Mustangs are often called *wild horses*, but their name actually means "stray" or "feral"—untamed, wide-ranging horses that live in herds and roam free. Mustangs are the descendants of horses brought to Mexico and Florida from Spain four hundred years ago. Small, fast, and spirited, many of these horses escaped to the wide North American West. Some mustangs were adopted by Native Americans, who used them for transportation, and then by North American settlers, who used them for exploring, trading, and even bringing mail across the Wild West as part of the Pony Express. Mustangs still exist in the United States today. Nearly forty years ago, in 1971, Congress officially recognized mustangs as "living symbols of the historic and pioneer spirit of the West, which continue to contribute to the diversity of life forms within the Nation and enrich the lives of the American people."

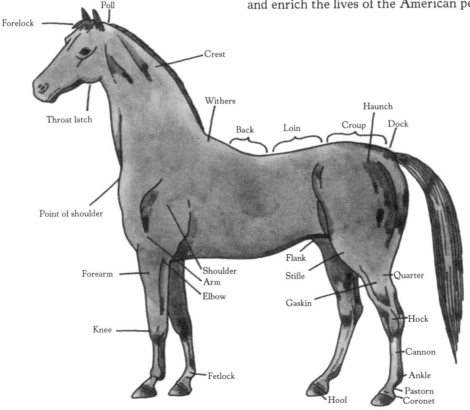

WALK, TROT, CANTER, AND GALLOP

A *gait* is the way a horse moves. There are *natural* gaits, which are basically walking and running the way a horse may do naturally; and *ambling* gaits, which are specialized ways of moving that generally involve humans training horses to walk and run in ways the horses probably never imagined. When you ride a horse for fun, you stick to the natural gaits—which is fun for the horse as well.

Walking is the slowest gait, moving along at about 4 miles per hour. When a horse walks, she puts her hooves down in this order: left hind leg, left front leg, right hind leg, right front leg. This creates a steady 1-2-3-4 rhythm.

A *trot* is the gait that's most comfortable for a horse. It's a bit faster than a walk, at about 8 miles per hout, and it's a two-beat gait. When a horse trots, she puts two legs down at the same time: left hind leg and right front leg together, then right hind leg and left front leg together: 1-2-1-2.

Cantering, which is a bit faster than a trot, is a three-beat gait. When a horse canters, it sounds a bit like someone drumming her fingers: 1-2-3, 1-2-3.

A *gallop* is a full-out run, with a quick 1-2-3-4 rhythm. When a horse gallops, she can go as fast as 25 to 30 miles per hour. This is the gait used by a horse when running away from predators or racing against other horses, and a horse can gallop for as long as a mile before needing a rest. The American Quarter Horse has the fastest gallop at 55 miles per hour.

Sailing Phrases

SAILING IS SOMETHING people now do for fun. But once upon a time, sailing ships were the only way to travel between continents, at least those that were separated by water. It took many sailors and many months to get from place to place. Ships were small worlds, complete with their own words and phrases. Even today, once you step aboard a ship, the usual words no longer apply. All of a sudden, a rope is a *line*. *Aye* is used instead of yes. Right and left become *starboard* and *port*. From the sailors and tall sailing ships that once roamed the oceans of the world come many of English's saltier phrases.

Above board
Up on the deck. Things that everyone can see in plain view.

Ahoy
Traditional Viking battle cry later used to hail and greet other vessels.

Bail
To get out of a tough situation. Comes from bucketing water from a boat that's taken too many waves or, as a last resort, jumping ship.

Batten down the hatch
To prepare for disaster, strengthen the defense. The hatch covers the entry into the halls and rooms below deck. Battens are strips of wood larger than the hatch, which hold down these covers in a storm.

Bear down
To focus on a goal, to sail quickly toward a landmark or another ship.

Cup of joe
Coffee. In 1913, President Woodrow Wilson appointed Josephus Daniels to be Secretary of the Navy. Daniels introduced women into the navy, and he also abolished wine from the ships, the result being that the strongest drink available to sailors was coffee, which was renamed "cup of joe" after Daniels's first name.

Flying colors
You've done well. Colored flags fly on the tallest mast to identify the ship. If a ship goes down in battle, the flags no longer fly; if a ship wins, the colors fly high.

Flotsam and jetsam
Odds and ends, this and that. Flotsam is the cargo from a wrecked ship that floats to the water's surface. Jetsam are things that are jettisoned, or thrown overboard, to protect the ship in a storm by making it more stable. (Sometimes jetsam are attached to a rope so that with some luck they can be retrieved after the storm, in which case they are called *lagan*.)

Footloose
Free-spirited, with nothing to hold you down. Name of the bottom part of a sail (called the *foot*) when it's properly secured and dancing happily in the wind.

Know the ropes
To have skill born from experience. Sailing ships have ropes, called *lines*, everywhere. Sailors know these intimately as they steer and capture and make use of wind.

Mayday
Help. The international distress call for trouble at sea. Comes from the French *m'aidez*, meaning "help me."

Rummage sale
The odds and ends of damaged cargo were sold when ships arrived in port. Comes from the French word *arrimage*, which means "ship's cargo."

Safe harbor
A cove to protect you and your boat from a storm.

Scuttlebutt
Gossip, small talk, and rumor. *Butt* is the nautical word for a wooden barrel. *Scuttle* is a square or rectangular hole, often cut in the deck or the side of a ship for light, air, or communication. Scuttlebutt is a medium-sized hole in the side of a water barrel into which sailors could drop a cup, pull out water to drink, and of course, trade tales and information while they did.

Show your true colors

To be your genuine, authentic self, with no fiction or pretense. Battleships flew flags that identified their names and their nations, according to the rules of engagement. In battle, some ships tried to confuse their opponents by hoisting flags other than their own. Once they got within close range, they would fly their true-colored flag and take aim.

Squared away

Fixed or solved. Comes from the look of sails on a square-rigged sailboat when trimmed and square.

Stem the tide

To divert an opposing force or trend. A boat with sufficient momentum, push, and wind could sail against and overcome the tide.

Swamped

Overwhelmed. A boat filled with water from tall and stormy waves.

Take the wind from their sails

To deflate someone's sense of achievement or pride. Comes from boats that sailed in such a way as to actually steal, by interrupting or getting in the way of, the wind another boat needed to sail.

The bitter end

The very last moment. A boat's anchor is connected by a rope to a post on the deck, and this post is called a *bitt*. If the rope unwinds fully off the bitt, it means the water is deeper than originally thought and the anchor isn't holding to the sea floor.

ALPHA BRAVO CHARLIE

Ever wonder what's going on when someone aboard a ship calls the coast guard and says, "I'm at coordinate Juliet 5"? She's using the International Phonetic Alphabet where every letter has a word, so no one ever has to ask "Did you say B or D?"

A Alpha	B Bravo	C Charlie	D Delta	E Echo	F Foxtrot
G Golf	H Hotel	I India	J Juliet	K Kilo	L Lima
M Mike	N November	O Oscar	P Papa	Q Quebec	R Romeo
S Sierra	T Tango	U Uniform	V Victor	W Whiskey	X X-ray
		Y Yankee	Z Zulu		

Worry Dolls

ORRY DOLLS, sometimes called trouble dolls, are small, handmade dolls from Guatemala. Parents and children have made these dolls for centuries to help soothe the fears of worried children. Traditional worry dolls, made in sets of six, are about a half inch to two inches in height and are usually made from bits of wood or clay, with colorful fabric or thread wrapped around the doll for clothing. Tradition has it that when a child is worried or anxious at bedtime, she can tell her troubles to one of these tiny dolls and then place it under her pillow. A different doll can be used each night for six nights in a row, by which point all worries should be gone.

Worry dolls were made originally from cast-off bits of fabric, splinters of wood, and other scraps people had on hand. Modern doll makers can stay true to this spirit by using household materials. Popsicle sticks, clothespins, toothpicks, stiff cardboard, pipe cleaners, or even plastic twist ties can be used to fashion the dolls' bodies. Thread, string, thin yarn, or even dental floss can be repurposed as doll clothes.

MATERIALS
- 2 flexible, plastic twist ties (each about 4 inches long)
- Embroidery thread or very thin yarn (6 strands, each about 20 to 24 inches long)
- 1 bead for the head (¼ inch or smaller, with a hole for threading)
- Permanent marker
- Glue
- Scissors

Making the body. Bend one twist tie in half. Twist it once or twice in the middle. The loop on top will be your doll's head, and the ends on the bottom will be the legs (Figure 1). Curl the very ends of the legs to make tiny loops for the doll's feet. Bend the other twist tie in half, and wrap it around the middle of the other twist tie to create the arms (Figure 2).

Making the clothes. Embroidery thread is perfect for this project, because it comes in thick strands. (Regular thread is too thin, unless you are making a very tiny doll, and most yarns are too thick, unless you are making a very big one.) So, using your embroidery thread or very thin yarn, cut 6 lengths of about 20 to 24 inches each. Then, take one length of the thread and wrap it around your doll frame, starting with the feet. Put the thread through the loop on the bottom of one foot to secure it, and then begin wrapping the thread around and up the leg. If your thread is long enough, you can continue wrapping up to the waist and then down the other leg; otherwise, end the wrap at the waist and use a second strand to wrap the other leg starting at the foot. Continue on using another thread for the midsection and one thread for each arm (Figure 3).

Tip: You can put a tiny bit of glue on the twist tie frame to help the thread stay on as you begin to wrap. To end a wrapped section, pull the thread tight and use glue to secure it. (Put a dab of glue on your finger and apply it to the ending point where threads are not secured. Press down and spread the glue in the same direction as the threads.)

Making the head and hair. Place the bead on top of the loop to make the doll's face (Figure 4) and use a permanent marker to draw a face on the bead. There should still be a bit of loop showing above the bead. This is what you'll be using as the "frame" for your doll's hair, as you tie thread all around it. Take a strand of embroidery thread and put just about 2 inches of it through the loop above the bead. Tie a double knot to secure the thread to the loop, and then cut the long side of the thread to match the other side. Then, tie another knot next to that, repeating the process until the entire twist tie above the bead is covered by thread (Figure 5). Then, push that loop of tied thread forward and down to make the hair cover the top of the bead (Figure 6).

How you style the hair is up to you. You can put a little bit of glue on your fingers and use it to smooth the hair down and keep the strands together. You can trim all the ends to make a shorter haircut. You can even separate all the tiny threads in each strand to make gigantic hair.

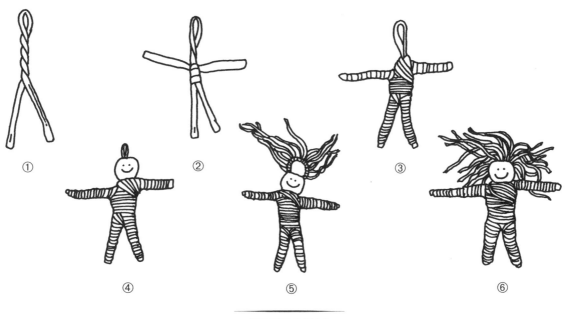

Measurements

FROM TIME IMMEMORIAL, humans have developed systems to measure distance, weight, and speed. Then they tried to get everyone else to agree to them. It's not an easy job. In the Roman Empire, no one was sure whether it was harder to be emperor or the official in charge of weights and measures at the local market.

The United States uses the U.S. Customary system of measurements, which is known in Great Britain as the Imperial System, so called because back in the day when the British ruled so much of the world, they made sure that all their subjects followed their standard of inches, feet, yards, ounces, and pounds.

The metric system was created in the 1790s by a group of French scientists who wanted a more rational basis for measurement than the human thumb. By contrast, the metric unit of distance, the meter, was said to be one 10-millionth of the distance between the Earth's equator and the North Pole (although, as the story goes, this distance was miscalculated, and the meter was wrongly measured for many years!). After World War II especially, many nations suggested that a worldwide system be adopted that would make trade and scientific exchange easier. That system is the metric-based *Système international d'unités*, abbreviated as SI, and is based on the meter, liter, and kilogram.

Most nations of the world have decided in favor of the metric system. The United States has officially adopted the metric system, but, like many countries, has not wanted to forgo its traditional measurements.

LENGTH AND DISTANCE

Inch	in. (")	In Rome, the width of an adult thumb, or the space between the first knuckle and tip of your pointer finger. Good to know if you need to measure and no ruler is nearby.
Foot	ft. (')	12 inches; based originally on the human foot
Yard	yd.	3 feet; originally the length from the nose to the top of the middle finger of an outstretched arm
Mile	mi.	1,760 yards, or 5,280 feet

There are actually two kinds of miles: stature miles, or miles on land, and nautical miles, or miles at sea or in the air. The measurement of a statute mile is based on the number of inches in a mile. The measurement of the nautical mile is calculated from the distance around the equator. That distance is divided into 360 degrees (or parts). Each degree is divided into 60 minutes. Each of the resulting 21,600 minutes is called a nautical mile. The equator is 24,902 miles long, which, when divided by 21,600 minutes, yields 1.15 miles, otherwise known as a nautical mile.

ARCHAIC MEASUREMENTS BASED ON BODY PARTS

The measurements of the U.S. Customary system come originally from Rome, where the inch was based on the width of the human thumb.

Digit	The width of a finger, about ¾ inch
Palm	The width of the palm, about 3 inches
Hand	4 inches; now used to measure the height of horses
Span	The size of an open hand, from pinky to thumb, about 9 inches
Cubit	The measurement of the forearm, about 18 inches
Fathom	Total arm span, measured from the fingertips, about 6 feet
Pace	A stride, about 5 feet
Millarium	1,000 paces; in Latin, mille passus; about 5,000 feet; the origin of our word mile

WEIGHT

Ounce	oz.	The abbreviation comes from the Latin *uncia*
Pound	lb. (#)	16 ounces. The abbreviation comes from the Latin word *libra*, meaning "weight and scale." A pound weight was called *libra pondo*, hence the abbreviation *lb*.
Ton	T.	2,000 pounds equal 1 ton, unless you are in Britain, where a long ton equals 2,240 pounds. To make the matter even more complex, the metric ton, or *tonne*, equals 1,000 kilograms and around 2,204 pounds.

APOTHECARY WEIGHTS

The troy system is also called the Apothecary system. It is used to measure things that are lighter than an ounce, like such as gold, silver, platinum, rubies, and precious stones or powders that pharmacists grind and combine to make medicine (and from there comes the name of the system, *apothecary* being the antique name for a pharmacy). This system predates the system we use now, and is based on the grain (there are 480 grains in a single ounce!) The troy system was replaced by the *avoirdupois* (French for "goods of weight") system, which is the basis of the system we use now.

Grain	The basic apothecary measurement; very light and small, equals $1/480$ of a troy ounce; originally based on the weight of a grain of barleycorn
Scruple	20 grains, or $1/24$ ounce
Dram	3 scruples, or 60 grains, or $1/8$ ounce
Troy ounce	480 grains, or 8 drams, or 24 scruples
Troy pound	12 ounces

VOLUME: DRY AND LIQUID

Teaspoon	t., tsp.	$^1/_3$ tablespoon
Tablespoon	T., tbsp.	3 teaspoons; 1 tablespoon equals ½ fluid ounce and 15 milliliters.
Fluid ounce	fl. oz.	2 tablespoons, or 6 teaspoons
Cup	c.	8 fluid ounces, or 16 tablespoons
Pints	pt.	2 cups, or 16 ounces
Quarts	qt.	2 pints, or 32 ounces
Gallon	gal.	4 quarts, or 8 pints
Peck	pk.	8 quarts of dry weight
Bushel	bu.	4 pecks
Barrel	bbl.	Has varied with time and use: 42 gallons if petroleum, 31.5 gallons if wine, and 30 if the barrel is filled with beer. The abbreviation *bbl* stands for the Blue Barrel, which holds 42 gallons.

MEASUREMENTS OF LAND

One acre	ac.	43,560 square feet, or 4,840 square yards, or .002 square miles
Square mile	sq. mi.	640 acres

METRIC SYSTEM PREFIXES

In the metric system, prefixes attach to basic units such as meter for distance, liter for liquid measure, and gram for weight. There are twenty prefixes in all, and each prefix raises or lowers the value by a power of ten.

Yottameter	Zettameter	Exameter	Petameter	Terameter	Gigameter	Megameter
Y	Z	E	P	T	G	M
1 septillion meters	1 sextillion meters	1 quintillion meters	1 quadrillion meters	1 trillion meters	1 billion meters	1 million meters
Kilometer	Hectometer	Decameter	Meter	Decimeter	Centimeter	Millimeter
k	h	da	m	d	c	m
1 thousand meters	100 meters	10 meters	1 meter (basic unit)	1 tenth of a meter	1 hundredth of a meter	1 thousandth of a meter
Micrometer	Nanometer	Picometer	Ferntometer	Attometer	Zeptometer	Yoctometer
µ—the Greek letter mu	n	p	f	a	z	y
1 millionth of a meter	1 billionth of a meter	1 trillionth of a meter	1 quadrillionth of a meter	1 quintillionth of a meter	1 sextillionth of a meter	1 septillionth of a meter

WORDS FOR REALLY LARGE NUMBERS

Name	In power of ten (and the number of zeros)
Billion	10^9
Trillion	10^{12}
Quadrillion	10^{15}
Quintillion	10^{18}
Sextillion	10^{21}
Septillion	10^{24}
Octillion	10^{27}
Nonillion	10^{30}
Decillion	10^{33}
Undecillion	10^{36}
Duodecillion	10^{39}
Tredecillion	10^{42}
Quattredecillion	10^{45}
Quindecillion	10^{48}
Sexdecillion	10^{51}
Septendecillion	10^{54}
Octodecillion	10^{57}
Novemdecillion	10^{60}
Vigintillion	10^{63}
Centillion	10^{303}

WONDERFUL MEASUREMENT WORDS TO KNOW

Ampere — Measures the amount of electrical current

Astronomical Unit — A distance measurement, equal to the distance from the earth to the sun

Butt — 2 hogsheads, or 126 gallons

Calorie — Measures heat that is produced from activity

City block — In Manhattan, a north-south block, 20 of which equal 1 mile

Clove — 7 to 10 pounds of wool or cheese; archaic term

Cord — 128 cubic feet of wood

Curie — Measures the intensity of radioactive decay

Danjon — Name of scale that measures the brightness of a solar eclipse

Dash — In cooking, a very small amount

Decibel — Measures the intensity of sound

Dol — Measures the intensity of pain

Elephant — A large paper size, 28 × 23 inches; archaic term

Ell — 45 inches; archaic term

Enhanced Fujita — Name of the scale, from 0 to 5, that measures tornadoes

Fathom — 6 feet; measures depth in the water

Femtosecond — Used in laser technology and measures time; 1 quadrillionth of a second

Furlong — 220 yards; used in horse racing

Gill — ¼ pint of liquid

Hertz — Measures the frequency of vibrations and waves; abbreviated Hz

Hide — 120 acres of land; archaic term

Hobbet — 2½ bushels

Hogshead — 63 gallons

Horsepower — Measures power; 550 foot-pounds of work per second

Jansky — Measures the strength of radio wave emissions

Jiffy — Equals $^1/_{100}$ second, or any short passing of time

Kip — 1,000 pounds

Langley — Measures solar radiation

League — 5.56 kilometers, or the distance that can be walked in 1 hour

Light-year — The distance that light travels in 1 year

Mil — Measures the thickness of wire; 1 mil equals $^1/_{1,000}$ inch

Morgan — Measures distance between genes on a chromosome

Mutchkin — ¾ of an imperial pint; archaic term

Parsec — 3.26 light-years

Pottle — 2 quarts, or ½ gallon

Quire — 25 sheets of paper

Ream — 20 quires, or 500 sheets of paper; 10 reams equals 1 bale

Rundlet — 18 wine gallons before 1824, after which it was a mere 15 Imperial gallons

Stone — 14 pounds

TORRO — Scale, from 1 to 10, for measuring the intensity of hailstorms

Electric Buzzer Game

HERE IS A SIMPLE GAME that you and a friend can build yourselves. The goal is to move a home-made wand the length of a curvy wire hooked up to a battery and a buzzer—without touching the wire. The secret to the game is the circuit of wires that you construct. The circuit is open and not electrified until the wand touches the curvy wire and closes the circuit. That closure sends electricity flowing through the whole circuit, and that's when the buzzer goes off.

One safety concern to state up front: When you put the game away, always disconnect the wires from the battery so it won't overheat. (You can draw a special reminder on the box and set up a place to hook one of the wires.)

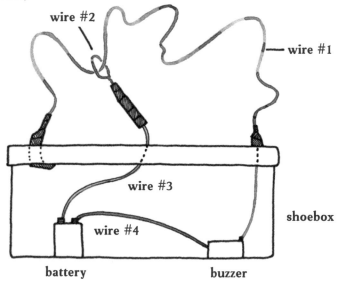

MATERIALS AND TOOLS

- Box . This can be a shoe box, or any box with a cover. Almost any box can be made to work.

- Copper wire, 16 or 18 gauge. You can also use a metal clothes hanger, but some can be hard to bend.

- Bell wire. Also known as primary wire. Coated in colorful plastic. Use a 16 or 18 gauge thickness.

- Electrical tape or duct tape (or both).

- A 9-volt battery. The battery can be changed out when it runs out of energy after a lot of play. For a battery that lasts longer, try a 6-volt lantern battery, which is larger, and also has two coils on top that make connecting the wires very easy.

- Buzzer. Ask at the hardware store. You'll need to pry off the top off to connect wires to it, but that's common and easily done.

- Tools such as wire strippers and wire cutters (which are often the same tool), long-nose pliers for twisting wires together, and a screwdriver.

Step 1

Assemble all your gear. Put the buzzer and the battery inside the box.

Step 2

Poke three holes in the top of the shoebox: one at the front center and one near each of the sides, as in the illustration. (If your box has flapped covers, just adjust the directions so that you make all three holes in one of the flaps.)

Step 3

The copper wire is the long game wire that bends and curves. We'll call it wire #1. Cut 36 inches of it, more or less depending on your box and how many curves you want (it can always be trimmed later). Work it into a wavy design. Pull the right end of the wire through the right hole in the box, and leave it to dangle below for the time being. Use some electrical tape to hold this part of the wire in place at the hole. Tape the wire at the top of the hole, and then wrap the tape around the wire for about an inch above the box. Leave the left side alone for now.

Step 4

The loop of the playing wand is also cut from copper wire. We'll call this wire #2. Know that the smaller the loop is, the harder the game will be. Cut 8 to 10 inches of copper wire and fashion a loop, wrapping the end several times around the rest of the wire to hold it fast. Set aside. Later on, it will be connected to wire #3.

Step 5

The handle of the playing wand is made from bell wire. This is wire #3. Cut an 18-inch piece of bell wire; depending on the size of your box, you may need more or less. With the wire stripper, remove 1½ inches of coating from each end. If you're just learning to use a wire stripper, work off a half an inch at a time, pressing hard enough to cut the plastic, but not so hard that you cut the wire. If you're new at this, cut a few extra inches of bell wire to give yourself room for mistakes.

Step 6

To make the playing wand, attach one end of this wire (#3) to the copper loop (wire #2). Make sure that the metal of both wires is touching. Wind the wires together (long-nose pliers can help). Then, wrap the connection with several layers of electrical tape, and cover 4 to 5 inches of the wand. All those layers should feel good in your hand and help you control the wand, and of course, protect your fingers from the heat of electricity coursing through the uncovered copper wire. The other end of this wire will eventually be connected to the battery. For now, pull the bell wire through the center front hole in the box, and let it dangle.

Step 7

The second piece of bell wire connects the buzzer and the battery inside the box. This is wire #4. Cut it 6 to 8 inches long, depending on the size

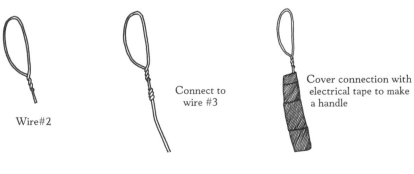

Wire#2

Connect to
wire #3

Cover connection with
electrical tape to make
a handle

of the box. Strip 1½ inches of covering from each end to open up the metal. Set it aside.

Step 8

Pick up the loop of the playing wand (wires #2 and #3) and thread it onto the curvy game wire (wire #1). Now you can connect the game wire to the box. Take hold of the left end. Wrap the last few inches of it with electrical tape. Once the game is put together, this will be a place for the playing wand to rest. Push this left end through the left hole in the box, and secure it with electrical tape on the underside. This end of the wire does not connect to the rest of the circuit.

Step 9

The battery and the buzzer are already in the box. Attach the right end of the long curvy game wire (wire #1) to the buzzer. Buzzers vary, but they are made to be connected to wires, which means the next step may be new to you, but it shouldn't be too hard. When you pop the top off the buzzer, you should see two coils. Next to them will be either one or two screws. Loosen one of the screws with a screwdriver, hook the end of the wire around it, and then retighten the screw so the wire stays put.

Step 10

Attach the playing wand (wire #3) to one of the battery's terminals.

Step 11

Pick up the shorter wire that connects the battery and the buzzer (wire #4). Hook one end tightly to the battery's other terminal. As you do, make sure this wire doesn't touch the wire that's already connected. If you think the wires need some help to stay in place on the battery, use some electrical tape.

Step 12

Working with the same wire (wire #4), hook the other end to the buzzer. (Rest the playing wand on the taped area of the curvy game wire—or ask someone else to hold it there for you. That way, it won't touch the curvy wire, close the circuit, and make everything buzz while you're trying to connect it.) Most buzzers will have a second screw inside, and you should connect this wire to that second screw. When you do, make sure that it doesn't accidentally touch the other wire connected there. Some buzzers may not have a second screw. If so, look around for any way to connect the wire. If the base of the buzzer is metal, all you'll need to do is touch the wire to the base, and it's good to go.

Step 13

Last thing, about safety. When you're done playing, you will need to unhook the short wire (wire #4) from the buzzer or from the battery (whichever is easier). Make that special place on the box where you can hook it until you're ready to play again.

The game is ready. If touching the wand to the game wire doesn't make the buzzer sound, double-check that all the connections are tight, and retest the game. If it still doesn't work, try a new battery.

Now that you know how the wiring works, you can change any part of the game. The wand can be made smaller or larger, and twists and turns to the game wire can be added, or taken away. Just cut new wires and use them to replace the old ones.

Being a Private Eye

L IKE BEING A SPY, being a private eye is all about observing, amassing information, and following clues to uncover a story.

Private eyes are also known as private investigators (PIs) or detectives. The first private detective agency was founded in 1833 in France by a man named Eugène François Vidocq. The Scottish detective Alan Pinkerton started the first U.S. agency, the Pinkerton National Detective Agency, in the 1850s.

Probably the most famous girl detective is Nancy Drew, the heroine of more than one hundred novels. From the first Nancy Drew mystery published in 1930 to the series published today, every adventure involves Nancy solving mysteries by using her powers of deduction (and her best friends).

Millions of girls have been inspired by Nancy Drew, and if you'd like to follow in her footsteps and start your very own private eye agency, here's what you need to know in order to do it. (Of course, the most important thing to know is that you should do this for fun—private eyes who charge money for their services are required by law to have a special private investigator's license!)

TOOLS OF THE TRADE

A private eye should always have on hand a small notebook (we prefer a 4-by-8-inch reporter's notebook or a stash of index cards) and a favorite pen, plus a few backups just in case. Binoculars, sunglasses, and a flashlight are also a good idea. She may also have a camera, for snapping surveillance photos, and a small tape recorder, for dictating notes; if she's really fancy, she may have a cell phone or GPS device. But the secret to being a good PI isn't the technology or the connections you have (employing your friends to act as snitches or lookouts), it's the ability to be patient, to notice little things as well as big things, and to watch, listen, and learn.

OTHER SKILLS

Beyond powers of observation (looking and listening) and deduction (drawing conclusions from bits of evidence), a successful PI should be able to communicate. That means she must be comfortable interacting with people—be able to ask questions when she needs to, and be able to clearly communicate her findings to her clients. She must also be able to write well: The end result of any case is the investigative report, which is a write-up of what the PI has observed over the course of her surveillance. Being able to present the facts clearly and simply is crucial. Another crucial skill is the ability to focus on the facts. That means relentless pursuit of the truth and reporting that is complete and unbiased. Opinions are for clients: They can draw their own conclusions from the facts a PI presents.

A few other things to remember: First, always obey the law. Second, never jump to conclusions; instead, simply gather evidence. And third, don't take matters into your own hands. Turn your evidence over to your client, and let her or him decide what to do with it.

One of the main techniques of a private investigator is the stakeout, which is all about watching, listening, and observing. During a stakeout, a PI stays hidden. She never interacts with the subject she's observing, and she never does anything illegal. She simply gathers data, like a scientist, or follows leads, like a reporter, and reports to the client what she's observed.

SETTING UP SHOP AND FINDING A CASE

First, make a name for yourself. Pick a name for your private-eye agency. If you're working on your own, this could be literally just your name (Emi Buchanan, PI; The Baird Sisters, Private Investigators). If you're working with friends, you could come up with a more descriptive name (Super Spies, Inc.; or PIE, Private Investigator Enterprises) or anything you think is catchy (The Daring Girls Detective Agency!).

Then, make a business card. This should have, at the very least, the name of your business. If you'd like, you can design a logo (a picture representing your business), or you can just have your business name in big letters.

Finally, to find a case, you have to network. That means letting other people know about your PI agency. Hand out your business card to friends and family (you never know who could be a potential client), put an ad in your school newspaper, or hang a sign on your locker. Let other people know what you're up to, and if a case happens to come along, you'll be the first person they think of.

How to Play Croquet

WIMBLEDON'S FAMED GRASS tennis courts were once croquet greens where Victorian women broke social convention by publicly competing in games of croquet. Many people know croquet from the memorable story of the Queen of Hearts' riotous game in *Alice in Wonderland*; others might know it as a fancy game with all-white clothes and a century's worth of complicated rules. But there is plenty of fun to be had playing croquet in your backyard or a nearby park or field, enjoying yourself and wearing whatever you please.

Croquet gear is usually sold as a set, complete with croquet mallets and balls, nine wire wickets, and two stakes. You may be lucky enough to find some old mallets in the attic or at a yard sale.

HOW TO SET UP AND PLAY

A regulation croquet court is generally 50 feet wide by 100 feet long. Set yours up to fit the space you have. The wickets are set into the ground in a figure-eight pattern. At the top and bottom of the court, there's an extra wicket and, behind it, a stake in the ground.

Croquet can be played as singles or in teams. Singles can decide to play with one or two balls. To begin the game, each player chooses a same-colored ball and mallet. The stakes that are part of the court show the game order of the colors, which is blue, red, black, yellow, green, orange. (Exceptions: If you play with four players, you'll use this order instead: blue, red, black, and yellow. If there are two sides, the formal rules of croquet suggest the sides should be blue, black, and green versus red, yellow, and orange.)

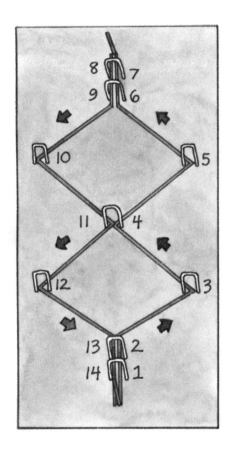

The game starts at the bottom of the court. Place the ball halfway between the bottom stake and the first wicket. Strike the ball with the mallet so it rolls through each wicket in order. The goal is to strike your ball through the wickets up the right side of the figure eight, through the double wickets at the top, and tap the top peg. Then, come back through the wickets on the left side of the court and under the double wickets at the bottom. Tap the bottom peg to finish. If you get there first, you win.

HOW TO USE THE MALLET

Strike the ball with the smaller side of the mallet, not the broad, longer surface. If you really need to whack the ball, hold the croquet mallet like a golf club and go for it. Otherwise, and most of the time, the mallet is never held like a golf club, and a calmer and gentler swing is used. Face the ball and your target. Hold the mallet in two hands, and allow it to swing from between your legs like a pendulum.

Line up the mallet, the ball, and your target. This may be the next wicket or your opponent's ball. Stand back and practice the swing. This is called "stalking the ball." Look for bumps and craters in the grass that may unexpectedly change the ball's course. When you're ready, step forward toward the ball and swing.

Here are some grips to try. In a Solomon grip, the knuckles of both hands line up in the front of the mallet. The thumbs are behind. In an Irish grip, the hands and knuckles line up behind the stick, with thumbs in front. In a standard grip, the knuckles of the top hand face front and the knuckles of the bottom hand face backward. Whichever you choose, move your hands up and down the mallet until you find a comfortable spot and the most control.

HOW TO SCORE

Every player hits balls through the wickets, in proper game order. Each wicket earns a point and a continuation shot. A continuation is a bonus shot. Continuations allow you to keep striking as long as you are getting things accomplished on the court. You can keep earning continuations as long as you strike your ball through a wicket, hit a stake, or hit an opponent's ball. The latter bears some explanation. Hitting your opponent's ball is called *roqueting*. You can do it only once in a turn, but it is an important and popular croquet move. You push their ball away from the wicket so that you can get ahead. Even better, a *roquet* gets you two continuation shots. This means you can set up a two-shot strategy for getting your ball through the next wicket—and without worrying that someone else will *roquet* your ball away!

Once you get into croquet, there are neat moves you can make. Here's one for when you roquet an opponent: Pick up your ball. Put it on the ground next to your opponent's so that they touch. Hold your ball down with your toe, and strike it. If this is done right, your ball stays where it is. Your opponent's ball, however, will have been hoisted across the green.

GOLF CROQUET

Several croquet games are played with six wickets, and golf croquet is one of them. If you're watching professional golf croquet (and there really is such a thing), the court will be large—84 feet wide by 105 feet long. At home, you'll use whatever size field you have. The stake goes in the middle, and the wickets are set up around it, as in the illustration on the next page.

Singles can play with either one or two balls, and two players can form a team, each with a ball of their own. Blue, red, black, yellow is the sequence of the balls.

The game begins when players strike the ball in from the corner near the fourth wicket. Each wicket and the stake has but a single point to give. Whoever hits her ball through a wicket first gets the point for that wicket. (In some games, players have colorful clips that snap onto a wicket to keep track of who won that point.) Once a player gets a wicket, every player starts to shoot for the next wicket. In other words, when one player gets the first wicket, everyone now goes for the second, whether or not they've made it through the first, and in this way, golf croquet is very different from regular croquet, where every player must get every wicket.

In golf croquet, each turn has only one shot. There are no bonuses, no continuation shots. The winner is the player who reaches the majority points first. It works like this: The shortest game is seven points. It is played with six wickets and the stake, but whoever reaches four points first wins the game. The stake is there in case both teams have three points and a tiebreaker is needed. The thirteen-point game uses the same six wickets. Then they are repeated in a backward order. The illustration shows how this works. There's a thirteenth wicket in case a 6-6 tie has to be decided. Of course, the game can be made more complicated. Professional golf croquet in particular has all sorts of fancy rules about faults and halfway lines, which you may want to learn about for more of a challenge.

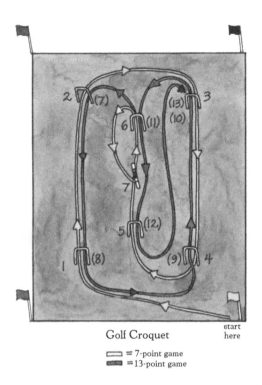

Golf Croquet

start here

▭ = 7-point game

▬ = 13-point game

THE QUEEN'S CROQUET GROUNDS

"Get to your places!" shouted the Queen in a voice of thunder, and people began running about in all directions, tumbling up against each other; however, they got settled down in a minute or two, and the game began. Alice thought she had never seen such a curious croquet-ground in her life; it was all ridges and furrows; the balls were live hedgehogs, the mallets live flamingoes, and the soldiers had to double themselves up and to stand on their hands and feet, to make the arches.

The chief difficulty Alice found at first was in managing her flamingo: she succeeded in getting its body tucked away, comfortably enough, under her arm, with its legs hanging down, but generally, just as she had got its neck nicely straightened out, and was going to give the hedgehog a blow with its head, it *would* twist itself round and look up in her face, with such a puzzled expression that she could not help bursting out laughing: and when she had got its head down, and was going to begin again, it was very provoking to find that the hedgehog had unrolled itself, and was in the act of crawling away: besides all this, there was generally a ridge or furrow in the way wherever she wanted to send the hedgehog to, and, as the doubled-up soldiers were always getting up and walking off to other parts of the ground, Alice soon came to the conclusion that it was a very difficult game indeed.

— *Alice's Adventures in Wonderland,*
Chapter VIII, by Lewis Carroll

Surfing

I T WAS IN 1778 THAT CAPTAIN JAMES COOK and his crew first encountered the Polynesian art of using planks of wood to ride waves. The European sailors, barely able to believe their eyes, dubbed it "the royal sport of kings." By the beginning of the twentieth century, Hawaii had become the surf capital of the world, with tourists flocking to the tropical beaches in hopes of learning how to ride the waves.

But surfing wasn't just the sport of "kings," it was the sport of "queens" as well. From its very start, surfing was something done by men and women, boys and girls. In fact, the ocean off the coast of Honolulu, just west of Waikiki, is named after Mamala, a figure in Polynesian mythology who was not only a shape-shifting goddess (who could take the form of a crocodile, shark, or woman), but also an accomplished surfer. Today, girls and women around the world surf both competitively and for fun.

SURFBOARDS

Most surf beaches have surf shops where you can rent boards, or you could borrow one from a friend or relative. There are a few basic kinds of surfboards: longboards, funboards, and shortboards.

Longboards, sometimes called Malibu boards, are 8 to 14 feet long. These foam boards are fast, with a rounded nose, and have one fin. Make sure to choose the correct height: The longboard should be 14 inches taller than you and at least 20 inches wide. These are considered the best boards for beginners, because their thickness and length make the board more stable for catching waves and standing up. Funboards, also called mini-mals, are a bit shorter than longboards and slightly more buoyant.

Shortboards, also known as thrusters, are kind of like the skateboards of the sea: They are shorter than other boards (5'8" to 6'10") and are used by accomplished surfers to perform tricks, fast moves, and sharp turns. Shortboards have three fins, and they are not recommended for beginners, as they require a different kind of balance technique from regular surfing, and as the shortboard is harder to master.

Whatever kind of surfboard you have, it's important to coat your board with wax; otherwise, it will be too slippery for you to stand on.

Some cold-water surfers wear wetsuits, snug-fitting, full-length bathing suits made out of neoprene or rubber that keep the surfer warm by trapping water between the wetsuit and the skin. The thicker the suit, the colder the water a surfer can endure. These suits are also called rash guards, because the suit protects skin from being scraped by the surfboard or sand. Wetsuits fit snugly, but they should not restrict range of motion.

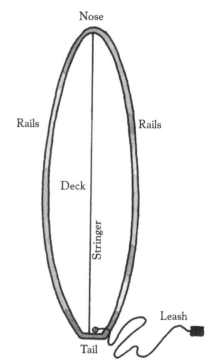

LEARNING HOW TO SURF

Surfboards are made to float: They have a natural center of gravity. The goal is to keep your board floating and centered even when you're on it. Lying on the board so close to the front that the nose dips into the water is called *pearling*; lying on the board too close to the back is called *corking*. Either way, you should adjust by moving toward the middle until both ends of the board are balanced. Once you find that sweet spot, you can mark the location using a Magic Marker or bit of wax to note where your chin lined up on the board in that position. That way, you have a guideline for the next time you ride.

Catching a Wave: Paddling

To find a wave, you have to paddle out to where the waves are. Lie on your stomach on the middle of the board, and raise your head slightly as you use your bent arms to paddle. Use the crawl stroke, alternating arms. Cupping your hands as you paddle helps you scoop through the water, pushing hard as your arm moves past your hip, and propelling you forward. Paddle past the breaking waves, and then point your board toward the beach and begin to paddle again as the waves come toward you. To catch a wave, you need to paddle at about the same speed as the oncoming wave. As the wave catches up with you while you paddle, that's when you pop up on the board to stand up and ride the surf.

Popping Up on the Board

This part involves jumping up from paddle position to standing on the board. You can practice the pop-up on your board in the water, but there are two dry-land drills that can help you get the "pop up" down: For the first one, think of it as if you were starting a race. Begin on your stomach ("On your mark!"), then press yourself up off the floor with your hands ("Get set!"), and then move into a race start position, that is, a crouch ("Go!"), with hands and feet touching the floor.

For the second, put the board down, and lie on your stomach right on the middle of the board. Keep your feet touching the board, and place your hands on the edge of the board as if you're going to do a push-up—because that's actually just what you're about to do! Do a push-up, and when you get to the top of your push-up, jump your feet forward so that you are in a crouching position. From there, stand up. Practice this until you can do it comfortably.

Standing on the Board

Once you're up, stand facing toward the beach with one foot in front of the other, knees bent to keep your center of gravity low, and grip the board with your feet. Crouch as low as you can go while still standing, making sure to stand over the middle of your board with your front foot angled at 90° to the deck. Extend your arms for balance, looking up. To turn, shift your weight to your back foot and lean in the direction you want to go. To speed up, shift your weight to your front foot. If you feel yourself falling and want to hop off, jump off to the side of your board feet first, rather than in front of or behind it (otherwise, you risk the board popping up and bopping you on the head).

ARE YOU NATURAL- OR *GOOFY*-FOOTED?

Being *natural-footed* simply means that you ride your board with your left foot in front. *Goofy-footed* means leading with your right foot. To determine whether you are natural- or goofy-footed, slide across a smooth floor while wearing slippery socks and take note of which foot you instinctively put forward as you slide. If it's your left foot, you are natural-footed. If it's your right, you are goofy-footed.

SURFING SAFETY AND ETIQUETTE

• Always surf with a buddy.

• Beginning surfers should always use a leash (a tether connecting the surfer to the board), and should always use a surfboard with a noseguard (a guard for the front of the board).

• Keep about 15 feet between you and other surfers.

- If you fall off your board, protect your head by bringing your arms to your head, covering the back of your head with your hands and your ears with your elbows. Come up facing the oncoming waves so you can be aware of what the water is doing.

- Don't cut in line: The surfer closest to the breaking wave has the right of way.

- Pay attention to the weather: Check on surf conditions before you go out, and don't surf in areas that are considered too dangerous for your skill level.

A WORD ABOUT RIP CURRENTS

Rip currents (which are sometimes referred to as *rip tides* or *undertow*) are narrow streams of water running from the shore out to sea. They are formed when water builds up at the shore instead of flowing sideways from breaking waves. Eventually the pressure from the buildup causes the water to turn back out to sea sharply, with a current cutting a path anywhere from 30 to 100 feet wide and moving as fast as 5 miles per hour.

The thing is, rip currents actually look like placid stretches of water—calm, waveless spots that seem like the perfect place to swim. In fact, they are just the opposite, and getting caught in a rip current can be deadly. The safest way to survive a rip current is to not be in one in the first place: Check with the beach lifeguards and look for posted signs about rip currents before you go in the water (many beaches will announce information over loudspeakers or block off areas prone to rips). When you do go in the water, pay attention and do not swim where there are no life guards present.

If you find yourself in a rip current, the most important thing is not to panic. The second most important thing to remember is not to fight the current: Swimming against the water will exhaust you. Instead, swim parallel to the shore. Raise your arm to signal for lifeguard help, and float on your back to conserve your energy. Float along the rip until it weakens enough for you to swim across it, and then swim parallel to the shore. Once you are past the rip, you can start swimming back toward the shore.

Notable Women IV: Eleanor of Aquitaine

ELEANOR OF AQUITAINE, born in south-western France in 1122 to a noble family, grew up to become perhaps the most powerful woman in Europe during the twelfth century.

Her name was actually Alia-Aenor, which meant "the other Aenor": She was named for her mother, Aenor de Rochefoucauld, who died soon after Eleanor was born. Her father was William X, the tenth duke of Aquitaine, a man known for his generosity and appreciation for music, arts, and fine education. When Eleanor was just eight years old, her younger sister and brother died, leaving her as the only heir to her father's legacy. This meant that when her father died, she would become the duchess of Aquitaine (and the owner of a bounty of other lands belonging to her father).

That day came when she was fifteen. Her father died of food poisoning on a trip to Santiago de Compostela, and on his deathbed he appointed King Louis VI as Eleanor's guardian. When word of this made its way to Paris, Louis VI (known as "Louis the Fat" for his imposing girth) was pleased: William's deathbed wish not only give Louis complete control over who would rule Aquitaine next, but also gave him a bride for his son, Louis Capet. Louis the Fat ordered young Louis and Eleanor to marry immediately, acquiring for himself in the process a dowry of the land William had bequeathed to his daughter: Guyenne, la Gascogne, le Poitou, la Marche, le Limousin, l'Angoumois, le Périgord, and Aquitaine. Eleanor was no longer Eleanor of Aquitaine, but Eleanor, future queen of France.

Although it was an arranged marriage, coming a mere two months after Eleanor learned of her father's death, it started out as a happy one. Eleanor was lively, intelligent, and beautiful; she was musical, composing songs and poetry, and she also knew how to read and write, unlike most people at the time. Louis was quite taken with her and consulted with her often for advice on political matters. But Eleanor's high spirits ultimately proved to be a mismatch to Louis's monkish temperaments. Louis had been trained as a priest, and it wasn't until his older brother died in a riding accident in 1131 that he even contemplated being king. But when Louis the Fat died just a month after Louis and Eleanor were married, that's exactly what happened: He was made Louis VII, king of France, and Eleanor was queen. Political life did not match up with the quiet life of devotion he had imagined for himself, and as time went on, Eleanor grew impatient, declaring that she had thought to marry a king, only to find she'd married a monk.

In 1147, Eleanor insisted upon joining Louis VII on a military expedition to the Middle East, which became known as the Second Crusade. He couldn't say no to her offer of thousands of soldiers from Aquitaine. And so she came, along with three hundred of her ladies-in-waiting, who dressed in armor and carried weapons, but did not fight. But Louis grew jealous of her political influence and bold behavior during this expedition, and the two became increasingly estranged, even after they returned to France (having sailed home on separate ships). Louis was suspicious that Eleanor had cheated on him, and there was another problem. They had two daughters, Marie (countess of Champagne, born in 1145) and Alix (born in 1151), but no son. This was cause for concern in the Middle Ages, as sons were considered crucial for carrying on the royal family line. The lack of a future king from Eleanor served only to increase the strain on their marriage, and by March 1152 it was annulled. As part of the annulment, Eleanor was given back all her lands. She was Eleanor of Aquitaine once again.

Just two months later, she married Henry Plantagenet, who was the count of Anjou and duke of Normandy—and, at just eighteen, also eleven years younger than her. The marriage was scandalous not only for the age difference, but for the fact that Eleanor was the one to propose. (No one found it scandalous, however, that before Eleanor made this proposal, two different noblemen had attempted to kidnap her in order to marry her and claim her lands.) This time there was no mistaking her political ambitions: She aimed to marry a king and not a monk. In marrying, she gave Henry the same lands she had brought to her marriage with Louis VII. Thus, in 1154, when Henry was made Henry II, the king of England, Eleanor of Aquitaine became "Queen of the English," and a large swath of southwestern France was put under English rule, sparking a fight between England and France that would last some four hundred years.

Together, Eleanor and Henry had five sons and three daughters. One son, William, died while still a toddler, but the rest of the children would grow up to play key political roles throughout Europe: There was Henry "the young" (who was named "co-king" during his father's lifetime but would die of dysentery before he was able to assume the role of king); Richard (who became king of England and was known as "Richard the Lionhearted" because of his bravery and military expertise); Geoffrey (who became duke of Brittany and earl of Richmond); and John, who would become king of England in 1199 (and whose reign, dramatized in Shakespeare's play *King John*, would eventually be considered the most disastrous in British history). Their daughter Matilda married Henry the Lion, duke of Saxony and Bavaria; their daughter Eleanor married Alfonso VIII, king of Castile; and Joan married William II, king of Sicily, and later Raymond VI, count of Toulouse. It is no wonder that historians have called Eleanor the "grandmother of Europe."

Her marriage to Henry was unhappy: Whereas she had been frustrated by her first husband for being too much of a monk, her second husband could have greatly benefited from some monklike restraint. Henry had constant affairs, and Eleanor resented his infidelity, especially when he refused to keep it secret.

They stayed married, but Eleanor returned to France in 1168 to hold court there, away from the rumors and Henry's indiscretions. Under her guidance and patronage, the court became a thriving center of artistic life, promoting poets, artists, and troubadours alike. Eleanor hosted the most famous of them, giving an audience to what would become enduring poetic traditions: "courtly love" (the idealistic, romantic songs describing the passionate devotion of knights to noble ladies) and the "legends of Brittany" (historical songs about Celtic traditions that gave rise to the medieval stories of King Arthur and the Knights of the Round Table, Tristan and Isolde, and many others). In time, Eleanor was summoned back to England by Henry, but her interest in and encouragement of the courtly arts continued.

By 1173, Eleanor wasn't the only person in her family angry by King Henry: Her three oldest sons, Henry, Richard, and Geoffrey, revolted against him in a bid to take over the crown, with Eleanor's full support. It did not go well. The sons were forced to flee to France, and although Eleanor, disguised as a man, tried to go with them, she was caught and captured by Henry's army. King Henry then arrested her for treason and held her prisoner, confined to her palace in Winchester, for the next sixteen years.

Her sons continued to fight King Henry, although they increasingly began to turn on one another as the fight wore on, even after the unfortunate death of their brother Henry the

Young in 1183. But when King Henry himself died just six years later, making her favorite son, Richard, the new king of England, Eleanor was finally set free.

When Richard left to fight in the Third Crusade, he appointed Eleanor in charge during his long absence, telling all the princes in the realm that the queen's word was law. She used her power wisely, traveling across England and releasing other prisoners King Henry had locked away, pardoning other offenses against the crown, and changing unfair laws that Henry had established. Her son John felt slighted by his brother's act of appointing their mother in charge instead of him, and he even plotted with the French king Philippe II to seize the throne of England, but Eleanor put a swift stop to that. And once that was done, she even managed to get the two brothers to reconcile their differences once Richard returned home. (Which he was only able to do after Eleanor herself rescued him from his capture by the duke of Austria, raising the ransom money to set him free and bringing him home, in person, herself.)

Richard died in March 1199, from complications of having been shot by an arrow, without leaving an heir to the throne. His brother John became king and, like Richard, relied on Eleanor for guidance, advice, and protection against his enemies. She continued to involve herself in political affairs, even into old age. Right after John assumed the crown, she helped defend Anjou and Aquitaine from her grandson, Arthur of Brittany, who laid claim to those lands. In 1200, when she was almost eighty years old, she crossed the Pyrenees, the mountain range dividing Spain and France, to take her granddaughter Blanche from the Spanish court and marry her to Louis VIII, the son of the French king, an arrangement she hoped would bring an alliance between England and France. In 1202, she was captured by Philippe's army and trapped in a castle at Mirebeau, but John intervened and was able to secure her freedom.

After this, she retired from political life and lived among the nuns in the Abbey of Fontevrault. She died there in 1204 and was buried next to her husband Henry II and her son Richard. An effigy of her on her grave depicts her with a book in her hands, a symbol of her learnedness, strong-mindedness, and wisdom. The nuns wrote of her upon her death: "She was beautiful and just, imposing and modest, humble and elegant. . . . [A queen] who surpassed almost all the queens of the world."

During the French Revolution her body was exhumed and her bones scattered, never to be found.

Stepping Stones

STEPPING STONES CAN TURN YOUR GARDEN, yard, or flower bed into a delightful walkway or meandering path. You can make stepping stones at home by pouring concrete into a mold, and then decorating the surface by making handprints, writing words, or adding stones, marbles, shells, and what have you.

WHAT YOU NEED

- Quick concrete, widely available at hardware stores (use the finer grain variety)
- Mold(s) (see below for examples)
- Trowel or old serving spoon, for mixing concrete
- 1-cup measuring cup
- Wire mesh, hardware cloth, or screen, cut smaller than the stepping stone
- Bucket, wheelbarrow, or other container to mix the concrete in
- Acrylic sealer (comes in a spray bottle)

Start by creating the mold. You can make your own by taping together pieces of cardboard in whatever shape you'd like. Use duct tape so it's extra strong. Any shallow cardboard box can be used as a mold (a pizza box is especially excellent). Plastic containers, like those that large plants come in, make good molds for round stepping stones, although you may want to cut them down to size before you start. Disposable pie tins are fine to use because they can be cut away from the dry concrete. Stay away from regular kitchen pots and pans, as the concrete will not come out, ever. Craft stores sell plastic molds in various shapes, and they are usually inexpensive, if you want to go that route.

Mix the concrete in a large, old bucket or in a wheelbarrow (clean it up before it dries). The bag of concrete will have directions for mixing it with water, so you'll want to follow those. It's a good idea to add water a little at a time, until the concrete holds its shape, but it isn't too loose, either. As much as you can, keep the concrete off your hands, as it can irritate them. And it definitely won't wash out of your clothes. Pour or scoop the concrete so that it fills the mold halfway up. Lay a piece of wire mesh or screen over the concrete. This material adds strength to the stepping stone, although it isn't absolutely necessary. Then, finish filling the mold. Air bubbles will collect inside. To remove at least some of them, tap the sides of the mold and shake it if you can.

In ten minutes or so, the concrete will have begun to set. Now is the time to add decoration to the top. If you want to use a stick to write your name (or anything else) in the concrete, wait until it sets just a few minutes more. Concrete takes several days to dry fully. When it's ready, take the stepping stone out of the mold. This is done by cutting the cardboard or plastic away, especially in a homemade mold. Spray acrylic sealer on the top, sides, and bottom. Let it set (or cure) for a few more days, or even up to a week, before putting it outside.

How to Say No / How to Say Yes

SAYING NO

When we were young, we had a favorite word. Not *supercalifragilisticexpialidocious*, but an even better (and shorter) word: *no*. You may know this word, too. It's a fantastic word: short, emphatic, and to the point, and as we grow older, we don't use it often enough.

It's true, sometimes saying no can be considered rude (especially if you're yelling it). But other times we forget about saying no because we worry that saying it may make a friend like us less, or because we're afraid to disappoint someone, or even because we have learned that saying yes is what girls are supposed to do. It can also just be hard to say no, especially to good friends. But remembering that you can say no even when you feel like you have to say yes—to hosting a sleepover when you'd rather not, or babysitting for a family friend, or even hanging out with a buddy when you just want some time alone—can feel like suddenly remembering to breathe.

Saying no is important. If you are in danger, or if someone is asking you to do something you are not comfortable with, saying no is a no-brainer. But *no* is useful even if you're not in peril. Saying no to something you don't want can help you make room to say yes to something else. And saying no takes confidence and bravery, two things necessary for living a full and daring life. So here are some ways to do it.

Just. Say. No.
Practice! Say it loud (*"NO!"*), say it in a tiny whisper, say it as if you're in a dramatic movie (*"Noooooooooooooooooooo!"*), say it like you're angry, say it like you're sad, say it like you're happy. Just practice saying it.

Be truthful, but don't elaborate
You don't have to make up reasons for saying no, and you shouldn't feel obligated to give huge explanations for why you are saying no. Keep it short. You don't have to feel guilty: Just say no.

Make it easy
As hard as it is to say no sometimes, it's often just as hard to hear it. You don't have to apologize for saying no, but it is possible to say no graciously when the situation calls for it. You can do this by being complimentary rather than apologetic ("I appreciate your considering me for this, but I have to say no. Good luck with your efforts!"), and you can also provide alternatives if it's appropriate ("Thank you for asking me, but I'm not able to do that right now. Why don't you check back in with me next week?").

Be polite but firm
Saying a gracious no does not equal saying yes. But sometimes people just don't want to take no for an answer. If you have said no and someone persists in the hopes of making you say yes, stick to your guns. Don't build false hopes with maybes: You have a right to say no.

Sleep on it
Not sure? Take some time to think it over before you answer. (Also, it's easier to say no and then change your mind than it is to say yes and try to back out.)

SAYING YES

Saying yes can be just as exhilarating as saying no, but it often doesn't come to us as easily. While we often are trained in the art of saying yes when it comes to helping other people, we're not always encouraged to say yes to doing things for ourselves or to doing things not traditionally done by girls.

Sometimes it's hard to say yes because it's risky, because we think that saying yes puts us in someone else's debt, or because saying yes feels greedy or aggressive. Sometimes we're so used to doing other things for other people that saying yes to someone's offer of help seems just plain wrong.

But saying yes can ground you in assertiveness even as it opens yourself up to adventure. Saying yes can mean making discoveries, trying something new, and maybe, just maybe, even changing the world one tiny bit. (Or at least your own world.) Here's how to do it.

Practice

There's a kind of acting game called *improv* (short for *improvisation*), in which two or more people essentially make things up as they go along. One reason this game is used by actors and comedians as a warm-up technique and even as public entertainment is because of the delightful fact that the only way the game can move forward is if all the people involved say yes to every made-up situation that arises. Someone pretends to be a giraffe? The other actors go with it. Someone trips and falls? It becomes part of the scene. Saying yes to whatever happens is the main principle of improvisation, because saying yes takes everyone to what happens next. Try some improv with friends or with your family, and see how fun it feels to constantly say yes.

Practice more: A little bit smaller now

Trying something new can be quite the adrenaline rush. Being nervous and getting through to the other side is part of the experience. To make it doable, start small. Say yes to little things that don't matter so much in the big picture, such as a friend asking you to let them go first in a game or your brother asking if he may borrow your pen. The more you say yes on a small scale, the easier it gets to say when the big questions come along.

Think about why you're inclined to say no

Often we'll have a gut response to a situation. Sometimes that gut response is because we definitely know what the right answer is, but other times it's hard to know. If you're asked something (to be the first student to read her book report aloud in class, for instance) and your gut response is to say no, ask yourself: If I say yes, will I be in danger? If I say yes, will I be putting anyone else in danger? In our example, going first, you may feel petrified, but reading aloud in front of the class is probably not going to put you or your classmates in danger. In this case, it's a safe bet to swallow your nerves and just say yes.

Say yes clearly and definitely

When you say it, don't be sheepish. Say it loud and proud. Even if what you say yes to doesn't work out the way you thought it would, you will learn something from the experience. (Even if what you learn is to say no next time!)

Sleep on it

Still not sure? As with saying no, for a big question, it is perfectly acceptable to ask for some time to mull it over before you respond.

SAYING MAYBE

We would be remiss not to point out the option of ambivalence, or having feelings of both *yes* and *no* that equal out to *maybe*. Sometimes you're just not sure whether to say yes or no, and that is okay. It's hard to choose, especially in those situations when you want to say both things at once. This is a time when sleeping on it—taking some time to consider things without giving an answer one way or another—or just going on record with a hearty "maybe" is perfectly all right.

Remember, although many people think *ambivalence* means not caring, it actually means caring strongly about two opposite things at once. It comes from the words *ambi*, meaning "both," and *valence*, "to be strong." It can certainly take strength to let go of certainty and see both sides of something. When that happens, just relax and embrace the power of maybe.

Dancing the Cotton-Eyed Joe

THE COTTON-EYED JOE is a much-loved country song and party dance, popular wherever you go. Lots of people like it because in the line dance version, there are no partners, just lots of friends dancing and having a good time. The dance varies from place to place, but with these basic steps you'll be able to join and follow the line anywhere.

BASIC VERSION

In the simplest version of the dance, everyone moves back and forth along the same line. The dance is sixteen counts, or four measures of four beats. To start, put your weight on your left leg because you'll be starting with your right.

Tap your right heel in front, twice (1, 2).
Tap your right toe in back, twice (3, 4).
Tap or stomp your right heel to the right side.
Cross it in front over your left thigh—and slap it with your left hand (1, 2).
Tap or stomp your right heel to the right side.
Cross it in back of your left thigh—and slap it with your left hand (3, 4).
Shuffle two counts to the right (1, 2).
Shuffle two counts to the left (3, 4).

Circle in place and do something fun with your hands, maybe pretend to spin a lariat, or make chicken wings with your arms (1, 2, 3, 4).

It goes by pretty quick. The second time through, start with your weight on your right leg and do all the moves with the left, and then shuffle to the left. To continue the dance, alternate the right and left sides.

TURNING VERSION

This second version is just a slight bit more complicated. Each time the dance repeats, everyone turns a quarter round to the left, and the line faces a new direction. This longer version has thirty-two counts, divided into four groups of eight.

Tap your right heel on the ground in front of you, twice (1, 2).
Tap your right toe on the ground behind you, twice (3, 4).

Tap front, tap back, tap front, tap back (1, 2, 3, 4).

Tap or stomp your right heel to the right side. Cross your right foot in front of your left leg, and slap it with your left hand (1, 2).
Tap your right heel to the right side. Cross your right foot in back of your left leg—and slap your foot with your left hand (3, 4).

Shuffle to the right for three counts and clap on the fourth (1, 2, 3, 4).

Shuffle to the left, and clap on the fourth count (1, 2, 3, 4).

Move three steps back and clap (1, 2, 3, 4).

Move three steps forward and clap (1, 2, 3, 4).

For the final four beats, break loose. Turn a circle, link elbows with a partner, and swing or circle back to back. Toss your hand over your head as if throwing a lasso, or dance some chicken wings. End up so you've done a quarter turn to the left. You're ready to start the dance again facing this new direction (1, 2, 3, 4).

Cross in front   Cross in back

"Cotton-Eyed Joe" is an old American folk song, and the lyrics have seen many variations. A version sung by the jazz, blues, and soul singer Nina Simone went something like this:

> *Where do you come from*
> *And where do you go?*
> *Where do you come from*
> *My cotton-eyed Joe?*
>
> *I come for to see you*
> *And I come for to sing*
> *I come for to show you*
> *My diamond ring.*
>
> *If it hadn't've been for*
> *Ol' cotton-eyed Joe,*
> *I'd a-been married*
> *A long time ago.*

Shooting Pool

POOL HAS AS ITS ANCESTOR THE LAWN GAME OF CROQUET. But even earlier than that was a game popular from the 1300s to the 1600s called *bilhard* in France, *biglia* in Italy, and *ground billiards* in English. Like croquet, it involved striking balls, using a mace or stick, through a hoop on one end of a grass court. When the game moved indoors, it was played on a table covered with green cloth, echoing the manicured grass of the traditional outdoor court. At first, the game was called *billiards* (from *bille*, "ball"), and it was played on a table without pockets. Eventually, tables were built with holes or pockets to catch the balls, and the game came to be called *pocket billiards*. It was later nicknamed *pool* because the billiard tables were often found in restaurants, bars, and other places where gamblers gathered to pool money together for the purpose of betting on horse races.

Women have always been enthusiastic pool players. Both fashionable and royal women played the game long ago; and in terms of competitive pool, there have been prominent women on the scene since the 1890s. May Kaarlus was a famed "trick shot" artist around the1900s; Ruth McGinnis toured the country in the 1930s and was rumored to have beaten nearly every man she played. The Women's Professional Billiard Association was formed in 1976, and nowadays professional women players organize tournaments and enjoy commercial sponsorship around the world.

There are hundreds of kinds of pocket billiards games—eight ball, nine ball, one pocket, and straight pool are just some of the games you may have heard of. Here are some basic rules about how to play.

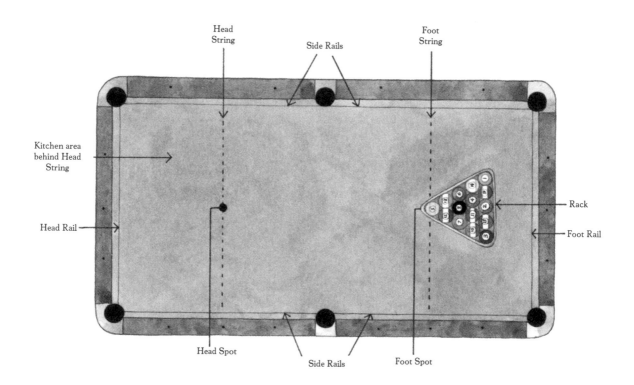

THE GAME

Pool is played on a rectangular, felt-covered table with six holes, or pockets (one at each corner and on either side of the long side of the table). Seven-foot-long tables are the standard, although tables can also be 8 or 9 feet long. The player uses a pool stick (sometimes called a *cue*), a white ball (called the *cue ball*, because it's the only ball the cue is allowed to touch), and a group of colored and striped balls numbered one through fifteen. Balls one through seven are solid colors (called *solids*) and balls nine through fifteen are striped (called *stripes*). The eight ball is black. The idea is to use the pool cue to move the cue ball and knock the other balls into any of the pockets—without sinking the cue ball.

BEFORE YOU PLAY

Pick a stick. Pool cues come in a standard length (about 57 inches), but range in weight from about 16 ounces (1 pound) to 21 ounces. It's important to choose one that feels right for you: If it's too heavy, your arm will get tired; if it's too light, it will give you less momentum when you hit the ball. So, go for a cue that's somewhere in the middle.

Also, keep in mind that most pool cues have been sitting around the pool hall for a while, so some will be newer than others. Check to make sure the one you pick is in good condition by looking at the tip of the cue, the end you use to hit the ball. If it's worn down, you don't want to use it. A good tip is rounded and extends a bit from the white end of the cue. Another thing to look for is whether or not the cue is level. Roll it on the table to check: A warped cue will wobble around as it rolls, but a level cue will roll smoothly. (Of course, you can also buy your own cue. Portable cue sticks come in two, three, and even four segments that can be screwed together for easy assembly once you're at a game.)

Chalk it up. Every pool table has a cube of blue chalk somewhere nearby. The chalk is applied to the cue tip before every shot to help prevent the tip from sliding off the ball. You don't need to grind it onto the tip of the cue—just lightly coat the tip with the chalk.

Rack the balls. Place all the balls (except the cue ball) inside the rack. Put the eight ball in the center and the one ball at the top. The other balls can be in any order, but make sure the balls around the perimeter of the rack alternate between solids and stripes. Then, with the one-ball side pointing away from you, slide the rack forward and press the balls toward the front of the rack; there should be a space between the base of the rack frame and the last row of balls. Move the rack so that the front ball is centered on the foot spot. Then, remove the rack from around the balls by gently lifting up the rack from the bottom. You'll know that you've racked correctly if you can see that all the balls along the perimeter are touching. If there are spaces between the balls, put the rack back on and try again.

Prepare to shoot: Make a bridge. Shooting, in pool, is the motion of the cue striking the cue ball, and to do it right, you need what's called a bridge. You can make this several ways using the hand that's not holding the pool cue.

The thumbs-up: Make a "thumbs-up" sign. Keep the sign but clamp your thumb down so it's in contact with your first knuckle. Now keep your thumb where it is, but open your fist so that your four fingers are extended. Keep your hand just like that and place it (about 5 to 10 inches away from the cue ball) so that your splayed fingertips are touching the table, creating a kind of tripod. The cue will rest on the crease between your outstretched thumb and the side of your hand.

The A-Okay: Make an "okay" sign. Then, keep the sign but turn your hand so that your three fingers point down. Place your hand so that your fingertips touch the table (about 5 to 10 inches away from the cue ball). The pool cue will go in the circle of the okay sign made by your thumb and forefinger.

Either way you make the bridge, your other hand should grip the pool cue toward the end of the stick. To slide the cue forward, keep your shoulder still and use your elbow, bending it back and forth to make the cue slide back and forth.

Make a break. Line up the cue ball on the head spot, across from the racked set of balls, so that it is in line with the one ball. Aim low on the cue ball and imagine striking through it with your cue. Make a few slides back and forth with your cue to warm up your shot, and then when you bring the cue forward to hit the ball, hit it as

THE LINGO

Bank shot
Hitting the cue ball into another ball, which then bounces off the side wall of the table.

Break
The first shot of the game, named for the way the shot breaks open the triangle of racked balls.

Combination
Hitting the cue ball into one ball, which then hits a second ball.

Cut
Hitting the cue ball so that it knocks into the side (rather than the middle) of another ball. This makes the ball travel at an angle, "cutting" left or right instead of rolling straight ahead.

Draw
Hitting the cue ball near its bottom, causing the cue ball to roll back toward you; also called *low English*.

English
Hitting the cue ball anywhere except its center.

Low English sends the ball back toward you, *high English* sends the ball away from you, *left English* sends the cue ball toward the left, and *right English* sends it toward the right.

Foot spot
The point on the table where the top ball of the triangular rack is centered.

Head spot
The point on the table where the cue ball is lined up.

Object ball
The first ball that the cue ball hits.

Rack
The triangular frame used to group the balls before playing a game.

Scratch
When the cue ball is accidentally sunk. When that happens, the other player can place the cue ball wherever she wants.

Sink
To hit a ball into a pocket.

hard as you can. Whether you're making a break or making a shot, remember to follow through, letting your arm extend in the direction of the cue ball rather than pulling up on the cue as soon as you strike.

PLAYING THE GAME: EIGHT BALL

Eight ball is probably the most popular game and the one that people mean when they talk about "playing pool." It's played with the cue ball and the fifteen colored, numbered balls. The goal is to sink all your balls before your opponent sinks hers. The most basic rule of the game, and the reason it's called eight ball, is that you have to sink the eight ball last. Here is how to play.

Rack all fifteen balls, putting the eight ball in the middle and the one ball in the front. Try to alternate striped and solid balls throughout the triangle as best you can.

Flip a coin to decide who gets to break. Then, alternate turns until someone sinks a ball. Whichever kind of ball is sunk first—a stripe or a solid—determines which kind of ball the player will be. If you sink a solid first, your goal is to then sink all the solids; if your first sunk ball is a stripe, your goal is to sink all the stripes. (And if you happen to sink one of each kind when you break, you get to pick which one you prefer!)

Whenever you sink a ball, you get another turn. Once you sink all the other balls, you may sink the eight ball. But if you sink the eight ball before you've sunk the rest of your balls, you automatically lose the game.

When it's time to sink the eight ball, you have to "call" which pocket you are aiming for, saying aloud, "Eight ball in the corner pocket!" or "Eight ball in the side pocket!" If you make it into the correct pocket, you win; if you miss, your opponent gets a turn. You win when you finally make the shot.

PLAYING THE GAME: NINE BALL

In this game, you use the cue ball and the balls numbered one through nine. Rack them in a diamond shape, with the one ball in the first row, two balls in the second, three in the third, two in the fourth, and the nine ball in the last row. (The balls in the middle rows do not have to be in numerical order.)

The goal is to sink the nine ball, but only after all the other balls have been sunk in numerical order. If you sink the right number ball correctly, you get another turn; if you sink the wrong ball, you lose a turn (but you don't remove the ball from the pocket—it's simply out of play). The winner is the player who sinks the nine ball (in the proper order) first.

Math Tricks

HERE ARE THREE easy-to-learn math tricks to wow your friends and family.

MIND READER

1. Choose any number. Do not tell it to me or anyone around you. Write it down.
2. Add 9.
3. Double your new answer.
4. Subtract 4.
5. Divide by 2.
6. Subtract your original number.
7. Your answer is 7!

This is actually plain algebra. Here are the equations that make it work:

- Let's use x to represent whatever number is picked at the beginning.
- When we add 9, the number becomes: $x + 9$
- When we double it, it becomes: $2(x + 9)$
- Using the distributive property, it becomes: $2x + 18$
- When we subtract 4, it becomes: $2x + 18 - 4$, which simplifies to: $2x + 14$
- We divide it by 2: $\frac{2x + 14}{2}$
- And so it becomes: $x + 7$
- Finally, subtract your original number, x, and you're left with 7.

No matter what number someone chooses, the result will always end up 7!

CALCULATOR POWER

Before class starts, or anywhere there's a calculator handy, use this trick and leave people wide-eyed.

1. Using a calculator, punch in the first three digits of your phone number.
2. Multiply your answer times 80. (Press =.)
3. Add 1. (Press =.)
4. Multiply times 250. (Press =.)
5. Add the last four digits of your phone number. (Press =.)
6. Again, add the last four digits of your phone number. (Press =.)
7. Subtract 250. (Press =.)
8. Divide by 2. (Press =.)
9. Does your answer look familiar?

FIVE MASTER

Look like a math genius by calculating high-number multiples in your head (or with a quick scratch on paper) with this trick for multiplying any number—and we mean *any* number—times five. It's this simple:

To multiply any number by five, cut the number in half, and then move the decimal one space to the right!

Examples:
44×5
Cut 44 in half to get 22 (or 22.0).
Move the decimal one space to the right to get 220!

426×5
Cut 426 in half to get 213.
Move the decimal one space to the right to get 2,130!

$\frac{1}{2} \times 5$
Change ½ to its decimal, 0.50.
Cut it in half to get 0.25.
Move the decimal one space to the right to get 2.5!

Words to Impress

ALTHOUGH CAUTION AGAINST BLOVIATING is always warranted, there is nothing more euphonious than an effulgent word. Whether ubiquitous, chimerical, or even ominous, the right amount of magniloquence can make you seem less a quidnunc and more like a salubrious speaker at the zenith of her powers.

Agnosia ("ag-NO-zha")
The inability to recognize objects through the senses.
Standing in line near the stinky bathroom, Katie wished for just a few minutes of agnosia.

Bloviate ("BLOW-vee-ate")
To talk for a long time, in a pompous manner.
When speaking in public, keep focused and resist the temptation to bloviate.

Borborygmus ("bor-bor-RIG-muss")
The noise made by a rumbling stomach.
As lunchtime neared, Jill could hardly hear her teacher over the sound of borborygmus.

Chimerical ("kye-MER-i-cull")
Wildly fanciful; highly improbable.
There was nothing Serena enjoyed more on a lazy summer afternoon than dozing off and letting her mind wander in chimerical daydreams.

Doppelganger ("DOPP-ull-gang-ur")
A person's double; a ghostly twin of a living person.
When Sarah yelled at her sister, their mom asked, "Sarah, is that you yelling, or your angry doppelganger?"

Effulgent ("eh-FULL-jent")
Resplendent; shining brilliantly; radiating light.
Eleanor's sparkly dress was effulgent in the spotlights during the winter concert.

Euphonious ("yoo-FONE-ee-us")
Pleasing to the ear.
Nola's euphonious singing filled the auditorium.

Herculean ("herk-yuh-LEE-un")
Of unusual size, power, or difficulty; resembling Hercules (of Greek and Roman myth) in strength or courage.
Dory made a Herculean effort not to yell at her brother when he interrupted her for the fifteen-thousandth time.

Imbroglio ("im-BROL-yo")
A difficult and complicated entanglement; a confusing situation.
Sidra and Sadie were embroiled in an imbroglio.

Inchoate ("in-KO-it")
A beginning or early stage; something vague or not fully developed; incipient.
Sandra had an inchoate idea for a story she wanted to write.

Jongleur ("zhon-GLUER")
A wandering minstrel (singer of folk songs).
Eleanor sang and juggled in the school hallway like a happy jongleur.

Larrikin ("LARR-ih-kin")
A person given to comical or outlandish behavior; a rowdy or disorderly person.
Sophia was a larrikin on the playground, by turns funny and rowdy.

Lugubrious ("loo-GOO-bree-us")
Excessively gloomy, dismal, mournful.
The school band played a lugubrious tune as it warmed up for the performance.

Magniloquent ("mag-NILL-o-quent")
Excessively grand and lofty in speech.
Randi interrupted Caroline, saying, "Are you done bloviating? It's time for me to wax magniloquent!"

Ominous ("AHM-in-uss")
Threatening; menacing; warning.
The dark and ominous clouds loomed overhead, threatening to spill open with rain.

Peregrinate ("PEAR-eh-grin-ate")
To journey, travel, or wander place to place, especially on foot.
In elementary school, she stayed in the same classroom all day. But once she started middle school, Lindsay discovered she was required to peregrinate, wandering from classroom to classroom for each subject she studied.

Quidnunc ("KWID-nunk")
A gossip or busybody; a nosy person.
Jane didn't want to get a reputation as a quidnunc, so she kept Nora's news to herself.

Redolent ("RED-ull-ent")
Suggestive or reminiscent; also, smelling of something, having an odor.
The cafeteria was redolent of the baked beans served earlier that day at lunch.

Salubrious ("sah-LOO-bree-us")
Promoting health and well-being.
Charlene's PE teacher recommended a salubrious walk in the fresh air.

Tabescent ("tah-BESS-ent")
Progressively getting smaller, wasting away.
Wendy saw the lights fade on the windshield in tabescent rainbow circles.

Tendentious ("ten-DEN-shuss")
Marked by a very strong, often controversial, point of view.
Julie was opposed to her mother's tendentious beliefs about bedtime.

Ubiquitous ("yoo-BIK-wih-tuss")
Seeming to be everywhere at once.
Much to her dismay, Rachel's little brother was ubiquitous at her playdate.

Undulant ("UN-dyoo-lunt")
Resembling waves; wavelike in motion.
Betty listened to the undulant music, letting the wash of sound roll over her.

Vacuous ("VAK-yoo-uss")
Empty; lacking in intelligence.
Emily studied for her math test so as not to appear vacuous.

Wizened ("WIZZ-end")
Withered; shriveled; dried up; shrunken.
Annie found a wizened old apple slice at the bottom of her book bag, a remnant of some long-ago snack.

Zenith ("ZEE-nith")
The highest point.
Yolanda's landslide victory as class treasurer was the zenith of her sixth-grade political career.

How to Paint a Room

WHEN YOU KNOW HOW TO PAINT A ROOM, you'll not only be able to use color to change your own bedroom—you'll also be able to hire yourself out and paint rooms in your neighbors' houses to earn money.

Before you begin, you'll want to know several things about painting. The first is that the preparation usually takes much longer than painting itself. Although it's not nearly as fun, it is very necessary. The second is that the paint always seems to run out just before the end, so make sure to get enough. The third is that paint is messier than you think and will stain the floor, your favorite jeans, your most-loved stuffed animal, and anything else that comes near it.

PREPARATION

Dust the wall with a cloth. Scrape any rough spots, and use sandpaper to smooth things out. The cover plates from electrical outlets and light switches need to be removed and put into a plastic bag with their screws, so they can be replaced when the painting is done. Remove nails or hooks. Use masking tape or painter's tape to cover doorknobs and to cover the edges of anything else that you don't want to paint. It will peel off easily when you're done. Fill any holes with spackle. Many people find this part fun. Let the spackle dry, and sand it so that it's even with the wall before you paint.

Lay down tarps, painter's cloth, or newspapers over the floor and furniture, and tape them down if necessary. Change into old clothes that you won't mind getting some paint on. Think about wearing a hat or a bandana around your hair. And make sure to have some windows open, to get some air in the room.

CUTTING IN

This is the painter's phrase for painting the edges where walls meet other walls or the ceiling, especially when the latter won't be painted or will be painted a different color. Paint these edges first. They are the hardest, but there are some tools and tricks that can help. Try using a paintbrush with bristles that are beveled or angled to fit into an edge. A rectangular contraption called a paint edger is useful. Some versions come with two small wheels along one side that move swiftly across the wall. You can also try painting by moving a plastic paint shield along the edge (or make your own from cardboard). Barring these aids, just paint very carefully, very slowly, and with a steady hand. If there are molding or baseboards or trim to be painted, attend to that before painting the rest of the wall.

PAINTING

You will be tempted to dive right in with color. All of us feel that way. But there is a step called priming that should be done. Primer is a base layer of heavy white paint. It provides a good surface for paint colors to attach to. It makes it possible to paint a lighter color over a darker color. And it makes the final color look nicer. Best of all, it takes only a half hour to dry before you can paint with your real color. We recommend it.

Professional painters dip the brush in water first and shake it out before they use it. They say this helps the brush hold the paint better. Mostly, painting is simple. Dip the brush in the paint. Let the extra paint drip back into the paint jar, scraping the excess paint on the edge of the can. Don't make too big a mess.

Rollers let you cover more wall faster. As with a brush, dip a roller in water, and shake it dry. Pour paint in the roller pan. Push the roller up and down in the pan to load it with paint. Whether you're using a brush or a roller, paint the walls with a sloping zigzag that looks like a W or an M. Try to paint over wet edges, and work with a few square feet at a time.

Wipe up splatters and drips immediately when they happen. If you need to take a break in the middle of painting, wrap the brushes tightly in plastic wrap. When you're done for good, wash the brushes and rollers well. Latex paint comes off with warm water and soapy detergent. To clean oil-based paints you'll need mineral spirits or turpentine (and an adult to help you with these if you are young).

FACTS ABOUT COLOR

The color wheel was drawn in 1666 by Sir Isaac Newton, after he saw a beam of sunlight refracted through a prism and began to understand the relationships of color.

The order of color in white light or in a rainbow is red, orange, yellow, green, blue, indigo, violet.

The *primary colors* are red, yellow, and blue. These colors are basic and can't be created by mixing other colors.

The *secondary colors* are green, orange, and purple. These are made by mixing primary colors.

Tertiary colors are the mixture of a primary color with the secondary color—for instance, the tertiary colors of blue are blue-green and blue-violet.

Adjacent or *analogous colors* are next to each other on the color wheel.

Complementary colors are directly across the wheel from each other.

A *triad balance* is any three colors on the wheel that can be connected by an equilateral triangle (like the three primary colors or the three secondary colors).

The *warm colors* are red, orange, and yellow.

The *cool colors* are blue, green, and violet.

The *neutral colors* are black, white, gray, tan, and brown.

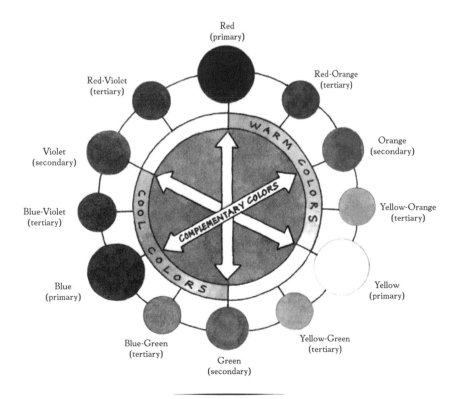

Running a Magazine

IN APRIL 1744, British novelist Eliza Haywood launched the first magazine written by a woman for other women readers. For two years, she published monthly installments of the magazine *The Female Spectator*, writing anonymously as four different characters: Mira, a witty and sarcastic married woman; Euphrosine, the beautiful, hardworking, and charming daughter of a wealthy merchant; the Widow of Quality, a wise widow who is able to see the good in everyone; and the Female Spectator, essentially Eliza's own point of view. Through the voices of these four women, she wrote essays aimed at the heart of what concerned women at the time.

In America, the first popular women's magazine would emerge eighty-six years later, in 1830. *Godey's Ladies Book* succeeded with women readers where other magazines had failed, in large part because of its editor, Sarah J. Hale. Hale (who is famous for writing the nursery rhyme "Mary Had a Little Lamb" and for her efforts to make Thanksgiving an American national holiday) came to the magazine as a writer herself, and she brought with her a writer's perspective on the interests and needs of women. *Godey's* (which cost three dollars for one year's subscription) featured poetry, short stories, fiction by popular writers, recipes, household tips, travel essays, sewing patterns, sheet music, and even job advertisements. With Hale at the helm, *Godey's* became a way for women to connect and to have a voice: Their letters were printed in the magazine, notices about local and national women's clubs and charity work were included, and women writers of fiction and nonfiction were published. Women artists were even employed to hand-tint each edition's color pages.

Today's magazines, like their early counterparts, are published on a regular schedule and feature a variety of articles usually organized around a single theme, topic, or interest. The difference now is how widely magazines are distributed, thanks to the printing press and the Internet, and just how many kinds of magazines there are.

There are magazines about things such as cars, clothes, television shows, trains, crafts, or sports; magazines for specific businesses or schools or organizations; magazines about celebrity gossip; magazines for men and women; magazines for boys and girls; even magazines about other magazines. The point is, just like Eliza and Sarah, you can create a magazine about pretty much anything you like—and as long as you have a group of friends who are interested in reading it, you'll be in business!

STARTING UP

Before you start your magazine, think about what you'd like it to be about. Then, look around and see if there are any other magazines already covering the topic you're interested in. This is called market research. Knowing what else is out there is useful, because you can see whether or not readers are interested (and it may also give you some ideas about what to do with your own magazine). Once you've done your research and decided to go ahead, start thinking about who you may want to have working with you.

WHO'S ON STAFF

Most publications rely on a group of people, called a *staff*, to work together. The number of people on staff depends on how big the company is. The bigger the company, the bigger the staff. Most major magazines have people working in the following positions.

Title	Job Description
Publisher	She is an overall manager, responsible for finding funding and thinking about the big-picture aspects of publishing and distributing the magazine.
Managing Editor	She is responsible for coordinating all the departments and making sure the work is flowing on time, according to schedule.
Editor in Chief	She is the boss of the editors and writers and has the final say about editorial content.
Editor	She is responsible for coming up with ideas for stories, assigning stories to writers, and giving feedback to writers about what they write.
Staff Writer	She is responsible for writing stories, columns, news, or features.
Editorial Assistant	She is the responsible for assisting the editor, which could mean researching, proofreading, answering phones, or getting coffee.
Copyeditor	She is responsible for checking the spelling, punctuation, grammar, facts, and other tiny details of the pieces turned in by writers. She uses special marks to let writers and editors know what needs fixing.
Proofreader	She checks for obvious formatting errors, misspellings, and other mistakes in the page layouts.
Art Director	She is responsible for the overall look of the publication, including cover design, photos, art, and style.
Typesetter/ Graphic Designer	She lays out the text and art electronically, using graphic design computer software
Production Manager	She is responsible for readying the magazine for publication and overseeing the process of going to press.

You don't have to have all of these positions—in fact, when you're doing your own magazine, you do all of those jobs at once! But if you're running a magazine with your friends, it's a good idea to assign a job title to each person and divvy up the work.

For a bare-bones publication, the most crucial positions are: editor (who will also act as a copyeditor and proofreader), writer, and art director (who will design the look of the magazine and also be responsible for getting any photos or art).

FOCUS

You've gathered your team. Now you need to ask yourself and your staff a few questions:
- What is your magazine about? Will it focus on topics concerning your school or community? Will it be a magazine for girls interested in spying? Try to figure out what you want your magazine to communicate to the people who read it.

- What should its name be? Your magazine name can be straightforward, fanciful, funny, catchy, or serious—but it should be something that gives people an idea about the magazine and what kind of publication it is before they even start to read it.
- How often should it be published? Weekly? Monthly? It's entirely up to you. Whatever you decide, it should be in keeping with the name and the mission of your magazine. (Something called *The Daily Anna* or *Fourth-Grade Weekly Review* probably shouldn't be published once a month!)
- How should it be done? You can decide to create your magazine using a computer, or you can do it all by hand. (In the olden days of publishing, that's what people did: Instead of cutting and pasting in a word processing program on a computer, they literally used scissors and glue to cut and paste typewritten content and place it where it was supposed to go.) You could also decide to handwrite your magazine, for a highly personalized look.
- What is its style? Talk with your team about what kind of look you want for your magazine. If you have an art director, this is a chance for her to put forth some ideas about how she thinks it should look. Otherwise, think about: Should we use photographs or drawings? Should we use color or keep it black and white? Do we want it to look modern or old-fashioned?

PLAN

Once you have the big picture established, meet with your editors and decide what topics you want to include. Ask yourself and your team: How many pages will we have in our magazine? How many stories can we fit in those pages? What kinds of stories should we tell? You may include: opinion columns (written by someone with a particular point of view on a subject they care about); product reviews (in which writers try out certain things and report on how well they worked); human interest stories (usually inspiring, personal stories about everyday people); essays (first-person stories); features (big, long stories about subjects important to the magazine and its readers); humor (including cartoons); and more. When deciding which kinds of stories to feature, you should remember to think about balance—that is, not having too many stories of the same kind—and about making sure every story holds interest for the reader.

SET A DEADLINE

Your deadline for getting everything done depends on how often your magazine will be published. For a monthly publication, you may decide to have a schedule like this: Two weeks for writers to turn in their writing. One week for editing, revising, and copyediting. One week to put it all together with any art or photos and get it ready for publication.

PUBLISH

Big magazines use big printing companies to publish their magazines, and they also use companies called distributors to get the magazines to stores. When you're doing it yourself, the printing company and the distributor are you!

If you have made your magazine using a computer, print it out and make sure everything is exactly the way you want it. If it's written out by hand, make sure all of the pages are correct and everything is finished and ready to go. Use a copy machine at the library or your school or an office supply store, and print as many copies as you feel like stapling together. Then share your magazine with eager readers!

How to Build a Raft

IN THE CLASSIC BOOK *THE ADVENTURES OF TOM SAWYER*, Tom sails down the Mississippi River on a small raft with his friend Huckleberry Finn. Meanwhile, Becky Thatcher, the girl Tom has a romantic crush on, stays home on dry land. We can't help but wonder: Wouldn't Becky have preferred to raft the Mississippi and see the world, unfettered? We'll never know, but here are directions for making a wooden raft, whether to journey down a slow-moving river or to pursue adventures on a nearby lake or stream.

How you will build your raft will depend on what materials are at hand, and on whether building the raft is a formal project or becomes a spontaneous act because you're at a lake and you found some wood. The long and short of raft building is that you need three basic things: a deck to sit on; a ballast, which is the layer just below the deck, and which supports the deck and also holds the flotation beneath; and some kind of flotation.

The other thing to realize is that the first two elements, the deck and the ballast, are almost always made of wood. Although wood looks heavier than water, it isn't, and that's why it floats. That said, you do need to keep your wood from becoming waterlogged, in which case it will become heavier than water and will sink. If you're not off in the wilderness, and your raft has become somewhat of a project, brush on a coat or two of polyurethane to keep the water out of your wood (or try some coconut oil, like some surfers use on their boards).

The materials for the ballast and for the deck are similar. They can be 1-by-4 or 2-by-4 wood planks, scrap wood, or fallen logs that you've collected in the woods. The deck can be made from a piece of plywood, although you will want to drill or cut some holes in it so water can drain off. It's also possible to use a wooden storage pallet for either element.

Finding the right flotation can be tricky, with the general rule being the larger the raft and the more friends you want on it, the more and stronger flotation you will need. Flotation can be from four big logs that have fallen in the forest (or which a neighbor has pruned from an oak tree). It also can

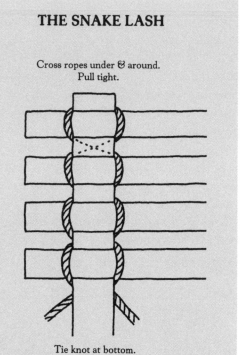

THE SNAKE LASH

Cross ropes under & around. Pull tight.

Tie knot at bottom.

If you're in the wild building a raft from fallen branches and you don't have a hammer or nails, grab rope and use the snake lash to hold the deck planks down.

be something decidedly less natural. Tire inner tubes can be put to work for you, as can large pieces of Styrofoam. A huge collection of empty plastic milk bottles or two-liter soda bottles can be used for flotation, with a similarly fulsome supply of duct tape to keep the caps on (and to keep the bottles full of air!); if you go this route, use lots of duct tape to secure the plastic bottles to each other and then to the boat. The last kind of flotation we can suggest are 55-gallon drums. These are often used to keep docks afloat on lakes. They are expensive to purchase new, and the used ones have quite possibly been filled with toxic stuff you want to stay away from. However, there are plastic, food-grade storage drums that can often be found at breweries and bakeries. When sealed tight with the air inside, they are another possibility for flotation.

In any case, the general rule of thumb is to go for more flotation rather than less. You just don't want to sink mid-river and a mile away from home.

There's one more thing. Depending on what materials you choose, you'll need to hold it together. The wood, obviously, can be nailed together, and drilled and bolted, if you wish. Rope is an option, and you'll need 50 to 100 feet to lash the raft pieces together. And duct tape, no matter what the materials, will be invaluable. We offer these specific directions, but to some extent, your raft will be the result of the materials you have and the decisions you make to hold it together.

WHAT YOU NEED

- **Deck** — Twelve to sixteen 4-foot-long pieces of wood. These can be 2-by-4s, or even 1-by-4s or fallen branches. You'll have to do some numbers to figure out the exact dimensions and how many pieces you'll need.

- **Ballast** — Two 6-foot-long pieces of wood (2-by-4s are a good choice, as are branches and 1-by-4s).

- **Flotation** — 4 big logs, 8 to 10 inches wide if you can find them, in lengths of 4 to 6 feet. (Or: inner tubes, a plethora of plastic jugs, or large storage drums.)

- **Rope** — 60 to 100 feet, depending. To hold together the logs for the flotation and whatever else needs to be bound together.

- **12d nails** — 80 to 100 of them, depending how many go in crooked and need to be pulled out and tried again.

- **Eyebolt** — Any larger size, to secure into the deck and so a rope can hold the raft to shore (optional, but good to have).

- **Tools** — Crosscut saw (or jigsaw), hammer, carpenter's square, measuring tape and pencil, screwdriver, hammer, sandpaper.

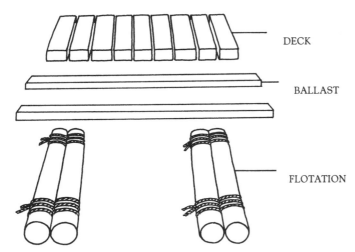

DECK

BALLAST

FLOTATION

Step 1. Saw all the pieces to the lengths needed for the raft.

Step 2. Lay out the wood for the ballast. To ready it for the deck pieces, use a measuring tape and pencil to mark a line every 4 inches or so, to make it easier to place the deck pieces once you start hammering. Smooth any rough ends with sandpaper.

Step 3. Lay out the wood for the deck. Hammer the deck wood to the ballast using two nails at either end.

Step 4. Choose the flotation for your raft, and do whatever preparation needs to be done—such as sawing off side branches from the logs, or duct-taping the plastic bottles. If you work with logs, it will be easier to put them together if they can float, so consider getting into the water and tying them together by wrapping the rope in a figure eight around them. Do this twice on each end, and tie off with a very tight square knot. You don't want it coming untied, but just in case, turn the logs over so the knot side is in the water, where it can be fixed if need be (and not hidden under the deck).

Step 5. Put it all together. Lift the deck and ballast on top of the logs (or other flotation). Attach using nails, or any method of getting the deck, ballast, and flotation to hold together. If you want to put an eyebolt on the deck so the raft can be tied to land when you're not on it, this is the time to screw it in. A screwdriver pushed through the hole and used for leverage will get the job done.

STEERING

If you've ever wondered how Huck and Tom steered down the Mississippi with a thin pole (or how Venetian gondoliers do the same), we're here with the answer. The raft is primarily moved forward by the water's current. When pushed backward, the pole, or sweep, propels the boat forward, and it's also handy for pushing off from mud. When pulled back toward you and the boat, the sweep steers. Drag it from side to side in the water to keep your boat going steady. Move the sweep to the left, and the boat will slowly move to the right. Move the sweep to the right, and the boat will slowly move to the left.

To make the steering pole or sweep, find a long branch that has fallen from a tree and whittle down any side branches.

HOW TO USE A HANDSAW

You have a saw, now what do you do with it? Place the wood you want to cut on a bench or a pair of sawhorses. Put the saw at the spot you want to cut, and pull it firmly toward you. Lift the saw away from the wood. Set the saw in the start spot again and, once again, pull it firmly toward you. This should be enough to set your cutting slot, called a kerf. Find a steady rhythm in which you pull firmly and push lightly. You don't need to force the saw—its weight will do the job for you.

You may also decide to use a crosscut saw with a hybrid blade, which lets you pull and push firmly. This makes the job go faster. When you get near the end of a cut, hold on to the wood so it won't fall off and splinter. As you cut, look at the angle where the saw meets the wood. For most cuts, that will be a 45° angle. A 90° angle will yield a fast, rough cut, and a 20° angle a very fine one.

April Fools' Day

N O ONE KNOWS THE EXACT ORIGINS of April Fools' Day. Some say it evolved from one of the ancient Roman holidays, Saturnalia or Hilaria. Saturnalia, which celebrated the Roman god Saturn, was held in mid- to late December and was a time of festive meals, gift giving, general happiness, and disorder. Hilaria was devoted to the Roman "mother of the gods," Cybele, and to the resurrection of her son, Attis, the god of vegetation who aided the death and rebirth of plants. Hilaria was celebrated with parades and processions, masks, disguises, and games. It took place a day after the spring equinox, a time when winter wanes and the light of day is finally longer than the dark of night. Others say April Fools' Day comes from the Feast of Fools, a medieval holiday in Europe that was held on New Year's Day. Villagers would elect a king of fools to lead the festivities and mayhem. They would change their positions in society, and it became a time for playing pranks and breaking rules.

Still another theory has it that April Fools' Day comes from All Fools' Day. This celebration emerged in the sixteenth century after Pope Gregory XIII replaced the Julian calendar with his Gregorian calendar. The Julian calendar had celebrated the New Year from March 25 to April 1, which was New Year's Day. The Gregorian calendar changed New Year's Day to January 1, as it is today. Many people resisted the change, however. They wanted to continue their traditional ways, and they believed that the New Year should start with the planting of the spring crops. Thus, April 1 was kept as a yearly celebration and called All Fools' Day after the usual New Year merriment.

Whatever the exact origin of our modern holiday, versions of gleeful spring festivals are found throughout the cultures of the world. The French April Fools' is called *Poisson d'Avril*, or "April Fish." Kids put pictures of fish on each other's backs, and people offer around gifts of chocolate fish. In Jewish traditions, the spring holiday of Purim celebrates the defeat of evil with costumes, parades, and hilarity.

In India, Holi is the festival of merrymaking that celebrates the full moon of spring. For centuries, on the eve of Holi, it has been the tradition to light bonfires all over India. The day after, called *Dhuleti*, is a buoyant carnival of parades. People dance and toss brightly colored powders at each other, so everyone's hair and clothing are filled with brilliant greens, pinks, yellows, blacks, and reds. They throw water balloons and dump buckets of cold water, or water that has been mixed with the Holi powders so that when it splashes, it is colorful, too. (You can find Holi colors at an Indian market or make your own Holi yellow by mixing turmeric spice with chickpea flour.)

Although there's no longer a king (or queen) of fools, April Fools' Day is a time for an extra dose of silliness and joy, when it's okay—nay, expected!—to be foolish and to play lighthearted pranks and pull off practical jokes.

Here are a few ideas for light-hearted pranks, all of which end by shouting, "April Fools !"

- **Hoax Pranks:** Spread incorrect news and elaborate hoaxes with a straight face. Make sure your news is harmless—like telling people that school is closed tomorrow (even hand out flyers!) or that there's a wild dog locked in a classroom or bathroom (then back it up by setting up in the room a recording of a big dog barking).

- **Salt and Pepper Prank:** Open up the shakers and put a napkin or plastic wrap at the top, so that nothing comes out. Or go a step further and put the opposite spice on top of the napkin or plastic wrap and rescrew the top, so when someone uses the pepper shaker, salt will come out, and vice versa.

- **Time Pranks:** Change all the clocks and wake up alarms so the alarms will go off at the crack of dawn, to set the day off in a topsy-turvy kind of way (and see how far into their routine everyone gets before realizing it's barely morning!).

- **Food Pranks:** Pull the bags out of all the cereal boxes and switch them around, so when your family goes to pour their cereal for breakfast, they get the wrong one. Or, tie a string around a yummy candy bar under the wrapper, and place the bar on the kitchen table or someone's desk (a teacher's even!). When they go to pick it up, yank the string so the candy bar jumps away from them.

- **Door Prank:** Paper over a closed door with large sheets of newspaper or a roll of wrapping paper. This is best done on a bedroom door while someone is sleeping inside. Or, prop a pillow on top of a cracked-open door so when someone opens it fully to walk through, the pillow lands on her head.

- **Drink Pranks:** Add food coloring to the milk container, so it is green (or red or blue) when poured. Works best in a carton (not a see-through plastic jug), because of the surprise factor. Or, use food coloring, water, and lemon juice to create a fake juice or fruit punch to serve to family or friends; watch their pinched faces when they expect something sweet and get sour instead.

- **Voice Mail Prank:** Rerecord your home voice mail in a different language, and ask your parents to call you at home (but don't answer, so they hear it!).

- **Toilet Prank:** Put some dish soap into the toilet. The next person who flushes will see bubbles everywhere. (Be nice and help clean up!) Alka-Seltzer tablets create bubbles, too, of a different sort. There's also the classic "toothpaste on the toilet seat" prank.

- **Thread Prank:** Put a spool of thread in your pocket, and then run the thread up your shirt and leave a tiny bit hanging out at the back of your neck. Ask a friend at school to please get the hanging thread off for you; enjoy her reaction when she pulls and pulls and ends up with a handful of thread.

- **Fake Bloody Finger Prank:** Cut a hole in the bottom of a paper cup or box. Stick your finger through it, and then add some ketchup or fake blood. Cover it up with the box lid or tissue paper. Tell someone to come see what you have found, and then lift off the lid or tissue paper. When they look in, wiggle your finger for a ghastly April Fools' present.

- **Shoe Prank:** Stuff tissues or toilet paper into your family members' shoes, so when they try to put them on, they can't get their feet in.

- **Swap Prank:** Move the dishes or cans from one cupboard to another, or from one shelf to another, or switch clothing between closets, or change the contents of everyone's backpacks. Or, switch roles with people: kids become parents, teachers become students, siblings become each other.

SYNONYMS FOR FOOLISH AND FOOLISHNESS

absurd	daft	hilarity	lunatic	off the wall	silly
batty	dotty	insane	mad	outlandish	skylark
cockeyed	eccentric	kooky	mayhem	preposterous	strange
comical	farcical	laughable	mischief	ridiculous	tomfoolery
crazy	fatuous	loony	monkey business	screwball	wacky
cuckoo	harebrained	ludic	nonsense	screwy	wild
daffy	high jinks	ludicrous	nonsensical	shenanigans	

Dominoes

NEARLY EVERYONE has a pack of dominoes tucked away on a top shelf or stashed in a toy box, but almost no one seems to know how to play them. Here's how.

DRAW DOMINOES

Befoe you begin, you'll need to "dig the boneyard," which is domino-speak for shuffling the tiles to lay facedown on the table, ready for play. (The domino tiles are sometimes called bones, and a small set of Double Six brand dominoes has twenty-nine of them.) In Draw Dominoes, each player picks seven dominoes and holds the dominoes so no one else can see them. The player with the tile with the highest double goes first. If no one has a tile with doubles, the player who has a tile with the highest sum of all the dots goes first. (If three or more people play, each starts with five dominoes, and after the first player is determined, the game order follows the direction of the clock.)

The first player begins the domino chain by setting the first domino down. After that, each player has to match a domino side to any edge of the dominos at the end of the chain, so that the sides that touch have the same number of dots. A double domino is put down at midpoint, perpendicular to the chain to form a "T". Future moves can be made in more directions.

If there's no match in your hand, pick from the boneyard until you find a match. When the boneyard is empty and you can't match, pass. The goal is to be the first to become tile free and, barring that, to have the lowest score left in your hand. One strategy is to make sure to get your large-value tiles out of your hand, especially near the end of the round. Another tip is to hold on to as many different numbers as possible, so you have more matching possibilities as the game wears on.

A round of Draw Dominoes ends in one of two ways. One player matches her last domino and wins. Everyone counts the points left in their hands. That total score goes to the winner. Bones go back to the boneyard for a shuffle, and the next round begins. The score is recorded on a tally sheet with everyone's name, and whoever reaches one hundred (or any predetermined number) first, wins the game.

Sometimes a round is blocked, which means that all players have passed and no matches are left. In this case, all hands are counted. The winner is the player with the lowest score in hand. The total of all the other hands, minus her own hand's value, is added to her score.

BLOCK DOMINOES

Each player chooses seven tiles (or five, if three players or more are in the game). The game is played like Draw Dominoes, except that the boneyard is put away, and whoever matches their tiles first, or has the lowest value in a draw, wins the round.

CONCENTRATION DOMINOES

Play alone or in a group. Shuffle all dominoes facedown and arrange them in neat columns and rows. The goal is to uncover dominoes that add up to twelve (that's if you are using a Double Six set; in a Double Nine set, the total will add to eighteen). The first player turns over two dominoes. If they equal twelve, she takes them, keeping them as a pair, and goes again. If they don't add up to twelve, both tiles are put back, facedown, and player two turns over two tiles. The key is to remember the values of the tiles that have been revealed and then turned facedown again when you need a tile of that value (that, and constantly adding four squares of dots in your head to calculate what equals twelve).

The game ends when all tiles have been claimed or when no combinations of twelve remain. The player with the most pairs wins.

DOMINO GLOSSARY

Blank --- 0
Double Blank ------------------------------------- 0-0
Ace --- 1
Deuce --- 2
The Trial -- 5-6
Snake Eyes -------------------------------------- 1-1
Puppy Paws ------------------------------------- 5-5
The Dog, also called Boxcars ----------------- 6-6

Double Twelve set ---------------------------------
   A domino set of 91 tiles, 0/0 to 12/12, for more complicated games like Mexican train or Solitaire
Pips --------------- The dots on the domino tiles
Spinner ----A double tile. Players can add new tiles to any side so the game can branch out in four directions.

DOMINO TOPPLING

The phrase *domino effect* describes a chain reaction that happens when one key element of a plan or plot stumbles and causes other elements to falter, too. It comes from the game of domino toppling, in which tens and hundreds and thousands of dominoes are stood on end in a pattern. One domino is tipped, and all the dominoes start to fall into the next with a lyrical clatter. The current world champion of solo domino toppling is Ma Li Hua, a twenty-four-year old Chinese woman, who won the title in 2003. She took forty-five days to set up 303,629 dominoes in a pattern on the floor of a Singapore stadium. Her dominoes toppled in four minutes. The world record for group domino toppling, held by a Dutch team, is four million dominoes.

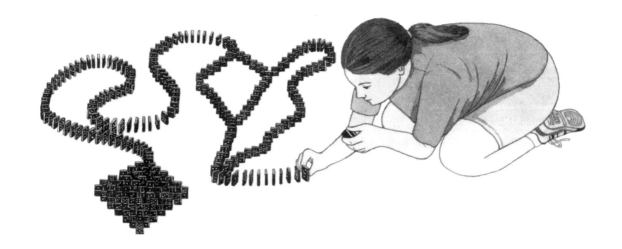

How to Practice Anything

THERE'S AN OLD JOKE THAT GOES, "How do you get to Carnegie Hall?" "Practice!" (Our music teachers when we were young told that joke, too, except the punch line was, "Practice, practice, practice!") You may have also heard the expression "Practice makes perfect." (Our same music teachers told us that, too, except their line was "Practice makes practice.") You may have noticed a theme here: Practicing seems to be the punch line for many a joke, as well as the main road to becoming really good at something. Here are some tips for how to practice anything—from a musical instrument to a speech, a sport, or even just doing homework.

Set the stage. Practicing something badly may be as ineffective as not practicing at all. So before you even begin, make it easy for yourself to practice well by choosing a quiet, uncluttered environment. This means turning off the television, clearing off a space on a desk or table, moving to an empty room, or otherwise making your surroundings conducive to concentration and productive work.

Check your attitude. As important as your practice environment is your attitude: Go into your practice session with enthusiasm and optimism. Having a positive outlook before you start can help you deal with the inevitable bumps along the way.

Set small goals. Start out with goals that you can reach. If you're practicing an instrument, trying to learn an entire piece in one practice session is a goal that may be too big to reach, which can leave you frustrated and even less likely to want to practice. The key to successful practice is to aim small. You will not only learn better what you're practicing, but also enjoy it more.

Bring snacks. Nobody can concentrate when she is hungry, thirsty, or tired, so make sure you have some snacks on hand for when your attention is flagging.

Relax. Before you practice, take several deep, slow breaths. Close your eyes and breathe in through your nose, filling your lungs with air. Then slowly blow the air out through your mouth. Do this several times to help bring yourself into a relaxed state of mind.

Start with the hard stuff first. Whatever you are practicing—whether it's a piece of music or a swimming stroke you're trying to master—take a look at what you have to do and figure out which parts are hard and which parts are easy. Then, work on the hard parts first. This will accomplish a few things: First, it will get the stuff you dread out of the way, and free you up to spend time on the things that come easier to you. (Think of the hard parts as dinner and the easier parts as dessert!) Second, it will make the hard parts seem easier. Starting out with the hardest part with a fresh mind is much easier than trying to tackle the tough stuff when you're tired from practicing everything else.

Break it down. Even if you have already started out your practice with small goals, it is always a smart technique to break it down even further. That means working in bite-sized chunks. If you're working on music, that may mean practicing one measure at a time; if you're memorizing a speech or lines from a play, that may mean practicing one sentence at a time. Practice those small bits until you are able to do them five times in a row. When you have that bite-sized chunk down, then you move on to the next one.

Put it back together. Once you've practiced in small bits, then your job is to put them back together. In our music example, that means going back to that first chunk of one measure at a time and making it twice as big: Now practice two measures at a time. In our speech example, that means going back to the beginning and practicing it two sentences at a time. Once you can do that,

keep enlarging those bite-sized chunks you've been tearing off until, eventually, you put it all back together. (It may not be your goal to do that in one practice session, but even with a smaller goal—half a page of a speech, half a dance routine, half a page of music—the principle of breaking it down and putting it back together still applies.)

Along the way: Look for connections. As you break things down and put them back together, look for connections along the way. If you're working on memorizing text, are there words or phrases that repeat? In dance, are there movements that return over the course of the dance? In music, are there measures, melodies, or patterns that are the same? Noticing these connections, and thinking about how they may relate to one another, helps you think creatively about what you're practicing.

Work in slow motion. For things such as homework, this means slowing down and not rushing through, reading carefully and not skimming. For things such as practicing an instrument or a dance routine, this means working in literal slow motion, like a super slo-mo instant replay in sports. Play or dance in very slow motion, paying attention to every small part. You may be surprised by how much harder it is to do it slowly than it is at regular speed. But that's exactly why super slo-mo practice is important: It shows you exactly where your trouble spots are. Once you're able to practice a part in super slo-mo successfully, bring it back to regular speed. You may be surprised by just how much you have improved.

Do-overs. The most important part of practicing comes when you're all done: Let your good work sink in, and then try it again tomorrow.

Calamity Jane

CALAMITY JANE WAS A FAMED PONY EXPRESS RIDER, frontierswoman, and scout. Born Martha Jane Cannary, she lived from 1852 to 1903. She spent much of her life in the Black Hills of North Dakota and became one of the more infamous women of her day. In her youth, Calamity Jane did everything. She saddled up her horse to scout land for the U.S. army. She worked as a nurse during a smallpox epidemic. She often dressed like a man to get her work done, as the long skirts and whalebone corsets of the day did not exactly suit her character. She was known to exaggerate when it fit her needs. Her friend Buffalo Bill Cody had this to say about her: "Before she was twenty, General Cook appointed her a scout under me. From that time on, her life was pretty lively all the time. She had unlimited nerve and entered into the work with enthusiasm, doing good service on a number of occasions." Her nickname "Calamity," it seems, was well earned. In 1896 Calamity Jane published her autobiography with this description of the adventurous years of her life.

LIFE AND ADVENTURES OF CALAMITY JANE
by HERSELF

My maiden name was Marthy Cannary. I was born in Princeton, Missourri, May 1st, 1852. Father and mother were natives of Ohio. I had two brothers and three sisters, I being the oldest of the children. As a child I always had a fondness for adventure and out-door exercise and especial fondness for horses which I began to ride at an early age and continued to do so until I became an expert rider being able to ride the most vicious and stubborn of horses, in fact the greater portion of my life in early times was spent in this manner.

In 1865 we emigrated from our homes in Missourri by the overland route to Virginia City, Montana, taking five months to make the journey. While on the way the greater portion of my time was spent in hunting along with the men and hunters of the party, in fact I was at all times with the men when there was excitement and adventures to be had. By the time we reached Virginia City I was considered a remarkable good shot and a fearless rider for a girl of my age. [. . .] Many times in crossing the mountains the conditions of the trail were so bad that we frequently had to lower the wagons over ledges by hand with ropes for they were so rough and rugged that horses were of no use. We also had many exciting times fording streams for many of the streams in our way were noted for quicksands and boggy places, where, unless we were very careful, we would have lost horses and all. Then we had many dangers to encounter in the way of streams swelling on account of heavy rains. On occasions of that kind the men would usually select the best places to cross the streams, myself on more than one occasion have mounted my pony and swam across the stream several times merely to amuse myself and have had many narow escapes from having both myself and pony washed away to certain death, but as the pioneers of those days had plenty of courage we overcame all obstacles and reached Virginia City in safety.

Mother died at Black Foot, Montana, 1866, where we buried her. I left Montana in Spring of 1866, for Utah, arriving at Salt Lake city during the summer. Remained in Utah until 1867, where my father died, then went to Fort Bridger, Wyoming Territory, where we arrived May 1, 1868, then went to Piedmont, Wyoming, with U.P. Railway. Joined General Custer as a scout at Fort Russell,

Wyoming, in 1870, and started for Arizona for the Indian Campaign. Up to this time I had always worn the costume of my sex. When I joined Custer I donned the uniform of a soldier. It was a bit awkward at first but I soon got to be perfectly at home in men's clothes. I acted as a pony express rider carrying the U.S. mail between Deadwood and Custer, a distance of fifty miles, over one of the roughest trails in the Black Hills country. As many of the riders before me had been held up and robbed of their packages, mail and money that they carried, for that was the only means of getting mail and money between these points. It was considered the most dangerous route in the Hills. [. . .]

I left Deadwood in the fall of 1877, and went to Bear Butte Creek with the 7th Cavalry. During the fall and winter we built Fort Meade and the town of Sturgis. In 1878 I left the command and went to Rapid city and put in the year prospecting [for gold]. [. . .] In 1881 I went to Wyoming and returned in 1882 to Miles city and took up a ranch on the Yellow Stone, raising stock and cattle, also kept a way side inn, where the weary traveler could be accommodated with food, drink, or trouble if he looked for it. Left the ranch in 1883, went to California, going through the States and territories, reached Ogden the latter part of 1883, and San Francisco in 1884. Left San Francisco in the summer of 1884 for Texas, stopping at Fort Yuma, Arizona, the hottest spot in the United States. Stopping at all points of interest until I reached El Paso in the fall. While in El Paso, I met Mr. Clinton Burk, a native of Texas, who I married in August 1885. As I thought I had travelled through life long enough alone and thought it was about time to take a partner for the rest of my days. We remained in Texas leading a quiet home life until 1889. On October 28th, 1887, I became the mother of a girl baby, the very image of its father, at least that is what he said, but who has the temper of its mother.

When we left Texas we went to Boulder, Colo., where we kept a hotel until 1893, after which we travelled through Wyoming, Montana, Idaho, Washington, Oregon, then back to Montana, then to Dakota, arriving in Deadwood October 9th, 1895, after an absence of seventeen years. My arrival in Deadwood after an absence of so many years created quite an excitement among my many friends of the past, to such an extent that a vast number of the citizens who had come to Deadwood during my absence who had heard so much of Calamity Jane and her many adventures in former years were anxious to see me. Among the many whom I met were several gentlemen from eastern cities who advised me to allow myself to be placed before the public in such a manner as to give the people of the eastern cities an opportunity of seeing the Woman Scout who was made so famous through her daring career in the West and Black Hill countries. [. . .]

Hoping that this little history of my life may interest all readers, I remain as in the older days,

Yours,

Mrs. M. BURK,

BETTER KNOWN AS CALAMITY JANE

What to Do When You're Bored

THERE SHOULD BE ENOUGH in this book to fill all your hours and days. Should you or your friends need a quick fix of something to do, our first advice is to step outdoors and see what happens. If you've already tried board games, cleaning your room, reading books (or the ads on the back of milk cartons), you're ready for our list.

1. Practice Dumb Tricks. Fill a cup of water half full, put an index card on top so it completely covers the rim of the cup, and turn the whole thing upside down. The card will stick to the cup and the water will stay in.

2. Have a Water Balloon Fight. A warm weather pleasure, obviously. Use wet sponges instead of balloons, and re-wet them in a bucket of water. They're just as fun as balloons, with no colorful latex fragments to pick off the asphalt after.

3. Make Beaded Safety Pins. Everyone loves these. Pull out whatever collection of beads are in the back of the closet and find some safety pins. There's a trick to it, though, which is that you need to pry open the coil on the safety pin so you can push the beads onto the top part of the safety pin that doesn't usually opens up. Use a small screwdriver or a pair of long-nosed pliers to do this. When you're done, close the coil back to its usual position so the beads will stay put.

4. Make a Set of Blocks. Get a 2-by-4 piece of wood and measure 2-, 4-, and 8-inch lengths along it. Saw the wood into pieces. Sand each block well to create a set of homemade wood blocks for a younger sibling or cousin.

5. Call the Oldest Member of Your Family. Seriously. She will appreciate the call. Be ready with pen and paper or with a recorder, to write down what she say when you ask her about your family's history or about the quirky things she and her siblings did as kids. If no one's home when you call, write down the funny things that your grandparents say and do. Or make up funny code names for every member of your family.

6. Start an Errands Club or a Babysitters Club. Adults in your neighborhood are always looking for kids to help with babysitting, car washing, dog walking, snow shoveling, lawn mowing, leaf raking and all sorts of yard work. They hate having to make several phone calls to find a helper. Organize your friends who are interested into a working club, and make a list of phone numbers or e-mail addresses. Post flyers or send e-mail announcements to the adults you know, letting them know to call the leader, who will find someone for them. The leader can be just you, or it can be a position you share with a friend. For your extra work, you'll earn a few dollars or a percentage from each job you assign.

7. Take Things Apart. Almost anything can be dismantled with a screwdriver (or a mini-screwdriver if the screws holding it together are very small) and Allen wrenches (for bolts and screws with a hexagonal top that an ordinary screwdriver won't fit). Use a hammer when you need it. The claw on the back can powerfully pull apart the most recalcitrant of metal boxes. Your best bet is to take apart televisions and old computers that are no longer in use until you get good and can put everything back together the way they came.

8. Plan a Party. Decide on a date and a theme (like April Fools' Day, Midsummer, or the end of school). Make an invitation list, draw up the invitations with a time, address, and RSVP (an abbreviation that stands for the French, *Répondez s'il vous plaît*, meaning "please respond"), and send them out. Jot down a list of fun things to do at the party. Oh, and probably you should run the party idea and date by your parents and get their okay.

9. Quizzes and Questions. Always good for when conversation wanes, and a must to battle the boredom of long car trips. Quizzes may seem dorky at first, but they turn fun pretty quickly. Try questions such as: What are your five favorite foods? Who do you admire most? What are your favorite movies, TV shows, and places to visit? Switch it around and ask about everyone's least favorite things. See if the conversation doesn't get interesting soon.

The game Twenty Questions begins with one person thinking of an animal, vegetable, or mineral. Everyone else gets twenty chances to guess what it is by asking questions that can be answered with a yes or a no ("I don't know" is also an okay response, when true). The traditional first question used to be "Is it bigger than a breadbox?" back when family kitchens had breadboxes.

10. Wax the Car. Your family's or a neighbor's. To wax a car, work one small section at a time by using a sponge to apply car wax to the painted surfaces of the car. Rub it in small circles. As you do, the wax will get hazy and white. That's when you buff it with a clean cloth—and move on to the next section. Try to keep the wax away from the black strips around the car windows, and any other part of the car that isn't painted (like the mirrors and the windows). After every section has been waxed and buffed, polish the whole car with a clean, soft towel. The most important thing to know: Don't wax on a hot day because the sun will bake the wax onto the car, and that is not a good thing.

11. Make an Ankle Bracelet. This four-strand braid can be made with embroidery floss, kitchen twine, or any string you find around the house.

Step 1. Start with two 40-inch pieces of twine. Fold each in half. At that fold (or the halfway mark), loop the two pieces through each other. Hold this spot tight with your fingers, or tape it to the table. There will be four strings to work with.

Step 2. Look at the two strings on the left. Cross the left string of this pair over the right string.

Step 3. Look at the two strings on the right. Cross the left string of this pair over the right string.

Step 4. Look at the two strands that are now in the middle. Cross the right strand over the left. Grab the two new left hand strands, and the two new right hand strands, and pull tight.

That's the basic stitch: left over right, left over right, right over left, pull, whether it's string—or your hair. When you're done, tie off the middle strands with a square knot (which is left over right and under, right over left and under), and cut off the remainder. Put it on your ankle, and tie the other two strands through the starting loop with the same knot. Or leave open to give to a friend.

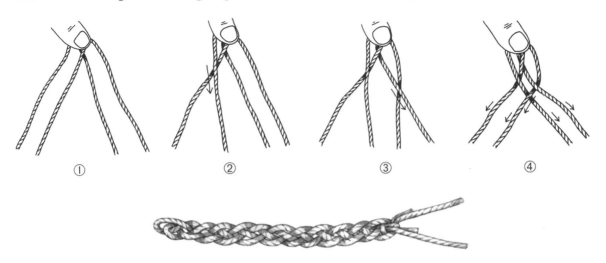

12. Plan a Carnival. You and your friends may no longer get excited about having your face painted, but what about planning and putting on a carnival for kids in the neighborhood? Carnivals are fun. If there is a cause that you care about, a carnival can be a good way to raise money for it. Here are some game and booth ideas to get you started.

- Face painting
- Beanbag toss. Cut target holes in the side of a box.
- Mini golf. Put a big box on the floor and cut small holes at floor level.
- Face and self-portrait drawing (have some mirrors available).
- Bob for apples. Place apples in a big bucket of water. Pull back your hair and grab them with your teeth!
- Fingernail painting and hair wrapping. Use quick-drying polish for the nails and embroidery threads for the hair.
- Soccer kicks (against a pitchback) or basketball throws, if there's a hoop around.
- Guess the number of marbles—or candy corn or pennies—in a jar.
- Squirt the balloons. Stretch a string between two poles or trees, and tie several balloons to it. Stand behind a line and hit the balloons with water from spray bottles or (although they are frowned upon by some) squirt guns.
- Sponge toss. Find a tall piece of cardboard or wood. Cut holes at various heights for people to show their faces through. Fill a bucket with water, and let everyone throw wet sponges.

13. Potato and Apple Stamps. There's usually an old potato or apple knocking around the bottom of the refrigerator. Cut one in half, etch a design (with a kitchen knife or craft stick), paint on the shape, and print on different sizes of paper. Useful for those party invitations or carnival signs.

14. Thumb Wrestling & Rock, Paper, Scissors. Sometimes when you're bored, doing something even more boring results in a burst of creative energy. If you're with a friend, try thumb wrestling, where you grab hands with your friend, four fingers locked together, and try to pin down the other person's thumb with yours. If you are still bored, up the ante to arm wrestling. Keep wrists straight and elbows on the table.

If you're still bored after all that, try Rock, Paper, Scissors. Count together to three and toss out a hand sign. (This can also be used to pick who goes first in games.) Here's the key to who wins.

Rock wins over scissors, because a rock is stronger ("Rock breaks scissors"). Scissors wins over paper, because scissors can cut paper ("Scissors cut paper"). Paper wins over rock, which surprises some people. It's because paper can wrap rock ("Paper covers rock"). Same hand signal: a tie. Do over.

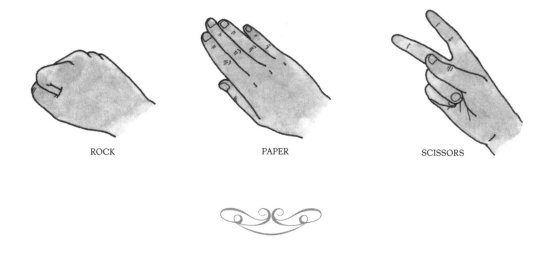

ROCK   PAPER   SCISSORS

Charades

THIS IS AN OLD PARLOR GAME OF PANTOMIME, or silent acting, whose repertoire of directions and delicate signals for fingers and hands have been passed on for many generations. It can get pretty funny, because there are so many chances for misunderstanding.

Divide into teams, or play one person at a time to the group. When it's your turn, pick a phrase, seven words or fewer, and it can't be a proper noun or name *only* (though names can be part of the phrase). With body motions and with the following signals, wordlessly give clues to the phrase so your audience can guess the phrase. You can start with a big concept, such as rowing motions if the phrase is *Row, Row, Row Your Boat*, or, if the phrase is more obscure, by indicating the number of words or the category, and then miming each one. Here are just some of the many charades signals.

The number of words in the title	Hold up the total in number of fingers
The specific word you are explaining	Hold up that number of fingers, after the audience has called out the number of total words
The number of syllables in the word	Lay that number of fingers against your arm
The specific syllable you are explaining	Lay that number of fingers on your arm, again, after your audience has called out the number of total syllables
Big concept	Sweep your arms back and forth
Movie title	Crank an old-fashioned, pre-digital movie camera
Title of a TV show	Make with your fingers the outline of a rectangular TV screen
Quote	Use your fingers to make pretend quotation marks in the air
Title of a song	Act like you're singing with a microphone in hand
Title of a book	Spread hands flat in front of you, as if you are holding a book
How long the word is	Pull your hands close together or far away
Past tense	When someone guessed the present tense, but the secret word is in the past tense, wave your hand over your shoulder. For present tense, when someone guessed a past tense word, wave your hand forward from your shoulder.
Exactly! You got it!	Tap your nose, i.e., *You hit it on the nose!*
The word sounds like	Cup a hand up by your ear; use this when giving a clue not to the content of a word, but to the way it sounds.
Shorter	Karate chop with your hand; use if someone has guessed a longer version of the correct word.
Longer	Put your thumb and first finger together, and pull them apart, for a longer version of a short word that has been guessed
Plural	Link your pinkies together. This means make a singular into a plural.
Proper name	Tap you head with an open palm
You're way off, let's start again	Sweep your arms wide, as if clearing the table

If people are stumped and cannot guess the phrase, you may have to start spelling letters for them. Chop your hand on your forearm (lightly, of course) up by the elbow for a letter at the beginning of the alphabet, and closer to the wrist for a letter nearer to Z. If you resort to the spelling chops often, we suggest picking easier phrases next time, or getting more creative in your pantomime.

There are ways to keep score and win at charades, but don't bother, because honestly, it really is all about having fun.

Yo-Yos

THERE IS A YO-YO TRICK CALLED "AROUND THE WORLD," and it couldn't be more appropriate, as the yo-yo has been quite the world traveler from the very start. Like so many things (paper, gunpowder, paper money, wheelbarrows, chess, and kites, to name a few), the yo-yo was invented in China. From China it made its way to Greece. The earliest surviving yo-yo, made from terra-cotta clay disks, dates to 500 BCE. In the sixteenth century, in the Philippines, a fearsome yo-yo-like weapon (basically a yo-yo made out of rocks and twine) was used by hunters to catch wild animals. When the yo-yo arrived in France in the 1700s, it was made of glass and ivory and was nicknamed *joujou de Normandie* ("toy of Normandy"). When it came to England a bit later, it was called a *bandalore*, an *incroyable*, and a *quiz*. By the time it immigrated to the United States in the mid-1800s, it was still called a *bandalore*, but in 1916 the magazine *Scientific American* published an article calling the toy a "yo-yo" (a Filipino word meaning "to return"), and that's the name that finally stuck. In 1928 a Filipino-American man named Pedro Flores demonstrated his handmade yo-yos to crowds in San Francisco. He had started a small company producing the toys, which he carved from wood with a string looped around the axle instead of tied to it, making it possible for the yo-yo to spin at the end of the string. Flores's demonstration was so impressive that a businessman named Donald Duncan who happened to be in the crowd not only bought Flores's yo-yo, he bought the company. By 1962, forty-five million yo-yos had been sold, and the rest, as they say, is history.

BEFORE YOU YO-YO

Choose your yo-yo

Yo-yos come in several different shapes. The three most popular styles are the "classic," the most basic design, featuring two sculpted plastic disks connected by an axle with a string looped around it; the "modified" shape, sometimes called "flywheel" or "modern," which is more rounded than the classic and also has a slightly larger gap between the disks where the string goes; and the "butterfly," which has angled sides and a wider string gap, making it possible to do tricks that involve catching the yo-yo on its string.

Adjust the string

A good rule of thumb is that the yo-yo string should be about as long as the distance from your belly button to the floor. If the string is longer than that, you can shorten it. Just unwind the string, put the yo-yo on the floor, and then bring up the string until you reach your belly button. Then, tie a loop at the end of the string that's left over.

Make the slip knot

Now the end of the yo-yo string has a loop, but that's not the loop that actually goes on your finger. You need to make a slip knot by taking the loop you just made, pulling a bit of the string next to it right through that loop, and then pulling it tight to create another loop. That is the loop that goes around your index finger (or, if you prefer, your third finger).

Check the string tension

If the string is too loose (usually evidenced by the yo-yo lazily spinning at the bottom of the string instead of coming back up to your hand), tighten it by first allowing the yo-yo to dangle at the end of the string, and then twisting the yo-yo clockwise before winding up the string. If the yo-yo is too tight (snapping back to your hand without spinning at all), let the yo-yo dangle at the bottom of the string and then twist the yo-yo counterclockwise.

Clear the area

Make sure you have a good amount of distance around you so that no person or thing can be hit by a flying yo-yo as you do your tricks.

YO-YO TECHNIQUES AND TRICKS

First, two important yo-yo terms: *sleeping* and *looping*. Sleeping, which is when the yo-yo spins at the end of its string, is the foundation for nearly every yo-yo trick. Looping is the opposite of sleeping, as it involves keeping the yo-yo in constant motion. Here are some yo-yo moves that use sleeping and looping. For all of these tricks, the key is patience and practice.

Gravity Pull

This is the classic, up-and-down yo-yo move: Releasing it from your hand and having it return to you. To do it, put your index finger through the loop and hold the yo-yo in your hand. Turn your hand so that your palm and the yo-yo are facing down, and then release the yo-yo and let it roll down. When it gets to the bottom, just before it finishes unwinding, give it a tug to pull the yo-yo up toward you again.

The Throw Down

Put your index finger through the loop and cup the yo-yo in your hand, palm up. Make sure the string is threaded so that it's coming off your finger *toward* you, not *away* from you. Bend your elbow to bring your hand toward you; your middle finger should be pointing back toward your shoulder. Flick your wrist away from your body to whip the yo-yo straight down toward the ground. Just as it gets to the end of the string, flick your wrist toward you to return the yo-yo to your hand.

The Sleeper

Begin by holding the yo-yo the same way as in the Throw Down maneuver. Flick your wrist strongly to send the yo-yo toward the ground. While the yo-yo spins its way down, turn your hand over so that it is palm down instead of palm up. Let the yo-yo spin at the end of the string for a second or two, and then give it a tug to send it back up again.

Walking the Dog

Unlike walking a real dog, this is best done inside the house, on carpet. To do this trick, throw a sleeper, and when the yo-yo reaches the bottom of its string, gently set it on the ground. The spinning motion will make the yo-yo move along the ground. Give the string a tug to bring your dog back from its walk.

Rock the Baby

This trick also starts with a sleeper, thrown from a little higher than usual, and this one is tricky. Bring your yo-yo hand just above your head, and throw the sleeper from there. Put your other hand between the string and your body, palm facing you and fingers extended. As the yo-yo descends, grab the string about a third of the way down using the pinkie and thumb of your free hand. Then, with your yo-yo hand, grab the string about six inches above where the yo-yo is dangling. Lift your yo-yo hand up so that it is above your other hand. This should create a triangle shape, with the yo-yo hanging in the middle of the string. Swing the yo-yo back and forth, like a baby rocking in a cradle. Give a tug with your yo-yo hand as you let go of the string to return the yo-yo.

Forward Pass

Hold the yo-yo in your hand, palm up, as in the Throw Down. Then, put your hand down at your side and turn your hand so that your palm faces behind you and the back of your hand faces front. Flick your wrist to send the yo-yo forward, in front of you. As it gets to the end of the string, give it a tug to return it and turn your hand so that it's facing palm up. Catch the yo-yo in the palm of your hand. This is harder than it sounds, so don't worry if you don't get it on the first try!

Around the World

Make sure that you have at least six feet of space around you and above you for this one. This trick starts with a forward pass. Throw a forward pass, but instead of returning the yo-yo when it gets to the end of the string, swing it up over your shoulder, over your head, and all the way around, making a big circle. When you've completed the circle and the yo-yo is back where it started, give it a tug to make it come back up from the end of the string.

FUN FACTS

The biggest yo-yo ever made had a 50-inch diameter and weighed 256 pounds. The all-wood toy made the 1981 *Guinness Book of World Records*.

Yo-yos have been to outer space—twice! Along with nine other toys, a yellow Duncan Imperial yo-yo was taken aboard the space shuttle *Discovery*'s April 12, 1985, trip. Astronaut David Griggs became the first person to yo-yo in space. Seven years later, in 1992, the shuttle *Atlantis* took a "high-tech" Silver Bullet 2 yo-yo along on its mission.

Rhetoric

RHETORIC IS, ESSENTIALLY, the art of persuasion. The word has its roots in the Greek word for *orator* (a person who speaks in public), and rhetoric today is still about using the spoken word in the service of elegantly communicating concepts and ideas. Rhetoric is concerned with not just what is said, but how we say it. This involves two other basic concepts from ancient Greece: *pathos* (emotion) and *logos* (logic). A good rhetorical speaker also keeps in mind three overarching principles: her audience (those to whom she is speaking); the concept of *kairos* (essentially, the crucial moment for speech); and decorum (the idea that the speaker's topic is especially suited to the occasion). Once upon a time, school children everywhere were taught rhetoric to help prepare speeches and write essays. These common rhetorical devices are used in speeches and literature to communicate ideas with thoughtfulness, logic, and passion.

Alliteration (uh-lit-uh-REY-shuhn) From Latin *ad*–, "to," and *litera*, "letter"
Repetition of the same sound at the beginning of several words in a row.
> *Step forward, Tin Man. You dare to come to me for a heart, do you? You clinking, clanking, clattering collection of caliginous junk!*
> —*Oz, from the movie* The Wizard of Oz

Anadiplosis (an-uh-di-PLOH-sis) From Greek *ana*, "again," and *diploun*, "to double"
Repetition of the last word or phrase of one sentence or clause to begin the next.
> *The love of wicked men converts to fear,*
> *That fear to hate, and hate turns one or both*
> *To worthy danger and deserved death.*
> —*Shakespeare,* Richard II

Anaphora (uh-NAF-er-uh) From *ana*, "again," and *phero*, "to bring or carry"
Repetition of a word or group of words at the beginning of the next phrases or clauses.
> *We shall not flag or fail. We shall go on to the end. We shall fight in France, we shall fight on the seas and oceans, we shall fight with growing confidence and growing strength in the air, we shall defend our island, whatever the cost may be, we shall fight on the beaches, we shall fight on the landing grounds, we shall fight in the fields and in the streets, we shall fight in the hills. We shall never surrender.*
> —*Winston Churchill*

Antimetabole (an-tee-meh-TA-boe-lee) From *anti*, "against," and *metabole*, "turning about"
Device whereby words are repeated in transposed order.
> *Ask not what your country can do for you—ask what you can do for your country.*
> —*John F. Kennedy*

Antistrophe (an-TIH-struh-fee) From *anti*, "against," and *strepho*, "to turn"
Repetition of the same words at the end of successive phrases or clauses.

> *In 1931, ten years ago, Japan invaded Manchukuo—without warning. In 1935 Italy invaded Ethiopia—without warning. In 1938 Hitler occupied Austria—without warning. In 1939 Hitler invaded Czechoslovakia—without warning. Later, in 1939, Hitler invaded Poland—without warning. And now Japan has attacked Malaya and Thailand—and the United States—without warning.*
> *—Franklin D. Roosevelt*

Asteismus (as-tey-IS-muss) From *asteios*, "of the city"
Polite or gentle mockery using wordplay, usually performed by latching on to another speaker's word and turning it around in an unexpected twist.

> *Benedick: Well, you are a rare parrot teacher.*
> *Beatrice: A bird of my tongue is better than a beast of yours.*
> *—Shakespeare,* Much Ado About Nothing

Chiasmus (kahy-AZ-muhs) "a diagonal arrangement"; from the shape of the Greek letter *chi* (X)
Repetition of ideas in reverse order, or a reversal in the order of words in two otherwise parallel phrases. (Unlike antimetabole, chiasmus does not involve repetition of words.)

> *By day the frolic, and the dance by night.*
> *—Samuel Johnson*

Dianoea (di-a-NOI-ah) From Greek, meaning "a revolving in the mind."
Use of animated questions and answers in the development of an argument; asking yourself questions aloud and answering them aloud to create a compelling and definitive argument

> *That man over there says that women need to be helped into carriages, and lifted over ditches, and to have the best place everywhere. Nobody ever helps me into carriages, or over mud-puddles, or gives me any best place! And ain't I a woman? Look at me! Look at my arm! I have ploughed and planted, and gathered into barns, and no man could head me! And ain't I a woman? I could work as much and eat as much as a man—when I could get it—and bear the lash as well! And ain't I a woman? I have borne thirteen children, and seen most all sold off to slavery, and when I cried out with my mother's grief, none but Jesus heard me! And ain't I a woman?*
> *—Sojourner Truth, 1851, Women's Convention, Akron, Ohio*

Epitrope (EP-ih-trope) From *epi*, "upon," and *trope*, "turn" ("to yield")
Device whereby things are turned over to the listener ironically, or submitted for consideration without spelling out specifically what the meaning is.

> *Go ahead, make my day.*
> *—Harry Callahan, played by Clint Eastwood, in the film* Sudden Impact

Metaphor (MEH-ta-for) From *meta*, "beyond, over," and *pherein*, "to carry"
Comparison made by referring to one thing as another.
> *No man is an island.*
> —*John Donne*

Metonymy (mih-TON-uh-mee) From *meta*, "change," and *onoma*, "name"
Device whereby one word or phrase is substituted for another with which it is associated; the substitution of one word for another which it suggests. (Closely related to this is *synecdoche*, where a specific part of something is used to refer to the whole—like saying "Nice threads" when complimenting someone's clothes.)
> *By the sweat of thy brow thou shalt eat thy bread.*
> —*Genesis 3:19*

Paromologia (para-MOLL-uh-ja) From *para*, "alongside," and *homologia*, "agreement"
Device whereby a weaker point is conceded in order to make a stronger one.
> *Sicinius: He's a disease that must be cut away.*
> *Menenius: O, he's a limb that has but a disease:*
> *Mortal, to cut it off; to cure it, easy.*
> —*Shakespeare, Coriolanus*

Syllepsis (si-LEP-sis) From *syn*, "together," and *lepsis*, "taking"
Device whereby a single word is used to have different meanings.
> *We must all hang together or assuredly we will all hang separately.*
> —*Benjamin Franklin*

Synchoresis (sin-ko-REE-sis) From *synchoreo*, "to come together, agree"
Device used to grant or yield a point in the service of making another.
> *What was [Roman] civilization? Vast, I allow: but vile.*
> —*James Joyce, Ulysses*

Tricolon (TRY-ko-lon) From *tri*, "three," and *kolon*, "clause"
Three elements of the same length in a series.
> *Veni, vidi, vici.*
> —*Julius Caesar*

Zeugma (ZOOG-muh) From the Greek word meaning "a yoking"
Device whereby two different words are linked to a verb or an adjective that is strictly appropriate to only one of them.
> *Here thou, great Anna! whom three realms obey,*
> *Dost sometimes counsel take—and sometimes tea.*
> —*Alexander Pope*

Bocce, Horseshoes, Shuffleboard, Lawn Bowling, and Quoits

BOCCE

To PLAY PROPER BOCCE, you need four balls per team and a *boccino* (or jack). Each team uses a different color of ball and can have from one to four players. A bocce court varies in size, but generally is twelve feet wide and eighty feet long, surrounded by a four- to five-inch wall. It's good to have a measuring tape to resolve heated disputes about whose ball is closer.

To begin, the *capos*, or team captains, call heads or tails and flip a coin to decide who tosses the boccino and goes first. When the play begins, both teams stand on the same end of the court and roll the ball from there. The first team tosses the boccino down the court and makes sure it rolls past the centerline. That team then rolls the first ball, trying to get it as close to the boccino as possible. Then it steps aside. Team 2 rolls its first ball. If team 2's ball is closer to the boccino than team 1's, then team 1 bowls next. If team 2's ball is farther, it keeps bowling. The principle is that whichever team (or player) has a ball closest to the boccino stands aside so the other team can bowl. This continues until all balls have been played.

To score: Whichever team has a ball closest to the boccino gains a point for that round. Players agree ahead of time on the number of points needed to win. It's often between ten and fifteen, depending on how long you want to play. After everyone collects the balls, walk to the other end of the court. The team that won the last point tosses the boccino and the first ball, and the next round begins.

Tips: Hold the ball like a grapefruit or orange, with your palm and fingers underneath it. To throw, crouch close to the ground and release the ball with the third and fourth fingers. Make sure that your foot doesn't step over the foul line.

Aim to roll your ball closest to the boccino, use your roll to knock the other team's balls away from the boccino, or push the boccino closer to your already-played balls.

Use the sideboards to ricochet the ball, but don't hit the back wall. If you do, your ball is out of play, or *dead*, until the next round (although some people play that if your ball hits another ball first, and then hits the back wall, it's okay).

ITALIAN PHRASES TO GO WITH BOCCE

Brava! ---------- Well done! (said of a girl or woman)
Bravo! ---------- Well done! (said of a boy or man)
No ---------- No
Sì ---------- Yes
Uffa! ---------- Oh, no! Ugh!
Scusami! ---------- Sorry!
Non c'è problema! ("Non cheh pro-BLEM-a!") ---------- No problem!
Non vale! ---------- That's cheating! Not fair!
Ma che dici? ("Ma kay DEE-chee?") ---------- What are you talking about?
Stai scherzando? ("Stai sker-ZAN-do?") ---------- Are you kidding?
Non scherzo! ("Non SKER-zo!") ---------- I am not joking!
Per carita. ---------- You must be joking.
Hai finito, no? ---------- You've finished, right?
Fa un freddo cane! ---------- It's freezing! (Literally, "It's dog cold.")
Non lamentarti, c'è chi sta peggio. ("Non lamen-TAR-ti, cheh key sta PE-jio.")
---------- Don't complain, there are people who feel worse.
Tutto è bene quel che finisce bene. ("TU-tto eh BE-ne kel key fi-NI-sheh BEH-neh.")
---------- All's well that ends well.

HORSESHOES

The goal of the game is to toss two horseshoes down a court so that one or both will ring the stake at the other end. Actual horseshoes were once used, but these days the game is played with special game horseshoes, which can be metal, rubber, or plastic.

In a formal horseshoe court, the two stakes are separated by forty feet. Each is dug deep into a sandpit, and there may even be concrete platforms around the sides for standing when you pitch the shoes. Life need not always be that formal. It's perfectly fine to make a court with whatever ground you have, whether it's pushing a stake into beach sand or hammering one into a corner of the backyard. Horseshoe stakes are often three feet tall, but they are hammered deep into the ground so that only fifteen inches stick out and so that the stake angles toward the horseshoes coming its way.

To play, each player (or team) stands at one end of the court and pitches two horseshoes toward the opposite stake. Each team's horseshoes are a slightly different color. Alternate tosses between teams so each player can try to knock the other player's horseshoes out of the way!

When thrown, the horseshoe needs to rotate in the air, so that when it spins toward the stake, it will drop down just a few inches in front of it and slide in for a ringer. To give it spin, grab hold of the bottom. There's often a small notch there. It should face up. Put your thumb on this notch. When you throw, you'll pull the notch in a bit with your thumb to give it some spin. Bend your knees. Focus your eye on the patch just in front of the stake. Step forward and pitch the horseshoe with a wrist flick to give it some spin. As with most types of throws, let the rest of your body follow through.

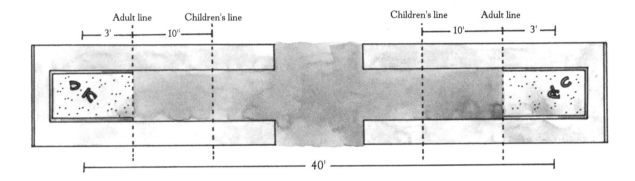

To score:

If the horseshoe rings the stake --3 points
If the horseshoe leans against the stake -------------------------------------2 points
If it is within six inches of the stake --1 point
If it is more than six inches away --0 points

To win: Score more points than the other team or reach a preset winning number, such as 10 or 21 or 42 points.

PLAYING SHUFFLEBOARD

Shuffleboard may be the most recognizable game in America, as well as the one whose rules are the least known. The court is a long rectangle, with triangular scoring zones at either end. The game is played with four scoring disks per side, which are pushed along with a long stick, or *cue*. The scoring triangle has spots worth ten, eight, and seven points, but if the puck touches any white line, it gets no score. If your disk lands in the dreaded ten-off zone, subtract ten points from your score.

All players start at the same end of the court. Eight disks, four in each color, are lined up in the ten-off area. After picking who goes first, each player takes a turn and pushes one of their disks downcourt with the stick so it lands squarely in a good scoring box. (When you push off, don't step past the foul line, which is at the top of the triangle.) Even better, you can try to knock someone else's disk away from a scoring box or even into the ten-off space.

When all disks are played, both players walk to the scoring zone and count the score for that round. Continue to play until someone earns 75 points, or any number that you decide upon ahead of time.

LAWN BOWLING

In lawn bowling, players take turns (also called *bowls*) rolling three or four balls each toward a target ball (called a *jack*, *boccino*, or *pallino*). The player whose ball lands closest to the jack wins the round (and bowls first in the next round). President George Washington asked his gardeners to install a lawn bowling court at his home at Mount Vernon. Rumor has it that Queen Elizabeth I of England was a big fan of the British form of the game, called "Bowls." Norse Vikings played a game called *Varpa*. Polynesians played *Ula Miaka*. The French played *Petanque* (pronounced "pe-tank") with metal balls and a jack called a *cochonnet* (pronounced "co-cho-nay"), which translates as "little piggy."

With a set of balls and a jack, the world of lawn bowling is yours. If you want to try lawn bowing but don't want to buy a set of unique balls for it, gather a bunch of old softballs, which are around the same size, and use a smaller ball as a jack. Set a course and some boundaries (the whole backyard or a part of it, lines drawn in the sand at the beach, or a course mapped in chalk on a parking lot, large driveway, plaza, sidewalk, or quiet street). Agree on some general rules and have fun.

QUOITS

Quoits (pronounced "kwoyts") was once a favorite game of sailors, passing the time at sea, as well as of emigrants on ships bound for new homes. With little to do on board, they would make circles from rope (there's always lots of rope on a ship), and toss them to a nearby target on the ship's deck. The game evolved into being played with steel circles, often weighing three to nine pounds each, although popular play used heavy rope circles, and there was even an indoor version for parlors and pubs.

You can play quoits with any target pins staked into the ground, which makes it an easy backyard game, and there are wooden sets in which each circle on a pin yields a certain number of points.

How to Organize a Tournament

ATOURNAMENT IS A GOOD WAY to organize multiple games with many players and/or teams and to keep a friendly competition going over an afternoon or a weekend. You can do a tournament with any kind of game, whether it be a sport or a board game. One person can be the chief of the tournament, and others can be timekeepers, announcers, or referees. Feel free to embellish with posters, scoreboards, and a "press box" with microphones.

The key to setting up a tournament is knowing how many players or teams are participating; it's easier to have an even number of teams or players, but an odd number is not insurmountable. Once you know who's playing, pick a tournament type and prepare the bracket, which shows the order in which games will be played and tells you who will play them. Here are the three main tournament types.

ROUND-ROBIN

In a round-robin tournament, each team plays a game against every other team. If the tournament includes four teams, assign a letter to each team and set up two playing fields, if you can, so two matches can be played at the same time. A round-robin bracket would look something like this.

Round 1	Round 2	Round 3
A plays B	A plays C	A plays D
C plays D	B plays D	B plays C

If two fields or playing grounds aren't possible, two teams rest (and provide commentary!) while the other two teams play that round. Keep a tally of each player's or team's wins and losses. The one with the best record wins—although if there's a tie, get ready for a playoff game.

SINGLE ELIMINATION

In a single elimination tournament, players and teams advance along the bracket toward a championship, but fall out with one lost game (and thus move over to the microphone to provide expert commentary on the continuing games). To start, use a blind draw (also known as picking out of a hat), so that players and teams are randomly assigned numbers—and their starting spots on the left side of the bracket. The winners of each round play each other. As the rounds progress, losing teams are eliminated from the

tournament. Winning teams move through the bracket to play in the quarterfinals and semifinals. The tournament ends with the final game and the crowning of the day's champion. (In some tournaments, the losers of the semifinals play each other for the third place title.)

DOUBLE ELIMINATION

A double elimination tournament offers a second chance to players and teams who lose their first game. The first-round losers play each other in a second round that is made up of all the players or teams that lost the first round. They then have a chance later on to meet the winners of the first round and even, potentially, win the championship. Double elimination brackets are easily found online, where one can type in the number of players and get an exact bracket for your group.

LAID-BACK STYLE

While it's not exactly a tournament, and it certainly doesn't need any organizing, don't forget the easygoing rhythm of the loser-takes-a-break and the first person in line (or whoever put a quarter at the edge of the pool table) plays the winner.

After you pick your tournament type, you will also need to consider game rules for the tournament. Games may be full-length with standard rules, or shortened versions to keep the action moving along. Some examples are: three rounds of horseshoes; ten-minute badminton matches; a contest of how many croquet wickets can be shot in two minutes; or, on the sillier side, five-shot contests aiming a water gun to vanquish a candle's flame.

Notable Women V: Arts and Letters

CLARA SCHUMANN was, most famously, the wife of composer Robert Schumann. But she was also one of the stars of nineteenth-century music, the first female concert pianist, and a composer in her own right.

Clara was born Clara Josephine Wieck in Leipzig, Germany, in 1819. Her father, Friedrich, was a music teacher, and her mother was a singer. They both played the piano, taught, and performed, and together ran a music store. Before Clara was even born, her father decided his daughter would be a musical prodigy. Her parents worked hard to make that happen: She not only studied piano from an early age, but also trained in voice, violin, counterpoint, composition, and score reading. She first performed in public when she was nine, and gave her first solo piano recital at age eleven. One year later, she embarked on her first concert tour.

As talented as Clara clearly was, this training did not come without a price. She didn't utter a word until she was over four years old. Her parents fought each other bitterly, blaming each other as the cause, and eventually divorced. Clara and her younger brother were cast back and forth between their parents before their father eventually took custody. Clara rarely saw her mother after that.

Her musical accomplishments continued, however. She composed her first concerto, *Piano Concerto in A Minor*, at age fourteen and premiered the piece with the Leipzig Gewandhaus orchestra, conducted by the famous composer Felix Mendelssohn, just two years later. She performed in salons throughout Leipzig and as a teenager made concert tours of Berlin, Dresden, Paris, and Vienna, where she was hailed as a musical genius and a virtuoso pianist of unparalleled musicianship.

She met Robert Schumann when he came to live and study music with her father in 1830. After seven years, he asked Clara's father permission for the two of them to be married. Her father refused, as Clara was just eighteen years old, and vowed to do all he could to prevent them from marrying before she turned twenty-one (at which age she was legally allowed to marry without his consent). He even threatened to shoot Robert if he came near Clara ever again. Clara and Robert filed a lawsuit against him and won. In the end, they married the day before her twenty-first birthday, September 12, 1840.

At first, they both taught music at the Leipzig Conservatory, but after a few years they moved to Dresden and then to Düsseldorf, where she concentrated on performing and he on composing and conducting. They had eight children, one of whom died in infancy. Robert Schumann enjoyed renown as a pianist and composer, but he battled with manic depression and mental illness, and his conducting post in Düsseldorf did not go well. In 1854, after a failed suicide attempt, he was committed to the asylum at Endenich, leaving Clara to run the family and continue in her musical career alone. Robert died in the asylum just two years after being committed.

Music gave Clara solace in the midst of tragedy. Clara moved with her children to Berlin in 1857, and continued to perform, teach, and promote her husband's work. She used her spectacular performing career to popularize his work through her many concert tours (thirty-eight of which she undertook outside Germany). In addition, she premiered works by Frederic Chopin and her good friend Johannes Brahms, who often stepped in as a babysitter to care for her children while she was on tour.

She was known as a thoughtful pianist, who combined a depth of feeling and a singing tone with technical precision. Her skills were considered to be equal or superior to those of Franz Liszt, the most famous pianist of the day.

As a composer in her own right, all of Clara's work dates from the time she was nine years old to 1853, the year before Robert's mental health deteriorated and she assumed responsibility for supporting her family. But in that span she wrote sixty-six pieces, including twenty pieces for solo piano, four pieces for piano and orchestra, and twenty-nine songs set to poetry by German poets including Heine, Rückert, and Goethe. Although women composers were not encouraged—indeed, composing was considered a man's art—Clara clearly relished the work. She wrote to her husband: "Composing gives me great pleasure. . . . There is nothing that surpasses the joy of creation, if only because through it one wins hours of self-forgetfulness, when one lives in a world of sound."

In 1878 the Gewandhaus in Leipzig held a celebration to honor the fiftieth jubilee of Clara's performing career, the centerpiece of which was Clara herself. She was feted with garlands and flowers as she came on stage to perform one of her last concerts, comprised solely of music by her husband, Robert Schumann. That same year she was appointed to the piano faculty of the newly established Hoch Conservatory, where she taught until

1892. Her last public performance took place in Frankfurt, in March 1891.

As she grew older, she performed less, as she grappled with painful rheumatism. But she remained a respected teacher of piano technique, and a trusted adviser for Brahms, who continued to be a steadfast friend. In March 1896, when she was seventy-seven, she suffered a stroke from which she never fully recovered. As her dying wish, she asked her grandson Ferdinand to play her husband's *Romance in F-Sharp Major*, which he had written for her. She died listening to his music on May 20, 1896, and was buried alongside him.

Marian Anderson was born in South Philadelphia on February 27, 1897. As a little girl, she enjoyed singing, especially as part of the choir of the Union Baptist church, but she didn't receive her first formal lesson until she was fifteen. Her congregation helped raise money for her to continue training. It paid off: When the budding opera star sang for the famed Italian conductor Arturo Toscanini, he pronounced, "A voice like yours is heard only once in a hundred years."

She made her debut with the New York Philharmonic on August 26, 1925, where her performance met with critical success. Three years later, she performed at Carnegie Hall, and then made a spectacularly well-received concert tour of Europe—a long way indeed from South Philly. But her most stirring performance was on the steps of the Lincoln Memorial in 1939.

She had planned to perform a concert at Constitution Hall, but the historic organization called the Daughters of the American Revolution (DAR) refused permission, because they did not like that the performance would take place before an "integrated" audience (that is, an audience of both white and black people). Marian appealed to the District of Columbia Board of Education, requesting the use of a public high school auditorium for the performance, but the board refused: The school was "whites only." Not all the members of the DAR agreed with the group's decision, and thousands of members—including First Lady Eleanor Roosevelt—resigned in protest. The Roosevelts (along with several powerful friends) went to the Secretary of the Interior Harold Ickes and proposed an open-air concert at the Lincoln Memorial. He agreed, and history was made. Marian performed to a crowd of more than 75,000 people of all colors and a radio audience of millions, famously opening the event with the patriotic song "My Country, 'Tis of Thee."

Her groundbreaking performances continued. During World War II and the Korean War, Marian cheered the troops with literally thousands of performances in hospitals and bases. At age fifty-eight, in 1955, she became the first African-American to perform with the New York Metropolitan Opera, singing the part of Ulrica in Verdi's *Un ballo in maschera* ("The Masked Ball"). She went on to become the first African-American to be named a permanent member of the company. She toured the Far East in the late 1950s as a goodwill ambassador of the U.S. State Department, traveling 35,000 miles in twelve weeks and making twenty-four concert appearances. In 1958 she was recognized for this work when President Dwight Eisenhower appointed her as a delegate to the Human Rights Committee of the United Nations. She sang at the inaugurations of Presidents Eisenhower and Kennedy and at the 1963 March on Washington for jobs and freedom. She was one of the original thirty-one recipients of the Presidential Medal of Freedom, given to her in 1963 for "especially meritorious contributions to the security or national interest of the United States, World Peace or cultural or other significant public or private endeavors." In 1965 she retired from singing, but continued her good work, winning the United Nations' Peace Prize in 1972.

In 1991, two years before her death, she was honored with a Grammy Award for Lifetime Achievement. She died in 1993, at age ninety-six, and is buried in the Eden Cemetery in Philadelphia, Pennsylvania.

Phillis Wheatley, who lived from 1753 to 1784, was the first published African-American poet. Born in what is now Senegal, Africa, she was kidnapped at age seven and brought to America in 1761 on the slave ship *Phillis,* from which she received her name. She was bought by the Wheatley family of Boston, who taught her to read and write and encouraged her poetic endeavors. She was tutored by John and Susanna Wheatley's son, Nathaniel, in Latin, history, English, geography, and religion. Their daughter, Mary, in particular encouraged her poetry. Eventually, the Wheatleys would free her.

Phillis's first poem, a tale of two men who had almost drowned at sea, was published in a Rhode Island newspaper when she was barely a teenager. This garnered her attention and also the support of a group of women who were willing to finance the publication of an entire book of her poetry. Her first book, published in 1773, brought her much acclaim. *Poems on Various Subjects, Religious and Moral,* was praised by the likes of George Washington and celebrated as far away as England. At first, however, readers were skeptical that a black woman could have really produced a book of such quality. Phillis actually had to defend herself in court before the book was even published, submitting herself to questioning by Boston luminaries including John Hancock and even the governor of Massachusetts. She proved her case, and the men wrote an attestant to her abilities that was published as the preface to her book.

With the book's publication, Phillis and Mrs. Wheatley traveled to London, where she met the likes of the Earl of Dartmouth, John Thornton, and Benjamin Franklin—all fans of her work. In the aftermath of Phillis's international literary success, the Wheatley family emancipated her on October 18, 1773 (although she stayed with the family until the death of her former master, John Wheatley). She met George Washington in person in March 1776, when he commended her for her poems. Later, she married and had three children, but unfortunately the marriage didn't last. She worked as a servant to support her family as a single mother, while trying to complete her second book of poetry. She died, before she had a chance to finish it, in 1784.

"On Imagination"
by Phillis Wheatley

Thy various works, imperial queen, we see,
How bright their forms! how deck'd with pomp by thee!
Thy wond'rous acts in beauteous order stand,
And all attest how potent is thine hand.
From Helicon's refulgent heights attend,
Ye sacred choir, and my attempts befriend:
To tell her glories with a faithful tongue,
Ye blooming graces, triumph in my song.
Now here, now there, the roving Fancy flies,
Till some lov'd objects strikes her wand'ring eyes,
Whose silken fetters all the senses bind,

And soft captivity involves the mind.
Imagination! who can sing thy force?
Or who describe the swiftness of thy course?
Soaring though air to find the bright abode,
Th'empyreal palace of the thund'ring God,
We on thy pinions can surpass the wind,
And leave the rolling universe behind;
From star to star the mental optics rove,
Measure the skies, and range the realms above.
There in one view we grasp the mighty whole,
Or with new worlds amaze th' unbounded soul.
Though Winter frowns to Fancy's raptur'd eyes
The fields may flourish, and gay scenes arise;
The frozen deeps may break their iron bands,
And bid their waters murmur o'er the sands.
Fair Flora may resume her fragrant reign,
And with her flow'ry riches deck the plain;
Sylvanus may diffuse his honours round,
And all the forest may with leaves be crown'd;
Show'rs may descend, and dews their gems disclose,
And nectar sparkle on the blooming rose.

Such is thy pow'r, nor are thine orders vain,
O thou the leader of the mental train:
In full perfection all thy works are wrought,
And thine the sceptre o'er the realms of thought.
Before thy throne the subject-passions bow,
Of subject-passions sov'reign ruler Thou,
At thy command joy rushes on the heart,
And through the glowing veins the spirits dart.

Fancy might now her silken pinions try
To rise from earth, and sweep th' expanse on high;
From Tithon's bed now might Aurora rise,
Her cheeks all glowing with celestial dies,
While a pure stream of light o'erflows the skies.
The monarch of the day I might behold,
And all the mountains tipt with radiant gold,
But I reluctant leave the pleasing views,
Which Fancy dresses to delight the Muse;
Winter austere forbids me to aspire,
And northern tempests damp the rising fire;
They chill the tides of Fancy's flowing sea,
Cease then, my song, cease the unequal lay.

Whittling

To WHITTLE, use a small knife to pare away shavings from the surface of a piece of wood. It's that easy, and it's as old as time. As long as there has been wood, there has been someone around to take a small knife and shape it into something new. Back in the days of the caves, that's how the wheel was invented: By some enterprising person with the vision to grab a stone flint and whittle a large chunk of wood into a circle.

Whittling is slow and gradual. It's perfect for passing time on a camping trip or hike in the woods, or a quiet hour in the backyard. It's also a fun way to sharpen your pencils.

A small knife like a Swiss Army knife or a pen knife is perfect for whittling. Gather some fallen branches from the backyard or nearby woods. Wood for whittling can also be purchased at craft and supply stores. Hold the knife in your stronger hand (right if you are a righty, left if you are a lefty), hold the wood in your other hand, and make sure to follow these three safety rules.

Rule 1. Always cut away from your hands, fingers, and all parts of your body. There may come a moment when you think, "It will be so much faster and easier if only I turn the knife this way toward me for just a second to make this tiny notch." Right at that moment is when the knife will accidentally slip and cut your hand, and the whole thing turns into a bloody mess. Believe us. We've seen it happen. So keep the knife facing away from you, all the time. Some whittlers choose to wear a protective glove on the hand that holds the wood.

Rule 2. Always keep the knife pointed away from other people. Always.

Rule 3. Always, always keep the blade sharp. You may think that a dull knife is safer. But when a knife is dull, you are more likely to force it, and that's when it's more likely to slip and cut you.

HOW TO WHITTLE

Some whittlers just take hold of a piece of wood, and follow their instincts. Others sketch what they want to make, perhaps an animal or a face, a small bowl or a toy boat. They work the sketch until it is just right, jotting down ideas and future directions as they come to mind. A sketch like this can be redrawn on the surface of the wood or kept in mind as a guide.

A good first project is to whittle the bark off of a fallen branch and turn the end into a point. Think of it as a stick you can use to roast marshmallows or hot dogs over a campfire, or as a stake to hold up a plant in the garden. Shape a piece of wood into a ball, by whittling half of it at a time. Then, turn it into a face. If you're at a campsite, whittle yourself a very useful fork and spoon. Whittle a shallow bowl from a larger piece of wood. Designs can be whittled into the wood, too: crosshatches for texture, and small notches and lines to show hair and other features.

If you're not feeling ready for a whittling knife and wood, no worries. Whittling can be done with a plastic picnic knife, or a butter knife, or even a wooden craft stick—as long as you have in hand a crisp apple or a potato or a bar of soap. Trace a design of a fish on the soap. Whittle away on all sides—you can work in a fin at the top or at the bottom. When you whittle soap, small mistakes can be fixed by rubbing in a small amount of water.

HOW TO SHARPEN A WHITTLING KNIFE

Sharpening a knife has become a long lost secret. A sharpening stone is inexpensive and can be purchased at a hardware store or a kitchen supply shop. The directions that come with it will tell you whether to add a little water or a touch of oil to the top of the stone, or to use it plain. In a pinch you can also use the long thin sharpening steels that are found in many kitchens. An old camping trick is to sharpen a knife on the rough bottom of a ceramic coffee mug, if you have one.

There are many sharpening methods, but this is the one that we like best. Face the knife away from you, and hold it against the stone at a 20° angle. Make clockwise circles along the whole blade. The blade will start to look shiny where it has been sharpened. Then, turn the blade so it faces you. Hold at the same 20° angle, and make counterclockwise circles until the second side is sharp, too.

Putting on a Show

All the world's a stage,
And all the men and women merely players
—William Shakespeare, *As You Like It*

THE GREEK PERFORMER THESPIS was perhaps the first person to perform a story solo on stage. He used masks to represent different characters and interacted with a group of singers (the Greek chorus) who commented on and narrated his actions. It is in Thespis's honor that actors the world over are called *thespians*. And in honor of the masks he used, the familiar sad and happy faced masks representing tragedy and comedy are today a universal symbol of the theater.

Probably the best-known figure in the history of the theater is the English actor and playwright William Shakespeare. He not only wrote some forty plays, but also told incredible stories and coined hundreds of words and phrases that are famous even now. ("It's neither here nor there," "a foregone conclusion," "to wear your heart on your sleeve," "pomp and circumstance," "as luck would have it," "the world's your oyster," "into thin air"—all from Shakespeare!)

Today, despite competition from television and movies, theater is still an important part of our culture. And every girl who's acted out a scene from her favorite story or show or book or even her own imagination knows how much fun it is to put on a show.

THE PLAY'S THE THING

To put on a play, you need a few things. The most important, of course, is imagination. The second most important thing is a script. Whether you go for Shakespeare or some other famous playwright, or whether you write the play yourself, you should be inspired by a story that leaps off the page. You need to ask yourself: What kind of play will you do? Will it be a musical? Will it be a famous play or something original? How many people will you need to play the parts? Once something captures your creative fancy, you need to turn your mind to the more practical aspects of putting on a show: Assembling your company.

THE COMPANY, CAST, AND CREW

Company is the term for all of the people involved in working on a theatrical production. *Cast* is the word for a group of actors in a play. And *crew* is the term for the people who do the *behind-the-scenes* work that supports the actors on stage. Here are some of the jobs involved in putting on a show.

Title	What she does
Producer	Responsible for the practical, business aspects of a theater production. She usually chooses the play, hires the director, and finds funding to pay all the people involved. She also sets ticket prices, determines performance dates, and develops marketing and advertising for the show.
Director	In charge of overseeing the entire production. She has a vision of the play, from how it should look to how it should be acted, and directs the cast and crew in making that happen.
Actors	A group of people who act out the roles in a play.
House Manager	Responsible for selling tickets, ushering audience members into the theater, and making sure the performance space is clean and inviting.
Stage Manager	Responsible for making everything run smoothly. She keeps track of blocking (where the actors go on the stage) and all stage directions; and makes sure actors follow the script and have the props and costumes that they need.
Assistant Stage Manager	Helps the Stage Manager and works backstage during the show.
Wardrobe Manager	In charge of finding, making, maintaining, and keeping track of costumes; wardrobe assistants may also help actors change in and out of costumes.
Wigs/Makeup Artist	In charge of choosing wigs, hairpieces, and face and body paints for each cast member; makeup artists will also help apply actors' stage makeup.
Lighting Manager	In charge of all things electrical, including spotlights.
Scenery Artist	Responsible for designing, building, constructing, and painting sets.
Prop Master	In charge of large and small items that are necessary for the play but not part of the actual scenery or set.
Sound Engineer	In charge of PA system, microphones, music, and sound effects.

For a small production, you don't need quite so many people. If you're doing a one-woman show, all you really need is yourself. But for a play among friends, you need a director, a few actors, and a few people for the crew.

ALL THE WORLD'S A STAGE

Another thing to consider when putting on a show is where you will perform. Perhaps your school or library has an auditorium you might use. Otherwise, stages can be made out of living rooms, bedrooms, basements, or even backyards.

For sets, scenery, and props, don't underestimate the power of paint, markers, creativity, and good old-fashioned elbow grease. With a few friends and some art supplies—from butcher-block rolls of paper to cardboard boxes to spare wood and someone who knows how to build things with it—you can create a backdrop for any scene.

As for costumes, check that trunk in the attic filled with your mother or grandmother's old fancy dresses; ask a big sister for hand-me-downs; troll some thrift stores for things that might fit the bill; or get a friend with a sewing machine to help make what you need. The easiest thing to do is use clothes you already have that look close enough to what's called for in the script. The audience can use their imaginations. And of course you need tickets and programs, which are always fun to make. You can have a crew member hand them out to the audience as they arrive.

REHEARSALS AND DRESS REHEARSALS

Rehearsing just means practicing, and you practice a play the same way you practice anything else: a little at a time. Once you begin rehearsals, you may decide to practice just the first few scenes one day and the last scenes the next. Closer to the performance date, you can rehearse going through the play from start to finish. The final rehearsal stage is the *dress rehearsal*, when everyone performs exactly as they would for an audience, in full costume and with finished sets and props (and special effects and music, if those things are part of the show). You may choose to have a few select and trusted audience members attend your final dress rehearsal, so that the actors have a chance to practice in front of other people.

OPENING NIGHT

Actors are a superstitious lot. In the theater, it is believed that wishing someone good luck will actually bring them bad luck. So on your play's big opening night, instead of wishing everyone luck, instead say what actors say: "Break a leg!"

PROJECTING YOUR VOICE

When singing and speaking on stage, an actor is aware of the space around her and uses her voice to fill that space. To do this properly, she must use her body to expand her voice, rather than simply yelling from the throat.

A silly exercise: Open your mouth, stick out your tongue, and pant like a dog. The muscles you are using to do this are your abdominal and intercostal muscles, along with your diaphragm, which runs along the bottom of your rib cage. Now, keep panting like a dog, but try to say, "Ha!" while you do it. Practice a few words like this, relaxing your throat and letting your belly muscles do the work. Then, try speaking normally, but still having your belly push your voice. It will be louder and yet gentler on your vocal cords.

Engaging these muscles is also key when singing. Normally, when we breathe in our chests expand and our bellies suck in a little; and when we breathe out our chests deflate and our bellies expand. When singing (and speaking on stage), breathing is slightly different. Breathe in by filling your belly, rather than your chest, with air, making your belly expand as you take in air; and breathe out by compressing your belly as you let air out. Practice with one hand on your belly to help you better notice how it expands and contracts with each breath.

THE ONE-WOMAN (OR ONE-GIRL!) SHOW

Sometimes the best kind of fun is acting out your favorite dramatic moments in private, all by yourself—the more dramatic, the better. One of the most famous examples of dramatic soliloquy—a speech addressed to yourself—is from Shakespeare's play *Hamlet*, in which Hamlet questions himself about the nature of existence. Even if you've never heard the whole thing, you may recognize it by its first six words: "To be, or not to be."

To be, or not to be—that is the question:
Whether 'tis nobler in the mind to suffer
The slings and arrows of outrageous fortune
Or to take arms against a sea of troubles
And by opposing end them. To die, to sleep—
No more—and by a sleep to say we end
The heartache, and the thousand natural shocks
That flesh is heir to. 'Tis a consummation
Devoutly to be wished. To die, to sleep—
To sleep—perchance to dream: ay, there's the rub,
For in that sleep of death what dreams may come
When we have shuffled off this mortal coil,
Must give us pause. There's the respect
That makes calamity of so long life.
For who would bear the whips and scorns of time,
Th' oppressor's wrong, the proud man's contumely
The pangs of despised love, the law's delay,
The insolence of office, and the spurns
That patient merit of th' unworthy takes,
When he himself might his quietus make
With a bare bodkin? Who would fardels bear,
To grunt and sweat under a weary life,
But that the dread of something after death,
The undiscovered country, from whose bourn
No traveller returns, puzzles the will,
And makes us rather bear those ills we have
Than fly to others that we know not of?
Thus conscience does make cowards of us all,
And thus the native hue of resolution
Is sicklied o'er with the pale cast of thought,
And enterprise of great pitch and moment
With this regard their currents turn awry
And lose the name of action.—Soft you now,
The fair Ophelia!—Nymph, in thy orisons
Be all my sins remembered.

How to Say Hello, Good-bye, and Thank You Around the World

GIVE OR TAKE A FEW DIALECTS, there are at least 6,700 languages in the world. Here is how to say *hello*, *good-bye*, and *thank you* in just a few of them.

LANGUAGE NAME IN ENGLISH (NATIVE NAME)	MAINLY SPOKEN IN . . .	HELLO	GOOD-BYE	THANK YOU
Amharic (Amharina)	Ethiopia	Selam, teanastëllën	Chou, tasanababata	Amesegenallo
Arabic (Arabi)	Throughout North Africa and the Middle East	Marhaba, ahalan, es salaam aleikom (to which one responds: wa aleikom es salaam), salaam, labas (used in Morocco)	Ma'a salama	Shukran
Balinese (Bali)	Bali and nearby islands	Depending on the time of day: selamat pagi ("good morning"), selamat siang ("good noon"), selamat sore ("good afternoon"), selamat malam ("good evening")	The person who stays says, "selamat jalan" ("peace along your way"). The person who leaves says, "selamat tinggal" (peace in your life). More simply, say, "sampai ketemu."	Terima kasi
Basque (Euskara)	Basque region near the border of Spain and France	Kaixo	Agur	Eskerrik asko
Bengali (Bangla)	Bangladesh, India, England	Nomoskar, a salaam alaykum	Bidaay, shuva-bidaay	Dhanyabaad
Bosnian (Bosanski)	Bosnia and Herzegovina	Zdravo, merhaba,	Do vidjenja	Hvala, hvala vam (implies extra respect)
Choctaw	Tribal language, Oklahoma and Mississippi, United States	Halito	Chi pisa lachike	Yakoke
Danish (Dansk)	Denmark, Greenland	Goddag, hejsa, hej	Farvel	Tak, mange tak
Dutch (Nederlands)	The Netherlands and Caribbean islands such as Suriname and Aruba	Hallo, goedendag, goeiedag, morgen	Tot ziens, dag	Dank u (polite form), dank je (informal)
English	North America, United Kingdom, Australia, and around the world	Hello, hi, hey, good to see you, greetings, g'day (Australia)	Good-bye, bye, bye-bye	Thank you, thanks (informal), thanks y'all
Esperanto	An international language created in 1887, which hoped to become a universal second language uniting all people on the globe	Saluton	Ĝis la revido	Dankon, donkon al vi
French (Français)	France and around the world	Salut, bonjour	Au revoir, adieu	Merci, merci beaucoup
German (Deutsch)	Germany, Austria, Switzerland	Hallo, guten tag, grüß dich (the "ß" is pronounced "s" and stands for a double s at the end of a word)	Auf wiedersehen	Danke, danke dir (informal), danke schön

LANGUAGE NAME IN ENGLISH (NATIVE NAME)	MAINLY SPOKEN IN . . .	HELLO	GOOD-BYE	THANK YOU
Greek (Elenika)	Greece	Yia sou, yassas (more formally or to several people)	Adio, yia sou and yia sas, which mean both "hello" and "good-bye"	Efkharisto
Haitian Creole (Kreyòl)	Haiti	Alò, bonjou	Orevwa, tchaw, babay	Mèsi, granmèsi
Hausa	West Africa	Sannu	Sai an jima	Na gode
Hawaiian (Olelo Hawai'i)	Hawaii	Aloha, aloha mai	Aloha	Mahalo
Hebrew (Ivrit)	Israel	Shalom, ma nishma, hi	Shalom	Toda, toda raba
Hindi	India and East Asia	Namaste, namaskar, helo (on telephone)	Alavidha, namaste	Shukriya, dhanyavaad
Hopi	Tribal language, Southwest United States	Hai (to call someone's attention). Um waynuma? To which one answers, "owí, nu' waynuma." Ha'u is said upon entering the kiva, or ritual room.	The person who stays says, "um ason piw a'ni." The person who leaves says, "nu' tus payni." The response is "ta'á, um ason piw a'ni."	Men say kwakwhá. Women say askwali or hevé.
Hungarian (Magyar)	Hungary	Szia (pronounced "see-ya," to one person), sziasztok (to more than one); similarly, hello and hellosztok	Viszlát (formal); szia (to one person) and sziasztok (to several) (informal)	Köszönöm, köszi
Icelandic (Islenska)	Iceland	Halló, góðan daginn	Bless, bless bless	Takk, takk fyrir
Igbo	Nigeria	Ndeewo, kadu	Ka o di, ka omesia	Imela, dalu
Indonesian (Bahasa Indonesia)	Indonesia	Selamat siang, halo, hai	Sampai jumpa. The person who stays says, "selamat jalan." The person who leaves says, "selamat tinngal."	Terima kasih banyak (formal), makasih (informal), thanks ya (very informal), trims (slang)
Inuit (Inuktitut)	Arctic Canada, Alaska, Greenland	Ai, ainngai	Assunai, ilaaniul	Nakurmik, quana
Italian (Italiano)	Italy	Buon giorno, ciao	Arrivederci, ciao, a domain, addio, pronto (on the telephone)	Grazie
Japanese (Nihongo)	Japan	Konnichi wa (emphasis on the second syllable), ohayo (good morning), moshi-moshi (said on the telephone)	Sayonara, jaa ne (said informally to friends), bye-bye	Arigato, domo arigato, arigato gozaimasu (when leaving an event that has not ended), arigato gozaimashita (for leaving an event that has ended); ja ma ta (see you!)
Kirghiz (Kirghizi)	Central Asia	Salaam	Ghosh	Rakhmat
Korean (Hangungmal in South Korea, and Chos Nmal in North Korea)	North and South Korea	Ahnyong, annyong haseyo (formal), yeoboseyo (on the telephone)	Ahnyong, chalga hasseyo	Kamsa hamnee-da (formal), komapsumnida (informal)
Kurdish (Kurdî)	Iraq, Iran, Turkey	Silaw. Roj baş (pronounced: "rozh-bash"); to which one answers, "bashem"	Xwahafiz	Shukur, sipas
Latin (Lingua Latina)	Ancient Rome and wherever Roman soldiers conquered	Ave, salve	Vale (said to one person); valete (said to several people at once)	Gratias ago tibi (GAT), gratias

LANGUAGE NAME IN ENGLISH (NATIVE NAME)	MAINLY SPOKEN IN . . .	HELLO	GOOD-BYE	THANK YOU
Lenape	Tribal language, Delaware Valley, United States	Hè	Làpìch knewĕl	Wanìshi
Malagasy	Madagascar	Manao ahoana, salama	Veloma	Misaotra
Mandarin Chinese (Pu tong hua)	China	Ni hao ma (ni hao wei, if on the telephone)	Zai jian	Xie xie
Maori (Te Reo Maori)	New Zealand	Kia ora	Haere rā (said by the person who stays), e noho ra (said by the person who leaves)	Kia ora
Mongolian (Mongol)	Mongolia	Sain baina uu, sainu	Bayarta, daraa uulzii (see you later!)	Bayarlalaa, gyalailaa
Navajo-Dine (Diné Bizaad)	Tribal language, United States	Yá'át'ééh	Hágoónee	Ahéhee'
Persian (Farsi)	Iran and the Iranian diaspora	Salaam	Kho'da hafez, masalaam	Tashakkur, mamnoon, merci, moshakir, mo'he'shaker'am
Pig Latin	Everywhere kids want to be silly and have fun by taking a word's first consonant, moving it to the end, and adding "ay"	Ello-hay	Ood-bye-gay	Ank-thay ou-yay
Polish (Polska)	Poland	Dzień dobry, cześć (pronounced cheshch), witaj	Do widzenia, nara	Dziękuję, dziekujemy (when said by several people at once), dzieki (to friends)
Portuguese (Portugues)	Portugal, Brazil, Angola, Mozambique	Ola, oi, bom dia (good morning), boa tarde (good afternoon), boa noite (good evening)	Adeus, tchau,	Obrigada (when said by a woman or girl); obrigado (when said by a man or boy)
Quechua	South America	Allillanchu	Wuasleglla	Yusulpaykia, paschi
Russian (Russki Yazik)	Russia	Privet	Do svidaniya, poka	Spasibo
Scottish (Scots)	Scotland	Guid mornin, guid efternuin, guide eenin, madainn mhath, hallo	Cheery, beannachd leat, mar sin leat	Thenk ye, tapadh leat (informal), tapadh leibh (formal)
Setswana	Botswana	Dumela mma (when saying hello to a woman or girl), dumela rra (when saying hello to a man or boy)	Samava sentle (meaning "go well," said by the person who stays), sala sentle (meaning "stay well," said by the person who leaves)	Ke itumetse (literally, "I am happy")
Spanish (Español)	Spain, Central America, South America	¡Hola!	Adiós, hasta luego (see you later), hasta pronto (see you soon)	Gracias, muchas gracias, te pasaste (in Latin America)
Swahili (Kiswahili)	Kenya, Eastern and Central Africa	Jambo, salama, hujambo	Kwa heri (good-bye to one person), kwa herini (good-bye to several people)	Asante

LANGUAGE NAME IN ENGLISH (NATIVE NAME)	MAINLY SPOKEN IN . . .	HELLO	GOOD-BYE	THANK YOU
Tagalog	The Philippines	Kamusta, hello, hi	Palaam	Salamat, salamat po
Tamil	India	Vanakkam, alo, hi	Poyittu varén	Nandri
Thai (Phasa Thai)	Thailand	Sawatdi, sawatdi ka (when said by a girl or woman), sawatdi krup (when said by a man or boy)	Sawatdi (ka/krup)	Khawp khun, kwawp khun ka (when said by a girl), khawp khun krup (when said by a boy)
Tibetan (Bod Skad)	Tibet and nearby	Oloy, tashidelek	Tashidelek	Tudiche (pronounced "*tu*-di-chey")
Turkish (Türkçe)	Turkey	Merhaba, selam	Güle güle, hoşçakal (pronounced "hosh-cha-kal")	Teşekkürler, teşekkür, teşekkür ederim, sagolun, sagol, mersi
Urdu	Pakistan	Asalam alaykum, namaste	Khuda-hafiz, salaam	Shukriya
Welsh (Cymraeg)	Wales	Hylo, sut mae?	Da bo chi (pronounced "dah-boh-khee"), hwyl (pronounced "hoo-il")	Diolch, diolch yn fawr
Wolof	Senegal, West Africa	Na nga def (to one person), na ngeen def (to several people, as in "hello, everyone")	Ba beneen	Jai-rruh-jef
Xhosa (isiKhosa)	South Africa	Molo (to one person); molweni (to two or more people)	Hamba ka-kahle (pronounced "kah-shlay," said by the person who stays); sala kahle (pronounced "sala kah-shlay," said by the person who leaves)	N'kosi
Yoruba	Nigeria and West Africa	Ago o, ba wo ni, to which the response is dadani esa, which means "i am fine." (In addition, there are another fifteen specific ways to say hello.)	Ó dà bò	E se é. O se (to someone your age or younger); e se (to someone older than yourself), e seun (polite form)
Zulu	South Africa and Lesotho	Sawubona (to one person), sanibonani (to several people)	Sala kahle (to one person, if you are leaving), salani kahle (to several people, if you are leaving), hamba kahle (to one person if you are staying), hambani kahle (to several people if you are staying)	Ngiyabonga (to one person), siyabonga (to several people)

Swimming

A SWIMMING STROKE is simply a way of moving your arms and legs to propel yourself forward in the water as smoothly as possible. There's the dog paddle, of course, but here are four more formal swimming strokes:

Freestyle

This stroke, probably the most common swimming style used today, was first developed around 1873 by an Englishman named John Arthur Trudgen. He based his technique on the way he saw Native Americans swim, with their heads in the water and their arms moving windmill style. This was new to Europeans at the time, who preferred to swim with their heads above water. It came to be known as "freestyle" for its use in swimming competitions where swimmers could swim in whatever style they preferred. As the "Trudgen" was the fastest for many swimmers, nearly all of them used that stroke in the "freestyle" laps. Soon *freestyle* overtook *Trudgen* as the name of choice (though it is sometimes referred to as "the crawl").

Begin on your stomach in the water, arms out in front of you, hands touching, and your head down. Keeping your left arm straight, pull your right hand down and back toward your legs. When your right arm is extended alongside your legs near the water's surface, turn your head to the right to take a breath. Take care to rotate only your head as you breathe, not your whole body. Reach your right arm over your head to meet your left arm at the starting position and put your head back down in the water. Repeat this on the left side. Throughout, kick your legs, alternating left and right, to help move your body through the water. The stronger your kick, the faster you'll go. After you get the hang of it, try taking a breath on every other stroke instead of every stroke, and then every third stroke.

Breaststroke

The breaststroke first appeared in the Olympics in 1904. It's the slowest of the four strokes and also one of the oldest: There are rock painting depictions of swimmers doing the breaststroke in Egypt's "Cave of Swimmers," dating back to the Ice Age. One of the advantages of the breaststroke is that you are able to see straight ahead when swimming. Also, as you lift your head up with every pull forward, you have an opportunity to breathe on every stroke.

There are two components to this stroke: the arms and the legs. For the arms, begin just underwater

with your arms extended and your head down. Your arms should be straight, with your palms facing outward. This means the backs of your hands and knuckles are touching each other, and your arms are hugging your ears. Move your hands out and back toward your body as though you are pushing the water away. As you bend your elbows to bring your arms in close to your sides, lift your head up and out of the water to take in a breath. Plunge your head back into the water, and bring your hands back together again, palms facing outward. Extend and straighten your arms to push your hands forward and begin the stroke again. For the legs, practice holding on to the side of the pool first. Begin on your stomach with your legs together and extended straight behind you. Bend your knees, flexing your feet as you bring your ankles back toward your bottom. Then, move your feet out to the side, bring them around in a circular motion, and end the way you started, with your legs together and extended behind you. When putting the arms and legs together, keep the following in mind: When your arms open (pushing the palms away from one another), your legs bend; when your arms are back and bent at your sides, your legs kick. The stroke all together, arms and legs, is: Extend arms, palms facing outward, with your head down and legs together and straight out behind you; move hands out and toward your body as you bend your knees and bring your feet back toward your bottom; bring your arms in at your sides as you lift your head out of the water for a breath and kick your feet out to the side in a circular motion; extend your arms, palms facing outward, head down, your legs extended behind you.

Backstroke

The backstroke is kind of like an upside-down freestyle: It involves moving the arms windmill style and a flutter kick with alternating feet, just like the freestyle, but it's performed belly-up instead of face-down.

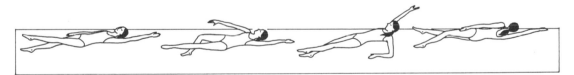

If you can float on your back, you can do the backstroke. Begin on your back with your arms at your sides. Lift one arm up and out of the water, keeping it straight and close to your body. When it reaches your ear, begin to lift up your other arm as you continue moving your first arm in a circular motion going under the water. Whenever one arm is up and out of the water, the other arm is below the water. Both arms move like windmills, circling around, and your feet should be kicking in a flutter kick, alternating left and right, to move you through the water. When doing the backstroke, aim for keeping your body flat, in a straight line, without your bottom sinking. A backstroker's tip for diminishing splash: try to lift each arm out of the water angled thumb-side first rather than bringing up your hand all at once, and when the arms go back into the water above your head, try to imagine entering the water pinkie finger first.

Butterfly

The butterfly, probably the most difficult of the four strokes, was developed in the 1930s and made its debut in the Olympics in 1956. This stroke involves using a dolphin kick, where both legs move up and down together, and an overhead arm stroke with both arms at the same time.

Although it's the undulating motion of kicking your legs and whipping your arms around at the same time that seems tricky, the real secret to this stroke is the kick. To do the dolphin kick, imagine that you are a mermaid, with a mermaid tail instead of legs. Keep your legs together and kick with the kind of fluid movement a mermaid would have swimming through the water. Practice kicking like this, and once you have the hang of it, try adding the arms: Kick with your head down and arms at your sides, and then, just after one of your mermaid kicks, swoop your arms up out of the water and over your head until they are straight in front of you, hands together. When your arms swoop up, your head and upper body does, too, so you can take a breath. And when your arms hit the water again in front of you, your head goes back down underwater. Keep your arms moving down through the water toward your legs, do another mermaid kick, and bring your arms up again out and over your head for another breath. Once you get the rhythm down, you can even try coming up for a breath every two strokes.

HOW TO DO A FLIP TURN

When competitive swimmers do laps, often instead of merely touching the wall and turning around to swim back in the opposite direction, they will do a flip turn, which is basically an underwater somersault, before pushing off the wall with their feet. Here's how to do it.

Before you flip. Start by doing a somersault on land, to get a sense of how it feels to do a forward roll. Then, move to the water to practice breathing: Breathing right can help keep you from getting water up your nose. Standing in the water, take a deep breath in through your nose with your mouth closed, and then when you bob underwater, exhale forcefully through your nose. Come back up. Do this a few times to get comfortable with breathing out through your nose while underwater.

PRACTICING THE FLIP

Middle of the pool: Standing flip. Stand in water that comes up to just above your belly. Hold your arms out in front of you. Close your mouth and take a deep breath through your nose. Jump forward into a tuck position—tuck your chin to your chest, bend your knees, and bring them up so they rest against your belly—as you somersault in the water. Remember to exhale, blowing the air out through your nose, as you flip over under the water.

Middle of the pool: Floating and swimming flip. Float facedown with your hands at your sides. Do a few quick kicks with your feet and then move into a tuck position as you do a somersault. Once you've tried this, try a somersault from swimming: Perform three freestyle strokes, then three or four kicks, and then do your somersault.

At the wall: Standing flip. Stand about a body length away from the wall. Hold your arms out and jump forward to do a somersault. Remember to blow air out your nose as you do the flip. About three quarters of the way through your somersault, extend your legs out of the tuck position and stretch to reach the wall with your feet. You should be on your back under the water when your feet hit the wall. Practice this several times so that you get a sense of how it feels to plant your feet on the wall and where in the turn you need to open up to get your feet there.

Doing the flip turn. Swim freestyle toward the wall until you are about a body length away. Then, tuck your chin to your chest and begin the somersault, blowing air through your nose as you do the flip. About halfway through your flip, open the tuck and extend your legs toward the wall. Push off the wall. You should be belly-up under the water, with your arms in streamline position (over your head, straight, fingers touching). Then, turn over so that you're on your belly, your back facing up, and begin kicking and swimming in the other direction.

Practical Life

SEW A HEM

The absolute simplest method of sewing a hem? Not sewing at all. Pick up some adhesive iron-on hem tape from a craft store, and all you need is an iron. But actually sewing a hem, with an actual needle and thread, is a handy skill to have, and what's more, it's very easy. So, gather a needle, thread, scissors, straight pins, and an iron. Try on the item of clothing that you need to hem, and fold the fabric to the length you need, using the straight pins to mark where the new hemline should be. (A good rule of thumb: On pants, a hem should be about one inch deep, and on skirts and dresses, about two inches.) Take off the item and turn it inside out; then, use an iron to press the new hem flat. Then, get a needle and about one yard of thread that matches the color of the fabric. Thread the needle, tie a knot in one end of the thread, and push the needle through the fabric at a seam point until the knot is flush against the fabric. Hand-stitch all along the top edge by pushing the needle and thread through the top side of the fabric and pulling it back through from the other side. Take care to keep the stitches even; if they are too tight, they can pucker the fabric. When you get to the end, make a double knot and cut the thread. Turn the item right-side out, and iron to finish.

SEW ON A BUTTON

Find the spot where the button was before it fell off and trim any loose threads that remain. Get a needle and about 12 to 18 inches of thread that matches either the color of the button or the color of the garment. Thread the needle to the halfway point of the thread, and tie the ends in a knot. On the back of the fabric, directly underneath where the button was, push the needle through to the top side and pull the thread all the way through. Slip the needle through one of the holes on the button and slide the button down until sits on the fabric. Pull the thread taut, then push the needle down through one of the button holes and through to the underside. Push the needle up from underneath and through another hole in the button. If there are four holes in the button, sew in a crisscross pattern, alternating holes. Do this until you get within a few inches of the end of the thread, and then tie a knot on the underside (pass the needle through the stitches on the back and tie). Trim the excess thread, and you're done.

SHARPEN DULL SCISSORS

Tear off a strip of tin foil, and fold it over a few times to make it thicker. Then, cut into the foil with the dull scissors.

PLUNGE A TOILET

Key to plunging a clogged toilet is the plunger itself: Make sure you have a plunger that not only has a bell (the rounded part at the end) but also a cup that sticks out just below the bell. To plunge, put the plunger in the toilet and center it on the hole. Press it tight: The cup part should go right in the hole and the bell part should create a seal around it. You'll know if you've made that seal when you try to pull the plunger back and it feels locked into place. Next, you'll need to pump the plunger in and out, pushing in and pulling it back quickly four or five times—without breaking the seal. This movement, especially the pulling back part, is what helps break up the clog. Then, pull the plunger all the way off the hole. If you hear a sucking sound, that means the clog is on its way to being broken. If you don't hear that kind of sound, repeat the plunge until you do.

STOP AN OVERFLOWING TOILET

Alongside nearly every toilet is a pipe connecting the toilet to the wall or the floor. What the pipe actually connects is the toilet and the water supply. If your toilet is overflowing, all you have to do to stop it is turn the valve on this pipe, and that stops the water from coming into (and out of) your toilet. If you don't have a pipe with a valve, never fear: You can stop the overflow another way. Just take off the tank cover, and lift up the float ball inside the tank; as long as you hold it up, the water will stop running. Hold it up while someone else shuts the water off at its main source.

UNSEAL A SEALED ENVELOPE

Place it in the freezer for a few hours. When you take it out, use your fingernail or a butter knife to gently lift the sealed edge.

PUT OUT A KITCHEN FIRE

For a grease or electrical fire: Use baking soda (not water) to put out the flames. For a fire in a pot or pan, put the lid on to cut off the oxygen supply (fire needs air to thrive), and turn off the heat. If the flames still aren't snuffed out by the lid, use baking soda. For an oven or microwave oven fire, close the door (or leave it shut if it's already closed), and turn off the heat.

Water is safe to use only on fires involving wood, paper, or cloth. Using water on grease fires can cause the grease to splatter, which will make the fire spread; and using water on electrical fires can put you at risk for serious shocks.

If you have a fire extinguisher, remember PASS: Pull, Aim, Squeeze, Spray. Pull the release pin, aim the nozzle at the far side of the fire, squeeze to activate the spray and hold the handle tight while you move the nozzle from side to side. And of course, if you've tried to put out a kitchen fire but it continues to spread, get to a safe place and call 911.

FIX A CLOGGED DRAIN

Sometimes a clog can be cleared with a simple homemade remedy. Pour a half cup of baking soda and then a half cup of vinegar into the drain. You may remember from second-grade science class how baking soda and vinegar interact with each other: Be prepared for foaming and fumes. If the drain has a cover, put it back on loosely, and then let it set for three hours or so before running the water again.

For a kitchen sink drain clogged with grease, try pouring in a half cup of salt, then a half cup of baking soda, and then an entire teakettle full of boiling water. Let it sit overnight to break up the clog. To prevent clogs in the first place, you may try this homemade drain cleaner, to be used on drains once a week. Thoroughly mix 1 cup baking soda, 1 cup table salt, and ¼ cup cream of tartar. Pour just a ¼ cup of this mixture into the drain, and then immediately pour 1 cup of boiling water down the drain. Wait for 10 seconds and then run cold water.

HANG A PICTURE

A good rule of thumb in general is to hang pictures so that the center of the picture is eye-level. For grown-ups, this is about 60 inches from the ground. Use a tape measure to measure up 60 inches on your wall where you want to hang the picture and mark the spot with a tiny bit of removable masking tape. That is where the center of the picture will go. To figure out where the nail should go in the wall, turn the picture over to the back and use removable masking tape to measure the distance between the hook or notch at the top (where the nail will be) and the middle of the frame. Then, take off that length of tape and put it on the wall, starting at the tiny bit of tape you put there to mark 60 inches and extending upward. Hammer a nail at the top of that length of tape, remove both bits of tape, and hang your picture on the nail.

For a picture frame that has two hooks in the back instead of one, it's removable masking tape to the rescue again: Use the tape to measure the distance between hooks (one end of the tape will be at one hook, and the other end will be at the other). Then, remove the tape and place it on the wall where you're hanging the picture. Make sure it's straight, and then hammer in one nail at each end of the tape, at the top.

For hanging a bunch of pictures: Roll out butcher-block paper on the floor, and lay the picture frames on the paper the way you'd like to have them hanging on the wall. Trace the outlines of the frames. Then, remove them (take them off the paper and place them on the ground in the same configuration, so that you don't lose track of which one you put where; or you may even write down on the paper which pictures go with which outlines). Use removable masking tape to tape the paper onto the wall, centered at eye level. Make sure the paper is straight, and hammer a nail for each picture right on top of the paper. Then, tear off the paper and hang the pictures.

GET INK OFF YOUR SKIN

Steep a tea bag (any kind of tea that comes in a bag is fine) in a cup of hot water for five minutes, and then let it cool to room temperature. Once it's totally cool to the touch, rub the tea bag on your skin where you have ink stains.

Calligraphy

CALLIGRAPHY COMES FROM THE GREEK WORDS *KALLOS,* which means "beauty," and *graphe,* which means "writing." So, more than just nice penmanship, calligraphy is the art of writing beautifully.

Before the printing press was invented in the mid-fifteenth century, books were written out by hand, using ink and quill pens on parchment paper or vellum. Scribes copied books, letter by letter, using refined alphabet scripts designed to both appeal to the eye and to fit as much information as possible in a small amount of space. Many cultures have a form of this kind of stylized hand script. The most famous are Chinese, Arabic, and Western or Roman calligraphies.

Western calligraphy, which we'll illustrate here, is also called Roman calligraphy because of its use of the Roman alphabet, which came to the west by way of Phoenician, Greek, and Etruscan letter systems around 600 BCE. The original Roman alphabet script reflected Roman principles of architecture, with designs based on the geometric shapes of the square, circle, and triangle (what we call Roman square capitals). A cursive version (later called Old Roman cursive) was created for everyday writing used by politicians, merchants, and schoolchildren, and this more informal, less geometrical script was used up until around the third century CE. Around that time, it morphed into what came to be called New Roman cursive, a more rounded and flowing style and the basis for one of the standard scripts used by modern calligraphers to this day.

Three basic styles of modern Western calligraphy that evolved out of the early Roman script are uncial, black letter, and italic. Uncial (pronounced "un-shull") was used by monks starting around the sixth century as they worked on copying and transcribing religions books. Black letter, sometimes also called Gothic, emerged around the 1300s as a narrow, stylized script that fit more letters on a page. And italic, the flowing script we most commonly associate with calligraphy these days, became popular toward the end of the 1400s.

With the invention of the printing press, and the advent of engraved copperplates in the seventeeth century, hand calligraphy began to fall out of style, save for handwritten correspondence and formal invitations (for which calligraphy is still used today). But its legacy lived on first as the basis of the fonts used by printers and engravers, and continues today in the contemporary typefaces found in word-processing programs on every computer.

WORDS ABOUT CALLIGRAPHY

- **Ascender** - The part of the letter that extends above a character's *x*-height
- **Baseline** - The line on which the letters sit
- **Descender** - The part of the letter that extends below the baseline
- **Majuscules** - Capital letters
- **Mean line (median)** - The line above the baseline, halfway between the baseline and the height of the capital letters. Lowercase letters (that don't have ascenders and descenders) fit between the baseline and mean line.
- **Minuscules** - Lowercase letters
- **Nib** - The tip of a calligraphy pen; the part of a pen or quill that comes in contact with the paper and deposits ink
- **Serif** - Lines on the ends of some letter strokes
- **X-height** - The distance between the baseline and the mean line; also, the height of the letter *x* in a script

ABCDEFGHIJKLM NOPQRSTUVWXYZ

a a d d m m

UNCIAL

Uncial comes from a Latin word meaning "ounce or inch." This calligraphic script is a majuscule script, meaning it uses only capital letters, and when it was first invented, a single letter took up about an inch of space, hence its name. Uncial is characterized by broad, round, open letters that are not joined with one another, and it was the main writing hand used by book scribes from the fourth to ninth centuries. During the seventh century, uncial lettering began to shrink in size, becoming more compact and developing ascenders and descenders (lines extending above and below the main part of the letters), and having some letters joined, as in cursive. This style, called *half uncial*, is most famously showcased in the ninth-century Irish illuminated text *The Book of Kells*. Uncial script in modern calligraphy resembles this later half uncial style.

Aa Bb Cc Dd Ee Ff Gg
Hh Ii Ij Kk Ll Mm
Nn Oo Pp Qq Rr Ss
Tt Uu Vv Ww Xx
Yy Zz

BLACK LETTER

Black letter script (also called Gothic, text letter, textur, textura, English, and Old English) was developed in northern Europe in the eleventh century, and even though it was used for German text up through the twentieth century, the script is difficult for our modern eyes to read. It began as an outgrowth of the rounded scripts like uncial, which as we saw above came to be more condensed over time. With the production of textbooks, which required book scribes to fit more information on the page, calligraphers made their letters even narrower. They also began to join characters, as in cursive; to create contractions and abbreviations; and to shorten the ascenders and descenders into stubs to take up less room. In the interest of taking up less room on the page, scribes also used what's called a *dual alphabet*, made up of lowercase letters (called *minuscules*) as well as capitals. The capital letters in this script became an opportunity for decorative embellishments such as flourishes and lines. This was a chance for individuality on the part of the scribe—there were conventions about flourishes, but no hard and fast rules. And so, while the lowercase characters were uniform, the ornate capitals were not, making each manuscript one of a kind. It was this script that became the inspiration for the first printing types in the mid-fifteenth century. In modern calligraphy, a readable version of black letter is the one most often used for formal certificates, diplomas, and invitations.

Aa Bb Cc Dd Ee Ff
Gg Hh Ii Jj Kk Ll
Mm Nn Oo Pp
Qq Rr Ss Tt Uu Vv
Ww Xx Yy Zz

ITALIC

The black letter script was called *Gothic* during the Renaissance because fifteenth-century Italians considered it barbaric and uncivilized. Instead, they favored a sloped style of handwriting, called *Italic* or *Chancery cursive*, which is today the most popular style of Western calligraphy. The credit for inventing Italic script goes to Italian scholar Niccolo Niccoli, who, in addition to being offended by black letter script, found the other hands too slow to write. His italic script used joined letters and fewer strokes per character, in much the same manner as the modern handwriting that we learn at school today. The biggest change he made was something small but telling: He transformed the lowercase letter *a* into a circular shape instead of the traditional two-story form.

TOOLS OF THE TRADE

Traditionally calligraphers used a quill pen and ink, but nowadays you can buy special calligraphy pens. The fanciest ones come with detachable nibs and special tubes of ink that you put in the barrel of the pen. Other kinds of calligraphy pens are actually markers, with the tips shaped to mimic a traditional nib. When you're just starting out, the markers are a good idea, as they are inexpensive and easy to find. But if you can't get to a store, you can always make your own homemade calligraphy tool: a double pencil.

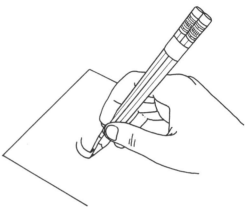

To do this, sharpen two No. 2 pencils. Use masking tape or clear tape to bind them together at the top (erasers) and bottom (sharpened pencil points). Hold the pencil at an angle so that both sharpened points touch the paper, and you are able to write with both pencils at the same time. When you start to write, you will see that the letter you make is quite large. That is okay—the large strokes produce the same effect as a very large calligraphy nib. As you write a letter, the pencils create an outline. You can make this decorative by using pens, markers, colored pencils, or crayons to fill in the space or punch up the outline.

WRITING IN CALLIGRAPHY

First, gather your materials: a calligraphy pen, paper, a pencil, and a ruler.

To make guidelines: On an unlined piece of paper, use a ruler to draw a straight line across the page with a pencil, making your baseline. Then, hold the calligraphy pen so that the nib is at a 90° angle to the baseline and mark out four nib lengths, starting at the baseline and moving up. Use a pencil and ruler to draw a parallel line at that height, to create your x-height. Mark out three more nib lengths up from that, and draw another line to mark the ascender height. Then, mark out three more nib lengths beneath the baseline, and draw a line to mark the descender depth.

Begin to write: Hold the pen at a 30° to 45° angle to the baseline, and practice drawing vertical strokes. Start at the top, and draw the pen down. Now try some horizontal strokes, drawing left to right. Never push the pen across the paper. Instead, think of it as drawing, pulling the pen across the page.

Making Antique Paper

OLD-FASHIONED-LOOKING PAPER is excellent for invitations to high tea, calligraphy scrolls, announcements of backyard theatrical productions, and, of course, bringing news to the queen.

- Boiled water
- Mug
- Black tea bags (or coffee, or instant coffee crystals)
- Paper
- Paintbrush
- Shallow pan or baking dish

To begin, set water to boil. (Ask for an adult's help with this if you are young.) When the water is ready, pour it into a mug with several black tea bags. A single mugful will do, unless you are making enough paper to reproduce the U.S. Constitution and the Federalist Papers all in one batch.

Moistening and tearing the paper's edges will add greatly to the antique effect. While the tea steeps, use a paintbrush to wet the edges of the paper, or simply dip the edges in standing water. Hold a ruler or other kind of straightedge a half inch in from each side, and tear along it. The torn paper will look soft and raggedy, and it will take the tea stain in a darker way.

When the tea has steeped for 20 minutes and you have finished preparing the edges, pour the strong dark tea into a shallow pan. Place the paper in the pan. Leave it to soak for a few minutes so the tea can stain the page. Remove the paper and let it dry on a dish towel. Squeeze excess water from the tea bags and rub them over the paper. You can also brush on the tea stain, so that some of the paper will look darker than the rest. To add even more furrow and wrinkle: After the edges have been treated and the tea stain applied, put the paper into a 200° oven, right on the rack, for 5 minutes.

Antiquing can be done with coffee, too. Make a superstrong cup of either instant or regular coffee, and apply as you would tea. To add extra depth and color to the paper, sprinkle a few instant coffee crystals on the paper. After a few minutes, wipe them away.

How to Debate

THE WORD *DEBATE* comes from the Middle English word *debaten*, which means "to beat." To debate has come to mean "to consider something deliberately and to engage in a formal argument by taking opposing points of view." Debates are loved by people who feel that political positions should be discussed vigorously and, at the same time, that people should learn how to disagree respectfully. For most people, debates take place informally and among friends. The idea is to focus a disagreement over a topic. Each side finds some common ground or a shared position that can be debated through a conversation in which each person argues for or against.

Probably the most famous debates in American history were the Lincoln-Douglas debates of 1858. Abraham Lincoln and Stephen A. Douglas were both running for the same U.S. Senate seat, in Illinois. They met seven times in formal debate, with the incumbent Douglas, a Democrat, arguing for slavery and Lincoln, a Republican, arguing against it (most memorably in his well-known "House Divided" speech). Both Lincoln and Douglas were eloquent debaters. They took up the issue of slavery, a topic that was on the minds of the citizens of the entire country at the time. Newspapers around the country transcribed their debate remarks and printed them in full. Lincoln lost the election, but only a few years later he served as president of the United States (from 1861 to 1865) and did abolish slavery.

PARLIAMENTARY DEBATE

This formal kind of debate is based on the process of the British House of Commons, in which speeches may not be written ahead of time, as is done in the U.S. Congress. Instead, they are spoken extemporaneously, on the spur of the moment. The only notes allowed are those jotted during the debate itself.

The moderator, called the Speaker of the House, presents the resolution, or motion, in rather formal language, such as "This house believes that world peace is a good thing" or "Be it resolved that world peace is a good thing." The debaters are divided into two sides, pro and con. The pro side argues for the house, that is, they argue for the statement's rightness. This team goes by several names: affirmative side, proposition side, or government side. The second side, the con side, argues against the resolution and is called the opposition, or negative side.

A formal debate goes something like this. Each side presents speeches that are prepared on the spot. After the topic is announced and sides are assigned, debaters have fifteen minutes of preparation time to consider how to support their position with evidence, examples, and arguments. (That's for the constructive argument part of the debate). Everyone jots down some notes during this time to use when the debate begins. Here's how it works:

First constructive argument by the affirmative side ---------- 7 minutes
First constructive argument by the negative side ---------- 8 minutes
Second affirmative argument by the affirmative side ---------- 8 minutes
Second affirmative argument by the negative side ---------- 8 minutes
Rebuttal by the negative side ---------- 4 minutes
Rebuttal by the affirmative side ---------- 5 minutes

Debaters can interrupt each other using the following points:

- **Points of Information,** when a debater stands up and says, "May I have a point, miss (or sir)?" The speaking debater can respond no or yes, in which case the interjector has fifteen seconds to pose her query.

- **Points of Misrepresentation** are raised when a debater feels that the other side is misrepresenting something they have said.

- **Points of Order** are raised when a debater thinks that the debate rules were violated.

- **Points of Personal Privilege** are called when a debater wants to complain that she or he has been unfairly and tastelessly insulted. This kind of ad hominem attack is not allowed in debates. Debaters are supposed to stick to the issues and use arguments and evidence, not personal attack, to win.

After the debate ends, people in the audience talk informally about it, and the judges decide who won.

LINCOLN-DOUGLAS-STYLE DEBATE

Lincoln-Douglas–style debates tend to focus on ethical and moral issues of concern, and allow the debators to cross-examine each other. The format is something like this:

Constructive argument by the affirmative side --- 6 minutes
Cross-examination by the negative side --- 3 minutes
Constructive argument by the negative side --- 7 minutes
Cross-examination by the affirmative side --- 3 minutes
Rebuttal by the negative side --- 6 minutes
Final rejoinder by the affirmative side --- 3 minutes

PRESIDENTIAL DEBATE

Every four years, the Republican and Democratic candidates for president meet in a series of debates. These are not formal parliamentary debates. They are organized by a special committee and hosted by a respected journalist, who poses a series of questions to the candidates. Each candidate has a few minutes to respond to the question, and then a few more minutes to take part in a free-flowing conversation with the other candidate. Each candidate then presents a short closing statement. Some debates are actually town hall meetings, during which audience members ask questions and candidates respond.

The Long and Short of It

Longest "Made-Up" Words in the Dictionary

Pneumonoultramicroscopicsilicovolcanoconiosis (45 letters)

This word, meaning "a lung disease caused by the inhalation of silica dust," was coined in 1935 by Everett Smith, then-president of the National Puzzlers' League, specifically for the purpose of becoming the longest word in any English dictionary.

Supercalifragilisticexpialidocious (34 letters)

This famous word comes from the song of the same title in the 1964 Walt Disney movie *Mary Poppins*. It's essentially a nonsensical word whose purported use is to make a speaker sound "precocious" when she uses it. (Believe it or not, there was an earlier claim to this word: In 1951, Alan Holmes and His New Tones recorded a song written by Patricia Smith and Don Fenton called "Supercalafajalistickespeealadojus," also known as "The Super Song." Disney was sued by the writers, but Disney won, and "Supercalifragilisticexpialidocious" is the song—and the word—we know today.)

Longest Real Words

Hepaticocholangiocholecystenterostomies (39 letters)

A genuine medical term for surgically created connections between the gall bladder and other organs

Hippopotomonstrosesquipedalian (30 letters)

This word (included in *Mrs. Byrne's Dictionary of Unusual, Obscure, and Preposterous Words*) means "pertaining to a very long word."

Floccinaucinihilipilification (29 letters)

This word, which means "an estimation of something as worthless," dates back to 1741 and was the longest word included in the first edition of the Oxford English Dictionary.

Antidisestablishmentarianism (28 letters)

A word meaning "opposition to the disestablishment of the Church of England"

Longest Words Used by Famous Writers

Honorificabilitudinitatibus (27 letters)

This word, meaning "honorableness," was used by Shakespeare in his play *Love's Labor's Lost* (Costard; Act V, Scene I), first published in 1598. It is also the longest word consisting entirely of alternating vowels and consonants.

Lopadotemakhoselakhogameokranioleipsanodrimypotrimmatosilphiokarabomelitokatakekhymenokikhlepikossyphophattoperisteralektryonoptokephalliokigklopeleiolagōiosiraiobaphētraganopterýgōn (183 letters)

Aristophanes, the Greek playwright who lived from about 456 BCE to about 386 BCE, made up this word to describe a dish of food.

Bababadalgharaghtakamminarronnkonnbronntonnerronntuonnthunntrovarrhounawnskawntoohoo-hoordenenthurnuk (101 letters)

James Joyce used nine 101-letter made-up words in his novel *Finnegans Wake*. This one appears on the book's first page and is supposed to represent a thunderclap.

Longest Place Names

Taumatawhakatangihangakoauauotamateaturipukakapikimaungahoronukupokaiwhenuakitanatahu (85 letters)

The Maori name for a hill in New Zealand, usually abbreviated to *Taumata*. The full name, celebrating the Maori chief Tamatea, roughly translates as "the summit of the hill, where Tamatea, who is known as the land eater, slid down, climbed up, and swallowed mountains, played on his nose flute to his loved one."

Shortest Words in the English Language

A and *I*

Shortest Two-Syllable Words

Io (pronounced "EYE-oh"; one of Jupiter's moons)

Ai (pronounced "AH-ee"; a three-toed sloth)

Aa (pronounced "AH-ah"; rough volcanic rock)

Shortest Words with Vowels Occurring in Alphabetical Order

Aerious (7 letters, 5 vowels), meaning "airy"

Hareiously (10 letters, 6 vowels), meaning "cruelly"

Shortest Word with Vowels Occurring in Reverse Alphabetical Order

Suoidea (7 letters, 5 vowels), which is the taxonomic group to which pigs belong

Shortest Words with One Double Letter

Aa (a type of lava) and *Oo* (a Hawaiian bird)

Shortest Made-Up Word to Appear in a Dictionary

Dord is a nonexistent word entered into the second edition of Webster's New International Dictionary by mistake in 1934. It was a simple typo: An editor wrote "D or d" in reference to a way the word *density* could be abbreviated (that is, with a capital *D* or a lowercase *d*), and this was misread as *Dord* and entered into the text. Dictionary editors and proofreaders didn't notice the mistake, and the word was included in the dictionary when it went to print, appearing on page 771. *Dord* was finally removed in 1939.

Windowsill Garden

MANY SCRAPS AND ODDS AND ENDS from the kitchen can be planted to make a small windowsill garden. To make this, you'll want to have on hand:

- A flowerpot, a pan, a bowl, or any kind of container that is at least 4 inches deep, so the roots will have room to grow
- Potting soil, which is regular soil mixed with lots of plant vitamins
- Wooden stakes, to support the plant as it grows
- Popsicle (craft) sticks, for marking the name of each plant, although you may consider this optional
- Water
- Lots of sunlight—a windowsill that faces south or west is best (north-facing windowsills get the least amount of light)

Planting is simple. Fill the container with potting soil. Plant the scraps or seeds. Water when the soil is dry. That said, plants don't always grow, and when they don't, you don't always know why. Plants can grow very slowly, which makes it easy to forget about watering them. Really, anything can go wrong, but much can go right, too.

Here are some possibilities for what to grow and how, but go ahead and experiment. Set up a large container of soil; you can pop in whatever seeds or plants come your way (like unroasted coffee beans, dried beans, seeds from apples, pumpkins, pears, lemons, and oranges). If a plant grows and you like it, transplant it into its own pot. In most cases, let the seeds dry out, and then plant. Many won't bear fruit, but they will be interesting nonetheless.

Avocado

Wash the pit. Set it aside for a few days, and when it's dry, peel away the brown outer layer. Spear several toothpicks into the sides. Suspend the pit-and-toothpicks over a glass of water, with the pit bottom a quarter inch in the water. This is an interesting way to do it because you can see the roots grow. The avocado pit will also grow if you just drop it in potting soil, which is the less dramatic but easier way to go.

Carrot

The ferny greens on top of carrots can be planted. Just leave some of the orange carrot on. It won't produce new carrots, but will grow into a nice plant.

Corn

Leave an uncooked piece of corn to dry in a shady spot. After a few weeks, cut the kernels off and plant them in potting soil. You can also try growing the kernels from a bag of popping corn.

Garlic

Separate individual cloves from a head of garlic. Plant them two inches down in the soil, with the pointy tips up. The garlic will sprout in about six weeks. Many months later, large tendrils will appear. These are called *scapes* (and some people use them in cooking). Eventually, when more than half the scapes yellow or turn brown, it's time to harvest. Dig up your new garlic bulbs. The scapes can be braided together, and hung in a dark place for a month so the garlic can dry. This cures the garlic and gets it ready to be eaten. (Garlic can be planted easily outside, too, in many climates. Plant the cloves in fall, and harvest them in early summer.)

Ginger

Cut off a section of fresh ginger, and plant it in potting soil. You can harvest new ginger in six to ten months, which, we agree, can seem like a very long time.

Grass Seed

While not a fruit or vegetable or even a kitchen scrap, grass seed is always fun to grow. It is sold in large bags, but you will need only a very small handful for this project. Toss the grass seed into your windowsill planter. Or, mix grass seed and potting soil, and pour into an old sock. Tie off the sock, place it in a bowl, and water regularly. Watch the sock puppet grow grass hair in about seven to ten days. The best part: If you trim the grass and keep it watered, it grows back. Fast.

Lentils

Plant six to eight lentils, any color. Cover with a quarter to half inch of soil. See what happens.

Peanuts

Shell some unroasted and unsalted peanuts. Plant four to six peanuts, covered with a bit of soil.

Pineapple

Cut the top off, and let it dry for a day. Plant it in shallow soil, as the pineapple gains most of its nutrition not from the soil but from the air.

Sweet Potato

Sweet potato can be grown into a vine, in two stages. Fill a glass with water. Stick toothpicks into the long side of a whole sweet potato. When you put it in the glass, the narrow end will be in the water. Two weeks later, it should have sprouted. That's when you will cut three or four of the shoots and plant them in potting soil. The sweet potato vine will grow up a wall or around a window. If sprouting and planting this seems too fussy, try just burying a sweet potato in your container of soil or, if it is spring or summer, directly into the ground outside.

Optical Illusions

WHAT IF WE TOLD YOU that you don't actually see with your eyes, but with your brain? It's true: Vision is part looking (done by your eyes) and part interpreting (done by your brain). The front of your eye is like a camera. When you look at something, light passes through several parts of your eye. Light first goes through the cornea (the clear part on the front of your eye), then the pupil (the dark part in the center of your eye, which is not really a spot but rather a hole through which light travels), and then the lens. Finally, it reaches the back of the eye, the retina, and an image of what you are looking at is formed. The only catch is, it's upside down. Your optic nerve sends the upside-down picture from your retina to your brain, and the brain then turns the picture right-side-up. And that's just for one eye. The brain must do this for both eyes, as it gets a different set of upside-down information from each one.

All of this happens in an instant, and sometimes the information the brain gets isn't perfect. So you may imagine that, with all the guesses your brain is making about what your optic nerves are reporting to it, some of those guesses may be wrong. You're partly right: Optical illusions are basically the things we see when our brain is guessing. As for whether or not those things are "wrong," let's just say not everyone sees "eye to eye" on that matter.

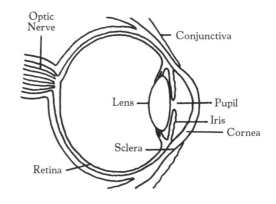

Before we show you some of the most well-known optical illusions, let's have a quick demonstration of the brain at work, making a best guess about what your eyes tell you.

The back of the eye is lined with sensitive photoreceptors, which function like film in a camera, imprinting images based upon how much light is received. But there's just one problem: There's a hole. At the optic nerve head, where neurons bundle together to form the optic nerve, there are no photoreceptors, so that one spot has no information to pass on to the brain. That is your "blind spot," and you have one in each eye. To find it—and see your brain at work, making its best guess about what you're seeing—take a look at the diagram below.

Close your left eye, and cover it with your hand. Now look at the plus sign with your right eye. You should still be able to see the dark circle on the right side of the page, even though you're not looking at it directly. But watch this: Continue to stare at the plus sign, and slowly move your head closer to this page. Move slowly, and keep staring at the plus sign. At some point as you move closer, the dark circle will completely disappear!

The circle disappeared because it entered your blind spot, and your brain made its best guess about what might be on that side of the page. With all the white space around the diagram, it's a pretty good guess that the right side of the page may be blank. But we can see how your brain's guess this time happened to be wrong. If you keep moving forward, or if you move backward, you will be able to see the circle again—just not when it's in your blind spot.

SIX WELL-KNOWN OPTICAL ILLUSIONS

Ebbinghaus Illusion

This illusion, like the Müller-Lyer illusion on the next page, is about relative size perception. The circle on the right, surrounded by smaller circles, appears larger to us; but in fact it is exactly the same size as the circle on the left, which is surrounded by bigger circles.

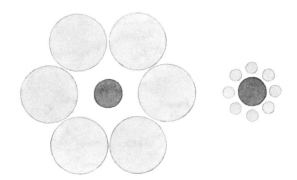

Rubin's Vase

This famous illusion was developed in the early 1900s by the Danish psychologist Edgar Rubin. The trick of this image is that it's flat—there is no depth or perspective to it to help the brain determine which part of the image is in the foreground and which part is in the background. Because of this, the image can be interpreted with either the middle space (what most people see as a vase or cup) or the surrounding space (what most people see as two faces in profile) as the most "important" part of it. Once you notice that there are two different ways to see the image, it's easy to switch back and forth from vase to faces and faces to vase.

The Müller-Lyer Optical Illusion

This illusion was created in 1889 by German psychiatrist Franz Müller-Lyer. All of the lines in this diagram are of equal length, but they appear to be all different lengths to us—possibly because of the way the brain interprets the directional arrow angles on the ends of the lines.

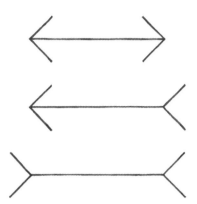

Impossible Triangle Optical Illusion

The "impossible triangle" uses shading, color variations, and perspective to create a shape that looks believable to us, although in fact it would be impossible to build such a triangle in three-dimensional real life.

Young Girl/Old Woman Illusion

This is another famous illusion that hinges on a lack of depth or shading to guide the brain in determining foreground and background. Look at it one way and it's a young girl in a fancy hat; look at it another way and it's an old woman. This illusion appeared on an anonymous German postcard in 1888. It's not known who the original artist was.

The Hermann Grid Illusion

This optical illusion was first reported by Ludimar Hermann in 1870. When one is looking at the grid, it appears that each intersection has a gray spot in the middle. But when one looks closely at an individual intersection, the gray spot disappears.

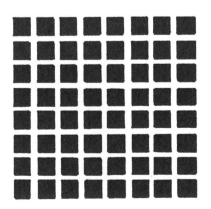

How to Start a Mother-Daughter Book Club

THE AUTHOR C.S. LEWIS ONCE SAID, "We read to know we are not alone." For many girls, talking about books with their friends or parents is a way to both connect with the important people in their lives and explore big ideas about the world.

Book clubs have a long and storied past. Women especially have been creating book clubs for as long as there have been books to read. Books pull us out of the immediate drama of our own lives and bring us to worlds we couldn't have imagined ourselves; and book club discussions introduce us to people we would otherwise never get to know so well. In the novel *The Mother-Daughter Book Club*, by Heather Vogel Frederick, four girls and their mothers start a book club, reading Louisa May Alcott's *Little Women* over the course of a year. The girls have their ups and downs, as do their parents. But the group stays together, pulled tight by the experience of reading the same book.

HOW TO START A CLUB

Choose some girls and their moms to join you. Four to six seems like a good number of mother-daughter pairs. (Part of the fun of a club is the other people and the points of view they bring, but a group that's too big can make it hard for everyone to be involved in the conversation.) Ask some people you know, as well as some you don't, because being in a book group together is a good way to get to know new people. It's best if members can really commit to meeting once every other month for a whole year. That way, everyone can take their time with the books, and there will be plenty of time to settle in and figure out how best to make your group work.

If you can't get enough people for a mother-daughter book club, you may consider other kinds of book clubs. You may start one for girls only, or for girls and boys, or for girls and their dads, or even for girls and their grandparents. It's also possible to have a short-term club, where a group comes together to read one or two books, and that's all.

It can take some time for a group to find its rhythm. Be patient. There are groups that start out strong and fade fast, and others that seem to take a while before everyone gets on the same page (so to speak). But some groups last from elementary school all the way through high school, providing a girl with a group reading experience that sustains her through girlhood and beyond.

Decide how often to meet. Every other month is good to aim for. It gives everyone enough time to read a book.

As for refreshments, book club meetings have been known to turn into elaborate events for which people spend a great deal of time preparing, cooking, and worrying. If doing this is truly fun for you, then go ahead. Otherwise, we suggest you steer clear of all that. It's about the reading, after all, and the camaraderie. Simple snacks are just fine.

With any luck the conversation will range freely and easily. For when it doesn't, here are some good go-around questions, which everyone in the circle can take a turn answering: *Who is your favorite character, and why? What was your favorite chapter, and why? What did you like best, and what did you like the least?* The best book conversations tend to be unpredictable and spontaneous, but starter questions such as these can get everybody's ideas flowing.

And finally, choose a book. The original *Daring Book for Girls* has a long list of classic books. But there are scads of books that aren't on that list. What you choose to read will depend on your age, your reading level, and what you like to read. Teachers and librarians are great sources of information about books, and they are wonderful people to ask for advice about what to read next.

In some groups, each member takes a turn picking a book for the next meeting. In others, the members meet every so often to decide together on books for the next few months or for the year ahead. You may decide to include only books available in paperback or at the library so that they are affordable to everyone.

You may also decide on a theme, such as reading several books in a row by the same author. Perhaps your group will decide to read books of historical fiction, bringing to life the volcanic eruption of Pompeii, the Underground Railroad, medieval Mongolia, or San Francisco during the Gold Rush. The next year could be devoted to books of fantasy and fire-breathing dragons from *Eragon* to *Beowulf*. The year after that could be spent reading *Anne of Green Gables* and other girl classics. It is up to you and your fellow book club members.

Miscellanea

1. Popcorn on the Stove

Pour 2 tablespoons of cooking oil in a large pot, enough to cover the bottom generously. Set the heat to a medium to medium-high flame. When the oil is hot, drop in three or four kernels. When they pop, sprinkle in a half cup of popcorn—this should be no more than a few layers deep. Cover the pan, but not too tightly. As the kernels get going, shake the pan back and forth on the burner. It will get noisy. Every so often remove the pan from the flame to cool for a moment, so that all the kernels can pop before they burn. When the popping noise slows, pour the popcorn into a big bowl with some melted butter and salt, or portion it into brown paper bags. To make sweet kettle corn, add a tablespoon of sugar to the butter and salt. Hot sauce or chili powder can be added, too.

Here's a secret recipe for if ever you are marooned on a desert island with only a microwave oven, a brown paper lunch bag, and 2 tablespoons of popping corn kernels. Put the popcorn into the bag. Fold the top over a few times so it stays put. Lay the bag in the microwave for a few minutes, and remove it when the popping noise stops. Add butter and salt.

2. The Five Longest Rivers in the World

The Nile in northeast Africa, the Amazon in South America, the Chang Jiang in China (also known as the Yangtze), the Mississippi-Missouri in the United States, and the Yenisey in Russia.

3. The Dance Moves to the YMCA Song

You'll never again have to second-guess the YMCA moves at a retro dance party or the seventh-inning stretch at a Major League Baseball game.

Y   M   C   A

Y   Raise your arms, like in a victory sign.
M   From the Y pose, bend your elbows and let the fingertips of each hand land on your head.
C   Curve both arms out to the left.
A   Touch your hands together overhead.

4. Homespun Wisdom for Stopping the Hiccups

Swallow a spoonful of sugar. Drink very cold water. Drink upside down. Eat a spoonful of peanut butter—pushing it to the top of your mouth. Tickle the roof of your mouth with your finger. Breathe into a paper bag. Hold your breath while you count to ten. Raise your arms over your head and take a few deep breaths. And the old reliable cure: Ask someone to scare you.

5. Hang a Spoon on Your Nose

Entertain young cousins at the table or turn ordinary dinnertime into silliness. There are two ways to do it. Method #1: Lay the spoon horizontally across the bridge of your nose. Find its center of gravity, and it will balance. Method #2: Rest the top part of the spoon on the tip of your nose. Good silver is too heavy, so grab a lightweight spoon instead. Tilt your head back. Rub the spoon's concave side a few times on your nose to get some friction going. You'll feel it start to stick. If this doesn't work, breathe on the spoon. If that doesn't help, rub the spoon with your finger (this gets some oil on it), and then stick it on your nose. It should definitely work now.

6. Make a Wineglass Sing

Like spoon hanging, this trick is good for the dinner table when conversation wanes, or while waiting for dessert. Good crystal is best, which makes this perfect for special dinners, fancy restaurants, and holiday meals. Wet your pointer finger, and rub it around the rim of the glass. Wet your finger again when it stops working. To form an orchestra, do this with glasses filled to different levels! (It works because your finger creates vibrations that bounce around the glass and through the water.)

7. Tin-Can Telephones

They really do work over a short distance. One person talks while the other listens, walkie-talkie style. Clean two metal cans (file any sharp edges that can hurt your fingers or ear). With a screwdriver or awl, or a hammer and nail, make a hole in the bottom of each can. Thread household string through one can, tie on the inside, and stretch it 9 or 10 feet, and tie it to the other can. The string should be tight and stretched so it can vibrate, which is the key to why this works.

8. Read a Topo Map and a Compass

Topos means "place" in Latin, and topo (or topography) maps show the elevation of terrain, which is what makes them such good guides to the woods. The lines on a topo map are hills and valleys and flatlands. Each line on the map has an elevation number. When the lines are close together, the terrain is sharp and steep. Lines that are far apart show land with a gentler slope. In either case, read for the direction of the numbers to see whether you're about to go up or down. A quick tip for what you need to know if you're hiking: When the trail crosses topo lines, you're either going up or down. If the trail follows the line, you're on steady ground, which is nearly always to be preferred.

To read a compass, hold it flat and still. The needle will move and then stop moving. When it does, twist around the outer circle of the compass so that N or North lines up with the arrow. That will give you your bearings. If used with a topo map, line up the compass with the word North on the map (which as we all know isn't just the top of the page).

9. Whistle Through a Blade Of Grass

Pluck a blade of grass that's at least about 3 inches long. Find the toughest grass you can with the widest blade. If there's a seam running down the middle of the grass, all the better: That means it's really wide.

Lay the blade across the outside of one thumb. Press the outside of the other thumb against the first thumb—first, the base of the thumb, and then the tip. This should create a small pocket between your thumbs, with the blade of grass stretched flat in between. The blade needs to be fairly taut. Blow into the pocket (try making a small slit with your lips); this should vibrate the grass and make a squawking sound. Moving the tips of your thumbs back and forth makes the grass pull more or less taut, changing the pitch.

10. Hide a Treasure in a Book
Find an old, already-read book, the thicker the better. Turn the first pages. On every page thereafter, take a few pages in hand and with a craft knife or scissor, cut a rectangle into the middle of the page. Continue cutting the same size rectangle from all pages until there is a cavity in the book. When seen from the shelf, it will pass as any old book, but its secret mission from here on out is to hide your treasure.

11. The Words to "Auld Lang Syne"
Come midnight on New Year's Eve, people sing the first line of "Auld Lang Syne" and then fake-hum the rest. The phrase *auld lang syne* comes from a Scottish folk song, and it means something like "old long ago." Here are the lyrics.

Should auld acquaintance be forgot
and never brought to mind?
Should auld acquaintance be forgot
and days of auld lang syne?

Chorus:
For auld lang syne, my dear,
for auld lang syne,
we'll take a cup of kindness yet,
for auld lang syne.

And here's a hand, my trusty friend
And give us a hand of thine
We'll take a cup o' kindness yet
For auld lang syne

Chorus:
For auld lang syne, my dear,
for auld lang syne,
we'll take a cup of kindness yet,
for auld lang syne.

ILLUSTRATION CREDITS

2: © iStock/Jan Tyler

43: Based on material from the American Studies department website, University of Virginia

47: Sharlot Hall Museum Photo, Prescott, Arizona

80-82: Ministry of the Environment, Government of Japan

96: clipart.com/©Jupiter Images Corporation

113: U.S. Army Photo

131: National Park Service

134: clipart.com/©Jupiter Images Corporation

154: © iStock/iShootPhotos, LLC

272: clipart.com/©Jupiter Images Corporation

ACKNOWLEDGMENTS

With special thanks to our editor Serena Jones and everyone at HarperCollins; to the Stonesong Press; to our wonderful illustrator, Alexis Seabrook; and to Serena's younger sister, Phoebe, for her talent in finding our title.

Andi Buchanan would especially like to thank her agent, Laura Gross; the Buchanan and Bineubaum families, most specifically Gil, Nate, and Emi; daring readers Sidra and Sadie (the inspiration for our card-playing girls) and Nola and Margo (the inspiration for our football throwers and catchers); Rachael Teacher; Barbara Card Atkinson; and Teacher Betsy's fourth-grade class, who proved to be excellent quillers and storytellers.

Miriam Peskowitz sends a round of applause and thanks to the writers of Wordspace, who have taught her everything from how to follow dreams to how to go car camping: Hilary Beard, Tamar Chansky, Meredith Broussard, Eileen Flanagan, Jude Ray, Andrea Ross, Eleanor Stanford, and Lori Tharps; to Deb Valentine; to Cheryl Bruttomesso and all of Samira's teachers, gym teachers, coaches, and friends; to Shirley Cruikshank; to Megan Pincus Kajitani and Alex Kajitani; to Sam Stoloff, who among many other things taught her how to whistle through a blade of grass; and to the Ricks-Dolgenos family, the Bromley-Zimmerman family, the McKenzie family, and the Lighte-Grant family: Peter, Julian, Hattie, and Tillie. Above all, thanks go to her mom and dad, Myra and Danny Peskowitz; to her other family, the Bairds; and to her daily inspirations for leading life with aplomb: Rob, Samira, and Amelia Jane.

Own all of the Daring Books!